The Anglo-Irish Experience, 1680–1

Religion, Identity and Patriotism

Irish Historical Monograph Series

ISSN 1740–1097

Series editors

Previous titles in this series

I. Ruling Ireland 1685–1742: Politics, Politicians and Parties, *D. W. Hayton*, 2004

II. Lord Broghill and the Cromwellian Union with Ireland and Scotland, *Patrick Little*, 2004

III. Irish Migrants in New Zealand, 1840–1937: 'The Desired Haven', *Angela McCarthy*, 2005

IV. The Fenian Ideal and Irish Nationalism, 1882–1916, *M. J. Kelly*, 2006

V. Loyalism in Ireland, 1789–1829, *Allan Blackstock*, 2007

VI. Constructing the Past: Writing Irish History, 1600–1800, *edited by Mark Williams and Stephen Forrest*, 2010

VII. The Making of the Irish Protestant Ascendancy: The Life of William Conolly, 1662–1729, *Patrick Walsh*, 2010

VIII. The Militia in Eighteenth-Century Ireland: In Defence of the Protestant Interest, *Neal Garnham*, 2012

The Anglo-Irish Experience, 1680–1730

Religion, Identity and Patriotism

D. W. Hayton

THE BOYDELL PRESS

First published 2012
The Boydell Press, Woodbridge

ISBN 978–1–84383–746–6

The Boydell Press is an imprint of Boydell & Brewer Ltd
PO Box 9, Woodbridge, Suffolk IP12 3DF, UK
and of Boydell & Brewer Inc.
668 Mt Hope Avenue, Rochester, NY 14620–2731, USA
website: www.boydellandbrewer.com

A CIP catalogue record for this title is available
from the British Library

Printed and bound in Great Britain by
CPI Group (UK) Ltd, Croydon, CR0 4YY

Contents

Illustrations

In memory of my parents

LEONARD ('TOM') HAYTON, 1912–1968

SHEILA CATTELL HAYTON, 1918–2009

and my aunt

MARJORIE HAYTON, 1904–1990

Acknowledgments

This book represents the culmination of a long period of research into various aspects of the period and grows out of work already completed as well as work in progress. Six of the chapters are substantial revisions of papers previously published in a different form, and contain new material as well as second thoughts. Two are entirely new. For permission to repeat some material already in print I must thank the American Society for Eighteenth-Century Studies, Cambridge University Press, the Eighteenth-Century Ireland Society, the Irish Economic and Social History Society, and the Lilliput Press.

For permission to consult and cite documents in private ownership, I am grateful to the duke of Abercorn, the marquess of Bath, the marquess of Normanby, the earl of Rosse, the Viscount de Vesci, the Viscount Massereene and Ferrard, the Viscount Midleton, Lady Ravensdale, and his grace the archbishop of Armagh. In respect of documents held in institutional libraries and archives, I must record similar obligations to the Keeper of Western Manuscripts of the Bodleian Library, Oxford; the British Library Board; Cambridge University Library; Cheshire and Chester Archives; the Governing Body of Christ Church, Oxford; the Folger Shakespeare Library; the Genealogical Office, Dublin; the Hardiman Library, National University of Ireland, Galway; the Henry E. Huntington Library and Art Gallery, San Marino, California; the Comptroller of Her Majesty's Stationery Office; Hertfordshire Record Office; the Irish Architectural Archive; the Centre for Kentish Studies, Maidstone; Kilkenny Borough Council; the Librarian, Lambeth Palace Library; the Record Office for Leicestershire, Leicester and Rutland; Liverpool Record Office; the Keeper, Marsh's Library, Dublin; the National Library of Ireland; the National Library of Wales; the National Records of Scotland; Northamptonshire Record Office; Nottinghamshire Archives; the Deputy Keeper of the Records of Northern Ireland; the Registry of Deeds, Dublin; the Representative Church Body Library; the Royal Dublin Society; the vicar of St Anne Shandon, Cork; Somerset Heritage Centre; the Curator, Tipperary South Riding County Museum; Surrey History Centre, Woking; the Board of Trinity College Dublin; West Sussex Record Office; and the Wiltshire and Swindon History Centre.

I must also thank the Yale Center for British Art for permission to reproduce the painting by Peter Tillemans on the cover, and the Trustees of the British Museum for permission to reproduce the cartoon by Gillray in Chapter 1. The map and family trees are the work of Ms Maura Pringle of the cartographic unit in the School of Geography, Archaeology and Palaeoecology at Queen's University, Belfast.

It is always a pleasure to acknowledge the assistance received – often well beyond the call of duty – from staff in archives and libraries, and although it is doubtless invidious to mention individuals, I would like to express my particular appreciation to Christopher Wright and Frances Harris at the British Library; David Griffin at the Irish Architectural Archive; Tom Desmond at the National Library of Ireland; Ian

Montgomery at the Public Record Office of Northern Ireland; Deirdre Wildy and Diarmuid Kennedy at the McClay Library, Queen's University Belfast; Ray Refaussé at the Representative Church Body Library; and Mary Kelleher at the library of the Royal Dublin Society.

Michael Page of the Surrey History Centre was responsible for the transcriptions of Brodrick family documents that are quoted in the text. Without his help the chapter on the Brodricks could not have been written. I hope he will recognise this book as the first instalment in the repayment of a very long-standing debt, and as an indication that he will not have too much more to wait for the publication of the edited collection of Brodrick letters on which we have been working.

Another vote of thanks must be accorded to the Huntington Library and its staff. I was awarded a Mayers fellowship during the academic year 2009/10, during which much of the research and writing of the final chapter was carried out, and the idea for this collection was conceived. I should also place on record my thanks to Barbara Donagan, Paul Griffiths, Susi Krasnoo, Ann and John Scheid, Michael Smith, and especially Nick Rogers, for doing so much to make my stay at the library enjoyable as well as productive.

Putting together a work of this kind necessarily involves trespassing upon the patience of others working in the same field, and I have been fortunate in receiving valuable assistance, in the form of advice, or the sharing of discoveries, from Toby Barnard, Tom Bartlett, John Bergin, Andrew Carpenter, Brenda Collins, Lee Davison, David Dickson, the late Arch. Elias, Neal Garnham, Raymond Gillespie, Stuart Handley, Andrew Hanham, Jacqueline Hill, Clyve Jones, the late David Lewis Jones, Jimmy Kelly, Patrick Kelly, Anne Laurence, Eoin Magennis, Robert Mahony, Anthony Malcomson, James McGuire, Ivar McGrath, Eddie McParland, Howard Nenner, Michael Page, Carole Rawcliffe, Andrew Sneddon, Joe Spence, Stephen Taylor, Roland Thorne, Patrick Walsh, and James Woolley. Colleagues in the School of History and Anthropology at Queen's University Belfast have also borne with these various preoccupations; in particular Sean Connolly, Peter Gray, Andrew Holmes, Keith Jeffery, Colin Kidd, Mary O'Dowd, and the late (and very much missed) Peter Jupp. During the six years in which I served as Head of School, I depended heavily on the School Manager, Frances Mercer, and successive secretaries, Catherine Boone, Angela Anderson, and Judith Cardwell; this book, and much else, would have been impossible had they not consistently and cheerfully lifted burdens from my shoulders.

I dedicate this book to the three people without whose encouragement and self-sacrifice I would certainly never have been able to go to university in the first place, much less consider an academic career.

D.W.H.
Belfast, 2011

Abbreviations

B.L.	British Library
Bodl.	Bodleian Library
C.J.	*Journals of the House of Commons*
C.J.Ire.	*Journals of the House of Commons of the kingdom of Ireland*
Coghill letters	*Letters of Marmaduke Coghill 1722–1738*, ed. D. W. Hayton (Dublin, 2004)
C.S.P., dom.	*Calendar of State Papers, domestic series*
D.I.B.	James McGuire and James Quinn (eds), *The dictionary of Irish biography* (9 vols, Cambridge, 2009)
E.H.R.	*English Historical Review*
HA	Huntington Library, Hastings papers
H.C. 1660–90	B. D. Henning, *The House of Commons 1660–1690* (3 vols, London, 1983)
H.C. 1690–1715	Eveline Cruickshanks et al. (eds), *The House of Commons 1690–1715* (5 vols, Cambridge, 2002)
H.C. 1715–54	Romney Sedgwick, *The House of Commons 1715–1754* (2 vols, London, 1970)
Hist. Ir. parl.	Edith Mary Johnston-Liik, *History of the Irish parliament 1692–1800* (6 vols, Belfast, 2002)
Hist. Jn.	*Historical Journal*
H.M.C.	Historical Manuscripts Commission report
I.A.A.	Irish Architectural Archive
I.H.S.	*Irish Historical Studies*
L.J.	*Journals of the House of Lords*
L.J. Ire.	*Journals of the House of Lords* [of the kingdom of Ireland]
N.A.I.	National Archives, Ireland
N.L.I.	National Library of Ireland
O.E.D.	*The Oxford English dictionary*
Oxf. D.N.B.	H. C. G. Matthew et al. (eds), *Oxford dictionary of national biography* (60 vols, Oxford, 2004)
P.R.O.N.I	Public Record Office of Northern Ireland
R.C.B.	Representative Church Body library
R.D.S.	Royal Dublin Society
R.O.	Record Office
S.H.C.	Surrey History Centre, Woking
T.C.D.	Trinity College Dublin
T.N.A.	The National Archives [of the U.K.]

Preface

The defeat of the Jacobite forces in 1690–91 confirmed in power in Ireland a Protestant landed class of predominantly English descent, most of whom still regarded themselves as representatives of the 'English interest' in the country. This fact may well render early eighteenth-century Ireland a 'colonial' society, as some historians have argued, even though the 'colonial' or 'planter' class which possessed economic and political power was ethnically various, and the process by which they had settled (and were in a few cases continuing to settle) in Ireland had been long drawn out. The majority, it is true, descended from families who had come over to Ireland in the various plantations of the sixteenth and early seventeenth centuries (the so-called 'New English'), together with a further substantial stratum deposited after the Cromwellian confiscations. But Protestant landed society also included 'Old English' families who had settled in Ireland long before the Reformation and had abandoned their Catholic allegiance – representatives of Anglo-Norman baronial dynasties such as the Butler dukes of Ormond and the Fitzgerald earls of Kildare, and even descendants of Gaelic lords, such as the O'Brien earls of Inchiquin, who traced their ancestry to the high-king Brian Boru.

Despite this diversity, the propertied elite of early eighteenth-century Ireland proved remarkably coherent. They were held together by a common Protestantism, and a sense that their security depended ultimately on the military backing of the English crown and parliament. Moreover, as landed proprietors their economic power was as yet unchallenged by any emerging commercial or manufacturing interests, and neither of the other major ethno-religious groupings in the country – the 'native' Irish Catholics and the immigrant Scottish Presbyterians in Ulster – rated as serious political rivals. Both were regarded by the English government and parliament as at least potentially disloyal (in the case of the Ulster Scots, even beyond the Anglo-Scottish Union of 1707).

It is thus easy to see why the eighteenth century has traditionally been depicted as the era of 'Protestant ascendancy', a phrase which historians have abstracted from the very specific sectarian polemics of the 1780s and 1790s and used to express the long-lasting dominance in Irish society of the Protestant propertied elite.[1]

1 W. J. McCormack, *Ascendancy and tradition in Anglo-Irish literary history 1789–1939* (Oxford, 1985); idem, 'Vision and revision in the study of eighteenth-century Irish parliamentary rhetoric' in *Eighteenth-Century Ireland*, ii (1987), pp 7–35; idem, 'Eighteenth-century ascendancy: Yeats and the historians' in *Eighteenth-Century Ireland*, iv (1989), pp 159–81; James Kelly, 'Inter-denominational relations and religious toleration in late eighteenth-century Ireland: the "paper war" of 1785–1788' in *Eighteenth-Century Ireland*, iii (1988), pp 39–67; idem, 'The genesis of "Protestant ascendancy": the Rightboy disturbances of the 1780s and their impact upon Protestant opinion' in Gerard O'Brien (ed.), *Parliament, politics and people: essays in eighteenth-century Irish history* (Dublin, 1989), pp 93–127; idem, 'Eighteenth-century ascendancy: a comment' in *Eighteenth-Century Ireland*, v (1990), pp 173–87.

Even if subject to periodic fits of insecurity – prompted by fear of Catholic insurrection, Jacobite invasion, agrarian violence or urban criminality – the members of this ruling class were generally comfortable in their enjoyment of social superiority and political power. They had secured political representation, and a degree of influence over the actions of government, through the re-establishment in 1692 of the Irish parliament, from which Catholics and all but a few Protestant Dissenters were excluded. The legislative capacity of this parliament, despite the restrictions imposed by Poynings' Law, had then been exploited to construct a 'confessional state' in which members of the established church enjoyed a monopoly of public office. Then in the final quarter of the century many of the residual limitations on the legislative autonomy of the Irish parliament were removed, to achieve something close to an eighteenth-century version of 'home rule', albeit at the cost of a partial dismantling of the confessional state, in which Presbyterians were admitted to full political rights while Catholics were relieved from many of their disabilities though still excluded from parliament and public office.

'Protestant Ascendancy', even if technically an anachronism, is clearly a useful way to describe the social organisation and governance of eighteenth-century Ireland. Another term, 'Anglo-Irish Ascendancy', was once as popular but seems to have fallen out of favour as historians have recognised the genuinely 'patriotic' sentiments of the most vocal Protestant parliamentarians, political agitators, and authors of the eighteenth century, who very obviously did not regard themselves as anything less than Irish. This was especially true in the years after 1760, as pressure built up for a constitutional equality with Great Britain, expressed through free trade and legislative independence. Yet it would be a pity to relinquish the adjective 'Anglo-Irish' altogether, since – for the first half of the century at any rate – it does express a highly significant element in the social and political culture of the Protestant landed class. These were people who, while genuinely coming to think of themselves as Irish, were still intensely aware of their English origins and connexions. Many had English relations, took English wives, or maintained English friendships. Some inherited or purchased English property. They visited England frequently, either on business or pleasure; bought and read books published in England, and imported pictures, furnishings, and even garden plants. Those in search of a legal education would attend the English inns of court. Some of those whom we will encounter in the following pages – great noblemen like the Butler dukes of Ormond, or the Boyle earls of Burlington, Carleton, Orrery, and Shannon – were almost permanent absentees; others, like the members of the Brodrick family, shuttled between Ireland and England, at ease in both countries.

In important respects, therefore, the 'Protestant ascendancy' was also an 'Anglo-Irish ascendancy', especially in the years c.1680–1730 with which this book is concerned, before the 'patriot' movement gathered impetus, and long before the Irish parliament emancipated itself from the tutelage of the Irish and British privy councils. Indeed, an essential characteristic of the period was the dominance in Ireland of a Protestant political culture which was in many respects distinctively 'Anglo-Irish'. We can observe this in the character of Irish political rhetoric, which often followed an English pattern, for example in the appearance in Ireland in Queen Anne's reign of 'Whig' and 'Tory' parties, and in the widespread assumption that the security of Ireland was determined by the strategic interests of the English crown in its European wars, or that Irish prosperity was bound up with the development of English overseas trading and colonial interests.

However, this was not a period of stagnation but of adjustment to new circumstances, leading to significant change. One important effect of the Williamite Revolution was to establish 'Protestant ascendancy' in Ireland on a much firmer footing, and to enable Irish Protestants to think more independently about their own destiny. While acknowledging the role played by the prince of Orange himself as their 'great deliverer', many commentators, especially among the clergy, came to see him less as the representative of English taxpayers (who had footed the bill for his army) than as the instrument of divine providence. In this mode of thinking, Irish Protestants were themselves a 'chosen' people under God's special protection. The military defeat of James II's 'popish tyranny' had not been simply an English (or English-financed) rescue. Much was made in contemporary literature of the defiance shown by Irish Protestants, especially at Derry, where the valour of the besieged inhabitants had defeated the might of Jacobite arms. They had done as much for themselves as others had done for them.[2] Developments after the Revolution encouraged further, and sometimes rather different, reflections on the nature of the Anglo-Irish nexus. The multiple kingdoms of England and Scotland were consolidated in a constitutional union, from which Ireland was excluded. The new entity of 'Great Britain' then emerged as a 'fiscal-military state' with European Great Power status, and an increasingly prosperous commercial empire. On the one hand, Irish Protestants were tempted by an expanding range of opportunities in the new imperial state; on the other, Ireland was relegated to a subordinate position in imperial governance and, increasingly, Irish interests were perceived as disadvantaged.

In a previous collection[3] I attempted to describe and analyse the ways in which Ireland was governed, and the ways in which Irish Protestants responded to government, between the Williamite revolution and the end of Sir Robert Walpole's prolonged stint as prime minister of Great Britain. The essays in this book are directed towards a different end; to understanding the political culture of the Irish governing class through relating it to the social background. The first two chapters consider changing perceptions of national identity: how Irish Protestants were viewed in England, and how (partly as a response to English stereotyping) they gradually came to see themselves unequivocally as Irish, and to root themselves more deeply and firmly in Irish soil. This is followed by two contrasting studies of landed families: one, the Ormond Butlers, a great aristocratic dynasty typical of the magnates who had been so influential in the past, now in terminal decline; the other, the Brodricks of Midleton, County Cork, a close-knit gentry family taking advantage of the opportunities available in Williamite Ireland to acquire office, wealth and property, and to construct a major landed and political 'interest'. Both families, however, encoun-

2 Thomas Bartlett, '"This famous island set in a Virginian sea": Ireland in the British Empire, 1690–1801' in *The Oxford history of the British Empire*, ii: P. J. Marshall (ed.), *The eighteenth century* (Oxford, 1998), pp 259–60.

3 D. W. Hayton, *Ruling Ireland, 1685–1742: politics, politicians and parties* (Woodbridge, 2004).

tered difficulties as a consequence of absenteeism and the challenges of maintaining a public position simultaneously on both sides of the Irish Sea.

Two chapters are devoted to a consideration of the nature of Anglo-Irish 'patriotism' in a context of limited legislative autonomy and the strategic demands of the emerging British empire. Despite occasional flourishes of national outrage on the part of opposition M.P.s in Dublin, at British governmental interference in Irish business and the undue influence of assertive English commercial interests over Irish economic affairs, a more pragmatic, constructive approach seems to have prevailed. This was certainly true of those holding government office, who recognised the dangers presented by a vociferous and aggressive patriotism, and the need to work within existing constitutional arrangements to do the best for Ireland (and for its Protestant people).

The final two essays consider issues of social reform and 'improvement'. During this period much attention was given – as it had been during the preceding two centuries – to the inculcation of 'civility' and the promotion of economic progress through the introduction of new agricultural techniques and manufactures, and an increase in trade. These social and material advances were seen to be facilitated by (if not dependent upon) the spread of the reformed religion. The 'charity school' movement of the period c. 1695–1725 provides a clear example of the merging of Protestant evangelicalism with social 'improvement', while a close examination of the activities of one family, the Rawdons of Moira, Co. Down, shows how this outlook could be affected by a matrix of personal as well as ideological influences.

In other respects too, Moira is an ideal place to end this exploration of Anglo-Ireland, since the history of the Rawdons – their fortune originating in an English connexion and their subsequent troubles also taking rise from the same source – illustrates perfectly the complexity of Anglo-Irish relationships. The vehement denunciation of absentee landlords published by their quondam agent, Thomas Prior, in 1729 might be taken to mark an important stage in shifting attitudes towards the English connexion:[4] the appearance of a fervent and uncompromising Irish patriotism (something that can also be detected in the later correspondence of the Brodrick family). Prior's pamphlet achieved a notable *succès de scandale*, and his ideas were immediately taken up in the Irish House of Commons. But lest we conclude prematurely that the pragmatism typical of 'Anglo-Irish' politicians and political families in the decades after 1692 had disappeared overnight, it is worth drawing attention to the response of another of Prior's employers, the Castle politician and practical patriot, Marmaduke Coghill (who lived in Dublin but held on to his family's small ancestral estate in Yorkshire): 'we have a bitter book published against absentees', and 'though it has some truths in it, it has many faults and is liable to many objections'.[5] In that carefully balanced phrasing we can still hear the authentic voice, and glimpse the cautious cast of mind, of the early eighteenth-century 'Anglo-Irish'.

4 Thomas Prior, *A list of the absentees of Ireland, and the yearly value of their estates and incomes spent abroad* ... (Dublin, 1729).

5 Coghill to Edward Southwell, 14 October 1729 (*Coghill letters*, p. 74).

Note on dates and quotations

Until 1750 the Julian calendar (referred to as Old Style) was still operative in England and Ireland, though the Gregorian calendar (New Style) was used across continental Europe. Dates are therefore given in Old Style, with occasional exceptions, denoted by N.S. However, the year has been taken to begin on 1 January and not on 25 March. Contemporaries often recorded both year dates during the period 1 January–24 March: where this usage appears in original documents it has been rendered as e.g. 1714/15; where the original takes the beginning of the year as 25 March, this appears as e.g. 1714[/15].

In presenting quotations from original sources, both manuscript and printed (including the titles of contemporary publications), spelling, capitalisation, and punctuation have been silently modernised unless there is ambiguity in the original.

1

From Barbarian to Burlesque

The changing stereotype of the Irish*

The Englishman's offensive practice of creating adverse social stereotypes of supposedly inferior national or racial groups has proved most attractive as a subject for study when it can be depicted as a weapon of colonial or neo-colonial exploitation. This is particularly true in relation to the development of Irish stereotypes, where a moralistic tone often intrudes.[1] With the exception of the work of literary specialists,[2] research into popular English impressions of Ireland and the native Irish has tended to concentrate on the periods in which caricature can be shown to have facilitated the justification of coercive policies and 'imperialist' domination. Sixteenth-century characterisation of the 'wild Irishman' as a barbarian and near-beast, a Caliban close to home, helped to legitimise the Elizabethan conquest and the rapacity of plantation schemes,[3] just as nineteenth-century cartoons of prognathous and blood-

* Published in its original form as 'From barbarian to burlesque: English images of the Irish c. 1660–1750' in *Irish Economic and Social History*, xv (1988), pp 5–31.

1 See for example John Kirkaldy, 'Irish jokes: no cause for laughter' in *Irish Studies in Britain*, ii (1981), pp 13–14; idem, 'English cartoonists: Ulster realities' in *Éire-Ireland*, xvi (1981), pp 27–42; Liz Curtis, *Nothing but the same old story: roots of Irish racism* (London, 1985); Patrick O'Sullivan, 'The Irish joke' in idem (ed.), *The creative migrant* (Leicester, 1994), pp 57–82. But see also Christie Davies, 'The Irish joke as a social phenomenon' in John Durant and Jonathan Miller (eds), *Laughing matters: a serious look at humour* (Harlow, 1988), pp 44–65; and in general Christie Davies, *Jokes and their relation to society* (Berlin & New York, 1998).

2 E. D. Snyder, 'The wild Irish: a study of some English satires of the Irish, Scots and Welsh' in *Modern Philology*, xvii (1919–20), pp 687–725; G. C. Duggan, *The stage Irishman: a history of the Irish play and stage characters from the earliest times* (Dublin, 1937); J. O. Bartley, 'The development of a stock character, i: the stage Irishman to 1800' in *Modern Language Review*, xxxviii (1942), pp 438–47; idem, *Teague, Shenkin and Sawney* (Cork, 1954), esp. ch. 6; J. M. Nelson, 'From Rory and Paddy to Boucicault's Myles, Shaun and Conn: the Irishman on the London stage 1830–60' in *Éire-Ireland*, xiii (1978), pp 79–105; Alan Bliss, *Spoken English in Ireland 1600–1700* (Monkstown, Co. Dublin, 1979); Deana Rankin, '"Shet fourd vor general nouddificaushion': relocating the Irish joke, 1678–1690' in *Eighteenth-Century Ireland*, xvi (2001), pp 47–72; and especially Joep Leerssen, *Mere Irish and fíor-ghael: studies in the idea of Irish nationality, its development and literary expression prior to the nineteenth century* (2nd ed., Cork, 1996), esp. pp 77–150. The first edition of Professor Leerssen's book had been published in Holland in 1986 but was not available to me when the original version of this essay was written.

3 There is an extensive literature on this topic: see in particular, E. M. Hinton, *Ireland through Tudor eyes* (Philadelphia, 1935); D. B. Quinn, *The Elizabethans and the Irish* (Ithaca, N.Y., 1966); Nicholas P. Canny, *The Elizabethan conquest of Ireland: a pattern established, 1565–1576* (Hassocks, Sussex, 1976); Nicholas Canny, *Making Ireland British, 1580–1650* (Oxford, 2001), ch. 1; Ciaran Brady, 'Spenser's Irish crisis: humanism and experience in the 1590s' in *Past and Present*, no. 111

lusting Fenians would vindicate Victorian repression.[4] By contrast, relatively little attention has been paid to the era in between, the late seventeenth and eighteenth centuries, in which the inhabitants of Ireland were generally regarded by the English as figures of fun rather than bogeymen, and 'Teague-land' became one of the first resorts of the English humorist. In the century following the Restoration of King Charles II, the stereotypical Irishman – appearing with predictable regularity on the English stage and in print, in plays, novels, mock-epic poems, essays, political tracts, ballads and jest-books – was transformed from a half-human savage into a ridiculous and contemptible gimcrack Englishman, whose limited capacities and comic idiosyncrasies offered cheap laughs and reassurance to the preening superiority of the metropolitan. Drinking, bragging in his cups, nursing his pride and forever taking up arms in defence of his 'honour', hunting fortunes, murdering logic and the English language, a certain kind of stock Irishman made his entrance into the world. The supersession of the frightful 'rough, rug-headed kerne' by the ludicrous figure of 'Captain O'Blunder' was to some degree a reflection of the changing political scene, in Ireland and in Britain: the reduction of Ireland as a strategic problem for English government following the subjugation of the Catholic interest. Equally, if not more important, as far as the members of the Irish propertied elite were concerned, it also marked a shift in perceptions of Irish national identity; the English public in the eighteenth-century now had a different view of who 'the Irish' were, as well as what they were like.

There was already a strong element of broad humour in the seventeenth-century 'stage Irishman'.[5] Jacobean dramatists introduced him most frequently as a simple peasant, foot soldier or servant, chiefly distinguished by his lisping speech. Other shorthand devices employed to fix the identification were name (Teague, Dermot, or Rory, say, for a male; Nora, inevitably, for a female), religion (indicated through invocations of 'Chreisht' and the saints, especially Patrick), habitat (bogs), diet (shamrock, watercress, buttermilk), or music (the harp). But these clowns were two-dimensional figures, whose characters were scarcely developed. The same is true of the few 'Irish gentlemen' and army officers to be found in pre-Restoration drama. Such humorous representations of the Irishman softened a little but did not fundamentally alter the image that had been stamped by Tudor conquistadors and reformers, of the Irishman as by nature 'wild' and uncivilised, even congenitally incapable of civilisation; regressive in his way of life, superstitious in his religion, licentious in his sexual mores, treacherous and savagely violent; in short, a dangerous barbarian. Although, naturally enough, this impression of a race of men inherently, and perhaps irredeemably, inferior, aroused powerful feelings of contempt among

(1986), pp 17–49; Willy Maley, *Salvaging Spenser: colonialism, culture and identity* (Basingstoke, 1997).

4 L. P. Curtis, jr, *Apes and angels: the Irishman in Victorian caricature* (Newton Abbot, 1971); Patrick O'Farrell, *England and Ireland since 1800* (Oxford, 1975), esp. chs 2–3; Ned Lebow, *White Britain and black Ireland: the influences of stereotypes on colonial policy* (Philadelphia, 1976); D. G. Paz, 'Anti-Catholicism, Irish stereotyping and anti-Celtic racism in mid-Victorian working class periodicals' in *Albion*, xviii (1986), pp 601–16. See also Roy Foster, 'Paddy and Mr Punch' in *Journal of Newspaper and Periodical History*, vii (1991), pp 33–47.

5 Leerssen, *Mere Irish and fíor-ghael*, pp 80–90.

the English, the ever-present undertone was one of fear. The credulity demonstrated by the English public in 1641–2 when fed with atrocity stories from the long-dreaded rising in Ireland testifies to the widespread belief in the reality of the 'wild Irishman'.[6] Even the playwrights, with their penchant for Irishness as comic relief, did not forget the savage in the shadows. Webster's howling Irishmen played a kind of football with the severed heads of their enemies. The purely comic characters, too, had their moments. In *Sir John Oldcastle* (1618) the Irish manservant talked carelessly of cutting his master's throat as soon as a suitable opportunity arose, throat-cutting being a practice particularly associated with the Gaelic Irish; and Dekker's *The honest whore* (1604) reminded its audience, in an arch reference to the achievements of St Patrick that was fast becoming a trope of English writers, that Ireland was 'a country where no venom prospers, but in the nation's blood'.[7]

The concept of the native Irishman (or on occasion, and with a significant ambiguity, the 'natural' Irishman) as barbaric persisted throughout the seventeenth century, although it gradually diminished in importance, and became one among several elements in the Englishman's perception of Irishness. During the prolonged crisis of the 1640s and '50s, when Puritan millenarianism and political insecurity were compounded with the traditional English sense of national superiority, it was still, in English eyes, the first point of definition of an Irishman. William Lithgow wrote in 1632 that 'the vulgar Irish ... live more brutishly than the undaunted or untamed Arabian, the devilish-idolatrous Turkoman or the moon-worshipping Caramines'.[8] Small wonder, then, that Oliver Cromwell himself, possessed like his compatriots with the tales of Irish cruelty gathered in Sir John Temple's best-selling history of the 1641 rising, could declare of the Irish that 'all the world knows their barbarism'; while the English press in the 1650s could pronounce the Irish people to be 'the most barbarous in the world'.[9] So affected were Parliamentarian troops by assumptions of Irish bestiality that some were prepared to swear on oath after the butchery of a Catholic garrison at Cashel in 1647 that the corpses included some with 'tails near a quarter of a yard long'.[10] Even in a later, less agitated, period an English commentator expressed his anxiety over prospects for Huguenot settlers in

6 Robin Clifton, 'The popular fear of Catholics during the English revolution' in *Past & Present*, no. 52 (1971), pp 26–7, 29–31, 49–50; K. J. Lindley, 'The impact of the 1642 rebellion on England and Wales, 1641–5' in *I.H.S.*, xviii, no. 70 (Sept. 1972), pp 143–70; Bernard Capp, *Astrology and the popular press: English almanacs 1500–1800* (London, 1979), pp 77–8; Anthony Fletcher, *The outbreak of the English Civil War* (London, 1981), p. 136; Micheál Ó Siochrú, *God's executioner: Oliver Cromwell and the conquest of Ireland* (London, 2008), ch. 2.

7 Quoted in Duggan, *Stage Irishman*, pp 243–5.

8 Quoted in Snyder, 'Wild Irishman', p. 159.

9 C. H. Firth (ed.), *The Clarke papers* ..., vol. ii (Camden Society, new ser., liv, 1894), p. 205; Maurice Ashley, *Oliver Cromwell* (London, 1937), p. 163; Joseph Frank, *The beginnings of the English newspaper 1620–1660* (Cambridge, Mass., 1961), pp 51, 183; Ó Siochrú, *God's executioner*, pp 63–4. See also John Morrill, 'The Drogheda massacre in Cromwellian context' in David Edwards et al. (eds), *Age of atrocity: violence and political conflict in early modern Ireland* (Dublin, 2007), pp 242–65.

10 Keith Thomas, *Man and the natural world: changing attitudes in England 1500–1800* (Penguin ed., Harmondsworth, 1984), pp 42–3.

Ireland by observing that 'if they be not encouraged in industry ... [they] will all turn Irish and barbarous'.[11]

Yet while the concept of barbarism remained – and indeed the expression 'wild Irishman' was not defunct even by the late eighteenth century, though its usage was by then merely conventional and jocose – this was not the same kind of barbarism in c. 1730 as it had been in c. 1650. For one thing, the strictly racist element in English prejudice was becoming diluted. William Petty's rebuttal of the theory that barbarism was innate in the Irish, a genetic inheritance from 'Scythian' or 'Phoenician' forbears, heralded, if it did not itself bring about, a significant change. In Petty's more sociological analysis, factors such as environment, history, and 'the influence of their governors and teachers' were responsible for the 'reprehensible manners' to be found in Ireland. Laziness, for example, was a consequence of lack of opportunity and encouragement to work, rather than any 'natural abundance of phlegm in their bowels and blood'.[12] The degree and extent to which attitudes were modified in this way should not be exaggerated. Theories of inherent barbarism survived, in the writings of Swift and Berkeley, to cite only the two most notable instances.[13] Furthermore, in much eighteenth-century commentary on the customs of the native Irish there remains a strong sense of racial, rather than national or religious, differentiation. But one may perhaps hear echoes of Petty in the assumption in some quarters that the native Irish, though barbaric in their culture and behaviour, were improvable, the corollary to an explanation of Irish barbarism as environmentally and historically conditioned. Belief in the potential of the civilising process was in tune with the reconstructive spirit of Restoration England, and no less consonant with its commercial opportunism. Thus we find an admirer of the 'wisdom' of the restored King Charles crediting that monarch with curing the 'ill ... humours in the natural Irish ... by sending wise and honest lord deputies, the increase of the English among them, and bring[ing] the Irish in some measure into trade and civility'; a pamphlet of 1677 grounding its arguments for the encouragement of trade in Ireland on the premise that this would be a means to 'wear off the barbarity of the common Irish ... for industry is the first step to civility'; and even Swift, in the persona of 'the Drapier', proposing means 'to civilise the ... natives, in all those parts of the kingdom where the Irish abound; by introducing among them our language and customs, for want of which they live in the utmost ignorance, barbarity and poverty'.[14]

[11] G. P. R. James (ed.), *Letters illustrative of the reign of William III from 1696 to 1708 ...* (3 vols, London, 1841), i, 429. See also Simon Clement, *The interest of England, as it stands with relation to the trade of Ireland, considered* (London, 1698), p. 12.

[12] Sir William Petty, *The political anatomy of Ireland* (London, 1691), pp 95–6, 98–101, 103–4.

[13] *Irish tracts 1728–1733*, ed. Herbert Davis, in *The prose works of Jonathan Swift*, ed. Herbert Davis et al. (16 vols, Oxford, 1939–74), xii, 19, 178; Joseph Johnston (ed.) *Bishop Berkeley's Querist in historical perspective* (Dundalk, 1970), p. 168. See also D. F. Bond (ed.) *The Tatler* (3 vols, Oxford, 1987), i, 256.

[14] 'Mr Houghton's ... observations on the wisdom and success of Charles the 2nd', 1680 (B.L., Brockman papers, Add. MS 42592, f. 5); *A letter from a gentleman in Ireland to his brother in England, relating to the concerns of Ireland in matters of trade* (London, 1677), p. 12; *The Drapier's letters and other works 1724–1725*, ed. Harold Williams, in *The prose works of Jonathan Swift*, ed. Herbert Davis et al., x, 169.

This subtle alteration in the response to encounters with Irish 'barbarity' did not make the language of denunciation any less brutal. What happened was a subtle shift in the direction of the invective. The crude manners of the native Irish were intimately connected with their poverty, both reflecting a physical, moral and spiritual degradation. For Swift and other Irish Protestant patriots, this represented a powerful argument against the defective political and economic system under which Ireland suffered. 'Nothing in so wretched and enslaved a nation as this can be worth entertaining your lordship with', the dean wrote to Lord Oxford in 1734; 'it is a mass of beggars, thieves, oppressors, fools, and knaves.'[15] For English observers, on the other hand, it was simply a fact of life. The poverty of the native Irish was axiomatic; with poverty went ignorance, and, in this line of thinking, with ignorance went stupidity. A stage Irishman could be introduced as 'a true half-witted bog-trotter'.[16] The picture of Irish rural society drawn by visiting Englishmen reinforced these pre-existing (and pre-induced) assumptions about a way of life that was squalid and depraved. An example from 1622, in a private letter, sounded the set note. 'The bad inhabitants of this good country' were

> scarce one remove from savages, if not in the same form of brutality. Their houses are like hog-sties ... and they themselves swine-like in all things but shape. Their habitats are swine-like, all live and lie together without any distinction of ages or sex, their houses are not to be gone but grope into, they making their doors as low and little as they can, and their ceilings' thatch as low as a man's head.[17]

Here are themes and analogies, including the traditional innuendoes of sexual promiscuity and perversion, which were to be utilised by numerous travel-writers.[18] In particular, they were taken up in three influential accounts published in the 1690s, which may be said to have re-established, and perhaps to have redefined, the popular idea of Irish 'barbarity': the anonymous *A brief character of Ireland* (1692), and *A trip to Ireland ...* (1699), which re-worked much of the same material; and the 'account of his conversation in Ireland' which formed the basis of the eccentric London bookseller John Dunton's *The Dublin scuffle* (also 1699).[19] All three dwelt on the poverty of the native Irish, their sordid and smoky cabins, crude and nauseating diet, and primitive customs, and even on the supposedly unprepossessing physical appearance, combined with gross lubricity, of their womenfolk. The underlying attitude

15 Swift to Oxford, 30 Aug. 1734 (*The correspondence of Jonathan Swift*, ed. Harold Williams (5 vols, Oxford, 1963–5), iv, 249).

16 Bliss, *Spoken English in Ireland*, quoting from John Durant Breval's *The play is the plot* (1718).

17 H.M.C., *15th rep.*, vii, 169.

18 The best known traveller not to have published his tale is Thomas Dineley; see his *Observations in a voyage through the kingdom of Ireland ... in the year 1681*, ed. James Graves (Dublin, 1870). His commentary is discussed in Constantia Maxwell, *The stranger in Ireland* (London, 1954), pp 101–6.

19 *A brief character of Ireland, with some observations of the customs, etc. of the meaner sort of the natural inhabitants of that kingdom* (Dublin, 1692); *A trip to Ireland, being a description of the country ... as also some ... observations on Dublin* (London, 1699); John Dunton, *The Dublin scuffle ...* (London, 1699; there is also a modern edition, with an introduction and notes by Andrew Carpenter (Dublin, 2000)). For Dunton, see Maxwell, *Stranger in Ireland*, pp 116–24; Dunton, *The Dublin scuffle*, ed. Carpenter, pp vii–xxvii; and *Oxf. D.N.B.* xvii, 366–7.

is revealed in Dunton's justification for his Irish sojourn, that 'having studied the manners ... of the Indians while in America, he now thought he would take a look at the Irish "savages"'.[20]

Another important difference from the prevailing climate of opinion in the late sixteenth and early seventeenth centuries is that in the presentation of this panorama of barbarity there was no element of fear. The *Brief character* scorned the notion of Irish fighting prowess: at the approach of the enemy 'the Teagues do only gaze about them to see what wood or bog lies nearest, and can best shelter or favour them in their retreat, or perhaps, by greasing their brogues, or anointing their joints, make ready for a more speedy flight'.[21] The tenor of the work, one of hearty contempt for almost everything in human form encountered on the island, evidently did not permit any apprehension of danger. In this the writer was, by and large, typical of his time. Generally speaking, Englishmen were now amused by the Irish rather than alarmed by them. However, changes in popular attitudes are seldom sudden and complete; we are faced with a slow transmutation of public perceptions rather than a mass Damascene conversion. In essence the *Brief character*, published immediately after the conclusion of the Jacobite war, was a piece of propaganda, having as a primary objective to debunk the ancient myth of Irish valour. Yet at the same time it reminded its readers of the brutality of previous Irish rebels: 'bloody they are, when they can overpower, and do it securely, and this is an effect of their cowardice, for that and their pride are curs of the same litter; witness their execrable butcheries and massacres of our poor and unarmed country folks'.[22] The preface to a published war play of 1690, *The royal voyage*, showed the same unease: 'the end of this play is chiefly to expose the perfidious, base, cowardly, bloody nature of the Irish'.[23] Certainly in December 1688, when there had been reports of Irish Catholic troops on the loose in the English midlands and south country, atavistic fears consumed the population. In the infamous 'Irish fright' malicious rumours were spread by Orangist agents that these regiments were indulging in an orgy of violence in revenge for the rejection of James II, and counties the length and breadth of England were 'raised with an alarm of Irish ... killing or burning all before them'.[24] Needless to say, they were said to be busy cutting throats wherever they roamed. This panic was the climax to a decade

20 Quoted in Maxwell, *Stranger in Ireland*, p. 119. Dineley compared Irish burial customs with those of the native 'Indians' of the Antilles (Dineley, *Observations*, ed. Graves, pp 28–30); the *Trip to Ireland* linked the native Irish with 'monsters' in Jamaica (preface); while the *Brief character* went so far as to imply an analogy with 'apes' (preface).

21 *Brief character*, pp 56–7.

22 Ibid., pp 35–6.

23 *The royal voyage, or The Irish expedition* (London, 1690), preface and pp 9, 28. Sir Francis Brewster's *A discourse concerning Ireland* (London, 1698) reconciled the notions of Irish cowardice and savagery by distinguishing between the 'ancient Irish', who were 'a poor, dispirited and cowardly people', and 'degenerate English papists ... the most desperate and troublesome enemies the Protestants have in that nation', who 'managed' their weaker-minded co-religionists in 1688 (p. 5).

24 J. R. Jones, *The revolution of 1688 in England* (London, 1972), pp 301–303; G. H. Jones, 'The Irish fright of 1688: real violence and imagined massacre' in *Bulletin of the Institute of Historical Research*, lv (1982), pp 149–53; Tim Harris, *Revolution: the great crisis of the British monarchy, 1685–1720* (Penguin ed., Harmondsworth, 2007), pp 298–9.

of Whig propaganda, seeking to terrify the English public with the traditional nightmare of bloodthirsty Irish papists.[25] That the programme worked so well proved the persistence in England of the popular reputation of the Irishman as a cruel savage, though it did require a political crisis to realise its full potential.

Nevertheless, if we examine more closely the anti-Irish writings of the 1680s and '90s we may detect signs of that ongoing process by which dread was being gradually replaced by derision. True, the native Irish were called 'a brutal race that Israel's God ne'er knew'; the horror-stories of 1641 were reworked, with contemporary embellishments recording planned massacres by the Jacobite forces and the inhumane treatment of Protestant prisoners; and, at the nadir of Whig taste, there was a revival of the canard of cannibalism – 'a virgin's haunch, or well-baked lady's breast, to them is better than a virgin's feast'.[26] More frequently, however, these same 'wild Irishmen' were portrayed as poor and ignorant. King James's Irish soldiers, the alleged pyromaniacs and mass-murderers of 1688, appeared in plays of the time as a rabble of hobbledehoys. The author of *Royal flight, or The conquest of Ireland* (1690) described 'Teague''s military preparations; 'to drink usquebaugh [whiskey] and pick his toes, mend his patched brogues and mundifie his clothes'.[27] A scene in *The royal voyage* extracted easy humour from the sight of a native Irishman keening over the corpse of a fallen comrade: 'Ah, brother Teague, why didst thou go?', with a chorus of 'aboo, aboo, aboo'.[28] Even the more measured treatment of Irish events in Colonel John Michelburne's play, *Ireland preserved*, or *The siege of Derry*, included Catholic Irish soldiers who were comic characters of the classic type, ridiculous in their appearance, their superstitious religion, and their manner of speech. The broadside ballads of the war years embodied what seems to have been a conscious effort to reassure English public opinion of the moral rectitude and military superiority of the Protestant cause in Ireland, by denigrating the intelligence, skill and bravery of the Jacobite rank and file.[29] The most famous anti-Irish satire of the period, the

25 See, for example, Jonathan Scott, *England's troubles: seventeenth-century English political instability in European context* (Cambridge, 2000), p. 199.

26 G. de F. Lord et al. (eds), *Poems on affairs of state* (6 vols, New Haven, Conn., 1938–75), ii, 383–4; iii, 16; Sir John Temple, *The Irish rebellion; or, An history of the beginning and first progress of the general rebellion raised within the kingdom of Ireland upon the ... 23 Oct. 1641 ...* (2nd ed., London, 1674; 3rd ed., London, 1679); John Vesey, *A sermon preached to the Protestants of Ireland in and about the City of London ...* (London, 1689), pp 28–31; diary of Simon Digby, Oct.–Dec. 1688 (Lambeth Palace Library, MS 3152); *The entring book of Roger Morrice 1677–91*, ed. Mark Goldie et al. (7 vols, Woodbridge, 2007–9), v, 291, 306; H.M.C., *5th report*, p. 380; newsletter, 13 Sept. 1690 (T.N.A., Powis papers, PRO 30/53/8/84).

27 Quoted in Duggan, *Stage Irishman*, p. 81. See also Rankin, '"Shet fourd vor general nouddificaushion"', pp 67–8. 'Mundify': to clean, often used in a religious sense to denote a purging of sins.

28 Quoted in Duggan, *Stage Irishman*, p. 79. See also Rankin, '"Shet fourd vor general nouddificaushion"', pp 67–70.

29 J. W. Ebsworth (ed.), *The Bagford ballads* (3 vols, Hertford, 1878–80), i, 297, 305–307, 373–6, 426–8; 'A collection of ballads, originally formed by John Selden ... and now forming part of the Pepys Library' (5 vols, B.L., Dept. of Printed Books, L.R.408. n.1), ii, 463–82; Henry Playford, *Wit and mirth: or Pills to purge melancholy* (4th ed., London, 1714–19), v, 165–6. [James Farewell,] *The Irish Hudibras, or Fingallian prince ...* (London, 1689), though a mock-epic aimed at a rather different audience, had a similar propagandist purpose. See Rankin, '"Shet fourd vor general nouddificaushion"', pp 60–64; Andrew Carpenter, 'Sectarianism in Marsh's Ireland: some literary

song 'Lilliburlero', was just such a burlesque, cast in the form of a dialogue between 'Teague' and his friend 'Morish', in heavy brogue, spiced with the obligatory invocations. The protagonists looked forward to the pleasure of some throat-cutting, but their sanguinary prognostications, delivered to a refrain couched in pseudo-Gaelic language, can hardly be described as blood-curdling.[30] English confidence, which had quickly returned after the hysteria of the 'Irish fright' in November 1688, is nicely captured in the contemporary political poem, 'The plowman', where two English rustics looked forward to settling accounts with the Irish. 'Never fear 'em', said one, 'we country boys, will piss on their beloved dear joys.'[31]

The most obvious cause of the modification of the stereotype of the Irishman in English print, the dilution of the element of savagery in the 'wild Irishman', was the changing political climate in late seventeenth-century Ireland. Repeated English military victories were encouraging a conviction of Irish inferiority on the battlefield. Furthermore, the land settlements that followed the successful wars of reconquest – especially the Williamite settlement – seemed to have shattered the economic (and thus the political) power of the Catholic landowning classes, while the flight of the 'wild geese' into Europe after the capitulation of the Jacobite garrisons at Galway and Limerick in 1691 had taken into a permanent exile the flower of the Catholic military cause. As some Irish Protestants soon realised, the 'youth and gentry' of Catholic Ireland had been effectively 'destroyed'.[32] For all that Catholics continued heavily to outnumber Protestants on the island, without the leadership of those whom contemporaries defined as the 'natural rulers', a rising on the scale of 1641, presumably now in the form of some spontaneous peasant *jacquerie*, was highly improbable. The only real threat came from the prospect of a Jacobite invasion, backed by foreign aid, but this too appeared increasingly unlikely. For the Jacobite pretender to accomplish his objective, the most practical scheme was a landing on the mainland of Great Britain, and preferably in England, followed by a quick strike towards London. King James II's bitter experience had taught his successor the futility of committing the main force to an Irish campaign. In 1708, 1715, 1719 and 1745 the danger to the English establishment came from landings (or attempted landings) in Scotland rather than Ireland, with the result that in the eighteenth century the Scottish Highlander replaced the Irish kerne as the Jacobite bogeyman. Growing English complacency is evinced by the statement of the attorney-general, Dudley Ryder, in 1715 that English Catholics constituted more of a problem than their Irish counterparts: 'though the number of papists is vastly superior to that of Protestants [in Ireland], yet the Protestants are able to keep them in order and prevent any trouble or danger from themselves, whereas we in England

evidence' in Muriel McCarthy and Ann Simmons (eds), *The making of Marsh's Library: learning, politics and religion in Ireland, 1650–1750* (Dublin, 2004), pp 197–202.

30 William Chappell, *Popular music of the olden time: a collection of ancient songs, ballads, and dance tunes, illustrative of the national music of England …* (2 vols, London, 1855–9), ii, 568–72; John Carswell, *The old cause* (London, 1954), pp 353–9; Lord et al. (eds), *Poems on affairs of state*, iv, 309–14.

31 Lord et al. (eds), *Poems on affairs of state*, iv, 302.

32 'The case of the sacramentall test …' (R.O. for Leicestershire, Leicester and Rutland, Finch papers, box 4950, Ire. 9).

that have much fewer papists here, are not sufficiently armed against ... rebellions and popery'.[33]

Alongside this lowering of the politico-military profile of the native Irish went a refinement in English Protestant attitudes towards the Catholic church. Religious allegiance had been one of the features that made the Irish rebel of the mid-seventeenth century such a terrifying figure. In the struggle for the Reformation, which the 'godly people' of England believed was reaching a climacteric in the 1640s and '50s, the Irish Catholic took a prominent place in the pope's divisions, as one of the shock troops of the army of Antichrist. By the end of the century, however, the cool breeze of reason began to dispel the enthusiasm of millenarian Protestantism. Anti-popery in the late seventeenth and eighteenth centuries lost little of its vehemence, especially at a popular level, as Colin Haydon has reminded us,[34] but its sights were adjusted to focus on the secular tyranny of continental monarchies and on the intellectual tyranny of Catholic 'priestcraft' over sceptical and rational enquiry, instead of assuming the existence of an armed international conspiracy against the reformed religion headed by the pope and the Society of Jesus and supported by fervent Catholic rulers like Louis XIV of France. Among the educated élite, contempt for 'popery' was acquiring a loftier ring. In denouncing the Church of Rome and its works in 1679, the Whig 'martyr' William, Lord Russell, declared that he despised 'such a ridiculous and nonsensical religion'.[35] Strikingly similar was the phraseology used by Sir Richard Cocks, an English Whig M.P. and anti-Catholic polemicist of the 1720s: 'a ridiculous, strange and detestable religion';[36] indeed, not so much a religion at all, in the eyes of many Protestants, as a political system, sustaining itself by persecution and by duping the gullible with mumbo-jumbo. The lady traveller Celia Fiennes observed Catholic devotions at St Winifred's Well in Flintshire from an altogether superior intellectual plane: 'There I saw abundance of devout papists on their knees all round the well; poor people [*that*] are to be pitied by us that have the advantage of knowing better.'[37] The essential characteristics were ignorance and superstition, enabling the ordinary Catholic to be deluded by his rascally (and mate-

[33] Dudley Ryder's diary, 2 Dec. 1715, *The diary of Dudley Ryder 1715–1716*, ed. William Matthews (London, 1939), p. 144).

[34] Colin Haydon, 'The anti-Catholic activity of the S.P.C.K., c.1698–1740' in *Recusant History*, xviii (1987), pp 418–21; idem, *Anti-Catholicism in eighteenth-century England, c.1714–80: a political and social study* (Manchester, 1993); idem, '"I love my king and country, but a Roman Catholic I hate": anti-Catholicism, xenophobia, and national identity in eighteenth-century England' in Tony Claydon and Ian McBride (eds), *Protestantism and national identity: Britain and Ireland c. 1650–c. 1850* (Cambridge, 1998), pp 33–52; idem, 'Parliament and popery in England, 1700–1780' in J. P. Parry and Stephen Taylor (eds), *Parliament and the church 1529–1960* (Edinburgh, 2000), pp 48–63. See also J. M. Black, 'The Catholic threat in the British press in the 1720s and 1730s' in *Journal of Religious History*, xii (1983), pp 364–81.

[35] William Cobbett, *The parliamentary history of England* (36 vols, London, 1806–20), iv, col. 1127.

[36] Sir Richard Cocks's diary, 15 Dec. 1699, *The parliamentary diary of Sir Richard Cocks, 1698–1702*, ed. D. W. Hayton (Oxford, 1996), p. 45); Cocks, A *true and impartial inquiry into the late bloody execution at Thorn* (London, 1727), p. 30. See also Samuel Johnson, A *letter from a freeholder, to the rest of the freeholders of England* (London, [1689]), pp 2–3; Mrs Mary Clarke to Edward Clarke, 29 May 1700 (Somerset Heritage Centre, Sanford papers, DD/SF 4515).

[37] *The journeys of Celia Fiennes*, ed. Christopher Morris (London, 1949), p. 181.

rially ambitious) spiritual governors. Lord Clarendon, lord lieutenant of Ireland in the 1686, wrote to his brother from Dublin Castle of the 'wonderful stupidity of the common people'. 'It is scarce possible for any that have not been here to believe the profound, ignorant bigotry the natives here are bred in by the priests, who to all appearances seem as ignorant as themselves.'[38] Ignorance was, as we have seen, one of the major defects that Englishmen ascribed to the native Irish, and those travel-writers and others who expatiated on the backward nature of Irish culture found religion a rich pasture. The stage Irish peasant of the late seventeenth century was usually portrayed as the illiterate tool of a barely more sophisticated hedge-priest, his piety chiefly characterised by indiscriminate devotion to the saints, from the ubiquitous Patrick down to 'St Holyhead'. The *History of Tom Thumb* being read to the 'common Irish' observed one wit, 'has passed current for the legend of one of their most famous saints'.[39]

From the Restoration onwards the English attitude towards Ireland, and all things and persons Irish, was settling into a permanent sneer. The 'wild Irishman' was a contemptible coward; even if a cunning cut-throat, at heart a coward. The emphasis throughout was on the inferiority of all things Irish. This was the habit of thinking which would prompt Dr Johnson to remark that an acquaintance had 'the misfortune to be an Irishman'. The adjective 'Irish' now denoted something deficient, and at least faintly comical.[40] A speaker in the English House of Lords in 1666 could refer to the 'Irish understandings' of those who disagreed with him.[41] To 'weep Irish' was to cry without tears, in other words to feign sorrow.[42] An 'Irish hurricane' was a dead calm;[43] 'Irish evidence' testimony that was worthless and corrupt, like that of the Irish witnesses to the Popish Plot, whence the expression derived.[44] A jury wishing to find a defendant guilty of perjury but 'not wilful' was instructed that this would be 'an Irish verdict',[45] while a stage character dragging away a drunk

38 *The correspondence of Henry Hyde, earl of Clarendon, and of his brother Laurence Hyde, earl of Rochester … from 1687 to 1690*, ed. S. W. Singer (2 vols, London, 1828), ii, 124–5. See also *Bishop Burnet's History of his own time*, ed. M. J. Routh (2nd ed., 6 vols, London, 1823), iv, 102; William Flower to R. Powell, 22 Sept. 1730 (N.L.I., Durrow papers, MS 11,479/5).

39 *Brief character*, p. 57.

40 Eric Partridge, *A dictionary of slang*, ed. Paul Beale (8th ed., London, 1984), p. 600, notes that 'Irish' took on a derogatory meaning c. 1690.

41 Cobbett, *Parl. hist.*, iv, 342. The perpetrator was the duke of Buckingham, a patron of Sir Robert Howard, for whom see below, p 12.

42 Cited without date in F. P. Wilson, *The Oxford dictionary of English proverbs* (3rd ed., Oxford, 1970), p. 876. It was used by Dineley in c. 1680 (*Observations*, ed. Graves, pp 18–19) and may well go back much further.

43 Cited, again without date, in Francis Grose, *A classical dictionary of the vulgar tongue*, ed. Eric Partridge (London, 1931), pp 200–201. For an example of its use (by Sir Robert Walpole) in 1723, see Albert Goodwin, 'Wood's halfpence' in *E.H.R.*, li (1936), p. 656 (repr. in Rosalind Mitchison (arr.), *Essays in eighteenth-century history* (London, 1966), pp 117–44).

44 Cited in Partridge, *Dictionary of slang*, p. 600 (an example from 1699). Cf. Lord et al., *Poems on affairs of state*, ii, 494; iii, 99; Sir John Hobart to William Windham, 31 May 1681 (H.M.C., *12th rep.*, ix, pp 185–6); Bartley, *Teague, Shenkin & Sawney*, pp 125–6.

45 Horace Walpole to Richard Bentley, 18 May 1754, *The correspondence of Horace Walpole*, ed. W. S. Lewis et al. (42 vols, New Haven, Conn., 1937–80), xxxv, 175).

by the heels spoke of giving his passenger an 'Irish sedan'.[46] There was also the phrase 'an Irishman's prize' to convey the notion of an apparent gain that proved to be valueless, 'gaining a loss'.[47] By 1700 the word 'Irishism' had been coined, for an inversion of logic or blundering with words – the association being already long established.[48] Some twenty years earlier an Irish Protestant had already conceded that the country was 'despised in England'.[49] Visitors to Ireland, even those as open-minded as Mrs Delany, the English wife of the dean of Down, expected to meet social 'oddity'.[50] Naturally, this persistent ridicule grated, and Protestant as well as Catholic Irishmen came to resent the use of 'Irish' as a byword for the second-rate; or, as Lord Abercorn put it, being 'made the subject of jests, by the worst-natured part of our neighbours'.[51] The impact was such as to persuade some to disavow their national identity. The first duke of Ormond was said to have been 'devilishly nettled' by a satire of Dryden's, 'which makes him an Irishman, whereas he was born in London'; while in 1712 the future lord chancellor of Ireland, Alan Brodrick, whose family had established themselves in County Cork some sixty years previously, could write, 'if I remove to England I shall be thought … (what of all things I would least choose to be) an Irishman'.[52]

Much of the blame for this state of affairs may be laid at the door of a publication that, more than any other, popularised the idea of the 'Irish joke': a collection of what were described as 'profound puns, learned bulls, elaborate quibbles ... and wise sayings of the natives of Teague-land', which began life in c. 1680 as *Bogg-witticisms, or Dear Joy's commonplaces*, became *Teague-land jests*, and went through many editions in the eighteenth century as *The Irish miscellany*.[53] This represented a new departure in English jest-books. Jokes at the expense of the Irish had been a rare occurrence in early seventeenth-century popular literature, and a survey of some of the more successful jest-books of the period 1660–1740 shows that in this highly derivative and conventional genre the 'Irish joke' was still a comparatively scarce item well

46 *Sir Robert Howard's comedy 'The committee'*, ed. C. N. Thurber (Urbana, Ill., 1925), p. 124.

47 *London Gazette*, 24–27 November 1759, cited in Philip Lawson, '"The Irishman's prize": views of Canada from the British press' in *Hist. Jn.*, xxviii (1985), p. 575.

48 *O.E.D.* cites a usage by William Pulteney in 1734, but cf. *The several addresses of some Irish folks* (London, [1702]), p. 4; Edward Ward, *The secret history of clubs* (London, 1709), p. 274.

49 Sir George Rawdon to Thomas Kirke, 27 May 1680 (B.L., Stowe MS 746, f. 27).

50 *Letters from Georgian Ireland: the correspondence of Mary Delany 1731–68*, ed. Angélique Day and Sybil Connolly (Belfast, 1991), p. 25.

51 Abercorn to Edward Southwell, 19 December 1713 (P.R.O.N.I., Abercorn papers, D623/A/3/6).

52 'Letters of Richard Thompson to his brother Henry', ed. J. J. Cartwright, in *Camden Miscellany*, viii (Camden Soc., new ser., xxxi, 1883), p. 3; Alan Brodrick to Thomas Brodrick, 1 Nov. 1712 (S.H.C., Brodrick papers, 1248/3/91–2). It is remarkable that even a tribute to the recently deceased Dublin Catholic lawyer Sir Toby Butler, who died in 1721, felt obliged to excuse its subject's rich brogue (*An elegy on the very much lamented death of Sir Toby Butler* … (n.d.: B.L., Dept. of Printed Bks, 112602.i.l[2])). For Brodrick and his family, see below, ch. 4.

53 J. O. Bartley, 'Bulls and bogg witticisms' in *Irish Book Lover*, xxx (1946–8), pp 59–62; Rankin, '"Shet fourd vor general nouddificaushion"', pp 55–60. I have used a mid-eighteenth-century version: *The Irish miscellany, or Teagueland jests* … (3rd ed., London, 1749).

into the eighteenth century, though registering a small increase in frequency.[54] In all probability, however, the compiler of *Bogg-witticisms* was catering to an existing or emerging market rather than opening up a new one. There are certainly indications that Restoration Englishmen (and women) were already starting to find the Irishman peculiarly funny. As a stage character he was enjoying a vogue, following the huge success of the 'droll' servant Teague in Sir Robert Howard's *The committee*, first performed in 1665.[55] Irish funerals are said to have become a fashionable attraction for London society, a fact both reflected in and encouraged by the attention devoted to such practices by playwrights, versifiers and travel-writers. And the phrase 'dear joy', on which *Bogg-witticisms* relied heavily for local colour, was beginning to be employed regularly in burlesque representations of the Irish. Nonetheless, the impact of the book must have been considerable, much more so at a popular level than the theatrical drolleries of Howard's Teague and his compatriots in Restoration drama, who were still prone to occasional reversion to traditional type.

Bogg-witticisms exploited traditional comic devices too: the use of a stylised brogue, with an epidemic of 'Oh, hone!', 'hoo hoo', 'boo boo', and so forth; reference to harps, shamrock, bogs and buttermilk; and many a stab in the direction of ignorance and idolatry. But more important was the introduction, or rather the appropriation to the Irish, of the bull, the essential 'Irishism', a blunder in speech with some ludicrous internal contradiction, defined as 'a sort of comical joke ... that is a preposterous kind of speaking; when you return my meaning as if by mistake'.[56] Previous jest-books had used this style of humour, but had not confined it to any particular national group: a few bulls might fall from the lips of the Welsh, but were just as likely to be perpetrated by indigenous English yokels. Now, however, the bull was identified with Ireland; this, above all, was to be the mark of the eighteenth-century Irishman. In 1741 Ireland was called 'that land of bulls'.[57] Few of the originals in *Bogg-witticisms* have retained their flavour unimpaired down the centuries. Two may suffice for illustration. An Irishman taxed with wearing one of his stockings inside out replied that 'he did it on purposh, vor dat dere vash a hole on de oder shide'; another, finding a corpse, 'did tauke him by the haund, and ausked him, if

54 This conclusion is based on a study of the following editions: *Cambridge jests, or Witty alarums for melancholy spirits* (London, 1674); [William Hickes,] *Oxford jests, refined and enlarged* (London, 1684); [idem,] *Coffee-house jests, refined and enlarged* (London, 1686); Humfrey Crouch, *England's jests refin'd and improv'd* (3rd ed., London, 1693); W.B., *Ingenii fructus: or, The Cambridge jests ...* (London, 1700); *Joe Miller's jests: or, The wits' vade-mecum* (London, 1739). From c. 240–350 items in each book, the number of recognisable 'Irish' jokes increased from none in 1674 to nine in 1739. Welsh jokes, beginning at eight, declined by half, while the number of Scottish jokes remained steady at two or three. A related publication, Francis Kirkman's 'dramatic miscellany', *The wits, or Sport upon sport* (London, 1662), contained one humorous Welsh character and no Irishmen. See also John Ashton, *Humour, wit, and satire of the seventeenth century* (London, 1883), pp 227, 319, 375.

55 Leerssen, *Mere Irish and fíor-ghael*, pp 90–92.

56 *Irish miscellany*, p. vi.

57 Henry Seymour Conway to Horace Walpole, 16 Feb. 1741 (*Corresp. of Horace Walpole*, ed. Lewis et al., xxxvii, 93). See also *Brief character*, p. 24; Ward, *Secret hist. of clubs*, p. 379.

he vaush dead? Bot he answered, and said noting.'[58] Such efforts caught the fancy of the English public. Proverbial phrases like 'the Irishman's prize' most probably derive from these stories. The author of *Bogg-witticisms* boasted that

> The bulls and witticisms, that have too frequently dropped from the mouths of dear joys, have made them so famous, that they are become the discourse of all sorts of companies. The Welshmen and Scots had a long time engrossed all the table talk of the town; and the jests and stories that were related concerning them, passed instead of a song or a fiddle. But Teague and his countrymen have clearly baffled Saint Taffy and Saint Andrew, for downright Dunstable, blunder and pun....[59]

Or, as the *Brief character of Ireland* ... expressed it, in a poetic 'epigram', 'one wond'ring at an Irish Teig, who spake much nonsense; and did everything mistake ... The wonder's not, says one, there's some such tools, but that there's half a kingdom of such fools.'[60] Not even the urbanity of *The Spectator* was proof against the fashion. Richard Steele, himself an Irishman by birth and upbringing, wrote of his fellow countrymen, albeit with a certain fond indulgence, 'there is seldom anything entertaining in the impudence of a south or north Briton, but that of an Irishman is always comic'.[61]

Several things were happening to the Irish stereotype in the half-century following the Restoration. The 'wild Irishman' was becoming less frightening, less of a 'bugaboo', and more an object of contempt. There was a tendency to concentrate on his supposed inferiority, his poverty, and the squalor in which he lives. He had also taken his place as a prime source of humour, on the stage and in literary works whether vulgar or polite. Along with this growing popularity as comic relief we find an elaboration of the physical aspects of the caricature. The stage Irishman in Restoration drama usually spoke a more specialised kind of brogue than his Jacobean counterparts, his linguistic peculiarities developed beyond a mere thickening of consonants, his conversation spattered with interjections in what might be described as kitchen Gaelic. His diet also became slightly more varied, or perhaps more specific, with the introduction of 'bonny clabber' (from the Irish *bainne clabair*, meaning sour milk) and the potato – soon to be 'the inevitable tuber'.[62] He was portrayed with a heightened attention to topographical detail. But still more significant is the evolution of what came to be regarded as typically Irish character-traits, beyond the traditional vices of ignorance, superstition, treacherousness and cruelty. This new set of national characteristics was less closely associated with the Irish peasantry and indeed in some respects was more readily applicable to the landed classes, enabling the creation of stock figures of a more elevated social status to set

58 Bartley, 'Bulls and bogg witticisms'. The latter had been anticipated by Sir Robert Howard (*'The committee'*, ed. Thurber, p. 56).

59 *Irish miscellany*, p. 3.

60 *Brief character*, p. 103.

61 D. F. Bond (ed.), *The Spectator* (5 vols, Oxford, 1965), i, 87; Leerssen, *Mere Irish and fíor-ghael*, p. 109.

62 Bartley, 'Development of a stock character', pp 443–4; idem, *Teague, Shenkin & Sawney*, ch. 6. The phrase is Duggan's (*Stage Irishman*, p. 216).

beside the servants and labourers over whose foibles the English public was accustomed to chuckle.

Perhaps the essential feature of the new breed of stage Irishman (applying the phrase more broadly than to mere theatricals) was pride, for that abiding sin begat a number of other prominent vices. False pride was a failing commonly attributed by the inhabitants of more prosperous regions to economically backward neighbours – Gascony may be the most obvious continental example – and the classic symptom, a misplaced pride in pedigree, can readily be found in English caricatures of the Irish (as well as Highland Scots).[63] More important, as far as Ireland was concerned, was the imputation of an overweening pride in nationality or race. Interestingly, the changing stereotype of the Irishman in the late seventeenth century was able to accommodate both arrogance and a tendency to fawn upon authority, an imagined failing derived from assumptions about the poltroonery of the natives.[64] Thus the *Brief character of Ireland* presented a picture of a cowardly nation who still displayed their racial pride by 'hugging their old ethnic customs' and refusing to be 'sociable with the English', towards whom they cast glances interpreted as a mute assertion of superiority ('I am too good for thee').[65] 'Nees', the burlesque Hibernicised Aeneas of the *Irish Hudibras* (1689) was said to show 'perfect pride and contempt for the English nation'.[66] Pride was edging out obsequiousness, however, and in the early 1700s Ned Ward's *London spy* could sum up the Irish as 'very poor and proud'.[67] Prickly national feeling could make an Irishman quarrelsome in company. In a different way, pride could also manifest itself in 'impudence', a perfect self-confidence that also came to be connected specifically with the Irish. They were supposed to be 'notorious for their impudence, and for standing in a lie which they have once told, by which means they are becoming a proverb among their neighbours'.[68] 'If any person does a scandalous thing' it became habitual to say that 'such a man has an Irish assurance', or on one occasion, when the radical pamphleteer John Toland was the subject, that he was 'an impudent and pragmatical Irish Teague'.[69] And impudence, it was soon noted, might bring unusual success with the fair sex. A seamstress informed *The Spectator* (again the Irishman Steele was the author) that 'A little prentice girl of mine has been for some time applied to by an Irish fellow, who dresses very fine, and struts in a laced coat, and is the admiration of seamstresses who are under age

63 For example, William Moffet, *Hesperi-neso-graphia: or, A description of the western isle* (London, 1716), pp 4–6, where a peasant woman proudly states that 'my father was a gentleman, the best but two of all his clan ... he was related to the best, of Macs and Os in all the west'.

64 For references to the 'fawning' Irishman, see Bond (ed.), *Spectator*, i, 88–9; Daniel Defoe, *The anatomy of Exchange Alley* (London, 1719), p. 37; *A modest defence of public stews* (London [?1720]), p. xviii.

65 *Brief character*, pp 9–10.

66 *Irish Hudibras*, preface.

67 Edward Ward, *The London spy*, ed. A. L. Hayward (London, 1927), pp 278–9.

68 *British Gazetteer*, 18 Jan. 1728/9.

69 *A modest argument, pro and con, enquiring into the cause why base and mean actions should be committed by the Irish in particular, more than any other nation* (London, 1731), p. 25; diary of Lady Cowper (Hertfordshire R.O., Panshanger papers, D/EP F29, p. 152). See also Bartley, *Teague, Shenkin & Sawney*, pp 123–4; *A lay-man's creed, very short ...* (London, 1713), p. 19.

in town'.[70] The 'ragged Irishman' began to appear in the guise of a brazen young spark; on the stage, for example, in the character of Roebuck, 'an Irish gentleman of a wild and roving temper' in Farquhar's *Love in a bottle* (1698), or as Major Fox in Shadwell's *The humours of the army* (1713), the latter nicely contrasted with an Irish companion, Major Outside, a dull provincial whose national origins were established more conventionally, with references to brogue, bulls, bonny clabber and potatoes.

With Roebuck and Fox we have moved up the social scale, not perhaps a tremendous distance, for these 'gentlemen' were still down-at-heel and shabbier versions of the English 'quality', but far enough from the hapless Teagues of Jacobean drama, and their descendants. The image of the Irishman as haughty and pugnacious, or as forward and 'frank', fitted more closely with the social profile of the adventurous man-about-town. The squirearchy in Ireland thus acquired the reputation they were to maintain throughout the eighteenth century, as duellists and lotharios. It was an adage that 'the Irish take you out and the Scotch take you in', referring to the Irishman's supposed propensity to take offence and offer a challenge at the slightest suspicion of an insult.[71] The character of the Irish fortune-hunter proved equally durable, achieving currency in every literary form, and by the second half of the eighteenth century had become the most popular species of stage Irishman. Nor was the gentrification of the Irish stereotype hindered by the prevailing emphasis on the inferiority and humorousness of all things Irish. Verbal eccentricities could drop from the mouths of gentlemen as well as peasants; ignorance could be as amusing in a squire as a bogtrotter, if not more so. In the case of drunkenness, often alleged by travel-writers to be a national pastime in Ireland, the adaptation was effected with particular ease. For the picture of Teague swilling his usquebaugh, the eighteenth century substituted the vision of the squireen drowning in the contents of his wine-cellar. 'Drinking is a most beastly vice in any country', preached Lord Chesterfield, a former lord lieutenant, 'but it is really a ruinous one to Ireland; nine gentlemen in ten are impoverished by the great quantity of claret which, from mistaken notions of hospitality and dignity, they think should be drunk in their houses.'[72] The theme of poverty gave a peculiar twist to the representation of the Irish landlord, making him a 'half-mounted gentleman', or a mock-squire, and thus, in the gathering preconceptions of the time, even more typically Irish. He was often shown as a penniless

70 Bond (ed.), *Spectator*, ii, 217. See also Theophilus Lucas, *Memoirs of the lives, intrigues, and comical adventures of the most famous gamesters and celebrated sharpers in the reigns of Charles II, James II, William III, and Queen Anne* ... (London, 1714), repr. in C. H. Hartmann (ed.), *Games and gamesters of the Restoration* (London, 1930), pp 148, 233–4.

71 *Corresp. of Horace Walpole*, ed. Lewis et al., xii, 254; and, for a similar contrast, W. M. Chappell and J. W. Ebsworth (eds), *The Roxburghe ballads* (9 vols, London, 1869–99), iv, pt 1, p. 224.

72 Chesterfield to Bp Chenevix of Waterford, 18 June 1747 (*The letters of Philip Dormer Stanhope, earl of Chesterfield* ..., ed. John Bradshaw (3 vols, London, 1905), ii, 822). It was an observation to which he often reverted: see, e.g., his letters to Thomas Prior, 23 Sept. 1746, 6 May 1747, and to Samuel Madden, 12 Dec. 1746 (ibid., 801–2, 809, 817). See also the report of a chief secretary, Sir John Stanley (Stanley to Swift, 20 Nov. 1713 (*Swift corresp.*, ed. Williams, i, 404)), the comments of another ex-viceroy, Lord Carteret (Cobbett, *Parl. hist.*, xii, 1254), and the reaction of a visiting absentee landlord, Sir William Courtenay (Charles Worthy, *The history of the suburbs of Exeter* ... (London, 1892), pp 178–9).

pretender to social status, believing himself to be the scion of a once royal house but riding a broken-down nag and with at most a single, unprepossessing, retainer, one whose excessive pride went with holes in his pockets and whose exalted pedigree, traced back to the high kings, was proclaimed in a strange accent and stranger grammar.

As the assumed national characteristics of the Irish increased in complexity, so there sprang up a greater variety of stock literary figures. The peasant was still portrayed, of course. On a slightly higher social plane there was also the Irish lawyer (usually an attorney rather than a barrister), and, beginning probably with Shadwell's 1681 play, *The Lancashire witches*, the cunning and villainous Irish priest.[73] Father Teague O'Divelly, Shadwell's creation, spawned many imitations, such as Foigard in Farquhar's *The beaux stratagem*, who emulated O'Divelly in his roguery, hypocrisy, ignorance and, inevitably, accent. The upper ranks of society came to be represented chiefly by military men, 'Irish captains', of whom the most perfect specimen was probably Sir Callaghan O'Brallaghan, the veteran hero of Macklin's *Love à la mode* (1760). An army career of one sort or another, being in reality the commonest resort of the exiled Irish gentleman, also provided in purely literary terms the ideal vehicle for a character remarkable – in the public mind – for his ready sword and desperate finances. As the first historian of the 'stage Irishman' pointed out, the Irish army officer so beloved of eighteenth-century dramatists was a man of little or no visible means of support, who, whether in London or at some leisure-resort such as Bath, exploited his military talents to impress a vulnerable heiress, or to uphold, in a duel or a tavern brawl, the honour of his native land. Moreover, there was generally a suspicion that he was not a proper officer at all, and that his commission, if indeed he had one, was only a militia rank.[74]

By far the most popular eighteenth-century stock character was the Irish fortune-hunter. The first such adventurer to walk the boards in the London theatre seems to have been 'Turlough … Macahone of the parish of Curoughabegely, in the County of Tipperary, esquire' in Farquhar's *The stage coach*, in 1704,[75] to be followed in due course by the pretended gentleman Shamwell in Miller's *The humours of Oxford* in 1730. The first to be described in detail was probably one Macdermot, in a poem by John Durant Breval in 1719.[76] In fact the association of the Irishman with the ruthless pursuit of the heiress was already sufficiently established to feature in *Bogg-witticisms*, where one of the stories featured 'a certain spark' engaged in the business, while in 1712 Addison was warning readers of *The Spectator*, in the assumed persona of an anxious parent, against 'fortune-stealers', among whom he singled out 'a tall Irishman, that has been seen walking before mine house more than once this winter'.[77] In *The humours of Oxford* Shamwell's preparations were said to have been

73 Leerssen, *Mere Irish and fíor-ghael*, pp 94–7.

74 Duggan, *Stage Irishman*, ch. 10, esp. p. 196.

75 *The complete works of George Farquhar …*, ed. Charles Stonehill (2 vols, London, 1930), ii, 16–17; Leerssen, *Mere Irish and fíor-ghael*, p. 103. Cf. Duggan, *Stage Irishman*, pp 272–3; Bartley, *Teague, Shenkin & Sawney*, pp 124–5.

76 Bliss, *Spoken English in Ireland*, p. 67.

77 *Irish miscellany*, pp 111–12; Bond (ed.), *Spectator*, iii, 125.

greatly assisted by an 'Irish society of fortune-hunters' in London. This seems to have been the invention of the author of a bantering account of social life in the capital published some years earlier, which supplied minutes of the society's meetings 'at a hedge-tavern near The Strand'. There were subcommittees 'for the affair of heiresses', 'for characters', 'to borrow monies', and 'to beat bailiffs', and the leading lights were 'Colonel MacBlunder', 'Mr O'Brazen', 'Sir James O'Vapour', and 'Captain Smell-Blood'.[78] Possibly the most famous satire in this vein was the ode penned by Sir Charles Hanbury Williams in 1743 on the occasion of the Irishman Edward Hussey's marriage to the duchess of Manchester, a rare prize. Williams's comments on what he called 'the Milesian race' – 'Nature ... denies them sense, but gives them legs and impudence' – provoked such a fierce reaction from Irishmen in London that the author was obliged to abandon the town and 'shelter his discontents in a foreign embassy' (being appointed minister to Saxony in 1746).[79] By the second half of the eighteenth century 'heroes that cross the Hibernian Sea, in search of widows' hearts' had become a frequent sight on the English stage.[80] Nor was any self-respecting picaresque novel complete without one: Tom Jones encountered Captain Fitzpatrick, once 'a gay young fellow' but 'rusticated ... so long, that he is become an absolute wild Irishman'; Roderick Random faced a luckless rival in Captain O'Donnell, an 'Hibernian hero' reduced to robbing his own servant and transferring his attentions to an apothecary's widow; and Humphry Clinker witnessed the downfall of the 'poor knight of Ireland', Sir Ulick MacKilligut, an ancient squire 'much out at elbows', whose amorous campaign aborted in a misconceived attack on his lady-love's pug.[81]

As will be apparent from some of these examples, there was still some overlap between what has been identified as the emergent 'squireen' stereotype and the old image of the 'wild Irishman'. The names given to stage Irish gentlemen, selected partly because they conveyed nationality at a stroke, the Os and Macs, Phelims and Ulicks, implied a character of native Irish origin. So too did the surviving taint of brogue – the involuntary exclamations of 'arragh' and such like, or, as Shamwell lets slip, 'my dear joy' – and so of course did his poverty, which immediately suggested the most obvious social prototype, the remnant of a once distinguished Catholic family, long since ruined by Cromwell and King William. George Colman's comedy *The Oxonian in town* (1769) differentiated between the 'pretended Irish jontleman', 'M'Skiffle', whose speech was 'rank brogue', and the 'true gentleman of Ireland'.[82] Nonetheless, the opening had been made for a caricature that would gather within

78 *A ramble through London: containing observations on men and things* (3rd ed., London, 1728), pp 23–30. See also *The Irish register: or a list of the duchess dowagers, countesses, widow ladies, maiden ladies ...and misses of large fortunes in England* (Dublin, 1742); *The adventures of Shelim O'Blunder, esq; the Irish beau ...* (London [1750]; John Oakman, *The life and adventures of Benjamin Brass, an Irish fortune-hunter* (2 vols, London, 1765).

79 *The works of the right honourable Sir Charles Hanbury Williams ...* (3 vols, London, 1822), i, 91–3; Horace Walpole, *Memoirs of King George II*, ed. John Brooke (3 vols, New Haven, Conn., & London, 1985), i, 138; A. P. W. Malcomson, *The pursuit of the heiress: aristocratic marriage in Ireland 1740–1840* (2nd ed., Belfast 2006), pp 102–3; *Oxf. D.N.B.*, lix, 140–45.

80 Duggan, *Stage Irishman*, p 271.

81 Leerssen, *Mere Irish and fíor-ghael*, pp 109–12.

82 Duggan, *Stage Irishman*, pp 274–5. See also Leerssen, *Mere Irish and fíor-ghael*, p. 140.

its scope the Protestant squire as well as the Catholic ex-squire. It was the addition of typical traits of personality to physical and cultural attributes that paved the way for the extension of the popular stereotype to members of the Protestant elite, a process clearly visible in the transition from Careless, the Irish gentleman in Howard's *The committee*, whose characterisation is bereft of national features and who is indistinguishable from his English counterparts, to the sparkish Irish squireens of early eighteenth-century comedies. This development, as we shall see,[83] was abetted by the changing sense of national identity among Irish Protestants. Whereas in the 1690s many had thought of themselves first and foremost as 'the English in Ireland', reserving the category 'Irish' for the 'popish natives', by the middle of the eighteenth century the passage of generations, together with a growing awareness that their own economic and political interests were separate from those of England, was transforming the previous 'Hiberno-English' into 'Anglo-Irish' and then to 'Irish' *tout court*. At least they were now ready to describe themselves, without much equivocation, as Irish. And Englishmen were quick to respond. In the constitutional controversies of the 1690s (over wool, forfeitures and judicial appeals) English polemicists preferred to speak of their antagonists as 'the gentlemen of Ireland'. In private correspondence the use of terms like 'the English Irish' revealed a perception in England of shifting national allegiances among their erstwhile brethren across the Irish Sea.[84] English sneering was thus interpreted, in many cases accurately, to be as much a slight on the Protestant squirearchy as on decayed Catholic landowners. English 'Country party' pamphleteers, reacting against complaints from Ireland of interfering and discriminatory legislation from Westminster, tipped their arrows with the poison of national satire. One author (who, by a colossal irony, may have been none other than the Irishman John Toland) wrote of Dublin parliamentarians and coffee-house philosophers as being infected with 'an Irish assurance', while the most successful of the English pamphleteers, John Trenchard (who also had Irish connexions) derided his opponents as 'fantastic viceroys' and 'squire-like governors of this wild and enchanted island', drawing an analogy between the Irish Protestant gentry and the jester Trinculo from Shakespeare's *The tempest*, who led by the nose the native Caliban.[85]

The historical mechanisms that lay behind these developments can only be conjectured. Undoubtedly some of the newer features of the staple Irishman, such as his distressed gentility and false pride, had their origins in the earlier image of the woodkerne, with his barbaric poverty and occasional *hauteur*. In other ways, too, we can detect continuity: the Gaelic tradition of hospitality was conveyed directly to the Anglo-Irish squirearchy, with the accompanying vices of prodigality and

83 Below, ch. 2.

84 Robert Harley to Sir Edward Harley, 25 Aug. 1694 (H.M.C., *Portland MSS*, iii, 554). See also *An inquiry into some of the causes of the ill situation of affairs in Ireland* (Dublin, 1731), p. 11.

85 Patrick Kelly, 'A pamphlet attributed to John Toland and an unpublished reply by Archbishop William King' in *Topoi*, v (1985), pp 81–90; [John Trenchard,] *A letter from a soldier to the Commons of England, occasioned by an address now carrying on by the Protestants in Ireland, in order to take away the fund appropriated for the payment of the arrears of the army* (London, 1702), p. 20; [F. E. Paget,] *Some records of the Ashstead estate* (Lichfield, 1873), p. 111; Sir Walter Scott (ed.), *A collection of scarce and valuable tracts …* (2nd ed., 13 vols, London, 1809–15), xi, 228.

drunkenness; the often deplored agricultural incapacity of the natives (manifested in a refusal to plough) was transmuted into the gentry's supposed fondness for living entirely on their rents and spurning opportunities for improving their land; Irish peasant licentiousness found an echo in the passionate addresses of the fortune-hunter. One could also make a strong case that the idea of the 'bull' represented a logical development from previous obsessions with Irish vocal distortions. Brogue naturally led to blunder. The extent to which the evolution was a literary phenomenon, isolated from social or political realities, is debatable. Changing conventions may have influenced the production of a polite version of the wild Irishman for the eighteenth-century stage.[86] Certain literary creations, such as Sir Robert Howard's 'Teague' or the procession of fools pilloried in *Bogg-witticisms*, may have had a vital effect in popularising a particular view of the Irish. It is also possible that the growth of a stereotype of this kind may have acquired a momentum of its own, so that elements once based on observation become in due course a caricature of themselves, and the stereotype a caricature of a caricature. It would be hard, however, to accept any assertion that these developments can be understood simply in terms of literary fashion. Some features of the new stereotype clearly derive from specific incidents or individuals. As we have seen, the origin of the phrase 'an Irish evidence' lay in the corrupt testimony given by the witnesses brought over by the earl of Shaftesbury to prove the Popish Plot, who turned about and swore against their patron.[87] The notoriety of the Irish fortune-hunter owed much to the exploits of adventurers like Edward Hussey and Richard Nugent. More generally, the appearance of the 'squireen' stage Irishman may also have reflected a collective appreciation of social change, in the same way as the earlier disappearance of the image of the Irishman as a ferocious savage. The wars and confiscations of the seventeenth century had left many old proprietors landless and in exile, some of them in England. The miserable Irish pseudo-gentleman who stumbled through the pages of *Bogg-witticisms* may have been a corruption of a widely encountered type.

To this end it may be useful to compare English images of the Irish with attitudes towards the Welsh and the Scots. The other nations of the Celtic fringe shared with the Irish a strangeness of language and culture. Their manner of speaking, clothes, and diet were all ridiculed.[88] Also, as inhabitants of mountainous terrain on the physical periphery of the state, they were subject to the same lowlander prejudice that informed the English view of the Irish. Daniel Defoe's *Tour through the whole*

86 Bartley, *Teague, Shenkin & Sawney*, p. 127.

87 K. H. D. Haley, *The first earl of Shaftesbury* (Oxford, 1968), pp 569–99, 643–61, 679, 681–2; J. P. Kenyon, *The Popish Plot* (London, 1972), pp 233–4; above, p. 10.

88 In general, see Bartley, *Teague, Shenkin & Sawney*, chs 3–4, 7–8. On attitudes to the Welsh, David Lewis, 'The Welshman of English literature' in *Y Cymmrodor*, v (1882), pp 235–41; W. J. Hughes, *Wales and the Welsh in English literature* (London, 1924), ch. 3; M. D. George, 'Some caricatures of Wales and Welshmen' in *National Library of Wales Journal*, v (1947–8), pp 1–12. On attitudes to the Scots, C. H. Firth, 'Ballads on the Bishops' Wars, 1638–40' in *Scottish Historical Review*, iii (1906), pp 257–73; idem, 'Ballads illustrating the relations of England and Scotland during the seventeenth century' in ibid., vi (1908–9), pp 114–28; G. M. Trevelyan, *England under Queen Anne* (3 vols, London, 1930–34), ii, 175–8; H. M. Atherton, *Political prints in the age of Hogarth* (Oxford, 1974), pp 208–27.

island of Great Britain, for example, emphasised the contrast between the dismal prospect of uplands, with their primitive pastoral economy, and the welcoming sight of an intensely farmed valley.[89] Above all, Welshmen and Scots were renowned for their poverty. The Welsh were depicted as a nation of cheese-eaters, for whom the mousetrap had proved the most beneficial of all technological advances.[90] A Welshman's wig was supposedly made of 'a disagreeable mixture of goats' beards, cows' tails, horses' manes, with a small addition of his wife's hair, or perhaps his daughter's'.[91] Beggary was the most common element in the English perception of the Scots. The 'Scotch itch', induced by rough clothing, or a prodigious infestation of lice, was proverbial. Surviving clansmen in 1746 were pictured running home from the rout at Culloden to 'beggary, oatmeal, and itch'.[92] The general impression formed of both nations was one of squalor. But the parallels with Ireland run closer still, especially in relation to the Welsh. Jokes about Welshmen, and to a lesser extent Scotsmen, preceded Irish jokes in the English jest-book tradition, sometimes depending for their impact on an idiosyncratic form of speech which gave rise to a species of 'bull'.[93] The Welsh and Scots were also satirised for obsessive devotion to long (and spurious) pedigrees, in defence of which, and of national honour, a Welshman would be quick to draw his sword, though if words actually turned to blows he would just as rapidly take to his heels.[94] Both stereotypes thus shared many features with the Irish, and the Welsh version, in particular, had the potential to have developed along very similar lines. Furthermore, before 1660 the Welsh had easily outstripped the Irish as a source of English humour, on the stage and in popular literature. Yet by the 1700s these positions had been reversed; and with a loss of prominence anti-Welsh humour also lost much of its vigour, relying on a few quirks of speech and occasional references to leeks and cheese.[95] The eighteenth-century stage Welshman was to differ little from the stereotypical English rustic. As for the Scotsman, his profile

89 Daniel Defoe, *A tour through the whole island of Great Britain*, ed. John McVeagh (3 vols, London, 2001), e.g. iii, 139. See also Thomas, *Man and the natural world*, pp 195, 258.

90 Edward Holdsworth, *Muscipula, sive kambromyomaxia* (London, 1709), translated by the author as *Muscipula sive Cambro-muo-machia: The mouse-trap: or, The Welsh engagement with the mice* (London, 1709), and retranslated and heavily embellished by Daniel Bellamy as *The Cambro-Britannic engineer: or the original mouse-trap-maker. A mock-heroic-poem in commemoration of St David's day* ... (London, 1722).

91 Ward, *Secret hist. of clubs*, p. 89.

92 Hanbury Williams, *Works*, ii, 69.

93 *Joe Miller's jests*, p. 37; Ashton, *Humour, wit & satire*, p. 183; Margaret Spufford, *Small books and pleasant histories: popular fiction and its readership in seventeenth-century England* (Cambridge, 1981), pp 183, 192. See also Charles Cotton, *Poems on several occasions* (London, 1689), p. 189.

94 *The distressed Welshman* (London, n.d.), p.20; *The Welchman's last will and testament* (London, 1719), p. 14; *British Gazetteer*, 18 Jan. 1728/9; Ashton, *Humour, wit & satire*, pp 220–22, 261; Hughes, *Wales & the Welsh*, p. 42; Bartley, *Teague, Shenkin & Sawney*, pp 62–5; John Ashton, *Chap-books of the eighteenth century* (Welwyn, 1969), p. 476; Trevelyan, *Eng. under Queen Anne*, ii, 176, 178; *English caricature 1620 to the present* (Victoria and Albert Museum, London, 1984), p. 93 and plate xii.

95 Hughes, *Wales & the Welsh*, pp 53–5; Bartley, *Teague, Shenkin & Sawney*, graph A, ch. 7, esp. pp 136, 142; Michael Duffy, *The Englishman and the foreigner* (Cambridge, 1986), p. 18. It is instructive to compare Hanbury Williams's poems on Edward Hussey (for which see above, p. 17) with a near-contemporary verse satire on the failure of a Welsh landed magnate, Morgan of Tredegar, to

in English satire was to remain relatively low, and his national stereotype relatively undeveloped, until the middle years of the eighteenth century.[96]

This comparison highlights political rather than social or purely literary factors. Trends in taste may account for modifications in the general presentation of all three stereotypes, but they cannot explain marked disparities in popularity or elaboration. Some variations in type can be seen to have a correspondence with social realities, or at least perceived social realities. In contrast to the Irishman, the stock Scotsman of eighteenth-century popular literature was a mendicant rather than a gallant, resolved to remedy his poverty at the expense of the English taxpayer by making his way to London to batten on the public purse instead of making his way to Bath to batten on the fortune of an unsuspecting widow. This was perhaps a reflection of English observation of the backwardness of the Scottish economy and of the penury of Scottish pedlars who hawked their wares over the English countryside, or the starveling lairds who were thought to be sucking at the vitals of the English court – the caravan of Scots who had followed James VI and I to England in 1603, and those who a century later allowed themselves to be bribed to pass the Act of Union.[97] More obvious still is the correlation between the literary profile of each national group and the threat each posed to the social and political order in England. It has been argued in the case of Wales that animosity was generated by substantial Welsh immigration into England in the sixteenth and seventeenth centuries.[98] Something similar may have occurred in the case of Ireland, though the extant evidence does not permit a confident conclusion. What is certain is that the hostility that excited English ridicule of the Welsh, Irish and Scots was fuelled by political crises. While stage Welshmen had existed long before the 1640s, it was the Civil War that made them more popular, as Parliamentarian writers focused on this outlandish element in King Charles's forces.[99] That the same degree of interest was not aroused by the king's Irish supporters may be attributed to the fact that the Irishman was as yet rather too outlandish, and too frightening, to be entirely an object of ridicule. By the end of the century the Welsh had been absorbed into the English religio-political system. The Catholic Irish, however, were still a threat, and the events of 1688–92, giving rise to a flood of anti-Irish propaganda, provided a stimulus to anti-Irish humour. In a similar way, the Jacobite rebellions raised the visibility of the Scot as the butt of English satire, and at last directed attention towards the Highlander, and away from the lowland 'Jocky' and 'Sawney', who as comic characters lacked the richness of 'Shenkin' (the Welshman) or 'Teague'.

Undoubtedly, another part of the explanation for the enhanced feeling of contempt shown by the English towards all things Irish in the late seventeenth and

obtain the Order of the Bath (printed in *Old Wales*, i (1905), pp 137–8), which contains almost no references to supposed national features.

96 Bartley, *Teague, Shenkin & Sawney*, graph A, ch. 8; Duffy, *Englishman & foreigner*, pp 18–20.

97 C. V. Wedgwood, 'Anglo-Scottish relations 1603–1640' in *Transactions of the Royal Historical Society*, ser. 4, xxxii (1950), pp 43–5; Firth, 'Ballads illustrating relations of Eng. and Scotland', p. 117; Bruce Galloway, *The union of England and Scotland 1603–1608* (Edinburgh, 1986), pp 117, 139–40.

98 Spufford, *Small bks & pleasant histories*, pp 56, 182–3.

99 Lewis, 'Welshman of Eng. literature', pp 235–6.

early eighteenth centuries should be sought within England itself. To explore very far in this direction would not be appropriate; suffice it to say that the Irish (and Welsh and Scots) were by no means the only victims of English superciliousness. English conformist humour constructed in this period an entire gallery of repellent national stereotypes. The Frenchman was 'a vain, over-civilised, pretentious dandy', caricatured as a monkey in finery. The Spaniard's besetting sin was arrogance; the Dutchman's, greed.[100] Nor did the English provincial fare much better at the hands of metropolitan satirists. Rural life was dismissed as insufferably dull; the archetypal landowner a clod-pated, muddy-booted Sir Tunbelly Clumsy or Squire Western. The bucolic oafs of Hampshire, a county nicknamed 'Hogland', the rascally attorneys of Norfolk or the horse-traders of Yorkshire, the simpletons of Essex; these and many other local types were in their own ways bywords for ignorance or a low craftiness just as the Irish were, though without the development of character visible in the stereotype of the Irishman.[101]

If we are to set rough chronological boundaries for the processes that this essay has sought to identify, we should probably begin at the Restoration and end at some point around the middle of the eighteenth century. Given the nature of the subject, and of the evidence, precise dating is impossible, but it does seem that the movements in public perception that have been outlined underwent a sharp acceleration after c. 1660, and possibly a further shift in c. 1690,[102] while by c. 1750 a new image (or images) of the Irish had not only been minted but had passed into circulation. He was no longer terrifying but contemptible; had become a prime source of humour and a proverb for all that was inferior or ridiculous; had become more varied in his shape and occupation; and finally had come to represent the Protestant planter class as well as the Catholic native. The features of the later eighteenth-century caricature were already fixed, so much so that Gillray's 'Paddy on horseback' (1779), the stage Irishman's belated debut in a published cartoon, merely translated into pictorial terms an image already familiar in print. Paddy was drawn in ragged costume, seated back-to-front astride a bull which he was urging towards London. From his saddlebag protruded a volume entitled *New systems of fortune-hunting*, and a list of likely ladies, headed by 'Lady Mary Rotten Rump, St James's Square, £30,000'.[103] By this time there were even signs of a backlash. It had begun at least as early as

100 Atherton, *Political prints in age of Hogarth*, pp 85–9; Duffy, *Englishman & foreigner*, pp 23–42; Capp, *Astrology & popular press*, pp 116–17.

101 Thomas Richards, *The (Latin) description of Hogland* (London, 1711) [a reply to Holdsworth's *Muscipula*]; *Memoirs of Thomas, earl of Ailesbury*, ed. W. E. Buckley (2 vols, Roxburghe Club, Westminster, 1890), ii, 656; Ward, *Secret hist. of clubs*, pp 112–20; Montague Summers, *Restoration comedies* (London, 1921), p. 382. *The humours of an Irish court of justice* (London, n.d.), a 'dramatic satire' possibly dating from the 1750s, has not only a stage Irishman (Jeremy Bilkshot, a miller of Carrick-on-Suir, Co. Tipperary) but also a stage Yorkshireman, complete with accent.

102 Bartley, *Teague, Shenkin & Sawney*, p. 127, detects a watershed in the development of the stage character in c. 1710: ignorant and superstitious peasants generally fall into the earlier period; amorous, fortune-hunting, bull-making officers into the latter. He explains this changeover simply by reference to the new ascendancy of sentimentality in the English theatre.

103 *Catalogue of prints and drawings in the British Museum ... political and personal satires* (11 vols, London, 1870–1954), v, 357–8. The replacement of 'Teague' by 'Paddy' should be noted.

'Paddy on Horseback', by James Gillray (1779)

1731, when an anonymous Irishman, 'not insensible that the Irish are more reflected upon than any other nation', published *A modest argument ... enquiring into the cause why base and mean actions should be committed by the Irish in particular, more than any other nation*, in itself an eloquent witness to the power of the enlarged stereotype.[104] One by one the author countered current canards: that the Irish were especially murderous and 'bloodthirsty', when 'in liquor' or 'in passion of pride'; that they were forward and brazen; and that they 'keep certain clubs, in a regular manner, for advancing the fortunes of their countrymen who have been bred gentlemen, and cannot attain, through some defects in their ancestors' management, their former hospitable way of living', by supplying the wherewithal 'to address a lady of fortune'.

Before Richard Brinsley Sheridan, and the appearance of the character of Sir Lucius O'Trigger, the most successful repudiation of the calumnies personified in the stage Irishman was to be found in his father Thomas Sheridan's farce, *The brave Irishman; or, Captain O'Blunder*, first performed in 1743.[105] Afflicted with only a mild brogue and an intermittent propensity to perpetrate bulls, O'Blunder (a direct literary ancestor of O'Trigger) was a proud and quick-tempered patriot. When the

104 See above, n. 69. The quotation is taken from p. 27. Previously the author had noted that the Irish were 'a people of late which the English ... have taken an antipathy to' (p. 23).

105 See Duggan, *Stage Irishman*, pp 196–9; E. K. Sheldon, *Thomas Sheridan of Smock Alley* (Princeton, N.J., 1967), pp 20–27; Leerssen, *Mere Irish and fíor-ghael*, pp 116–18. The quotations are taken from Thomas Sheridan, *The brave Irishman: or, Captain O'Blunder* (Dublin, 1759), pp 8, 10–11, 21–22.

Frenchman, Monsieur Parbleu, calls him 'de vild Irishman, de potato face', he is straight away on his feet, blade drawn, to avenge this 'affront to an Irish shentleman'. The playwright's trick was to lead the audience to expect another Shamwell, but instead to reveal O'Blunder as the hero of the piece – genuinely brave and chivalrous, one whose conduct was living proof of the inaccuracy of the stereotype. The captain is a real gentleman; as Sheridan says, one may see it 'by his dress and behaviour'. On cue he vigorously disavows the Irish reputation for fortune-hunting. When it is suggested that an Irishman would desert a lady on discovering her to be penniless, he retorts, 'We play no such dirty tricks in our country.'

With Captain O'Blunder we are at the beginning of another phase in the development of the stage Irishman, one in which Irish writers would themselves participate. The further elaboration of the comic image in the late eighteenth and early nineteenth centuries, and the resurrection of the 'wild Irishman' as a simian terrorist in the Victorian era, are beyond the scope of this essay, though what has been shown of earlier experience suggests some possible explanations. Of particular interest in this context is the emergence in Victorian caricature of a dual image. In one drawing Britannia protects her sister Hibernia from an ape-like, stone-throwing Land Leaguer with 'Anarchy' written on the ribbon of his billycock hat.[106] The notion that there were two Irelands, a modern West Britain, with a recognisably English civilisation, and a traditional morass of barbarism, recalls the distinction between the 'wild Irish' and the English of Ireland'. Political pressure and agrarian violence had turned the clock back.

106 *Punch*, 29 Oct. 1891, reproduced in Curtis, *Apes and angels*, p. 41.

2

Anglo-Irish Attitudes

Shifting perceptions of national identity*

In eighteenth-century Europe units of government tended to be 'composite states' rather than 'nation states', and political loyalties were often correspondingly local or dynastic. Thus where 'national identity' existed it was not necessarily 'national' in the modern sense of being ethnocentric and exclusive. In this political world splintered or overlapping identities were commonplace. The position of the Protestant elite of early eighteenth-century Ireland – caught between dependence on the English connexion, and dependence on Irish property – was not therefore unusual. It was, however, unusually delicate. These dual loyalties, though sometimes complementary, could pull in different directions. When English and Irish interests were in active opposition, public figures (and, indeed, private commentators) could not continue to be simultaneously 'English' and 'Irish' but were obliged to make a choice. Alternatively, the 'Anglo-Irish' might find themselves in a no man's land between two 'nations'; neither properly English, nor truly and entirely Irish.[1] Even those who asserted allegiance to Irish interests most strongly and vociferously, the self-conscious 'patriots' among the political classes – especially those in opposition to government – could suffer self-doubt, since their national identity was to some degree compromised by the narrow confessional basis of their politics.

As Toby Barnard has observed, in a subtle analysis of the 'crises of identity' besetting Irish Protestants in the Restoration period, discussion of the Anglo-Irish predicament has been plagued by conceptual confusion, as historians have failed to distinguish between 'identity', 'mentality' and 'ideology'.[2] This can manifest itself in a tendency to pass swiftly from assertions of the divided or uncertain identity of Irish Protestants to assumptions about the effects of that uncertainty on attitudes and political beliefs. To separate 'identity' from 'mentality' and 'ideology' is far from easy, however, and in fact may not always be desirable. Although different things, these were often interconnected, and interdependent. To give one example: the Dutch cultural historian Joep Leerssen has argued convincingly that eighteenth-century

* A revised and expanded version of an earlier paper, 'Anglo-Irish attitudes: changing perceptions of national identity among the Protestant Ascendancy in Ireland, ca. 1690–1750' in *Studies in Eighteenth-Century Culture*, xvii (1987), pp 145–57.

1 R. F. Foster, *Modern Ireland, 1600–1972* (London, 1988), ch. 8. J. C. Beckett, *The Anglo-Irish tradition* (London, 1976), is in its entirety a prolonged meditation on this problem, but see esp. chs iii, v.

2 T. C. Barnard, 'Crises of identity among Irish Protestants, 1641–1685' in *Past and Present*, no. 127 (May 1990), pp 40, 46–9.

Irish 'patriotism' was a local manifestation of a Europe-wide movement.[3] In doing so he has emphasised the elements of 'civic humanist' discourse in Irish 'patriot' writings: the elevation of the public good over private interest, the importance of maintaining the liberty of the individual and the power of representative institutions, and the ongoing conflict between virtue and corruption. But his primary purpose in making this case seems to have been to distinguish between eighteenth-century 'patriotism' and nineteenth-century nationalism, and one of the foundations of his thesis is that eighteenth-century patriots lacked an historical basis for their assertions about independent Irish statehood. In other words, their sense of national identity was imperfectly formed or imperfectly founded, their position as a 'middle nation' setting limits that could not be overcome.[4]

Whether rightly or wrongly, historians have used Irish Protestants' doubtful or conflicted sense of 'national' identity as a key to understanding more general features of political culture and political behaviour, although they have been unclear as to how this should best be characterised. Leerssen is obviously right to stress the essentially non-specific, non-national, quality of eighteenth-century 'patriotism', since in different contexts it could relate to multi-national composite states (Poland-Lithuania, or Denmark-Norway), or sub-national independent units (the Kingdom of the Two Sicilies, or any one among the crowd of German electorates). Yet we still have to account for the passion that could be manifested in Ireland: the effusions of apparently genuine 'national' feeling that occurred during parliamentary debates in Dublin, sometimes overflowing into a broader public discourse and occasionally – as in the agitations over 'Wood's Halfpence' in 1722–5 and over the 'Money Bill Dispute' in 1753–7 – resulting in tumultuous public demonstrations against English misrule. And this depth of feeling has to be reconciled with the sectarian character of public life in Ireland, and the Anglocentrism pervading its political culture, which would suggest that Irish Protestants were still governed by a primary loyalty to the English connexion.

One formula for resolving these contradictions gained currency in the 1970s. Developed by the late J. G. Simms, it was enshrined in the eighteenth-century volume of the Royal Irish Academy's *New history of Ireland*. It derived from the obvious (perhaps too obvious) analogy between the new 'patriotism' of the political elite in Ireland and emerging collective identities among planter groups in colonial America. Irish Protestants' sense of 'Irishness' was thus attributed to a growing consciousness that their economic interests were separate from, and indeed incompatible with, those of the mother country.[5] The idea of 'colonial nationalism' fitted the model of Anglo-Irish relations created by nineteenth-century Catholic nation-

3 J. T. Leerssen, 'Anglo-Irish patriotism and its European context: notes towards a reassessment' in *Eighteenth-Century Ireland*, iii (1988), pp 7–24.

4 Ibid., p. 24.

5 J. G. Simms, *Colonial nationalism 1698–1776: Molyneux's 'The case of Ireland … stated'* (Cork, 1976); T. W. Moody and W. E. Vaughan (eds), *A new history of Ireland*, iv: *Eighteenth-century Ireland 1691–1800* (Oxford, 1986), esp. pp 104–22, 196–235. See also Patrick Kelly, 'Archbishop William King (1650–1729) and colonial nationalism' in Ciaran Brady (ed.), *Worsted in the game: losers in Irish history* (Dublin, 1989), pp 85–94.

alists, that Protestant Ireland was in essence an English colony, even a 'garrison'. In the same way it was, and occasionally still is, attractive to those 'cultural critics' intent on analysing the literature produced by the 'Anglo-Irish ascendancy' through the prism of post-colonial theory.[6] And for a short time it also played a part in the controversy between historians over whether eighteenth-century Ireland was best defined as an English 'colony' or whether its superficially colonial features – the sharp political distinction between landed and landless, and even the sectarian exclusiveness of the governing class, were in fact typical of the European '*ancien regime*'.[7] Although debate has tended to focus on differing interpretations of social structure and social relations, the character of the Anglo-Irish constitutional connexion can furnish subsidiary arguments in favour of the analogy between Ireland and English colonial possessions overseas.[8]

However well the concept of 'colonial nationalism' seemed to encapsulate the limitations and contradictions inherent in eighteenth-century Protestant 'patriotism', it remained an anachronism, a phrase coined in the late nineteenth century to describe movements for autonomy in the dominions of the British Empire.[9] Consequently it soon proved inadequate as a conceptual tool for understanding the self-image of Irish Protestants in this earlier period. The most obvious weakness was that to impose such a definition on eighteenth-century Irish 'patriotism' involved the application of objective rather than subjective criteria, and required historians to ignore Irish Protestants' own perceptions of their identity. The members of the propertied elite in eighteenth-century Ireland did not regard themselves as a 'colonial' caste. Very few were prepared to adopt the term 'colony' about their own kingdom, or to concede the constitutional subordination implicit in colonial status. As Professor George Boyce observed some time ago, and others have endorsed, 'Anglo-Irish political thinking held no brief for the idea that they were colonists, or that Ireland was in any respect like Virginia or Maryland.'[10] But if we try to understand the 'Ascendancy' class on its own terms, by examining the ways in which contemporaries described themselves, especially in the first half of the eighteenth century, complexities soon cloud the process. While 'colonial nationalism' may be summarily disposed of, it is not easy to see what should take its place. In the documents left behind by the generation that had witnessed the Williamite revolution

6 For a recent example, see S. D. Moore, *Swift, the book and the Irish financial revolution: satire and sovereignty in colonial Ireland* (Baltimore, Md, 2010), pp 50–51.

7 S. J. Connolly, 'Eighteenth-century Ireland: colony or *ancien régime*' in D. G. Boyce and Alan O'Day (eds), *The making of modern Irish history: revisionism and the revisionist controversy* (London, 1996), pp 15–33; Ian McBride, *Eighteenth-century Ireland: the isle of slaves* (Dublin, 2009), pp 100–3.

8 For example, James Kelly, *Poynings' Law and the making of law in Ireland 1660–1800* (Dublin, 2007), esp. pp 358–65.

9 Richard Jebb, *Studies in colonial nationalism* (London, 1905). For Jebb and his ideas, see John Eddy and Deryck Schreuder (eds), *The rise of colonial nationalism: Australia, New Zealand, Canada and South Africa first assert their nationalities 1880–1914* (Sydney, 1988).

10 D. G. Boyce, *Nationalism in Ireland* (London, 1982), pp 106–8; S. J. Connolly, *Religion, law and power: the making of Protestant Ireland 1660–1760* (Oxford, 1992), pp 105–6; Thomas Bartlett, 'Ireland, empire, and union, 1690–1801' in Kevin Kenny (ed.), *Ireland and the British empire* (Oxford, 2004), p. 70.

it is hard to find clear and unequivocal statements of national identity. Some were happy to identify themselves as Irish, for some of the time; others were not.

The elucidation of contemporary perceptions of 'national identity' in this period is indeed fraught with risk. Evidence may be found across a great variety of source materials, and conclusions based on a sampling of this evidence will inevitably be open to criticism on the grounds that they are impressionistic. Moreover, it is particularly important to set such fragments firmly in context, both in terms of author and circumstances. The hazard of dragging out of context *obiter dicta* of individuals like Swift or Berkeley scarcely requires emphasis. To underline the point, we might consider one further example, the Irish born freethinker and radical pamphleteer John Toland, from whose published writings and private correspondence might be gleaned a variety of conflicting statements about nationality.[11] In the late 1690s and early 1700s, Toland showed public sympathy for the assertions by the English legislature of superiority over the Irish. He was at this point a client – even a financial dependant – of the London financier Sir Robert Clayton, who as a governor of the Irish Society had a vested interest in determining constitutional conflicts in favour of Westminster. Toland was also a protégé of Robert Harley, one of the leaders of the 'Country party' in the English parliament, which was pushing through a resumption of Irish forfeited estates in the teeth of Irish Protestant opposition. In the 1720s, when Toland's personal and political fortunes had changed, and he had found a new patron, the Irish parliamentary 'patriot' Viscount Molesworth, he took the opposite view of Anglo-Irish controversies.[12] In other respects too, Toland varied his colours according to the nature of the surrounding foliage. In his political writings for an English public, he occasionally masqueraded as an Englishman (or very occasionally a Briton), but when travelling on the continent, and in need of hospitality from Irish exiles, he was prepared to allow that Ireland was his 'native land'.[13]

This essay follows the argument made by other historians who have examined the question of 'identity formation' in eighteenth-century Ireland, that if we take the long view we can detect a shift in the self-image of the Protestant propertied elite, towards the belief that they themselves constituted the Irish 'nation'.[14] There have

11 For Toland see S. H. Daniel, *John Toland: his methods, manners and mind* (London, 1984), pp 12–27; Justin Champion, *Republican learning: John Toland and the crisis of Christian culture, 1696–1722* (Manchester, 2003); *Oxf. D.N.B.*, liv, 894–8; *D.I.B.*, ix, 397–401.

12 *The miscellaneous works of … John Toland …* (2 vols, London, 1747), i, pp lii–liv; ii, 318–22, 459–63; A. B. Worden (ed.), Edmund Ludlow, *A voyce from the watch tower*, part v: *1600–1662* (Camden Society, ser. 4, xxi, 1978), p. 42; Patrick Kelly, 'A pamphlet attributed to John Toland and an unpublished reply by Archbishop William King' in *Topoi*, iv, (1985), pp 81–90; John Toland, *The art of governing by partys* (London, 1701), pp 105–6; Giancarlo Carabelli, *Tolandiana* … (Florence, 1975), pp 219, 223–4; J. G. Simms, 'John Toland (1670–1722): a Donegal heretic' in *I.H.S.*, no. 63 (Mar. 1969), p. 315; J. B. Duke-Evans, 'The political theory and practice of the English commonwealthsmen, 1695–1725' (Oxford Univ. D.Phil. thesis, 1980), pp 213–15, 217–18, 220, 228–9.

13 Toland, *Works*, ii, 349, 381, 405, 407–9, 429, 459, 466.

14 See, for example, Nicholas Canny, 'Identity formation in Ireland: the emergence of the Anglo-Irish' in Nicholas Canny and Anthony Pagden (eds), *Colonial identity in the Atlantic world, 1500–1800* (Princeton, N.J., 1987), pp 159–212; Thomas Bartlett, '"A people made rather for copies than originals": the Anglo-Irish, 1760–1800' in *International History Review*, xii (1990), pp 11–25;

been, and may well continue to be, disagreements over when the process began,[15] but the balance of evidence seems to suggest that, despite earlier foreshadowing, the first significant signs of change were visible in the aftermath of the Williamite Revolution. By the time of the Wood's Halfpence imbroglio in the 1720s momentum had gathered, and by the middle of the eighteenth century an Irish Protestant nation had emerged. But it is impossible to impose a more precise measurement, especially given the difficulties inherent in the evidential base. What was happening was a gradual, piecemeal shift in understanding.

We already have ample evidence of the ways in which Protestants in Ireland in the 1690s, whether Irish bred, Irish born, or recent immigrants who were merely Irish based, alluded to themselves as the agents of the 'English interest' in Ireland, in contrast to the 'Irish interest' represented by the 'native' Catholics, or the 'Scottish interest' of the Presbyterians of Ulster. Jim Smyth has drawn particular attention to a pro-Union pamphlet by an Irish Protestant, which he would date to the early 1690s (but in any case cannot be later than 1707), whose author makes a very clear distinction between 'the English planters' in Ireland and 'the Irish', to the point of criticising ill-informed Englishmen who 'consider not the English stake here, but look upon all here in effect to be Irish'.[16] A host of other examples could be supplied: parliamentary addresses, representations and petitions from 'the King's [or the Queen's] English subjects of Ireland', contemporary histories such as William King's *State of the Protestants of Ireland*, defining Williamite loyalists as the 'English interest';[17] political squibs appealing to the finer feelings of the Protestant reader with such phrases as 'every honest Englishman who loves his country';[18] and, in an extreme example, one pamphlet which argued the case for generous treatment of Ireland by the English parliament speaking on behalf of 'the English of Ireland' as though they were a distinct 'people'.[19]

By the 1720s, however, the term 'English interest' had acquired a very different political usage, denoting those in the Dublin administration and the Dublin parlia-

idem, 'The rise and fall of the Protestant nation, 1690–1800' in *Éire–Ireland*, xxvi, no. 2 (1991), pp 7–18; idem, 'Protestant nationalism in eighteenth-century Ireland' in Michael O'Dea and Kevin Whelan (eds), *Nations and nationalisms : France, Britain, Ireland and the eighteenth-century context* (Oxford, 1995), pp 79–88; S. J. Connolly, *Divided kingdom: Ireland 1630–1800* (Oxford, 2008), pp 225–9. Jim Smyth, however, has warned against exaggerating the extent of the transformation, and underestimating the persistence of Irish Protestants' anxiety and underlying attachment to the British connexion (Jim Smyth, *The making of the United Kingdom, 1660–1800* (Harlow, 2001), pp 138–44).

15 Canny, 'Identity formation in Ireland', pp 201–2; Jim Smyth, '"Like amphibious animals": Irish Protestants, ancient Britons, 1691–1707' in *Hist. Jn.*, xxxvi (1993), pp 788–9.

16 *Considerations concerning Ireland, in relation to England. And particularly in respect of an union* (n.d.). See Smyth, '"Like amphibious animals"', p. 788, n. 13. For a contemporaneous instance of the use of the term 'Irish interest' to mean Irish Catholics, see James Bonnell to John Strype, 18 Oct. 1692 (Cambridge University Library, Baumgartner papers, Add. MS 1, f. 104).

17 William King, *The state of the Protestants of Ireland under the late King James's government* … (Dublin, 1713), p. 49.

18 *The recorder's speech: with the principles of the Whigs defended* ([Dublin,] 1711), pp 9–10.

19 Sir Francis Brewster, *A discourse concerning Ireland and the different interests thereof* … (London, 1698), preface.

ment who supported English government at all costs, on issues like the dispute between the English and Irish Houses of Lords over appellate jurisdiction in Irish cases, or the infamous patent awarded to William Wood. In particular, the native-born or native-educated clergy of the Church of Ireland generated a well of anti-English sentiment, as they watched helplessly the granting of plum appointments to newcomers.[20] One such episcopal immigrant in George I's reign (in fact a Welshman, and Welsh-speaking at that) regarded this hostility as quite 'ridiculously national'.[21] Conversely, the 'patriot' opposition in parliament and in the country at large could be said to represent the 'Irish interest'. Robert Molesworth, the 'patriot' *eminence grise* (who also happened to be Toland's patron by this time), could be praised by an admirer after his decease as 'the best of friends to poor Ireland's rights', while a eulogy on another of the country's parliamentary defenders, the Dublin alderman John Stoyte, called upon 'Irish druids' to join in lamentations for his passing.[22] Similar instances of the raising of national consciousness can be found in literary circles. During Queen Anne's reign Irish Protestant writers like the playwright George Farquhar or the essayist Richard Steele had carelessly ridiculed their compatriots,[23] but in February 1722 another (albeit inferior) dramatist, William Philips, grandson of the Plantation servitor Sir Thomas, contributed to the 'patriot' cause an allegorical denunciation of foreign exploitation, entitled *Hibernia freed*, which proved an enormous success among Irish exiles in London when put on at the Theatre Royal in Lincoln's Inn Fields.[24] 'I never knew a play so clapped', reported the *Freeholder's Journal*, 'and must own I was a little surprised (tho' I have seen a much worse performance), until a friend put me in mind that half the audience were wild Irish'.[25] Philips based his story on a narrative contained in the recently published work by the Irish Catholic antiquarian Hugh MacCurtain (Aodh Mac Cruitín), which in turn was derived from that of the 'Old English' Catholic historian Geoffrey Keating.[26] The hero was the Gaelic high king, O'Brien, and the villains the Dane

20 Patrick McNally, '"Irish and English interests": national conflict within the Church of Ireland episcopate in the reign of George I' in *I.H.S.*, xxix, no. 115 (May 1995), pp 295–314; Philip O'Regan, *Archbishop William King of Dublin (1750–1729) and the constitution in church and state* (Dublin, 2000), chs 7–9.

21 Bp Evans of Meath to [Abp Wake of Canterbury], 19 Mar. 1718/19 (Christ Church, Oxford, Wake papers, Arch. W. Epist. xiii, no. 46). Cf. same to [same], 28 Dec. [1719], 12 Jan. 1719[/20] (ibid., nos 139, 142). One clergyman in the diocese of Derry, contemplating the prospects for a successor to the ailing Bishop Hartstonge in 1717, went so far as to write, 'I abhor the thoughts of an Englishman' (—— to Hugh Howard, [1717] (N.L.I., Wicklow papers, MS 38,369/18)).

22 *A funeral elegy on the … death of Robert Vis[count] Molesworth … by* M.B. ([Dublin, 1725]); *An elegy on the … death of Alderman J[ohn] S[toyte]* (Dublin, 1928), pp 12, 25.

23 See above, pp 13, 15, 16, 18.

24 Joep Leerssen, *Mere Irish and fíor-ghael: studies in the idea of Irish nationality, its development and literary expression prior to the nineteenth century* (2nd ed., Cork, 1996), pp 326–7; John Kerrigan, *Archipelagic English: literature, history and politics 1603–1707* (Oxford, 2008), pp 322–4; *D.I.B.*, viii, 100–2.

25 *Freeholder's Journal*, 21 Feb. 1722, quoted in C. J. Wheatley, *'Beneath Iërne's banners': Irish Protestant drama of the Restoration and eighteenth century* (Notre Dame, Ind., 1999), p. 49.

26 Hugh McCurtin, *A brief discourse in vindication of the antiquity of Ireland: collected out of many authentic Irish histories and chronicles …* (Dublin, 1717); Brian Ó Cuív, 'Irish language and literature,

Turgesius and his henchman Erric. Although the play's conclusion acknowledged the future necessity of English conquest to bring to Ireland economic and social progress, its overarching theme was the ennobling ideal of love for country, and the immediate impact was to stimulate patriotic and anti-English sentiment.

Specific examples like this might suggest a process both rapid and smooth, almost a natural development, but that would be misleading. Indeed, Philips's tedious drama, although on the surface it appears to show an Irish Protestant, of Plantation stock, heartily embracing the Gaelic past, has hidden shallows of a rather different kind: the imagery of violent intrusion and usurpation, especially the Dane Erric's violation of an Irish maiden, was redolent of contemporary Jacobite literature, and we know from other evidence that Philips himself may well have had Jacobite sympathies.[27] The characters of the Irish chieftains could also have recalled for the audience not merely great figures from the distant Irish past, but contemporary Tory and Jacobite politicians (not least the second duke of Ormond, whose identity is suggested by the name in the play given to O'Brien's principal supporter, 'Herimon'). Before concluding that old ideas about national identity had already given way to new, we would do well to consider the behaviour of another theatre audience, and a scene enacted at a Dublin playhouse two years later, in January 1724, at the height of the controversy over Wood's Halfpence, when supporters of the two warring factions in the Irish House of Commons almost came to blows, the government party headed by Speaker Conolly, and the opposition led by St John Brodrick. The Brodrick party had arranged on a previous occasion for a particular tune to be played between acts, which was associated with a scurrilous ballad against Speaker Conolly then going the rounds of Dublin society. To prevent a repetition, Conolly's friends arrived armed with cudgels, 'with a resolution to have [the opposing faction] drubbed off the stage if they had appeared'.[28] The ballad –'Sir Owen MacHugh' – was a transparent reference to Conolly's low social origins in County Donegal, and presumed descent from 'native Irish' Ulstermen.[29] The occasion was a defeat for one of Conolly's supporters in a disputed by-election for County Westmeath, which had been taken to the Commons on petition, and decided in favour of the opposition candidate. The first stanza is enough to give the flavour:

> Sir Owen Makue
> For ever may rue
> The vate of De Vestmead elexin elexin
> For ere shince dat day
> Oh hone I may say
> I have lost my support and protexin protexin

1691–1845' in Moody & Vaughan (eds), *New hist. Ire.*, iv: *Eighteenth-cent. Ire.*, p. 394; Leerssen, *Mere Irish and fíor-ghael*, p. 316.

27 Kerrigan, *Archipelagic English*, pp 322–3.

28 Philip Perceval to Visct Perceval, 30 Jan. 1723/4 (B.L., Egmont papers, Add. MS 47030, ff 57–8). On this episode, see D. W. Hayton, 'Two ballads on the County Westmeath by-election of 1723' in *Eighteenth-Century Ireland*, iv (1989), pp 7–30.

29 For a detailed discussion of Conolly's pedigree (and contemporary misconceptions about it), see Patrick Walsh, *The making of the Irish Protestant ascendancy: the life of William Conolly, 1662–1729* (Woodbridge, 2010), pp 11–15. See also, below, pp 80–81.

Obviously, there were still formidable obstacles to be surmounted before an Irish Protestant could proudly call himself an Irishman. The first was the ingrained habit of identifying Irish Catholics as 'the Irish' *tout court*. This can be seen regularly in Williamite commentaries on events during the war of 1689–90, when King James's forces were invariably referred to as 'the Irish'. 'The Irish army' was encamped before Derry; in an action near Limerick a number of 'the Irish' were killed; and when Marlborough took Kinsale in 1690 the defeated garrison were simply 'the Irish'.[30] In 1699 a newspaper announcement of festivities on 1 July (Old Style) explained that it was 'the anniversary of the overthrow of the Irish, at the Boyne'.[31] This terminology made no concession to the traditional ethnic division between 'Old English' Catholics, the pre-Reformation settlers, and the Gaelic 'Old Irish', a distinction which, if it was recognised at all, was now usually treated historically, devoid of contemporary relevance.[32] The way in which the two groups were merged in the popular mind is suggested by a mock-elegy to an Old English lord deputy, Tyrconnel, which referred to him as 'general of the bog-trotting army'.[33] Beyond the military context there are abundant examples of the word 'Irish' being used as short-hand for Irish Catholics, usually in relation to subversive political activity, or threats to public order. Thus in 1695 the Whig politician Alan Brodrick noted that there had been opposition to the meeting of an Irish parliament by anxious vested interests, 'among which were all the Irish'.[34] A scare-mongering broadside of 1689 reported with affected horror the story of Catholic civilians – 'the Irish' – taking the opportunity of a Catholic government in Dublin and a breakdown in order in the countryside to exact a bloody revenge on Protestants,[35] while the agent for the County Wicklow estates of the absentee English family of Wentworth claimed, once the Williamite regime was safely established, that during the 'late troubles' his property had been plundered by local Catholics; that is to say, he had been 'a great sufferer by the Irish'.[36] When returning Jacobite exiles were arrested for not possessing the

30 *Account from Colonel Kirk of the relieving of Londonderry* ... (Edinburgh, 1689); *An account from Lymrick, of the taking a castle above the English-town* ... (London, 1691); *An account of the taking of the new fort in Kinsale by the forces of the earl of Marlborough* (1690). Many other examples could be given.

31 *Post Boy*, 8–11 July 1699.

32 For examples see Rowland Davies, *The truly catholic and old religion, shewing that the establish'd church in Ireland, is more truly a member of the catholic, than the church of Rome* (Dublin, 1716), preface; Ralph Lambert, *A sermon preach'd in Christ's-Church, Dublin, on Wednesday October 23d. 1717. Being the anniversary commemoration of the happy deliverance from the Irish rebellion and massacre in 1641* (Dublin, 1717), p. 17.

33 *An elegy to the memory of Richard earl of Tyrconnel, late deputy of Ireland, and general of the bog-trotting army, who departed this life in Limerick, on Tuesday August the 8th, 1691* ([Dublin,] 1691).

34 Alan Brodrick to St John Brodrick, 17 Dec 1695 (S.H.C., Brodrick papers, 1248/1/278–9). A similar usage occurred in a memorandum of about the same time, which declared that 'the Irish with their spoils make themselves favourites to men of public employments', but displayed a certain confusion of kind by prefacing this remark with the assertion that 'the people of Ireland', meaning the Protestants, 'think themselves treated like enemies' (quoted in Connolly, *Divided kingdom*, p. 227).

35 *An account of a late, horrid and bloody massacre in Ireland of several thousands of Protestants* ... ([Dublin,] 1689).

36 Letter of John Cully, 6 Dec. 1693 (B.L., Wentworth papers, Add. MS 22192, f. 11).

requisite licence for re-entry an English newspaper simply called them 'several of the Irish'. And a slightly different, but equally telling, example appears in the judicial testimony of a representative of the petty gentry of County Clare (from obviously Catholic stock himself and probably a recent convert to the established church) who during proceedings in a notorious legal case in 1701 deposed that he had been robbed by men who 'by the tone of their speech ... seemed to be Irish-men'.[37]

Similar connotations adhered to the word 'native', and by extension 'nation', when used by Protestants in the late seventeenth and early eighteenth centuries to describe the inhabitants of Ireland. In almost every case phrases like the 'native Irish', 'the natives' and 'the Irish nation' were intended to denote Irish Catholics. Sometimes the context was historical, as with that most popular genre of clerical pronouncements, the commemorative sermon preached each year on 31 October, the anniversary of the outbreak of the Irish rebellion of 1641. A typical harangue delivered in 1712 by the Roscommon-born Bishop St George Ashe of Clogher (a former provost of Trinity College, Dublin) identified Catholics as 'the natives of our kingdom' and explicitly contrasted papists with Protestants, as representing the 'Irish' and 'English' interests in the kingdom.[38] Similar instances abound (including an occasional published example from a Presbyterian minister).[39]

Another obvious context in which the same usage predominated had again a strong clerical bias, namely the literature of proselytism: tracts urging the conversion of Catholics by compulsion, education, or evangelism, especially petitions, addresses, sermons and pamphlets relating to the charity school and charter school movements.[40] A petition to the lord lieutenant in 1711 argued for the establishment of a chartered corporation to facilitate 'the conversion of the popish natives', in order that 'the whole nation may in time be made both Protestant and English';[41] while John Richardson, the County Cavan rector who was the greatest contemporary enthusiast for education and proselytism through the Irish language (into which he translated various devotional works) described how alternative schemes had consistently failed in A *short history of the attempts that have been made to convert the popish natives of Ireland* (1712). Richardson later celebrated the conversion of one Irish Catholic in his parish by preaching a sermon, subsequently published in a bilingual edition, declaring that it was 'The true interest of the Irish nation' to

37 *The tryal and conviction of Patrick Hurly; late of Moughna, in the county of Clare, gent. in his majesty's court of king's bench in Ireland* ... (Dublin, 1701), p. 3. Hurly had been indicted for claiming a 'sham robbery' of his father's property, as part of a campaign to secure an indictment of high treason against the former Jacobite Sir Donough O'Brien of Dromoland, Co. Clare, whose lands he coveted. See the extensive documentation in N.L.I., Inchiquin papers, MSS 45,346–57.

38 St George Ashe, A *sermon preached to the Protestants of Ireland, now in London, at the parish church of St Clement Dane, October 23, 1712* (London, 1712), pp 5–7, 20–22.

39 E.g. Theophilus Bolton, A *sermon preach'd in St. Andrew's, Dublin, before the honourable House of Commons, on Monday, the 23d of October, 1721* (Dublin[, 1722]), p. 3; Richard Howard, A *sermon preached in Christ Church, Dublin; before their excellencies the lords justices, on Tuesday October the 23d, 1722* ... (Dublin, 1722), pp 14, 17; Joseph Boyse, A *sermon preach'd at Wood-Street on the 23d of October, 1716* ... (Dublin, 1716).

40 See below, ch. 7.

41 Sir Charles S. King (ed.), A *great archbishop of Dublin: William King D.D.* ... (London, 1906), pp 296–7.

embrace the reformed religion.[42] This usage was still current as late as 1730, when the campaign for charity schools brought pressure to bear on government with a published proposal 'for obtaining his majesty's royal charter, to incorporate a society for promoting Christian knowledge among the poor natives'.[43]

But it was not only evangelical clergymen, with a vested interest, who identified the 'natives' or 'nation' of Ireland with the Catholic population. Not surprisingly, humorists who turned their attention to Ireland treated the Gaelic Irish, in whose appearance and manners they found so much amusement, as 'the natives', or, in the words of one comical dialogue, 'the old Irish nation'.[44] The same assumption was also found in more straightforwardly political writers, even those sympathetic to the 'patriot' cause, such as William King, in his frequently reprinted *State of the Protestants of Ireland* (1689), or the Irish M.P. Henry Maxwell, in his appeal for an Anglo-Irish union in 1703.[45]

No less of a deterrent to the assumption by Irish Protestants of an Irish national identity, at least in the early decades of the eighteenth century, was the changing image of the Irishman in the popular literature and public discourse of late seventeenth- and early eighteenth-century England. As we saw in the preceding chapter, Restoration comedy had varied the former stereotype of the blood-crazed Irish savage, and, with the assistance of a best-selling jest-book, *Bogg-witticisms*, had promoted the character of 'Teague' or the 'dear joy' as a rich source of humour, ridiculous and contemptible where he had once been a monster of ignorance, violence and cruelty. The adjective 'Irish' gradually became a byword for anything inferior, and Irish Protestants were obliged to confess that their country was now despised in England. What was worse, the 'stage Irishman' was no longer drawn exclusively from the lower orders of society. The down-at-heel Irish gentleman was becoming a familiar figure in plays, novels, and cheap print; often an army officer, whose life was devoted to chasing widows, duelling, and boasting about his supposedly ancient lineage. Such individuals as Sir Ulick McKilligut, or Shelim O'Blunder, usually bore an obviously 'native' Irish name, as a clear sign for the more obtuse reader; and indeed they were often characterised as poverty-stricken Catholic claimants to gentry status, possibly ruined Jacobites – specimens of the 'pretended jontleman', as one dramatist put it – rather than the 'real gentlemen of Ireland'.[46] But at the same time there was little or

42 John Richardson, *A short history of the attempts that have been made to convert the popish natives of Ireland, to the establish'd religion: with a proposal for their conversion* (London, 1712); idem, *The true interest of the Irish nation: in a sermon preached in the church of Belturbet, on Sunday the 23d of October, 1715* ... (Dublin, 1716), esp. pp 9, 13, 21. See also Francis Hutchinson, *A letter to a Member of Parliament, concerning the imploying and providing for the poor* (Dublin, 1723), p 11.

43 *An humble proposal for obtaining his majesty's royal charter, to incorporate a society for promoting Christian knowledge among the poor natives of the kingdom of Ireland* (Dublin, 1730).

44 *Hesperi-neso-graphia: or, A description of the western isle in eight cantos* (Dublin, 1724), p. 4; *Bopeep, a dialogue between Bob Byass, late quæstor of the fiscus, and Simon George, a country gentleman* ... (Dublin, 1715).

45 King, *State of the Protestants*... (1713 ed.), table of contents and pp 33, 71, 87, 91, 120; [Henry Maxwell,] *An essay towards an union of Ireland with England* (Dublin, 1704) p. 9. For Maxwell, see below, ch. 5.

46 G. C. Duggan, *The stage Irishman: a history of the Irish play and stage characters* (Dublin, 1937), pp 274–5; above, pp 15–18.

nothing in the way they were described that could be regarded as denominationally specific, and often the satire was expressly intended to include Protestant squires within its scope. English Country Party polemics over the Westminster parliament's resumption of the Irish forfeited estates in 1699–1703, which were directed against the complaining 'poor Protestant purchasers', those who had bought or leased lands from the original grantees and were now to be dispossessed, exploited the conventions of anti-Irish humour, labelling their opponents as 'some Irish folks', and attributing to them what were seen as typically Irish 'bulls' and blunders.[47]

As early as 1713 the sixth earl of Abercorn objected strongly to his countrymen being 'made the subject of jests by the worst part of our neighbours'.[48] Paradoxically, however, as Abercorn's comment implies, with its reference to fellow countrymen, the effect on an Irish Protestant of having his Irishness rammed down his throat in this way was to produce a patriotic reaction. In 1731 an Irish author, presumably a Protestant, was sufficiently moved to reply in print, and at some length, to the scandalous 'reflections' to which his (or conceivably her) compatriots were subjected. This was probably a direct response to an extraordinarily popular mock-travelogue published in 1728 – going rapidly through six editions – which had described in detail the activities an 'Irish society of fortune-hunters' in London.[49] The indignant reply first focused on the accusation of fortune-hunting, although it then strayed to the more general (and equally objectionable) depiction of the Irish gentleman as a beggar hiding his poverty under false display, a condition which allegedly produced other such disreputable traits as welching on debts and cheating shopkeepers:[50]

> We may, and do daily see, several persons, as well others as the Irish, that carry a fine outside, flashy appearance, but if you examine into their fortunes, or way of living, they both bilk their tradesmen they deal with ... and impose upon the major part of mankind in their behaviour; that to deem one set of people more than another in this way, is entirely groundless.

This pamphlet was unusual in its unqualified assumption that the Protestant as well as Catholic inhabitants of Ireland could be comprehended under the description Irish, and even that together they constituted the Irish 'nation'. There are, however, other examples which show that as early as the first decade of the eighteenth century, the adjectives 'Irish' and 'native' were beginning to be deployed in a new way, to refer to Protestants as well as Catholics. This usage was alongside the

47 John Trenchard, *A letter from a souldier to the Commons of England, occasioned by an address now carrying on by the Protestants in Ireland* ... (London[, 1702]), pp 16, 20; idem, *The several addresses of some Irish folks to the King and the House of Commons* ([London, 1702]).

48 Abercorn to Edward Southwell, 19 Dec. 1713 (P.R.O.N.I., Abercorn papers, D/623/A/3/6). For a similar example a generation earlier, see Sir George Rawdon to Thomas Kirke, 27 May 1680 (B.L., Stowe MS 746, f. 27), writing from Lisburn, Co. Antrim: 'I need not give you any account of this neighbourhood, which [the bearer] can answer your expectations of, if you please to make any inquiry of it, or of my passages in this remote corner of the world, so much despised in England'.

49 *A trip through London: containing observations on men and things* (London, 1728).

50 *A modest argument, pro and con, enquiring into the cause why base and mean actions should be committed by the Irish in particular, more than any other nation* (London, 1731), p. 26.

traditional form, so that in examining each case context is a crucial. For example, Tory resentment at the jobs and pensions handed out by King William and his Whig ministers to religious and political refugees from the continent, especially French Huguenots, produced xenophobic rants from high-flyers in Ireland as well as in England. (In Ireland the unwillingness of many Huguenots to conform to the established church gave additional offence.) In denouncing the preference supposedly given to European 'foreigners', Tory pamphleteers noted particularly that they had been favoured at the expense of the 'natives', meaning the Protestant inhabitants of England and Ireland.[51] In writing in this way they were carrying over English party rhetoric without thinking through the implications. A similar instance is that of the Church of Ireland clergyman Ezekiel Burridge, who in a political essay written in 1700 found himself having to distinguish Irish from English Protestants, since at this point their interests were in conflict. Although in pressing his argument he repeatedly used the word 'Irish' in the traditional way as a short-hand for 'Irish Catholic' (for example, 'Irish proprietor' for dispossessed Catholic landowner) he also on occasion introduced a significantly different form: the crown's 'Irish subjects', or on one occasion 'the people of Ireland', which clearly referred to the Protestant population.[52]

Move forward two decades, and the position becomes even less clear-cut. Not only was the 'Irish interest' now a standard term for the 'patriot' opposition in both houses of parliament, and for its supporters out of doors; even the term 'native', which had once been exclusively reserved for the Gaelic 'Old Irish', could be used more loosely. Of course, we can still find examples of contrary meanings cheek by jowl in the same source. A tract of 1721, putting forward a complex analysis of the economic, social, and political implications of the controversial project for an Irish national bank, produced the obscure and ambivalent argument that 'we must apply ourselves heartily to the conversion of the natives, and make it [Ireland] a Protestant nation'. In the first clause 'natives' clearly meant the Gaelic Irish; in the second 'nation' must have been intended to comprehend both Catholic and Protestant.[53] Individual examples could be multiplied, but the overall picture is that of a gradual shift from the simple identification of the 'Old Irish' as the 'natives' of Ireland to a more complex situation in which a new understanding of the composition of the Irish 'nation' had emerged, sometimes inclusive, relating to all the inhabitants of the country, and sometimes exclusive, as a synonym for what modern historians would call the 'political nation'. Thus for Swift in 1720, in the *Proposal for the universal use of Irish manufacture*, the 'natives' were clearly the Catholics, but eight years later, in his *Short view of the state of Ireland*, he used 'natives' in a generic sense, relating to

[51] *A letter to the French refugees concerning their behaviour to the government* ([Dublin,] 1711), p. 8; *A long history of a certain session of a certain parliament, in a certain kingdom* (Dublin, 1714), p. 34.

[52] Ezekiel Burridge, *A short view of the present state of Ireland; with regard particularly to the difficultys a chief governor will meet with there in the holding of a parliament, written in the year 1700* (Dublin, 1708), pp 14, 16, 18, 22–24. See Canny, 'Identity formation in Ireland', p. 202; Smyth, '"Like amphibious animals"', p. 788.

[53] *A letter to the gentlemen of the landed interest in Ireland, relating to a bank* (Dublin, 1721), p. 7.

all the inhabitants of Ireland, before slipping back to the customary meaning.[54] An even finer instance of mental shape-shifting occurs in Thomas Prior's very influential pamphlet of 1729, *A list of the absentees of Ireland*. The passage is worth quoting in full.[55] Dismissing the ambitions of absentee Irish (Protestant) landlords to be preferred to great employments in England, Prior wrote:

> We may be soon cur'd of any vain expectations of that kind, if we consider that our country-men are so far from being caress'd, that they are generally slighted, and hated in other countries: it must be owned, that the poverty of some of our natives, and the extravagance of many of our men of fortune have brought us into discredit and contempt; so that of all nations, we have the misfortune to be the least regarded by those, who get most by us: and yet such is our folly, that many of our people choose to spend their estates, in a mean obscure way abroad, under the contempt and hatred of all about them, rather than live at home in plenty, honour, and esteem.

It is interesting to ponder what Prior thought he meant by phrases like 'our countrymen', 'some of our natives', 'many of our people', and, looking to the future, perhaps the most significant, 'of all nations'.

What seems to me to be the most plausible pattern into which these tesserae of evidence can be fitted would postulate that two concepts of nationality were current among Anglican Protestants in Ireland in the first few decades after the Williamite revolution. On the one hand the tradition continued of reserving 'Irish' for the indigenous Gaelic and Catholic inhabitants – 'the natives'– with Church of Ireland Protestants, especially the landowning elite, regarding themselves as belonging to the 'English interest'; on the other, it is possible to detect an emerging concept of national identity that extended to all those living on the island and might even be applied primarily to the Protestant inhabitants, whose representatives occasionally arrogated to themselves the privilege of constituting the real Irish nation. It was perfectly possible for an Anglo-Irishman like Robert Molesworth, born in Dublin of English immigrant stock, and with one substantial estate in County Dublin and another in Yorkshire, to think of himself in different contexts as Irish and English, and to move easily between the two kingdoms, settling first in England, as an Englishman, and then in Ireland, as a 'patriotic' Irishman, as he followed the most promising prospects for personal advancement.[56] The County Cork lawyer and antiquarian Sir Richard Cox, though Irish born, consistently emphasised the English heritage he shared with his fellow Protestants.[57] His best known work, *Hibernia Anglicana*, a history of 'English Ireland', published in London in 1689, traced the

54 Jonathan Swift, *A proposal for the universal use of Irish manufacture* ... (Dublin, 1720), p. 15; idem, *A short view of the state of Ireland* (1727/8), pp 4, 5, 11.

55 Thomas Prior, *A list of the absentees of Ireland* ... (Dublin 1729), p. 24.

56 Molesworth to [James Vernon], 30 Jan. 1699 (*C.S.P., dom.*, 1699–1700, p. 36); notes for speech by Molesworth in the Irish House of Lords, [1719] (H.M.C., *Various collections*, viii, 824); Duke-Evans, 'English commonwealthsmen', pp 213–15. For Molesworth see Hugh Mayo, 'Robert Molesworth's *Account of Denmark*: its roots and its impact' (PhD thesis, University of South Denmark, 2000); *H.C. 1690–1715*, iv, 826–35; *Oxf. D.N.B.*, xxxviii, 530–32; Finola O'Kane, *Landscape design in eighteenth-century Ireland: mixing foreign trees with the natives* (Cork, 2004), ch. 1.

57 For Cox, see *The autobiography of the rt hon. Sir Richard Cox* ..., ed. Richard Caulfield (Cork,

long-drawn-out conflict between Irish and English (or British) 'nations' in medieval and early modern Ireland.[58] But another pamphlet, the *Essay for the conversion of the Irish*, embodied the assumption of contemporary Scripture-based ethnography that the peoples of the British Isles, including the Gaels, shared a common origin, and accepted that native Irish Catholics were capable of embracing English civility if they could be brought over to the Protestant faith.[59] Even more interesting is his apparently contradictory statement, in a private letter, that in a particular political crisis he had 'behaved himself like a true Englishman, which ... is not inconsistent with a tender affection for my native country'.[60] In the same way Lord Abercorn could be quoted in the context of local estate management as regretting that he had insufficient 'English' tenants to offset the presence of so many 'Irish', while in national politics he viewed the Protestant community not just as 'the inhabitants of Ireland', but as 'the whole nation'.[61] It would have to be said that this ambivalence over the composition of the 'nation', and the place that Protestants of English extraction occupied in it, does not seem to have worried contemporaries; certainly not to the extent of encouraging them to reflect upon the question and to embark upon sustained self-analysis. Indeed, such political theorising as occurred in the early eighteenth-century Dublin press tended to ignore the difficulties that might arise from a 'mixed' or 'middle' identity. Henry Maxwell's *Essay upon an union of Ireland with England* (1704) blithely talked of Ireland both as a 'colony' or 'province' of England and as a 'nation' or 'kingdom' in its own right.

It is tempting to try to draw a distinction between Irish Protestants of comparatively recent vintage – those descended from seventeenth-century settlers (especially the beneficiaries of the Cromwellian confiscations), or even the minority who had themselves been born in England and had come over to Ireland to make their careers – and those whose connexion with the country went back many generations. But it is exceedingly difficult to demonstrate this in practice: for every seventeenth-century settler who thought of himself as English, one could find another, even a very recent arrival, like Archbishop Thomas Lindsay of Armagh, a leading supporter of the 'Irish interest' in the House of Lords after 1714, who developed pronounced 'patriotic' sensibilities. In theory it might also be possible to contrast absentees (either permanent or periodic), who maintained establishments on both sides of

1860); T.C. Barnard, *A new anatomy of Ireland: the Irish Protestants, 1649–1770* (New Haven, Conn., & London, 2003), pp 1–2; *Oxf. D.N.B.*, xiii, 865–7; *D.I.B.*, ii, 937–8; below, p 54.

58 Richard Cox, *Hibernia Anglicana: or, The history of Ireland from the conquest thereof by the English, to this present time* (London, 1689); Leerssen, *Mere Irish and fíor-ghael*, pp 315–16; Colin Kidd, *British identities before nationalism: ethnicity and nationhood in the Atlantic world 1600–1800* (Cambridge, 1999), pp 169–71.

59 Cox, *An essay for the conversion of the Irish; shewing that 'tis their duty and interest to become Protestants* ... (London, 1698).

60 Cox to earl of Nottingham, 9 Nov. 1703 (B.L., Hatton-Finch papers, Add. MS 29589, f. 310). See also Jim Smyth. '"No remedy more proper": Anglo-Irish unionism before 1707' in Brendan Bradshaw and Peter Roberts (eds), *British consciousness and identity: the making of Britain, 1533–1707* (Cambridge, 1998), p. 320.

61 Abercorn to R. Plumer, 15 Oct. 1717 (P.R.O.N.I., D/623/A/4/9); same to Edward Southwell, 19 Dec. 1713 (ibid., D/623/A/3/6).

the Irish Sea, the genuinely 'Anglo-Irish' as Toby Barnard has described them, with those whose entire property was in Ireland.[62] But again the distinction breaks down at the level of the individual: Robert Molesworth is an obvious example of someone with land and interests in both Ireland and England who was still able to show himself a vocal parliamentary patriot (in the 1690s and early 1700s, and again in the 1720s). Another, rather different, case would be that of the pro-Castle politician Marmaduke Coghill, who also owned property in County Dublin and in Yorkshire, and whose 'patriotism' was of a more discreet and – he would have argued – constructive, but none the less determined, variety.[63]

In fact, the practice of thinking in different ways about nationality, and of altering self-identification from English to Irish and vice versa, was widespread among Protestants in Ireland in the early eighteenth century, and for some almost a habit, to which they paid little attention and of which they may not even have been aware. Even when Swift calculatingly addressed his fourth 'Drapier's letter' to 'the whole people of Ireland', he slipped back into using 'Irish' to refer to the Catholics and 'the true English people of Ireland' for the Protestants, describing, of all people, the arch-patriot William Molyneux, whose *Case of Ireland* ... (1698) was to acquire almost iconic status as a statement of the country's constitutional rights as an historically independent kingdom, as 'an English gentleman born here'.[64] Of course, Swift was in one sense arguing for the rights of Irish Protestants as Englishmen who happened to be domiciled on the wrong side of the water. What is perhaps a clearer instance of the coexistence in the Protestant mind of the two concepts of nationality comes from a poem written in 1694 by a Church of Ireland rector, Edmund Arwaker. Recalling the recently concluded Jacobite war, Arwaker at first told his readers how 'Hibernia, that unhappy land,/ Her empress Albion durst withstand,/ And strove to wrest the sceptre from her hand'. However, when the war is over we find that Hibernia has been subjected, not to 'Albion' but to 'her sovereign', and, 'pleased with the blessings of his gentle reign', she could sing 'her liberty regained,/ Which, if unconquered, she had ne'er obtained'.[65] In other words, we begin with the notion of Gaelic Ireland struggling to throw off the imperial domination of England, and end with a quite different scenario, William, king of Ireland, saving the Protestant kingdom from the tyrant James.

In postulating the existence of an Irish kingdom which embodied Protestant political interests, Arwaker's insipid and otherwise uninteresting literary effort can be seen to give early expression to a concept that was to become popular during the first half of the eighteenth century, and eventually become dominant: that of the Protestant Irish nation. However, the movement towards a widespread acceptance of the idea was both slow and haphazard. Before Protestants could fully accept their new, unambiguous national identity, the notion of Irishness itself required further development. In the first place, something had to be done about the Catholics,

62 Barnard, 'Crises of identity', p. 47.

63 For Coghill, see below, ch. 6.

64 *The Drapier's letters and other works 1724–1725*, ed. Harold Williams, in *The prose works of Jonathan Swift*, ed. Herbert Davis et al. (16 vols, Oxford, 1939–74), x, 79, 81, 85.

65 Edmund Arwaker, *An elegy on his excellency Lieutenant-General Tolmach* (London, 1694), pp 5–6.

whose presence in the background would always threaten to spoil the idealised picture of a Protestant 'Hibernia'. The most radical solution is to be found in Molyneux's celebrated *Case*, which simply denied the Gaels their separate, special status as the aboriginal Irish. It was, wrote Molyneux, 'manifest that the greatest body of the present people of Ireland, are the progeny of the English and Britons [in this context, the Welsh] that from time to time have come over to this kingdom, and there remaining a mere handful of the ancient Irish at this time, I may say, not one in a thousand'.[66] And given that property – 'a stake in the hedge', in contemporary parlance – was assumed by the dominant political ideology to be the essential qualification for active citizenship, the Protestants, as the propertied class, would thus constitute the 'political nation' in Ireland.

It was not necessary to go as far as rewriting an historical ethnography in order to relegate the Gaelic peasantry from their place as 'the Irish, properly so called'. The means more readily at hand was a systematic denigration of their innate character and customary way of life, all aspects of which were represented as primitive, barbaric, and squalid. The clergyman Thomas Sheridan, for example, wrote in 1728 in the periodical *The Intelligencer*:[67]

> When I travel through any part of this unhappy kingdom ... it raises ... in my breast ... a sincere compassion for the natives, who are sunk in the lowest degree of misery and poverty, whose houses are dunghills, whose victuals are the blood of their cattle, or the herbs in the field, and whose clothing to the dishonour of God and man is nakedness.

Thirty years later the chief baron of the exchequer, Edward Willes, when on circuit, reported from the Mournes that 'the cabins in the rough part of the mountains I apprehend to [be] much like the Indian huts, and the inhabitants not much better', while in the 'golden vale' running from County Tipperary into County Limerick, though the land was much richer, 'the common people are most wretchedly poor. The man, his wife and his children, a calf, a goat and a porker and some poultry lie all together in a worse cabin than you read of among the Creeks and Cherokees of America.'[68] The standard view was that without the good example that Protestants had established, the ordinary Catholics would 'let all run into its original wilderness, and live like cannibals one upon another, or like their native wolves, from whom they are now but one degree removed'.[69] The impression built up in popular literature and reinforced by the patronising descriptions of travellers was one of barbarism and near-bestiality. It was reflected in the adjectives commonly chosen to distinguish the Catholic 'natives': the 'wild Irish', the 'mere Irish', and the significantly ambiguous 'natural Irish'. The cumulative effect was to make the erstwhile 'natives'

66 William Molyneux, *The case of Ireland's being bound by acts of parliament in England, stated* (Dublin, 1698; repr., with introduction by J. G. Simms, Monkstown, Co. Dublin, 1977), pp 34–5.
67 Jonathan Swift and Thomas Sheridan, *The Intelligencer*, ed. James Woolley (Oxford, 1992), p. 86.
68 *The letters of Lord Chief Baron Edward Willes to the earl of Warwick 1757–62: an account of Ireland in the mid-eighteenth century*, ed. James Kelly (Aberystwyth, 1990), pp 39, 52.
69 *Some account of the Irish* ... (London, 1753), esp. pp 33–4.

appear less than human, and by depriving them of a claim to citizenship, facilitate the appropriation by the Protestant gentry of an Irish national identity.

In overcoming the obstacles to their developing sense of Irishness, early eighteenth-century Protestants in Ireland also made particular use of two elements in the traditional symbolism of Irish nationality: St Patrick as the country's patron saint, and Hibernia as her classical personification. Although some writers resorted to the invocation of St Patrick as a shorthand means to identify an Irish 'Teague', the saint's feast day was in fact celebrated with enthusiasm by Protestants as well as Catholics. Swift wrote towards the end of Queen Anne's reign that he had encountered in London crowds of expatriate Irishmen marking the occasion by wearing crosses about their persons, and in 1698 there had been a newsletter report that even King William had 'done the Irishmen the honour to wear the cross in his hat'.[70] It is not difficult to see why Patrick should have meant so much to the established church. It was of course, essential for Church of Ireland controversialists to establish the true apostolic succession of its bishops and clergy, and in this case, an unbroken line back to St Patrick was a *sine qua non*. In a response to a Catholic tract, *The reformed churches proved destitute of a lawful ministry ...*, an Anglican writer noted how, by the use of ecclesiastical registers,

> We were able to prove the regular succession of the a[rch]b[isho]ps of Canterbury, from Austin [Augustine] to Dr Will[iam] Wake, the present a[rch]b[isho]p who is the eighty-first from the first foundation of the see. In like manner we are able to prove the succession of the a[rch]b[isho]ps of Armagh, from St Patrick to Dr Hugh Boulter, the present archbishop, who is the ninety-six[th] from St Patrick.[71]

Equally important was the fact that contemporary Anglican theology, imbued with the influence of patristic scholarship, emphasised the importance of returning to the practices of the 'primitive' church, while in a specifically Irish context one of the principal themes of ecclesiastical historiography in the two centuries following the Reformation had been the determination of Protestant writers to demonstrate the purity of early Christianity in Ireland, and its independence from Rome. Thus St Patrick appeared not only as the first predecessor of the Anglican primate but in the more general sense as the founding father of Irish Protestantism and thus a natural emblem of Protestant Irishness.[72]

In a similar way Hibernia provided a national symbol, reaching back to a remote and idealised classical past beyond any contemporary association with what was seen as the sordid world of the papist Gaelic peasantry. The sororal relationship with Britannia also expressed perfectly what was to become the common Protestant view of the Anglo-Irish relationship: an alliance of equals, in this case elder and younger sibling (or, as Swift imagined it, in his unpublished unionist polemic, 'The story of

70 Swift, *Journal to Stella*, ed. Harold Williams (2 vols, Oxford, 1948), ii, 640; newsletter, 18 Mar. 1697[/8] (Folger Shakespeare Library, Washington, D.C., Newdigate newsletters, L.C. 2751).

71 Thomas Breviter, *The mission of the clergy of the Church of England and Ireland vindicated ...* (Dublin, 1728), p. 3. See also Davies, *Truly catholic and old religion*.

72 Bridget McCormack, *Perceptions of St Patrick in eighteenth-century Ireland* (Dublin, 2000), ch. 3; Kidd, *British identities before nationalism*, pp 171–2.

the injured lady' (1707), bride and bridegroom). 'Hibernia', 'Hibernian', and other derivations such as 'Hibernicus' (the pseudonym adopted by the journalist James Arbuckle, among others[73]), were common currency in eighteenth-century 'patriot' literature, and in polite correspondence, too, where, for example, Lord Orrery might acknowledge that the beauty of the Irish countryside had 'turned me into an Hibernian'.[74] It may not be too far-fetched to suggest that this phraseology had the additional attraction of enabling an Irish Protestant to avoid calling himself or herself 'Irish'. I would not wish to press the point, for clearly a fondness for circumlocution and classical nomenclature can also be ascribed to literary convention; but in the light of what has been said about the changing English stereotype of the Irish, it does seem a plausible explanation for the frequency with which elaborate synonyms were devised. One 'patriotic' ode, dating from as late as 1780, proclaiming the simultaneous decline of 'old England' and the rise of a new, a purer Irish nation, displayed a particularly fertile invention. Even though the title drew a contrast between 'the characters of the English and Irish', nothing and no one was described as 'Irish' in the text itself; instead Ireland was 'Hibernia', 'Ierne', 'this green isle'; its young female inhabitants were 'daughters of the Hibernian soil', 'virgins of the Atlantic shore', and 'daughters of the Atlantic plain'.[75]

It is worth asking why 'Britishness', as an umbrella national identity, did not offer the early eighteenth-century Irish Protestant an intellectual and semantic escape-route from dilemmas over allegiance, especially in the light of the extensive recent discussion of the rise and apparent decline in the modern period of a sense of 'British' national identity, and in particular the detailed exploration of eighteenth-century 'Britishness' in Professor Linda Colley's influential study, *Britons* (1992).[76] The answer seems simple. Despite the uncontentious usage of 'British' and 'Briton' to refer to the pre-Gaelic settlers of Ireland, which was adopted by various writers – particularly those of an historical or antiquarian bent – to 'undermine the historical supports of Old Irish ideology',[77] for most adherents of the established Church of Ireland the overpowering difficulty with the terms 'Briton' and 'British' was that they implied a community of interest with the Ulster Scots, who were indeed occasionally referred to as 'British'.[78] Antagonism between the established

[73] James Arbuckle, *A collection of letters and essays on several subjects, lately publish'd in the Dublin Journal* (2 vols, London, 1729). See also *Advice to the freeholders of Ireland; concerning the present elections* ... ([Dublin, 1715]); *The present state of Ireland consider'd: in a letter to the Revd. Dean Swift* ([Dublin, 1724]); [James Digges Latouche,] *A freeholder's fourth address, to the merchants, traders, and others, the freemen and citizens of the city of Dublin* ... (Dublin, 1749).

[74] Constantia Maxwell, *The stranger in Ireland* (London, 1954), p. 154.

[75] *The contrast; or, A comparison between the characters of the English and Irish in the year 1780* (Dublin, 1780).

[76] Linda Colley, *Britons: forging the nation 1707–1837* (New Haven, Conn., & London, 1992). See also Bradshaw & Roberts (eds), *British consciousness and identity*; Tony Claydon and Ian McBride (eds), *Protestantism and national identity: Britain and Ireland c. 1650–c. 1850* (Cambridge, 1998).

[77] Kidd, *British identities before nationalism*, p. 170.

[78] *The parallel: or Persecution of Protestants the shortest way to prevent the growth of popery in Ireland* (Dublin, 1705), pp 24–5; *Reasons why the bill to prevent the growth of schism ... should not be extended to Ireland* ([1714]). The point is made in Connolly, *Religion, law & power*, p. 118; and T. C. Barnard,

church and the Presbyterian community in Ulster was one of the driving-forces of early eighteenth-century Irish politics, producing bitter party divisions in Queen Anne's reign, between Whigs, who favoured some degree of toleration for Protestant Dissenters and a united front against the threat from popery, and Tories, who took the opposite view, that the graver danger to the establishment in church and state came from Presbyterian 'schismatics'. Even as late as the 1730s these passions could flare in response to an attempt by the British ministers to admit Dissenters to full political rights by removing the requirement that holders of public office take Holy Communion in the established church. In 1733 one High Church broadsheet, entitled *Some queries upon the demand of the Presbyterians to have the sacramental test repealed*, demanded to know 'whether the Scottish Ulster Presbyterian farmers, tradesmen and cottagers ... be not a more knavish, wicked, thievish race than even the natural Irish of the other three provinces'.[79] This phraseology suggests more than mere political hostility, or a belief in Presbyterians' inherent disloyalty, but a real sense of cultural superiority based on ethnic difference. Indeed, when Ulster Presbyterians appeared in the popular literature of the period their way of life and manner of speaking were portrayed pejoratively, in terms of their Scottish lowland origins.[80]

On the rare occasions on which the term 'British' did appear in the public or private utterances of Irish Protestants, it was used with a clear purpose, to express or encourage solidarity against the threat posed by Catholics and Jacobites. Thus in the period of uncertainty immediately following the Williamite revolution we find earnest Churchmen like the accountant-general James Bonnell or the future bishop, John Stearne, willing to countenance a unity of interest with Dissenters and to encompass all the various Protestant communities on the island under the adjective 'British'.[81] Sermons commemorating the rebellion of 1641 were a particularly appropriate occasion on which to recall shared sufferings, with a view to future action.[82] In England and Scotland, of course, this community of interest was given institutional expression, in the Anglo-Scottish union of 1707, which created the constitutional entity of 'Great Britain'. During the next half-century Whig politicians and writers in both countries, for obvious political reasons, emphasised the necessity of the union, and cited the expansion of overseas commerce as one very valuable outcome. Consequently the idea of a 'British empire' grew in importance.[83]

'Protestantism, ethnicity and Irish identities, 1660–1760' in Claydon & McBride, *Protestantism & national identity*, p. 208.

79 *Some queries upon the demand of the Presbyterians to have the sacramental test repealed at this session of the parliament* ([Dublin,] 1733).

80 See, for example, *The wouns of the kirk of Scotland* (Dublin, 1743).

81 James Bonnell to John Stearne, 18 Oct. 1692 (T.C.D., MS 1.6.13, ff 189–90, a reference I owe to the kindness of Dr J. I. McGuire); John Stearne, *A sermon on the prayer of Moses, at the xii. verse of the xc. psalm* (Dublin, 1695), p. 9.

82 See, for example, Edward Smyth, *A sermon preach'd in Christ Church, Dublin, on Saturday the 23d of October, 1703; being the anniversary thanksgiving for discovering the Irish rebellion, which broke out in the year 1641* (Dublin[, ?1703]), p. 9; Henry Downes, *A sermon preach'd in Christ Church, Dublin, on Friday October 23d 1719. Being the anniversary commemoration of the happy deliverance from the Irish rebellion and massacre in 1641* ... (Dublin, 1719), p. 17.

83 David Armitage, *The ideological origins of the British empire* (Cambridge, 2000), ch. 7; idem, 'The British conception of empire in the eighteenth century', repr. in idem, *Greater Britain, 1516–1776:*

By c. 1750 the imagery of the British imperial nation was beginning to seep into political discourse in Ireland, occurring in the writings of 'patriot' ideologues like Henry Brooke, or the younger Sir Richard Cox (grandson of the historian).[84] But in the Irish context it seems to have been used only as a replacement for 'English' in descriptions of the political nation over the water: 'British' liberties being cited, for example, as against the previous invocation of the 'English' tradition.[85]

We might still question, perhaps, the extent to which the 'patriotism' of men like Brooke and Cox represented a genuine 'national' feeling in anything approaching the nineteenth-century sense. Brooke, after all, could be regarded as a classic exemplar of the transferable, eighteenth-century version of 'patriotism' to which Professor Leerssen and others have directed attention. Before establishing himself in Ireland in the 1740s, he had been active in literary and political circles in England, in particular among the 'Leicester House' set gathered around the heir to the throne, Frederick, prince of Wales, which espoused a 'British' patriotism in opposition to the administration of Sir Robert Walpole.[86] Like Robert Molesworth in the late 1710s, it was only after his return to reside in Ireland that his patriotism took on a distinctively Irish tinge. The way in which the mere fact of residence could lead to the acquisition of a sense of Irishness is highly suggestive, and particularly so in the case of those transplanted Englishmen – clerics or government placemen – who became in due course staunch upholders of the 'Irish interest' in economic and political matters. The tendency of imported administrators to 'go native' was a traditional feature of English government in Ireland. An Irishman observed in 1702 that 'had we a new set [of officials] taken out of London, that had no knowledge or engagements in Ireland, yet in seven years they would carry a grudge in their hearts against the oppressions of England; and as their interest in Irish ground increased, so would their aversion to the place they left'.[87]

'Patriotism' in this sense can look very much like self-interest writ large, which would account for the fact that resentment against English misgovernment, or English parliamentary interference in Irish affairs, often manifested itself most acutely at times of financial insecurity, when harvests were bad, trade was poor, and rents slow to come in; for example in 1698–1703, 1723–5 and again in 1729–31. It would also help to explain the intensity with which the Irish parliament and 'public

essays in Atlantic history (Aldershot, 2004), ch. xii. See also T. C. W. Blanning, *The culture of power and the power of culture: old regime Europe 1660–1789* (Oxford, 2002), pp 301–16.

84 Henry Brooke, *The farmer's six letters to the Protestants of Ireland* (Dublin, 1749), p. 6; Sir Richard Cox, *An examination of the facts, and a detection of the impudent falsehoods, and gross misrepresentations, contained in a pamphlet, intitled, A critical review of the liberties of British subjects* (Dublin, 1750), p. 51.

85 An exception might be Charles Lucas's pamphlet of 1748, *A free-man's answer to the freeholder's address*, which he published under the pseudonym 'Britannicus' (Jacqueline Hill, *From patriots to unionists: Dublin civic politics and Irish Protestant patriotism, 1660–1840* (Oxford, 1997), p. 104); however, another of his contributions published in the same year, *The British freeholder's political catechism* ... (Dublin, 1748), confirms the general point.

86 Christine Gerrard, *The patriot opposition to Walpole: politics, poetry, and national myth, 1725–1742* (Oxford, 1994), pp 46, 76–77, 79, 88–9, 114–15, 140; *Oxf. D.N.B*, vii, 895–7; *D.I.B.*, i, 874–5.

87 Quoted in W. E. H. Lecky, *A history of Ireland in the eighteenth century* (new ed., 5 vols, London, 1892), i, 401.

opinion' agitated against decisions by government or parliament at Westminster that would adversely affect the Irish economy, as compared to their more muted protests over the denial of Irish constitutional rights. In the late 1690s, the claim by the English House of Lords to a final appellate jurisdiction over legal cases in Ireland certainly angered Irish peers, but it was the discriminatory Woollen Act passed by the English parliament in 1699, and the Forfeitures Resumption Act a year later, both of which hit Irish landowners in their pockets, which produced the loudest and most prolonged response, with the publication of Molyneux's *Case* and the organisation of county addresses against the resumption, the so-called 'national remonstrance'.[88] Similarly the renewed controversy over the appellate jurisdiction in 1717–19 aroused patriotic opinion in the Irish parliament but no great agitation in the country at large.[89] Moreover, the passage at Westminster of the Declaratory Act of 1720, which was intended to settle these issues by asserting the right of the British parliament to make legal judgments in Irish cases and to legislate for Ireland, even though expected to stir up a hornet's nest, in fact elicited not a whimper of protest when the Dublin parliament resumed sitting in the following year.[90] By contrast, the granting of a royal patent to William Wood to coin halfpence and farthings for Ireland, which Swift and others interpreted as a deadly danger to the Irish economy, produced not only a parliamentary storm but a raging in the press, and violent public demonstrations.

A case could also be made, though rather more tentatively, that many of the manifestations of Protestant 'Irishness' in the first half of the eighteenth century paralleled nothing so closely as English provincial self-consciousness. Englishmen had, after all, been accustomed for generations to think, and talk, of their county as their 'country'. Thus the annual feasts organised for Irish Protestants in London, following the preaching of a sermon to commemorate the outbreak of the 1641 rising, had their counterparts in similar festivals held in the metropolis (on different occasions) for Cumbrians, Suffolk men, or Wiltshiremen.[91] It might even be argued that the pride Irish Protestants were coming to display in their own capital city and its various institutions, symbolised by the magnificent new parliament-house, differed only in scale rather than essence from the civic pride of the populace of the larger English provincial cities like Bristol, Norwich and York. In Ireland, however,

88 J. G. Simms, *The Williamite confiscation in Ireland 1690–1703* (London, 1956), pp 125–6; D. W. Hayton, *Ruling Ireland, 1685–1742: politics, politicians and parties* (Woodbridge, 2004), pp 82–3.

89 Isolde Victory, 'The making of the Declaratory Act of 1720' in Gerard O'Brien (ed.), *Parliament, politics and people: essays in eighteenth-century Irish history* (Blackrock, Co. Dublin, 1988), pp 9–29; D. W. Hayton, 'The Stanhope/Sunderland ministry and the repudiation of Irish parliamentary independence', in *E.H.R.*, cxiii (1998), pp 610–36.

90 R. E. Burns, *Irish parliamentary politics in the eighteenth century* (2 vols, Washington, D.C., 1989–90), i, 109–33; Hayton, *Ruling Ireland*, pp 228–32. Cf. Bp Evans to [Abp Wake], 9 Apr. 1720 (Christ Church, Oxf., Arch W. Epist. xiii, no. 161).

91 *Daily Courant*, 19 Oct. 1713; H.M. C., *Townshend MSS*, p. 130; 'The Wiltshire Society' in *Wiltshire Notes and Queries*, ii (1896–9), p. 35; J. D. Marshall, 'Cumberland and Westmorland societies in London, 1734–1914' in *Transactions of the Cumberland and Westmorland Antiquarian and Archaeological Society*, lxxxiv (1984), p 239; and in general Peter Clark, *British clubs and societies 1580–1800: the origins of an associational world* (Oxford, 2000), pp 274–301.

the distinction between national and civic pride is harder to make. As the national capital, Dublin had a symbolic importance, and most of its institutions were to some degree national institutions – not only parliament but the university, the King's Inns, even the Dublin Society. Outside Dublin, there is some evidence of a provincial or local allegiance with which a more truly national feeling might be contrasted. In politics, for example, regional loyalties sometimes helped to bind together factions. Speaker Conolly, himself an Ulsterman, was said to have found a particular band of support among 'the northern members', while his great rival for the leadership of the Irish Whig party, Alan Brodrick, commanded a 'Munster squadron' of M.P.s from his own native province.[92] But, as Professor Oliver MacDonagh once observed, localism did not take a powerful hold on the emotions of the 'Anglo-Irish': 'In the minds of the planters of the Williamite era, Ireland was ... undifferentiated internally.'[93] This observation still holds true in essence, I think, even though historians have begun to trace in this period the beginnings of an associational culture in relatively remote areas of provincial Ireland which could reflect a distinctive local pride. Much of what has been unearthed still looks very much like local manifestations of country-wide phenomena – freemasons' lodges, for example, loyal societies, and 'patriot clubs' in the 1750s.[94] Until we can find an Irish equivalent of the strong county and regional identities visible among the English, it is hard to resist the conclusion that the very Irishness of those whom Professor MacDonagh found no difficulty in calling 'Anglo-Irish' was in itself a kind of localism, with Protestant Ireland a '*petite patrie*' in the greater English cultural and political world.

Yet there were important ways in which Protestant Irish patriotism did embody and represent a distinctive sense of national identity, at least at the end of our period. By c. 1750 Irish Protestants were not only well aware that their economic and political interests were separate from, and might often be in conflict with, those of Great Britain but had even succeeded to some degree in rooting themselves in the Irish past. The most influential 'patriot' ideologue, Molyneux, whose *Case* was reprinted many times during the century, after writing Gaelic Ireland out of existence, began the history of the seventeenth-century Irish nation with the Norman invader, Strongbow, and identified his fellow Protestants as heirs to the medieval Irish constitutional tradition. A similar effect was achieved, as we have seen, through the systematic denigration of the culture of contemporary Gaeldom and the elaboration of national symbols appropriate to Protestant Ireland. At the same time, Protestant antiquarians and historians, including two Englishmen who were translated to bishoprics in the Church of Ireland, William Nicolson of Derry and Francis Hutchinson of Down and Connor, were discovering traces of a civilisation in the distant Irish past comparable in its sophistication to the worlds of classical

92 Hayton, *Ruling Ireland*, p. 113. Cf. below, pp 80–81.

93 Oliver MacDonagh, *States of mind: a study of Anglo-Irish conflict 1780–1980* (London, 1983), pp 15–16.

94 D.A. Fleming, *Politics and provincial people: Sligo and Limerick, 1691–1761* (Manchester, 2010), pp 148–57; Jacqueline Hill, 'Loyal societies in Ireland, 1690–1790' in James Kelly and M. J. Powell (eds), *Clubs and societies in eighteenth-century Ireland* (Dublin, 2010), pp 181–202; Bob Harris, 'The patriot clubs of the 1750s' in Kelly & Powell, *Clubs & societies*, pp 224–43.

antiquity.[95] Their findings, together with the work of Catholic Irish scholars, were presented to an English-speaking audience which (if we may judge by the subscription lists to published works) included many representatives of the propertied elite.[96] A 'more positive attitude' to the Gaelic Irish heritage, and even by extension to the Gaelic Irish present, was already present in Protestant Ireland in the 1740s, marked by the publication in 1744 of *The ancient and present state of County Down*. Compiled by the antiquarian author Walter Harris,[97] it was the first fruit of the efforts of a circle of antiquaries and Anglican evangelicals who in the same year formed themselves into the Dublin-based Physico-Historical Society, intended to co-ordinate a county-by-county survey of Irish geography, topography and antiquities. Behind this ambitious project lay a mixture of motives, including the desire to promote the 'improvement of Ireland' through the initiative of the landlord class, but one of the most obvious results of the society's work was the refutation of current English calumnies against the Irish population, and the vindication of Irish culture from the blanket accusation of barbarism.[98] The same confusion is visible in the polemical writings of the Dublin apothecary Charles Lucas, whose vigorous opposition to the oligarchy of the Dublin corporation turned him into the *enfant terrible* of Irish politics. Although his basic political opinions are best described as ultra-Protestant, producing anti-papist invective on behalf of ordinary Protestant tradesmen, he also adopted an historical perspective which implied sympathy for the wrongs the native Irish had suffered in the sixteenth and seventeenth centuries. At one point he even seemed willing to deny one of the mainstays of the Protestant political creed, that the frequency of rebellions in the kingdom had been owing to the innate perfidy and cruelty of the natives, blaming instead the 'oppressions, instigation, evil influence and connivance of the English'.[99]

Of course, the period c. 1745–90, which in retrospect appears as the heyday of Protestant patriotism, was also the zenith of Protestant self-confidence, after the demise of Jacobitism and before the rise of separatist republicanism and the pressure for full Catholic emancipation. Anglo-Irish attitudes in the era of revolution would subsequently return to their former complexity, with a renewed ambivalence about identity and allegiance. None the less, by the mid eighteenth century Irish

95 William Nicolson, *The Irish historical library: pointing at most of the authors and records in print or manuscript, which may be serviceable to the compilers of a general history of Ireland* (Dublin, 1724); Francis Hutchinson, *A defence of the ancient historians: with a particular application of it to the history of Ireland* (Dublin, 1733); Leerssen, *Mere Irish and fíor-ghael*, pp 315–25.

96 Ann de Valera, 'Antiquarian and historical investigations in Ireland in the eighteenth century' (MA thesis, University College Dublin 1978), ch. 12.

97 For Harris, see *Oxf. D.N.B.*, xxv, 474–5; *D.I.B.*, xiv, 485–6.

98 Eoin Magennis, 'A "beleaguered Protestant"? Walter Harris and the writing of *Fiction unmasked*' in *Eighteenth-Century Ireland*, xiii (1998), pp 87–8, 92–98; T. C. Barnard, 'Improving Ireland's past' in idem, *Improving Ireland?* (Dublin, 2008), pp 113–19.

99 Seán Murphy, 'Charles Lucas and the Dublin election of 1748–1749' in *Parliamentary History*, ii (1983), pp 94, 96; Hill, *From patriots to unionists*, pp 84–91; S. J. Connolly, 'Precedent and principle: the patriots and their critics' in idem (ed.), *Political ideas in eighteenth-century Ireland* (Dublin, 2000), pp 141–3; Jim Smyth, 'Republicanism before the United Irishmen: the case of Dr Charles Lucas' in D. George Boyce, Robert Eccleshall and Vincent Geoghegan (eds), *Political discourse in seventeenth- and eighteenth-century Ireland* (Basingstoke, 2001), pp 251–2.

Protestants had succeeded in creating a brand of patriotism that was more genuinely 'national' than 'colonial' in character. This was one aspect of a maturing political culture; the underlying process that was also reflected in such apparently diverse phenomena as the growth of a lively domestic 'Grub Street' press and the erection of the grandiose public architecture for which Georgian Dublin is famed. While Welsh aristocrats and gentlemen were abandoning their national culture in a keen pursuit of Anglicisation,[100] and some unionist Scots were developing a specifically 'North British' identity,[101] the Irish landowning elite was following a very different path. If, as one influential historical sociologist has argued, the early modern period of British history was marked by a systematic process of 'internal colonialism', perpetrated by the English core at the expense of the 'Celtic' periphery,[102] in early eighteenth-century Ireland, at least in cultural terms, this trend was clearly being put into reverse.

100 Philip Jenkins, *The making of a ruling class: the Glamorgan gentry 1640–1790* (Cambridge, 1983), pp 209–10, 213–14.

101 Colin Kidd, 'North Britishness and the nature of eighteenth-century British patriotisms' in *Hist. Jn.*, xxix (1996), 361–82.

102 Michael Hechter, *Internal colonialism: the Celtic fringe in British national development 1536–1966* (London, 1975), esp. pp 109–19.

3

Aristocratic decline

The fall of the house of Ormond*

For the Irish landed aristocracy the Williamite Revolution marked an ebb tide. Rebellions and religious wars had destroyed or weakened many older noble dynasties, while families which would in later years come to dominate the political life of Hanoverian Ireland – the Ponsonbys, Hills, Beresfords and their ilk – were still clambering out of the ranks of the gentry. Of the magnates whose rivalries had determined the course of Irish politics during the conflicts of 1640–90, some, like the Bourkes and Talbots, had been expropriated because of their Catholic political loyalty; others, such as the Annesleys and the various branches of the Boyles, had drifted into absenteeism; while a few great families, pre-eminently the Fitzgerald earls of Kildare, had lapsed into a vegetative state as the genetic inheritance of political talent that had run through their lineage dried up (temporarily in the case of the Kildares). With one important exception, Irish politics in the half-century after 1690 was dominated by 'new men'. The exception was James Butler, second duke of Ormond, to all intents and purposes the leader of the Tory party in Ireland in Queen Anne's reign, and twice lord lieutenant, 1703–7 and 1710–13.

Ormond was set apart from his contemporaries not only by his illustrious family history, the breadth of his acreage and the size of his disposable income – profoundly impressive if judged by the criterion of his extravagant expenditure rather than by the actual balances in his accounts – but also by his possession of that traditional appurtenance of noble power, a large personal retinue. His annual rent-roll, variously estimated at its fullest extent as between £22,500 and £25,000 (Irish), [1] could be matched among his Irish contemporaries only by the Boyles, earls of Cork and Burlington, but they were absentees with substantial landed interests in England.[2] Ormond, though spending much of his time after 1689 on the continent (doing his duty as an army officer) or at Westminster, remained in essence an Irish magnate,

* Originally published as 'Dependence, clientage, and affinity: the political following of the second duke of Ormonde' in T. C. Barnard and Jane Fenlon (eds), *The dukes of Ormonde, 1610–1745* (Woodbridge, 2000), pp 211–41.

1 'The state of the late duke of Ormond's debts ...', 21 July 1688 (B.L., Holland House papers, Add. MS 51326, f. 58); *A state of the value of the forfeited estates of James, late duke of Ormond* ([?1720]).

2 T. C. Barnard, 'Land and the limits of loyalty: the second earl of Cork and first earl of Burlington (1612–98)' in idem and Jane Clark (eds), *Lord Burlington: architecture, art and life* (London, 1996), pp 167–99; David Dickson, *Old world colony: Cork and south Munster 1630–1800* (Cork, 2005), pp 72–9.

his power based in his family's traditional domains in Counties Kilkenny and Tipperary. He also retained a large number of personal followers and dependants: those employed in his household and in the management of his estate, clients who owed their advancement to his patronage, and ambitious young parliamentarians who acknowledged his leadership. All would have described themselves, and been described by contemporaries, as 'friends of the duke of Ormond'.

Historically, the most important function of a magnate's retinue was to assist him on the field of battle: in defence of the realm, or in pursuit of his own interests. A few historians would argue that this was still the case as late as the civil wars of the mid seventeenth century, but the restoration of the monarchy in 1660 had ushered in a different political world. With the exception of the earl of Argyll, who rose in armed rebellion with his clansmen against King James II in 1685, and various Jacobite lords and chieftains in England and Scotland in 1715, magnates now eschewed military force in favour of subtler modes of self-advancement. Kinship and connexion remained important, but in ways that did not require the lord or his dependants to pick up a sword. A retinue had a political rather than a military role. In the reign of Charles II, with the struggle for power centred on the court, the first duke of Ormond's lengthy tenure of the Irish viceroyalty had enabled his followers to colonise the bureaucracies of church and state. After the Revolution and the ensuing war, attention turned towards the parliament in Dublin as offering a more accessible route to public eminence. It was there that the followers of the second duke were expected to settle their obligations.

In this new political world the Ormonds did not lack resources. Admittedly, some of their traditional advantages had been devalued. The ramifying Butler genealogy was of less value in constructing a parliamentary 'interest' than it had been in providing the fifteenth- and sixteenth-century Ormonds with men-at-arms, since many of the second duke's relations were Catholics. On the other hand, the family's local power-base afforded opportunities for the development of electoral patronage. Even more important was the influence the duke could exert to facilitate employment and advancement for his supporters, not just within his own household and estate, but also in central and local government (both in Ireland and England), in the legal profession, the army, and the established church. Directly or indirectly, Ormond could channel a remarkable variety of preferments in the direction of those who applied for his favour. At the same time, however, the foundations of the family's power were crumbling. The vast estate was being devoured by debt; encumbered and mortgaged in almost every part. It was poorly managed, and top-heavy with superfluous staff. Expenditure consistently outran a rental income which itself fell far short of expectations. Thus Ormond inevitably came to depend less and less on his own personal resources and more and more on his privileged access to crown and public patronage.

The context of a great estate in terminal decline affords particular interest to the exploration of Ormond's role as a magnate. Despite modest abilities, he was showered with honours and appointments, especially in the reign of Queen Anne, when, besides the Irish lord lieutenancy, he rose to the highest rank in the army – captain-general in succession to Marlborough – before losing everything in the political crash that followed the Hanoverian succession, when he fled to the exiled Jacobite court to escape impeachment. There is a peculiar fascination in the problem of understanding how his glittering public career could have been built upon treacherous foundations; how his political 'connexion' not only endured but, as we shall see, apparently grew in strength just at the time that his financial affairs were coming to a crisis; and how, by various means, his followers' allegiance was sustained until the catastrophe of Jacobite exile.

The pathology of the decline of the Ormond estate has already been subjected to detailed investigation. The restructuring of tenurial arrangements and selling of freehold property were charted in T. P. Power's study of eighteenth-century Tipperary,[3] while the late W. G. Neely described similar processes happening in County Kilkenny,[4] but their conclusions have to be fitted into a broader picture. Put crudely, Ormond's problem was that outgoings were far in excess of income. Danger signals were already visible long before his succession to the dukedom. His grandfather, the first duke, had bequeathed a mountain of debt, the total stated in May 1688 at £98,500, serviced by annual interest payments of £6,000.[5] There were two main causes: a low return on the estate (where it was common for abatements of rent to be granted or arrears indulged) and uncontrolled expenditure. Administrative costs were bound to be high, but even so the Ormonds employed far too many people, with the result that the estate always ran at a loss. No element was profitable, not even the palatinate of Tipperary, where the family controlled (and received fees from) the local law courts.[6] The first duke had been driven to borrow heavily, and the more he borrowed, the more he seemed to need.

The accession of the second duke only accelerated the decline. Collection of rents slowed even further, on the pretext that the depredations of both sides in the Jacobite war had destroyed stock, retarded agricultural production, and made money scarce. The receivers' accounts from 1690 show that the granting of substantial abatements, and an acceptance that other rents could never be collected (had become 'desperate', in the agents' parlance), had reduced the maximum available to a little over £17,000 p.a.[7] Simultaneously, expenditure was spiralling: during the 1690s the annual sum spent merely on the household, even in those less expensive years when Ormond was on campaign, amounted to between £2,000 and £3,000.[8] Frequently the duke maintained three separate establishments; sometimes four. Kilkenny Castle retained the splendour with which it had been adorned in his grandfather's time, a

3 T. P. Power, *Land, politics and society in eighteenth-century Tipperary* (Oxford, 1993), pp 76–82, 118–25.

4 W. G. Neely, 'The Ormond Butlers in County Kilkenny' in William Nolan and Kevin Whelan (eds), *Kilkenny: history and society* … (Dublin, 1990), pp 123–6.

5 Power, *Land, politics & soc.*, p. 120.

6 Ibid., pp 4–6.

7 N.L.I., Ormond papers, MS 2,561 (unfoliated).

8 Household and 'small' accounts of the duke and duchess, 1694–1707 (ibid., MS 2,547 (unfoliated)); 'A particular of several affairs relating to his grace the duke of Ormond' (ibid., MS 2,545 (unfoliated)). See also household inventories, 1628–1715 (ibid., MSS 2,521–5, 2,527–9, 2,552–5),

visitor describing it as 'the most worth seeing of anything I have yet seen in Ireland'.[9] Even in the absence of the duke in 1702 the castle staff included a dancing master, chasseur ('dog keeper'), gardener, porter, three grooms, and fourteen other servants.[10] Then there were the properties in England: Ormonde House in St James's Square, Westminster, and a house in Richmond Park, both with a complement of staff.[11] To make matters worse, when Ormond was campaigning, or when he presided over the Irish government, he felt himself to be under an obligation to entertain, which eroded any profit from the acquisition of an official salary.[12] 'The duke of Ormond has made him eighteen *aides-de-camp*', reported Bishop Burnet's nephew in April 1712, after the announcement of the promotion to captain-general, 'and intends to appear in very unusual splendour and at a very great expense in Flanders. He will have the honour of running farther into debt by being made a general.'[13]

Other persistent charges on domestic expenditure were even less justifiable (and less likely to figure in the ducal accounts). Ormond was an energetic womaniser: a contemporary lampoon sneered that he was 'as silly as poor', and that 'his courage and wit lies in keeping a whore'.[14] His second duchess, evidently not always sinned against, was reputed to have lost a fortune at the gaming tables.[15] Both husband and wife seem to have been compelled to spend money, either for self-indulgence, or as a way of expressing their exalted social status. Whatever the reason, they were immune to the sternest warnings. Ormond's friends impressed upon him the need to retrench, with lessons in domestic economy the simplicity of which foreshadowed Mr Micawber. Time and again he promised to comply,[16] but exceeded even their

9 Edmund Denton to Richard Norris, 30 Mar. 1703 (Liverpool R.O., Norris papers, 920 NOR 1/252).

10 Return of the number of Protestant inhabitants, St Patrick's parish, Kilkenny, 1702 (N.L.I., Ormond papers, MS 11,048/157).

11 'Lady duchess's list of debts paid by her', received Jan. 1721[/2] (N.L.I., Ormond papers, MS 11,067). For Ormonde House, see A. I. Dasent, *The history of St James's Square* ... (London, 1895), pp 89–93; *Survey of London* (47 vols so far, London, 1900–), xxix, 118–20. An undated account of the staff retained in Ormonde House during the later seventeenth century lists forty-one household servants, together with a gentleman of the horse, ten stablehands, a chasseur, two chairmen and seven watermen (B.L., Wentworth papers, Add. MS 22267, f. 68). There are inventories of the contents of both houses at T.N.A., FEC 1/O.34/3–4, FEC 1/O.40. 'A particular of several affairs relating to his grace of Ormond (N.L.I., MS 2,545) recommended that the 'establishment for the family' (in Ireland and in England) be fixed, and 'put in an easy method for the steward to understand, and to follow'.

12 See bills of fare for Ormond at Dublin Castle, 1711 (formerly B.L., Ormond papers, Loan 37/8).

13 Thomas Burnet to George Duckett, 8 Apr. 1712 (*Letters of Thomas Burnet to George Duckett 1712–1722* (Roxburghe Club, London, 1914), p. 5).

14 'A new Protestant litany', Feb. 1711[/12] (B.L., Add. MS 40060, f. 88); *Memoirs of the life of his grace James, late duke of Ormond* ... (London, 1738), pp 6–17, 48–9, 62–8, 74–82, 92–103, 190–202, 208–14, 221–34, 261–72, 283–6; G. De F. Lord et al. (eds), *Poems on affairs of state: Augustan satirical verse 1660–1714* (7 vols, New Haven, Conn., 1963–75), vi, 440; *The prose works of Jonathan Swift*, ed. Herbert Davis et al. (14 vols, Oxford, 1963–75), viii, 133; entry of the arms of William Butler, illegitimate son of the duke of Ormond, 6 July 1705 (Genealogical Office, Dublin, MS 103, p. 4).

15 [Erasmus Lewis] to [Robert Harley], 17 June 1708 (H.M.C., *Portland* MSS, iv, 493).

16 In 1707 Sir Richard Cox expressed his pleasure that Ormond was at last 'retrenching' (Cox to Edward Southwell, 26 Apr. 1707 (B.L., Southwell papers, Add. MS 38155, f. 23)).

generous allowances. 'Is it not a lamentable story', complained one of his advisers, Archibald Hutcheson, to another, Sir Richard Cox, in 1711, at a time when property was being sold off in yet another systematic attempt to set the duke's affairs to rights,

> that with all the present great incomings of his grace his debts, instead of lessening, are upon the increase ... and if in the present prosperity things run thus, how swift must the destruction be when the tide shall turn. And is there any longer an encouragement to toil in the stopping up of auger holes when the master of the vessel is tearing up the planks? Can a ship long swim in such circumstances as these? Surely you and his grace's other friends in Ireland should frequently mention to him the state of his affairs, the necessity of the utmost frugality, and all other honest methods for the retrieving them. I am persuaded you do so, and will choose rather to lose his friendship than not be really his friends and rather to disoblige him by these necessary alarms than suffer him to sleep securely on the brink of a precipice, and to drop unwarned into irretrievable ruin.[17]

Yet at the same time payment of servants' wages was happily allowed to run into arrears, and tradesmen's bills were regularly refused.[18] Occasionally this might bring embarrassment, though usually to the duchess rather than the duke himself. In 1711, for example, while Ormond was feasting his friends and followers in appropriately regal fashion in Dublin Castle, his wife was preparing to barricade herself into the Richmond Park house in order to withstand the assaults of bailiffs.[19]

In practice, cutting back on spending was out of the question. Instead, Ormond continued to borrow, and to mortgage and remortgage his assets: land, office, pensions, and hereditary privileges such as the right to collect the prisage (customs duty) on wines imported into Ireland. Mortgages were of course only short-term expedients, and while expenditure continued to outrun income at an alarming rate all that was achieved was an accumulation of greater encumbrances on the estate. By borrowing to pay his debts, Ormond was exchanging one dependency for another. Ultimately, he was obliged to realise the value of his properties by sale, though this went against the grain.[20] The diminution of his patrimony was something that disturbed him greatly, and to which he was brought to agree only after all other solutions had manifestly failed.

The history of the management of the Ormond estate after 1689 is exceedingly complex, involving a succession of agents, managers, commissioners, and trustees. To begin with, the second duke inherited his grandfather's servants and advisers: Valentine Smyth as steward, and Charles Gosling as receiver-general of rents. But it was soon clear that the difficulties created by the first duke's huge borrowings demanded a different approach. In 1691 the superintendence of Ormond's affairs

17 [Hutcheson] to Cox, 11 Aug. 1711 (N.L.I., Ormond papers, MS 2,474, pp 361–2).

18 Thomas Burnet to George Duckett, 8 Apr. 1712 (*Letters of Thomas Burnet*, p. 5); 'Lady duchess's list of debts paid by her', received Jan. 1721[/2] (N.L.I., MS 11,067); William Betts to Sir Edward Turnor, 31 Dec. 1701 (West Sussex R.O., Shillinglee papers, Ac.454/851); *The case of the creditors of the late duke of Ormond* ... ([?London, 1715]); Neely, 'Ormond Butlers', p. 125.

19 [Hutcheson] to Cox, 11 Aug. 1711 (N.L.I., MS 2,474, pp 361–2).

20 Sir Richard Cox to Ormond, 8 Jan. 1697[/8] (N.L.I., Ormond papers, MS 2,456, pp 323–7).

was entrusted to a commission presided over by the second earl of Longford (who had married the widow of Ormond's uncle) and consisting of Longford's nephew Francis Cuffe, the attorney-general of the Tipperary palatinate Joseph Coughlan, John Price, and Richard Warburton.[21] These commissioners faced an uphill task. The slow recovery of the Irish economy obliged them to concede further abatements of rent, while Ormond's creditors became ever more insistent. Longford was perhaps not the best man for the job, for he was struggling with his own debts,[22] and in 1694 the commission was wound up, with responsibility given to an individual, another veteran of the first duke's service, William Worth, an experienced lawyer who was a baron of the Irish exchequer.[23] However, Worth continued to consult the former commissioners, especially Warburton, who had devised a novel means of raising money on the Irish properties by changing the nature of tenures.[24] In return for a substantial fine, a tenant holding a lease for years would be able to exchange it for a lease for lives, while those already holding lives-leases would be offered a perpetual renewal. Warburton's scheme was adopted, and brought into effect by means of two private acts of parliament, an Irish act of 1695, to vest lands in trustees to be sold or leased to clear Ormond's debts; and an English act of 1697 to permit the sale of woods and the granting of leases for lives renewable in perpetuity.

Under these two statutes management of the estates reverted to a commission, in which Worth was joined by Edward Corker, M.P. for Ratoath (Co. Meath), the Irish surveyor-general William Robinson (another old client of the Butlers), and Sir Richard Cox, a County Cork lawyer who had begun his career under the patronage of the Boyles, but who had contrived an introduction to Ormond and was resolved to attach himself to the duke's interest.[25] Between 1697 and 1700 the new commissioners raised considerable sums, through fines and sales. But Ormond was dissatisfied. He resented the alienation of ancestral lands, the more so when the weight of debt did not seem appreciably lighter, and was suspicious of the commissioners,

21 Ormond to Valentine Smyth, 2 Sept. 1690 (ibid., p. 45); Ld Longford to Charles Gosling, 6 July 1692 (ibid., pp 151–6); Longford et al. to Josias Haydock, 7 Sept. 1692 (ibid., p. 165); Longford to Ormond, 14 Nov. 1691 ('Letters of Lord Longford and others on Irish affairs, 1689–1702', ed. Patrick Melvin, in *Analecta Hibernica*, xxxii (1985), p. 76); same to John Ellis, 11 Dec. 1691 (ibid., pp 84–5); Power, *Land, politics & soc.*, pp 120–21.

22 Longford to Gosling, 8 Dec. 1692, 17 Aug. 1695, 28 Jan. 1695/6 (N.L.I., MS 2,456, pp 179, 215, 255).

23 For Worth, see F. E. Ball, *The judges in Ireland 1221–1921* (2 vols, New York, 1927), i, 358–9.

24 Power, *Land, politics & soc.*, pp 77–8.

25 T. C. Barnard, 'The political, material and mental culture of the Cork settlers, c. 1650–1700' in Patrick O'Flanagan and C. G. Buttimer (eds), *Cork: history and society* (Dublin, 1993), p. 343; draft bill in *attorney-general of the palatinate of Tipperary* v. *Peter Hayden*, [?1711–14] (N.L.I., Ormond papers, MS 11,044/260); Cox to Ormond, 8 Jan, 1697/8 (H.M.C., *Ormonde MSS*, n.s., viii, 35). For Robinson, see John Rotton to Henry Gascoigne, 27 Nov. 1688 (N.L.I., MS 2,454, p. 305); Rolf Loeber, *A biographical dictionary of architects in Ireland 1600–1720* (London, 1981), pp 88–97; G. D. Burtchaell, *Genealogical memoirs of the Members of Parliament for the county and city of Kilkenny* ... (Dublin, 1888), pp 86–7; *D.I.B.*, viii, 552–3; for Cox, *The autobiography of the rt hon. Sir Richard Cox* ..., ed. Richard Caulfield (Cork, 1860); *Oxf. D.N.B.*, xiii, 865–7; *D.I.B.*, ii, 937–8. For evidence that Cox was looking beyond Ormond for other possible patrons, see earl of Rochester to Thomas Keightley, 24 Apr. 1701 (N.L.I., Inchiquin papers, MS 45,721 /1).

who were indeed taking advantage of the new system of tenures to obtain life-leases for themselves. The projected sale of the town of Arklow (in County Wicklow) to Colonel John Allen for £9,000 was a particularly sore point, since it remained uncompleted after eighteen months, and gave rise to a tedious lawsuit. Ormond's father-in-law, Lord Rochester, and other friends in England may have prompted his distrust of his Irish commissioners. By February 1701 Worth was reported to have 'fallen under the duke of Ormond's displeasure and the severe censure of most persons about and in London'.[26]

The consequence was another private act of parliament, passed at Westminster (with Rochester chairing the Lords' second-reading committee).[27] Despite Ormond's own reservations about granting perpetual leases, this measure reinforced the provisions of the two previous acts and permitted tenants to transform their holdings into fee farms, paying a lump sum in order to free themselves from future fines for renewal. It established a body of English-based trustees to whom the commissioners would be responsible, including Rochester, the financier Sir Stephen Fox, who held a number of mortgages on Ormond property, and the rising Tory politician (and future lord chancellor) Simon Harcourt. A new name was also added to the Irish commission, that of Francis Annesley, an Irish lawyer long since transplanted into England. Annesley was a close associate of Harcourt, who seems to have become by this time one of Ormond's closest advisers.[28]

The 1701 reorganisation set the pattern for future management. The policy of granting fee farms was followed consistently, with further private acts of the Irish parliament, in 1704, 1707 and 1710, extending the time for these arrangements to be made. There was a substantial input from Ormond's English trustees, particularly Fox, whose position was strengthened by virtue of the sizable personal loans he had already made and was continuing to make on the security of lands and the prisage. The Irish commissioners found their advice ignored. Whereas they had recommended 'moderating' the conditions on which fee farms were granted, in order to encourage potential purchasers, the duke insisted that 'the old rates' be adhered to.[29] New pairs of eyes detected inefficiency at all levels, and gradually the local administration of the estate was transferred to different hands. Samuel Booth, seneschal of the manors in County Kilkenny, was removed in 1701. Worth was discharged in 1705. Gosling's successor as receiver-general, Alderman Josias Haydock of Kilkenny, was replaced in 1708 by an Irish barrister and M.P., Robert Fitzgerald. Three

26 Cox to Ormond, 30 July, 24 Sept. 1700, 28 Jan. 1700[/01] (N.L.I., Ormond papers, MS 2,457, pp 31–2, 39–40, 63–7); Michael Hickie to Sir Donough O'Brien, 6 Feb. 1700/01 (N.L.I., Inchiquin papers, MS 45,311/2).

27 *L.J.*, xvi, 666.

28 Annesley to Harcourt, 25 Aug. 1701 (N.L.I., MS 2,457, pp 153–7; Worth et al. to Ormond, 26 Aug. 1701 (ibid., p. 161); Worth to Harcourt, 10 Sept. 1701 (ibid., pp 175–6); Sir Robert Southwell to Benjamin Portlock, 21 Feb. 1701/2 (ibid., p. 191); Cox et al. to Ormond's trustees, 9 Mar. 1701/2 (ibid., p. 211). For Annesley, see *H.C. 1690–1715*, iii, 34–9; for Harcourt, ibid., iv, 200–222; *Oxf. D.N.B.*, xxv, 130–34.

29 Cox to Ormond, 3 Mar. 1701[/2] (N.L.I., MS 2,457); Cox et al. to Ormond's trustees, 9 Mar. 1701/2 (ibid., p. 211); Cox and Worth to George Clarke and John Ellis, 12 Mar. 1701/2 (ibid., p 218).

years later Ormond dismissed the auditor of his Irish household, Ulysses Burgh, who had by some unspecified offence 'given the finishing stroke to all his roguery', and inquiries were set on foot into the conduct of other collectors and receivers.[30] Fitzgerald's superintending responsibility was broadened, and he was eventually given sole charge of affairs in Ireland, until, worn out by the unequal struggle with Ormond's insolvency, he begged leave to 'retire to my own house', and was replaced in his turn in February 1712 by Richard Nutley, an English Tory who had originally come to Dublin in 1701 as counsel to the English parliament's forfeiture trustees, and was close to Rochester and Harcourt.[31]

The Irish statute of 1710 had placed all Ormond's property under the control of trustees – Rochester, Sir Stephen Fox and his son Charles, William Robinson (now Sir William), Ormond's former private secretary John Ellis, and two Irish-born lawyers, Archibald Hutcheson and William Sloper.[32] The Dublin banking brothers, Henry and Sir Alexander Cairnes, were also becoming more intimately involved, as they advanced money to the duke on various securities. Henry, in fact, became the designated recipient of all Ormond's rental income.[33] This new management team was prepared to make radical changes. In 1711 they began a thorough reappraisal that resulted in a concerted effort to set Ormond's affairs on a sound basis. Debts were consolidated into a few large loans; a plan of retrenchment was adopted (though, needless to say, ignored by the duke and duchess); property was sold outright rather than let in long leases or fee farms.[34] An act was even rushed through the Westminster parliament to enable Ormond to surrender to the crown the regalities of the Tipperary palatinate, in return for cash.[35] It was not acted upon but kept in reserve. But despite these extraordinary exertions the situation at the time of Ormond's flight to the Pretender in 1715 was, if anything, worse than it had been in 1688. Debts had increased again, to £110,500, while the alienation of

30 Worth to Ormond, July 1701 (ibid., p. 113); 'A particular of several affairs relating to his grace of Ormond' (ibid., MS 2,545); Neely, 'Ormond Butlers', p. 123. For Booth, see Worth to Ormond, 10 Sept.1701 (N.L.I., MS 2,457, p. 167); same to Harcourt, 10 Sept. 1701 (ibid., pp 175–6); Burtchaell, *Genealogical mems*, pp 82–3. For Haydock, see order signed by Ormond, 24 June 1701 (N.L.I., MS 2,457, p. 89); Cox to Ormond, 4 July 1709 (ibid., Ormond papers, MS 2,473, p. 203); order for payments to Haydock, 1701–2 (ibid., MS 11,044/265); copy of bill in chancery in *Butler v. Haydock* (ibid., MS 11,048/153). For Fitzgerald, see Bp Hartstonge of Ossory to Ormond, 26 July 1705 (H.M.C., *Ormonde* MSS, n.s., viii, 168). For Burgh, see John Ellis and Sir William Robinson to 'Mr Clayton', 18 Aug. 1711 (N.L.I., MS 2,474, p. 373).

31 Instructions to Robert Fitzgerald, 1710 (N.L.I., MS 2,545); John Isham to Sir Justinian Isham, 9 June 1713 (Northamptonshire R.O., Isham papers, IC 2224). For Nutley, see John to Sir Justinian Isham, 15 Feb. 1702[/3] (ibid., IC 2198); Ball, *Judges*, ii, 72; *Hist. Ir. parl.*, v, 365–6.

32 Indenture, 25 Apr. 1711 (N.L.I., MS 2,545); copy of act, 1710 (ibid.); Robert Fitzgerald to John Cotton, 3 Aug. 1710 (ibid., MS 2,473, pp 417–18). For Hutcheson, see *HC 1690–1715*, iv, 449–52; for Sloper, *H.C. 1715–54* (2 vols, London, 1970), ii, 425–6. Additional notes in the files of the History of Parliament Trust make it clear that Sloper was born in Ireland, of an Irish landed family, in contradiction to the published biographical entry.

33 [Hutcheson] to Cox, 11 Aug. 1711 (N.L.I., MS 2,474, p. 353).

34 [Same] to same, 11 Aug. 1711 (ibid., pp 349–69); John Cotton to —, 5 Jan. 1711[?/12] (ibid., p. 513). See also Hugh Henry to Hutcheson, 2 Sept. 1714 (ibid., MS 2,477, pp 37–8); Neely, 'Ormond Butlers', pp 123–4; Power, *Land, politics & soc.*, pp 80–81.

35 Francis Annesley to [Ormond], 20 June 1712 (N.L.I., Ormond papers, MS 2,475, p. 427).

property (by fee farm leases and outright sales) had depressed the rental income – in theory £16,000, in practice as little as £5,400, insufficient to meet Ormond's ordinary expenditure.[36] In all probability, Ormond's departure was a blessing in disguise for the estate. The palatinate was finally extinguished by an Irish statute, albeit on political grounds, thus disposing of one drain on income. Although the duke had been attainted by the British parliament and not the Irish, property in both kingdoms was forfeit, and was administered efficiently by the Forfeited Estates Commissioners until 1721, when Ormond's brother Arran was allowed to buy it back. By this time the Butler family had long ceased to occupy the commanding heights in either national or local politics in Ireland.

In this tortuous and depressing story we may observe two salient points. In the short term, the chronic economic weakness of the estate did not necessarily reduce the political 'interest' possessed by its owner, since the management of decline opened up new possibilities for existing and prospective clients. In the long term, however, the erosion of Ormond's property meant that these benefits formed a constantly diminishing resource.

Ormond's financial embarrassments may occasionally have made life difficult for some of his employees, such as the rent collectors, whose remuneration was calculated on commission (sixpence in the pound), but for many others a tempting vista opened. The successive commissions, agencies and trusts established to administer Ormond's affairs provided employment, and at least some of those involved were paid salaries: Robert Fitzgerald received the far from negligible sum of £400 a year between 1709 and 1712, and under him there were jobs for an auditor, at £100 a year, various clerks, costing altogether a further £150, and a solicitor, at £20.[37] Probably previous commissioners (though not trustees) had also been paid; they were certainly regarded as employees.[38] Those appointed in 1701 were provided with sufficient funds to accommodate themselves in offices in Dublin, and to engage staff. Their chief clerk, Ormond's steward and man-of-business Stephen Sweet, demanded £200 a year in salary.[39] Other rewards came indirectly. It was a well established custom on the estate for agents to make arrangements on favourable terms for themselves, their families and friends, and, not surprisingly, two of the commissioners responsible for the restructuring of leases in 1697–1700 profited materially. William

36 State of Ormond's rents, Michaelmas, 1710 (ibid., MS 2,545); state of debts, 1711 (ibid.); 'A particular of several affairs relating to his grace of Ormond' (ibid.). Cf. 'The case of the earl of Arran' [1716] (Bodl., MS Carte 125, f. 91); Neely, 'Ormond Butlers', p. 124.

37 Instructions to Fitzgerald, 1710 (N.L.I., MS 2,545). It was customary for tenants to pay a fee to Ormond's solicitor for drawing up a lease (Longford to Ormond, 14 Nov. 1691 ('Letters of Longford', ed. Melvin, p. 76); same to John Ellis, 11 Dec. 1691 (ibid., pp 84–5)).

38 See for example, Alan Brodrick to Thomas Brodrick, 10 Mar. 1702/3 (S.H.C., Brodrick papers, 1248/2/84–5), referring to Francis Annesley.

39 Annesley to Harcourt, 25 Aug. 1701 (N.L.I., MS 2,457, pp 153–7); Worth et al. to Ormond, 26 Aug. 1701 (ibid., p. 161); Worth to Ormond, 10 Sept. 1701 (H.M.C., *Ormonde MSS*, n.s., viii, 40); earl of Ranelagh to same, 16 June 1705 (ibid., 160). See also Josias Haydock to Sir Thomas Hales, 18 July 1698 (Somerset Heritage Centre, Bouverie of Brynmore papers, DD/BR): 'Whatever lies in my power to serve Mr Hales in shall not be wanting, tho' being only a servant I have nothing to dispose of, that being the province of his grace's commissioner, who has a great many that depend on him.'

Worth was accused of enlarging his own fortune substantially while at the same time the estate was losing over £30,000,[40] while Sir Richard Cox was obliged to admit that he had invested £1,500 himself in Ormond lands, sugaring his explanation with elaborate protestations of innocence.[41] These were only the two most prominent examples. Among many other beneficiaries we may count the commissioner, Robinson, who converted his lease of Sherwood Park, Co. Carlow, into a freehold purchase; the legal adviser, sometime agent, and palatinate official Thomas Medlycott, who acquired property near Clonmel in about 1698; the receiver-general, Haydock; the commissioners' clerk Stephen Sweet; and Ormond's private secretary Benjamin Portlock.[42]

Throughout Ormond's household administration and land management a kind of parasitism prevailed, with the duke's dependants happily feeding off the estate. At the lowest level receivers and agents retained money in their own hands for long periods. In 1708 the receiver-general Haydock was caught with £5,000 unaccounted for, and two agents, Silvester Cross and John Pacy, were observed to be exceedingly slow in making up their books.[43] Haydock was said to have abused his position to build up his own local influence, which, as far as Ormond was concerned, was another dangerous temptation. At the top of the scale, commissioners and trustees commonly portrayed themselves as disinterested,[44] yet at the same time figured prominently among the duke's creditors, or those making purchases of his property.[45] The most obvious example is Sir Stephen Fox, whose claims to altruism have been tentatively endorsed by one biographer.[46] However, contemporaries had their suspicions, and the circumstantial evidence does not show him to advantage.[47] He had always been Ormond's biggest creditor, and by 1700 was owed over £16,600. A series

40 Worth to Ormond, 14 Aug. 1701 (N.L.I., MS 2,547, p. 137); 'A particular of several affairs relating to his grace of Ormond' (ibid., MS 2,545). For further evidence of the acquisition of land by the Worth family in County Tipperary, see map of holdings in Donoghill, 1759 (Tipperary South Riding County Museum, Clonmel, O'Callaghan papers, Acc. 1985:119).

41 Cox to Ormond, 8 Jan. 1697[/8], 16, 22 May 1699 (N.L.I., MS 2,456, pp 323–7, 369–73, 397–8).

42 'The case and complaint of Mr William Robinson', 8 Sept. 1688 (ibid., MS 2,453, pp 33–8); 'Arrears of rents in collectors' hands', 1690/1 (ibid., MS 2,561, f. 7); rentals of Ormond estate 1689–1704 (ibid., Ormond papers, MS 2,562, no. 860); Cox to Ormond, 30 July 1700 (ibid., 2,457, pp 31–2); 'memorandum about Portlock's land ...' (ibid., MS 11,053/8); Loeber, *Biog. dict.*, p. 92; *H.C. 1690–1715*, iv, 790–93; W. P. Burke, *History of Clonmel* (Waterford, 1907), p. 318; T.N.A., FEC1/O.29–30, 46, 91; FEC1/O. 122/65,74.

43 Neely, 'Ormond Butlers', p. 123; Robert Fitzgerald to [Ormond], 29 Dec. 1708 (N.L.I., MS 2,473, pp 143–8).

44 See, for example, [Hutcheson] to Cox, 11 Aug. 1711 (N.L.I., MS 2,474, pp 349–69): 'I entered into his grace's affairs upon the pure motive of good nature and compassion'.

45 Hutcheson would be an exception, although he benefited from Ormond's electoral influence as lord warden of the Cinque Ports, when returned for Hastings in the British general election of 1713. See below, p. 68.

46 This at any rate would seem to be the implication of the discussion in Christopher Clay, *Public finance and private wealth: the career of Sir Stephen Fox, 1627–1716* (Oxford, 1978), pp 177–8. Dr Clay does admit, however, that 'the dealings between Ormond and Sir Stephen ... are extremely hard to follow in detail' (p. 177).

47 Robert Fitzgerald to [Ormond], 29 Dec. 1708 (N.L.I., MS 2,473, pp 143–8).

of deeds and settlements were then effected, ostensibly to reduce the level of debt, and involving the assignment of further securities and eventually sales of land. But Fox continued to advance money, to answer what were said to be Ormond's 'urgent occasions', and by 1709 the debt had risen again, to £19,500.[48]

Those employed by Ormond, or who were involved in his business affairs (such as Fox or the duke's other bankers, the Cairnes brothers), benefited in the short term from the connexion. But the law of diminishing returns applied. Favourable leases and discounted sales provided immediate gratification but no lasting attachment, and, as the rent roll shrank, fewer receivers or agents were needed, and fewer opportunities arose to gratify tenants with abatements or postponements of rent. Nor was it simply a matter of Ormond's patrimony and retinue dwindling together. The granting of perpetual leases and fee farms, and the sale of freeholds, helped to raise up other propertied interests. There was always a risk that Ormond's agents would use the authority they derived from the duke to enhance their own influence, and when Ormond had no more to give, they might make use of this in quite another way. This indeed happened in the case of Haydock, who, after his dismissal as receiver-general, exploited his standing among the tenantry to promote parliamentary candidates in opposition to Ormond's nominees, and became one of the leaders of the Whig faction in Kilkenny city.[49]

The operation of these processes can be seen in the decline of Ormond's electoral influence, which in theory ought to have been extensive (and indeed, in the aftermath of the Williamite peace settlement was assumed by his agents and advisers to be extensive) but which in practice turned out to be limited and grew feebler as the estate was gradually broken up. In 1692 the concentration of Butler estates in Kilkenny and Tipperary ensured that there would be a strong representation of his tenants among the freeholders of both shires, and in several parliamentary boroughs he was either the ground landlord or the largest single proprietor. The two constituencies in the city of Kilkenny – Kilkenny itself and St Canice (or Irishtown) – were obviously subject to pressure from the castle. (In the case of St Canice, the bishop of Ossory could make a claim to patronage but successive bishops tended to defer to ducal wishes since they were themselves ducal nominees.) Elsewhere in County Kilkenny Ormond was landlord of Callan, lord of the manor of Knocktopher, owned the castle that dominated Gowran, and held substantial property in Inistioge and Thomastown.[50] In Tipperary he was ground landlord in Clonmel,

48 N.L.I., Ormond papers, MS 2,526, is a lengthy statement of accounts between Ormond and Fox, 1700–11. See especially pp 9, 21, 23, 25, 30–33; also Clay, *Public finance & private wealth*, pp 322–3.

49 Ebenezer Warren to Haydock, 15 Dec. 1715, 24, 28, [?29] Sept., 15 Oct. 1717 (N.L.I., Ormond papers, MS 11,058/3); Burtchaell, *Genealogical mems*, pp 81–2; W. G. Neely, *Kilkenny: an urban history, 1391–1843* (Belfast, [1989]), pp 140, 144.

50 For a general survey of electoral politics in County Kilkenny in this period, see T. P. Power, 'Parliamentary representation in County Kilkenny in the eighteenth century' in Nolan & Whelan (eds), *Kilkenny*, pp 305–32. For Kilkenny city and St Canice, see Edward Worth to Charles Gosling, 23 July 1695 (N.L.I., MS 11,048/143); list of Ormond's tenants in Kilkenny city (ibid., MS 11,048/145); Bp Hartstonge to [Ormond], 1 May [1707] (N.L.I., MS, 2,472, pp 132–5); same to Josias Haydock, 7 June 1709 (ibid., MS 2,473, pp 190–3); Neely, *Kilkenny*, pp 134–40. For

administrative headquarters of the palatinate, and could also exert a proprietorial claim over Fethard.[51] Even without the less predictable county elections, this clutch of boroughs could have produced a squadron of some fourteen M.P.s had Ormond been able simply to nominate. But this was far from the case.

Even before his commissioners embarked on the programme of reconstruction that so diminished his patrimony, the duke did not have things his own way in the two counties that traditionally served as the core of Butler power. Other substantial landowners had emerged following the Cromwellian confiscations to challenge the family's predominance in county politics: the Cuffes, Deanes, Floods, Flowers, Ponsonbys and Wandesfords in Kilkenny, and the Hamertons, Pennefathers and Moores in Tipperary. And despite Ormond's proprietorial pretensions, he often faced opposition in the boroughs as well, or at the very least was obliged to negotiate with rival interests. The Cuffe and Weymes families in Callan, the Agars in Gowran, the Deanes and Ponsonbys in Inistioge, Lord Massereene and the Harrisons in Thomastown, the Moores in Clonmel and the Everards in Fethard: all possessed substantial influence in their own right, even if some were inclined to co-operate with Ormond.[52] Not all the boroughs were predictable: Kilkenny, in particular, was by Irish standards a popular election, with a relatively numerous and expensive freeman electorate.[53] Nor could Ormond always trust his own agents: in 1692 the deputy clerk of the crown in the palatinate, Matthew Jacob, spurned ducal direction with breathtaking impudence. Ormond's chief tenant at Gowran, Charles Agar, also flouted his authority; and in Kilkenny itself Josias Haydock was said to have indulged in 'indirect and underhand dealing' (a transgression that, unhappily for Ormond, was forgotten when Haydock was subsequently appointed receiver-general of his rents).[54]

The general election of 1692 would certainly have brought home to Ormond the limitations of his electoral muscle. Lord Longford reported the outcome at some length:[55]

> Before the commissioners left Kilkenny they took all the prudent cautions they could, by discoursing with as many of those who could influence the other corporations as we met with, and we gave directions to his grace's receivers to prepare the electors in

Callan, see orders for payments to Josias Haydock (N.L.I., MS 11,044/265); Joe Kennedy, 'Callan – a corporate town 1700–1800' in Nolan & Whelan (eds), *Kilkenny*, pp 301–2. For Gowran, see Ld Longford to John Ellis, 10 Oct. 1692 ('Letters of Longford', ed. Melvin, pp 100–101). For Thomastown, see T.N.A., FEC1/O.36. For Knocktopher, see Burtchaell, *Genealogical mems*, pp 87–9.

51 Burke, *Clonmel*, pp 167, 215, 240, 308, 441; Longford to Ellis, 10 Oct. 1692 ('Letters of Longford', ed. Melvin, pp 100–101).

52 'History of the Irish parliament' project, notes on Callan (P.R.O.N.I., ENV/5/HP/14/3); Power, 'Parliamentary representation', pp 320, 322–3, 325; idem, *Land, politics & soc.*, pp 224–7.

53 Power, 'Parliamentary representation', p. 311. At least 400 freemen were polled in 1715 (*C.J.Ire.* (2nd ed.), iii, 123).

54 Longford to John Ellis, 10 Oct. 1692 ('Letters of Longford', ed. Melvin, pp 100–101); Longford et al. to Haydock, 7 Sept. 1692 (N.L.I., MS 2,456, p. 165); proposal of Charles Agar, n.d. (ibid., Ms 11,048/156).

55 Longford to John Ellis, 10 Oct. 1692 ('Letters of Longford', ed. Melvin, pp 99–101).

their respective collections for such recommendations as his grace should think fit to make to them.

The results were bitterly disappointing. Superficially, it might have appeared that the county elections had gone well: in Tipperary the chancellor of the palatinate, Sir John Meade,[56] shared the representation with the independently inclined Stephen Moore, while in Kilkenny the two men whom Ormond's commissioners had recommended, Colonel William Ponsonby and Richard Coote, were elected after a contest. But it is unclear how much of this was owing to Ormond's backing, since each of the successful candidates possessed a powerful interest of his own. Of the four, no one but Meade had any connexion with Ormond, or, indeed, was politically congenial to him. Moreover, Ponsonby and Coote had only been endorsed in return for the promised election of two of Ormond's followers (Thomas Medlycott and Richard Warburton) at Inistioge, where Ponsonby was said to have 'so overruling an interest ... that he could dispose of ... that borough as he pleased'.[57] In the event Ponsonby ratted, and neither man was returned. Elsewhere, Ormond secured one seat in Kilkenny, for the viceroy's nephew, but only after last-minute manoeuvring; took another single seat at Gowran, for Richard Warburton's uncle, in the teeth of resistance from the Agars; and saw his supporter Richard Connell chosen for St Canice (a man who, it must be said, was himself an active participant in the factional politics of that corporation and of Kilkenny[58]). But his recommendation of Joseph Coughlan was rejected at Clonmel, and his attempt to find a seat for the English revenue commissioner William Culliford failed utterly, first at Thomastown, where the combined Massereene and Harrison interests were too strong for Ormond's local allies,[59] and then at Callan, where his seneschal Samuel Booth, fleeing from a likely defeat at Fethard, 'procured his own return'.[60] In parliament Booth would presumably have acknowledged Ormond's political leadership, as would William Robinson at Knocktopher, but both owed their seats to their own efforts.

The tally did not improve in the next general election, in 1695. Of the shire knights only Meade, re-elected for Tipperary, could properly be described as an adherent of Ormond, and a Tory petition against the return of Ponsonby and Agmondisham Cuffe for County Kilkenny indicates a defeat there for the candidate backed by the ducal interest.[61] On the positive side, Ormond held a seat in Kilkenny city (through the return of the recorder, Standish Hartstonge), may also have kept one in Gowran, and could rejoice in Richard Connell's continued success in St Canice and the election of the young Edward Worth (nephew to his commissioner,

56 'Officers in the liberty courts from Mr Kearny', 8 Aug. 1688 (N.L.I., MS 11,044/251).

57 Longford to John Ellis, 10 Oct. 1692 ('Letters of Longford', ed. Melvin, p. 100).

58 Burtchaell, *Genealogical mems*, pp 85–6; Kilkenny corporation minute book 1690–1717, pp 184, 213, 215, 226, 244 (Kilkenny corporation archives; N.L.I., microfilm P.5136); St Canice corporation minute book 1661–1718 (Kilkenny corporation archives; N.L.I., P.5143); Power, 'Parliamentary representation', p. 317.

59 Power, 'Parliamentary representation', p. 320; W. J. Pilsworth, *History of Thomastown and district* ([Kilkenny,] 1953), pp 10–11, 13, 80.

60 Longford to John Ellis, 10 Oct. 1692 ('Letters of Longford', ed. Melvin, p. 101).

61 Power, 'Parliamentary representation', p. 307.

Baron Worth) at Knocktopher. But the members chosen for Callan and Thomastown, though politically acceptable, were returned on their own interests,[62] the election for Fethard of the recalcitrant palatinate official Matthew Jacob could hardly be regarded as a triumph, and Inistioge once again showed itself immune to Butler influence.

Nevertheless, from being able to return no more than five M.P.s, and probably nearer three, Ormond's electoral connexion suddenly expanded in the general election of 1703. The High Churchman Sir Henry Weymes took a seat for County Kilkenny, alongside Meade for Tipperary; both Ormond's candidates were chosen in Kilkenny city; and the single seats held by Ormondites in St Canice, Gowran and Knocktopher were retained. Moreover, in several other boroughs the Butler interest seemed to have made a comeback. In Callan followers of the duke took both seats; Thomas Medlycott was finally returned in Clonmel; and even Inistioge elected Ormond's private secretary, Benjamin Portlock.

How had this recovery been achieved? Obviously, Ormond's appointment as lord lieutenant in 1703 had done wonders for his prestige, and it would be tempting to ascribe these successes to the uncritical enthusiasm of Irish Protestants for an Irish-born viceroy, and a rediscovered deference of local families for the house of Ormond. There were certainly manifestations of popular devotion to the duke: in a progress through the Irish countryside in the summer of 1703 he encountered groups of ordinary people piping and dancing on the road before him, in 'spontaneous' demonstrations of joy, and mounted squires and borough aldermen arrayed in welcome. At Clonmel, for example, his train was greeted by 'the sheriff, and all the gentlemen and freeholders of the palatinate'.[63] But if we look closely at the elections, other forces may be detected. In the first place, the gains were made not by the exertion of ducal influence but by resident landed proprietors exploiting their own interest to bring in friends who also happened to be followers of Ormond. In Callan the result was decided by the intervention of James Hamilton and Sir Henry Weymes,[64] while Portlock's election at Inistioge reflected the arrival of Stephen Sweet as a prominent member of the local landowning community.[65] These men were doubtless inspired by admiration and affection for the duke, but there was also the additional encouragement of 'party' loyalty, as Whig and Tory sentiment suffused the Irish body

62 Ibid., pp 320, 325. Arthur Bushe, one of the members returned for Thomastown, had been associated with Ormond's circle for some years, through his friendship with John Ellis. He may even have been employed in a small way in the management of Ormond's affairs at the outset of his legal career. See Bushe to Ellis, 7 Apr. 1689, 20 Nov. 1690 ('Letters of Longford', ed. Melvin, pp 64, 70); Henry Ryder to Ormond, 30 Sept. 1691 (B.L., Ellis papers, Add. MS 28877, f. 115); Bushe to Ellis, 24 Sept. 1701 (ibid., Add. MS 28888, f. 188). In 1702 his brother Amyas thanked Ellis for recommending him for appointment as 'one of his [grace's] deputies for the county of Kilkenny', possibly a deputy governor (Amyas Bushe to Ellis, 4 May 1702 (ibid., f. 215)). For the brothers, see *Hist. Ir. parl.*, iii, 333–4.

63 Account of Ormond's progress from Waterford to Lismore, July 1703 (N.L.I., Ormond papers, MS 993, pp 264–5).

64 — to Ormond, 12 Oct. 1706 (B.L., Southwell papers, Add. MS 38153, f. 74); Kennedy, 'Callan', p., 296.

65 'Hist. Ir. parl.' project, notes on Inistioge (P.R.O.N.I., ENV/5/HP/14/5); Power, 'Parliamentary representation', p. 323.

politic. Ormond was an icon to the Tory faithful, so an attachment to Tory principles may well have been as important as loyalty to the Butler family in determining the choices made by local borough-mongers. Certainly partisan hostility was a major factor in the conflicts that erupted in the larger corporations. Kilkenny was a prime example, its ruling oligarchy divided into Tory and Whig factions, who fought each other in municipal and parliamentary elections.[66] The cohesion of the Tories in the corporation, a number of whom were also involved in the affairs of St Canice (where they had things very much more their own way, and received strong support from the bishop), contributed significantly to the election of Ormondites in both the 1703 and 1713 elections.[67]

The apparent revival of the Ormond interest in 1703 was therefore something of an illusion; less a recrudescence of old-fashioned magnate power than the arrival of a new phenomenon: a 'party' grouping composed of country gentlemen and urban politicians. If we turn our attention back to Ormond himself, we can see that during Queen Anne's reign his trustees' policy of selling land was seriously compromising his ability to return M.P.s of his own choosing. In four boroughs the residual Ormond interest had quite disappeared; the Callan and Clonmel property conveyed to trustees, Gowran Castle sold, and Knocktopher now dominated by the Langrishe family, even if Ormond remained the titular lordship of the manor.[68] In consequence, the 1713 general election was a low point for Ormond's electoral interest. Although the returns included a flock of M.P.s who were, or had been, close associates, only a few successes could be ascribed directly to Butler influence. In Kilkenny the Tory Sir Henry Weymes shared the county representation with the Whig William Ponsonby, while in Tipperary George Mathew, Ormond's kinsman and son of the first duke's land agent, secured a place as a shire knight after announcing his conversion to the established church.[69] Although both Weymes and Mathew probably benefited from Ormond's backing, each possessed a strong proprietorial interest himself. In Kilkenny city the solicitor-general, Sir Richard Levinge, and his running-mate, the local recorder, Darby Egan, were elected, but after a strenuous contest that apparently cost Levinge the unprecedentedly large sum of £200.[70] 'I never took so much pains in my life', he wrote, 'nor ever spent so much money on any election in Ireland, which, if I had not done, the duke had been in danger of losing his interest in his own city, and at his own door.'[71] The voters of St Canice, in returning Ormond's old clients Sir Standish Hartstonge and Sir Robert Maude, were doing their bishop's bidding rather than the duke's, after the Tory faction in the corporation had packed the freeman roll

66 Neely, *Kilkenny*, ch. 7; Power, 'Parliamentary representation', pp 312–14.

67 Sir Richard Cox to Edward Southwell, 27 Mar. 1707 (B.L., Add. MS 38155, f. 3); Power, 'Parliamentary representation', pp 316–17.

68 Kennedy, 'Callan', p. 302; N.L.I., MS 8,019/2; Hubert Butler, *In the land of Nod* (Dublin, 1966), p. 18; survey of the property of Lewis Chaigneau in Gowran, 1711 (N.L.I., 21.F.55(2)); Burtchaell, *Genealogical mems*, pp 87–9; surveys of electoral interest in Irish constituencies, 1713 (B.L., Southwell papers, Add. MS 34777, ff 22, 28–9, 42–4).

69 *Hist. Ir. parl.*, v, 211.

70 Cox to Southwell, 29 Sept., 31 Oct., 7 Nov. 1713 (B.L., Add. MS 38157, ff. 17, 19, 21).

71 Levinge to Edward Southwell, 13 Feb. 1713/14 (Sir Richard G. A. Levinge, *Jottings of the Levinge family* (Dublin, 1877), p. 57).

with reliable men.[72] Callan was now controlled by Sir Henry Weymes, who brought in Ormond's former servant Silvester Cross.[73] At Gowran the Huguenot Chaigneau family, purchasers of the castle, were not yet ready to challenge the Tory Agars, who were happy to provide Levinge with an insurance policy in case the Kilkenny contest went against him. Other Tory successes were at Knocktopher, where Edward Worth, aided and abetted by John Langrishe, returned himself and the counsel to the barrack commissioners, Roscarrick Dunkin;[74] Thomastown, whose choice of the brothers Arthur and Amyas Bushe was allegedly accomplished by the efforts of Dean Marsh and the Hewetsons;[75] and Fethard, in which another local interest, that of the Everards, was sufficient to secure the election of the head of the family, Sir Redmond Everard, and Cornelius Callaghan, a lawyer who held a mortgage on the Everard estate.[76] At Clonmel and Inistioge, on the other hand, all vestiges of Ormond influence had vanished, and each borough returned a pair of Whigs.[77]

In all, it must be doubtful whether at this election Ormond was personally responsible for the election of a single member. A recommendation from Kilkenny Castle was still important in the city itself, and to a lesser extent in the county, and Ormond's agents and receivers of rent may well have been required to communicate the duke's preferences to his tenants. But even in Kilkenny itself it was the energy of the local Tory faction (supplemented by hard cash) that proved decisive. Most Tory successes, including the election of retainers like Silvester Cross, resulted from the efforts of lesser landed families and Tory factions in boroughs, many of which had grown up in the protective shade of the house of Ormond, and had now come to maturity. By 1713 Ormond was a party leader rather than a traditional magnate: the figurehead of the Tory interest in Kilkenny and Tipperary, no longer its proprietor.

The steady decline of Ormond's electoral influence, only briefly masked by the apparent gains that ensued when he assumed the viceroyalty in 1703, reflects the more general history of his political following in the period 1689–1715. An underlying transformation may be detected in the nature of the obligations that bound men to his 'interest'. Direct dependence, through employment in his household or estate, was supplemented and then replaced, first by a kind of clientage, the cement of which was the influence the duke could bring to bear as a patron, interceding with the crown, state bureaucracy, established church, or other public bodies; and

72 St Canice corp. min. bk 1661–1718, pp 231, 236–7, 262, 269, 275, 278 (N.L.I., mic. P.5143). The influence exerted by Bishop Hartstonge over the borough can be seen in the fact that his nephew, Sir Standish, served as portreeve from 1711 to October 1713, just before the election, at which point he was succeeded by his son, and that after 1707 at least ten clergymen were admitted to the freedom of the corporation (ibid., pp 231–79, passim).

73 Survey of electoral interests, 1713 (B.L., Add. MS 34777, f. 33); Power, 'Parliamentary representation', p. 325; 'Hist. Ir. parl.' project, notes on Callan (P.R.O.N.I., ENV/5/HP/14/3).

74 Survey of electoral interests, 1713 (B.L., Add. MS 34777, ff 42–4).

75 Ibid., f. 22.

76 N.L.I., reports on private collections, 293 (Barton papers); list of documents relating to articles of marriage of John Everard, 1721 (Tipperary S. Riding Co. Museum, Acc. 12985: 180); Power, *Land, politics & soc.*, pp 84, 226.

77 Survey of electoral interests, 1713 (B.L., Add. MS 34777, ff 42–4); Sir Richard Cox to Edward Southwell, 29 Sept., 21 Nov. 1713 (B.L., Add. MS 38157, ff 17, 26); list of 'burgesses' and freemen of Inistioge, 5 Oct. 1713 (N.L.I., MS 11,048/164).

eventually by an even weaker form of connexion, deriving from personal affection or a common political outlook.

Ormond did, of course, continue to maintain a substantial private establishment, comprising household servants and those employed in the administration of his property. The household may even have expanded, as a result of his enforced peregrinations, between the English court and Dublin Castle, and on military service abroad. The first duke seems to have been attended by two private secretaries, one stationed in Ireland and the other in England. The second duke replaced the Irish secretary, Henry Gascoigne, in about 1693 with a young Cambridge don, Benjamin Portlock,[78] but when a further vacancy occurred two years later, on the resignation of the English secretary, John Ellis, to take a position in Whitehall, Ormond did not move quickly to find a replacement. Portlock may have acted for a time as a peripatetic secretary, accompanying his master on his travels, with Stephen Sweet acting in a subordinate capacity as domestic steward and clerk.[79] It was some years later, presumably responding to an increase in business consequent on his elevation to the lord lieutenancy, that Ormond added a second private secretary, David Kennedy, who may have been based primarily in England. He also employed Edward Southwell in the more prestigious role of chief secretary during his viceroyalties, and Henry Watkins as his military secretary when on campaign, which meant that in 1712–13 he was being served by four secretaries.[80] Apart from the secretaries, however, only a few other members of the household staff were of any political significance. Chaplains might in due course rise through the ecclesiastical hierarchy to a level at which they could be useful: four became bishops (Welbore Ellis, John Hartstonge, William Moreton and Sir Thomas Vesey) and two became deans (Peter Drelincourt and John Hinton).[81] And occasionally Ormond seems to have employed a promising young man as an usher, or gentleman of his bedchamber – in his private as opposed to his viceregal persona – but, as was the case with Silvester Cross, who enjoyed a position of this kind for a time, it was usually reinforced by another, more remunerative appointment (for Cross a collectorship of rents).[82]

Employment in the administration of the estate offered at first a greater range of possibilities, and even something approaching a career structure. It was possible to

78 H.M.C., *Ormonde* MSS, n.s., viii, p. xxxiii. Portlock's name first appears in the household accounts for 1695 (household and small accounts of the duke and duchess of Ormond, 1694–1707, 11 May 1695 (N.L.I., MS 2,547 unfoliated))). See the biographical entry in *Hist. Ir. parl.*, iii, 108–9.

79 Valentine Smyth to Charles Gosling, 10 Apr., 1697 (N.L.I., MS 11058/3); Sir Richard Cox to Ormond, 24 Sept. 1700 (ibid., MS 2,457, pp 39–40); household accounts, 1698 (ibid., MS 2,547).

80 For Kennedy, see Sir Stephen Fox to Kennedy, 3 Feb. 1710[/11] (N.L.I., MS 2,474, p. 197); Kennedy to Sir William Robinson, 12 Nov. 1711 (ibid., pp 397–401); same to Col. Butler, 1 Jan. 1711[/12]) (ibid., p. 481); Arthur Hebburne to David Kennedy, 12 Mar. 1705/6 (H.M.C., *Ormonde* MSS, n.s., viii, 224); lease of Ormonde House to Kennedy and earl of Arran, 1712 (T.N.A., FEC1/O.16); *Hist. Ir. parl.*, v, 16. For Watkins, see *H.C. 1690–1715*, v, 810–13.

81 *Oxf. D.N.B.*, xvi, 902–903; xviii, 261; xxv, 638–9; xxxix, 92–3; lxvi, 392; Valentine Smyth to Charles Gosling, 10 Apr. 1697 (N.L.I., MS 11,058/3); Hinton to Ormond, 14 Nov. 1705 (H.M.C., *Ormonde MSS*, n.s., viii, 193).

82 Bp Hartstonge to [Ormond], 31 Oct. 1710 (N.L.I., MS 2,473, pp 480–3); Cross to [Ormond], 22 Jan. 1710[/11] (ibid., MS 2,474, pp 139–43); Burtchaell, *Genealogical mems*, p. 103.

rise through the ranks, from rent collector to receiver, agent, and ultimately commissioner, and several who began in the lower reaches came to acquire a more exalted status. Four secured seats in the Irish parliament; Thomas Crawford and Silvester Cross, who had both started as collectors, Richard Connell, a former seneschal, and John Pacy, a receiver and agent.[83] However, opportunities shrank with the depredation of the estate. In 1688 there were seven collectors, responsible to a receiver-general; by 1711 there were four, and it was proposed to concentrate all their work in the hands of a single receiver.[84] Again, seneschals had been appointed in 1688 for each of the counties in which Ormond possessed extensive manorial rights – Carlow, Kilkenny and Tipperary – as well as for individual manors elsewhere – but in 1701 the suggestion was made that these offices be consolidated into one.[85] There was also a significant drawback to the service, in that the frequent fits of anxiety to which Ormond and his advisers were subject, over the level of income and the efficiency of its collection, created chronic insecurity of tenure.

Beyond his household and estate, Ormond had inherited the right of appointment to a number of miscellaneous posts. Included in his household accounts were the salaries of the master of Kilkenny School, the masters of the diocesan schools of Cashel and Ossory, and curacies in nine parishes in Ossory diocese.[86] He also had the right to nominate the master of the free school a Clonmel, and held the advowson in numerous ecclesiastical livings, one as far distant as Ahoghill, County Antrim.[87] But the most valuable source of patronage was the palatinate of Tipperary. Although on balance a financial liability, it provided ten or so offices which were in Ormond's gift, with which he could attract the kind of recruits who were most useful to him politically: lawyers. There were places for two judges (the chancellor, or seneschal, and second judge, or master of the rolls), each of whose emoluments, in salary and fees, amounted to about £100 p.a.; an attorney-general, at £35 p.a.; and various minor officials – chirographer, prothonotary, treasurer, escheator, exami-

[83] For Crawford, see arrears of rents in collectors hands, 1690/1 (N.L.I., MS 2,561, f. 12); rentals 1689–1704 (ibid., MS 2,562); Crawford to John Ellis, 2 Nov.1698 (B.L., Add. MS 28883, f. 241); same to same, 13 Sept. 1701 (ibid., Add. MS 28887, f. 284); Crawford to Ormond, 16 July 1705 (H.M.C., *Ormonde* MSS, n.s., viii, 166). For Cross, see rentals 1689–1704 (N.L.I., MS 2,562, nos. 596–610, 745–60). For Pacy, see accounts, 1703, 1705 (ibid., MS 2,547); Sir Richard Cox to Ormond, 29 Apr. 1704 (H.M.C., *Ormonde* MSS, n.s., viii, 69); Pacy to [Ormond], 17 Oct. 1707 (N.L.I., MS 2,472, pp 449–50). For Connell, see Burtchaell, *Genealogical mems*, pp 85–6.

[84] Rentals 1689–1704 (N.L.I., MS 2,562); 'A particular of several affairs relating to his grace the duke of Ormond' (ibid., MS 2,545).

[85] 'The case and complaint of Mr William Robinson', 8 Sept. 1688 (ibid., MS 2,453, pp 33–8); Sir Richard Cox to Ormond, 24 Sept. 1700 (ibid., MS 2,457, pp 39–40); William Worth to Ormond, 10 Sept. 1701 (H.M.C., *Ormonde* MSS, n.s., viii, 42). Until at least 1701 it was the custom for seneschals to act by deputy (William Worth to Simon Harcourt, 10 Sept. 1701 (N.,L.I., MS 2,457, pp 175–6)).

[86] Instructions to Robert Fitzgerald, 1710 (N.L.I., MS 2,545); Sir Richard Cox to Ormond, 9 Dec. 1709 (ibid., MS 2,473, pp 259–61).

[87] Sir Richard Cox to Ormonde, 5 Aug. 1704 (H.M.C., *Ormonde* MSS, n.s., viii, 105); — to same, 2 May 1705 (ibid., 153); Cox to Benjamin Portlock, 5 July 1705 (ibid., 163); John Hinton to Ormond, 14 Nov. 1705 (ibid., 193); Bp Moreton to same, 8 Jan. 1705/6 (ibid., 209); William Ponsonby to same, 8 Dec. 1706 (ibid., 268); Cox to Edward Southwell, 5 Jan., 22 May 1714 (B.L., Add. MS 38157, ff 45, 96).

nator, register, and clerk of the crown and peace.[88] Perhaps predictably, jobs were often provided for the sons of local gentry families or for those, like William Ellis (clerk in 1688) or Standish Hartstonge (second justice in 1701), already associated with the Ormonds. Occasionally, employment in the palatinate courts would be the first rung on a ladder of preferment that extended to dizzy heights. Francis Bernard, for example, began his legal career as attorney-general in the palatinate, moved to the chancellorship, and thence to national eminence as a judge of common pleas.[89] His predecessor as attorney-general, Thomas Medlycott, while not achieving the same distinction, nonetheless acquired in due course a perfectly respectable position as a revenue commissioner.[90]

The examples of Bernard and Medlycott demonstrate the degree to which Ormond needed access to the higher spheres of patronage in order to reinforce the loyalty of his employees. Those whom he paid out of his own pocket may have constituted a personal retinue (in the traditional sense), but such service, for limited rewards, was unlikely to satisfy a young man of parts. Thus the duke was obliged to capitalise on his position as lord lieutenant in 1706 to recommend Francis Bernard for the solicitor-generalship of Ireland,[91] while for Thomas Medlycott he found a minor office in England (as deputy steward of Westminster) and seats in the Irish and British parliaments.[92] A similar story could be told of others whom Ormond had first employed in his own affairs: John Pacy, given a life patent as keeper of the Parliament House in Dublin; Benjamin Portlock, made taster of wines in Ireland, again for life; David Kennedy, a commissioner of appeals; and, most spectacularly, the estate commissioner William Robinson, who rose to occupy the key post of deputy vice-treasurer in Dublin Castle, and Richard Nutley, one of the duke's legal advisers, who in Ormond's second viceroyalty became a judge.[93]

Ormond's popularity among Tories in both Britain and Ireland guaranteed him a hearing when he spoke on patronage matters to government ministers of his own kidney.[94] But he also controlled a substantial slice of crown and official patronage himself by virtue of a remarkable portfolio of appointments. A striking feature of his biography – until 1715 of course – is that, despite limited political talent, he

88 'Officers in the liberty courts from Mr Kearny', 8 Aug. 1688 (N.L.I., MS 11,044/251); Burke, *Hist. Clonmel*, pp 424–37, 443.

89 Draft bill in *Attorney-general of the palatinate of Tipperary* v. *Peter Hayden* [?1711–14] (N.L.I., MS 11,044/260); order for sergeant-at-arms in *Duke of Ormond* v. *Thomas Hopkins*, 2 May 1709 (ibid., MS 11,044/271); Ball, *Judges*, ii, 199; *Hist. Ir. parl.*, iii, 173–4.

90 Draft bill in *Attorney-general of the palatinate of Tipperary* v. *Peter Hayden* [?1711–14] (N.L.I., MS 11,044/260); *H.C. 1690–1715*, iv, 790–93.

91 Ormond's proposals for legal appointments, 7 Jan. 1705/6 (N.L.I., Ormond papers, MS 993, pp 266–7).

92 Medlycott to Ormond, 3 May 1705, Ormond to Lord Treasurer Godolphin, 10 May 1705 (H.M.C., *Ormonde* MSS, n.s., viii, 154–5); *H.C. 1690–1715*, iv, 791–2.

93 Ormond to lords justices, 20 Oct. 1705 (N.L.I., Ormond papers, MS 992, p. 250); same to same, 15 Apr. 1707 (ibid., MS 993, p. 254); *Hist. Ir. parl.*, v, 265–6; vi, 168–9; *D.I.B.*, viii, 553.

94 Though he could not persuade ministers against their better judgment: see the failure of his attempts to secure an English bishopric (Hereford) for John Hartstonge, when the lord treasurer, Oxford, was committed to an alternative candidate (Adam Ottley to Bp Ottley of St David's, 1, 6, 10 Jan. 1712[/13] (National Library of Wales, Ottley papers, 1613–14, 1616)).

was honoured with several high offices of state. William III made him lord high constable of England in 1689 and a gentleman of the bedchamber. He later served Queen Anne for two terms as lord lieutenant of Ireland. He also enjoyed a long and gratifying military career – gratifying, that is, in terms of offices and dignities rather than successes in the field. He held commissions as colonel of the second troop of lifeguards from 1689 to 1712, and colonel of a cavalry regiment on the Irish establishment from 1703 to 1713, as a major-general in 1692, lieutenant-general in 1694 and general of horse in 1702; was commander of the land forces sent to Cadiz in 1702; and finally captain-general in 1712. And among a sheaf of public honours, he was lord lieutenant of Norfolk and Somerset, high steward of Bristol, Exeter, and Westminster, chancellor of the universities of Dublin and Oxford, and lord warden of the Cinque Ports.

Each of these appointments carried the opportunity for patronage. As steward of Westminster and warden of the Cinque Ports he could name his deputy, and both positions were highly sought after. He was also able to determine who would be his vice-chancellor at Trinity and at Oxford, and was assumed by a host of applicants to be able to influence the disposal of other places, honours and distinctions. Equally important, in this context, was the possibility of interfering in parliamentary elections in the university constituencies. Although Ormond does not seem to have made his presence felt in Oxford, Trinity paid him the compliment of returning, at different times, Joseph Coughlan, the attorney-general of the palatinate, and Edward Southwell.[95] Similar possibilities opened up in the Cinque Ports, and here Ormond did make recommendations, with mixed success: in 1713 Archibald Hutcheson was elected at Hastings, while the military secretary Henry Watkins failed at Rye.[96]

Ormond's long military career placed at his disposal an even greater array of jobs and favours. Most obviously, the raising of his regiment in Ireland in 1703 was expected to 'give him an opportunity of obliging a great many gentlemen that went over with him'.[97] But the power of patronage did not disappear when commissions were filled. As a regimental commander and staff officer, Ormond took decisions that affected the welfare and prospects of his subordinates in many different ways. He oversaw the sale of commissions, permitted absence, recommended candidates for promotion, administered courts martial, and issued vital operational orders concerning the recruitment, billeting, clothing and feeding of troops. His surviving private papers are replete with letters from anxious officers, especially when he was viceroy and had ultimate direction of the Irish military establishment. In the 'first age of party' the army was as heavily politicised as any area of public life in Britain and Ireland and it was natural for a pro-Ormond faction to develop among regimental officers, in opposition to those who looked for political leadership to the duke of Marlborough. Clearly, professional soldiers of a Tory cast of mind regarded Ormond as their party chieftain, while others attached themselves to him in the hope of preferment. But of these only a few were really close enough to justify being counted as his 'friends', most notably the major-generals Robert Echlin and

95 *H.C. 1660–90*, i, 360–2; *H.C. 1690–1715*, ii, 484–91.

96 *H.C. 1690–1715*, ii, 763, 771.

97 John Isham to Sir Justinian Isham, 12 Oct. 1705 (Northants R.O., IC 2205).

Thomas Pearce, and Ormond's *aide-de-camp*, Theophilus Oglethorpe.[98] Echlin and Pearce held parliamentary seats in Dublin, where they were joined by three of the captains in Ormond's own regiment, his namesake James Butler, Hugh Morgan and Sir Richard Vernon.

But it was the viceroyalty that provided the richest reserves of patronage. Just how much of this was available to the lord lieutenant himself, either directly by nomination or indirectly through recommendation, has emerged from the studies of Dr Patrick McNally.[99] The largest complement of offices was to be found on the military establishment, and here the lord lieutenant made most decisions himself, without reference to a higher authority. He also determined the disposition of barracks, the appointment of garrison commanders, and controlled expenditure on the military contingency fund, sometimes referred to as his 'privy purse'. As far as the civil establishment was concerned, his authority was circumscribed by the existence of numerous life patents and reversions, by the fact that the recently constituted revenue board with its rapidly growing bureaucracy was responsible to the English Treasury, and not to him, and by the practice of reserving decisions on places in the judiciary to ministers in Whitehall. In the same way, he could only offer advice to the monarch and to ministers on the choice of bishops. But this still left a substantial reservoir of patronage under direct control, and the expectation that in all major decisions his voice would at least carry weight. Once again Ormond's surviving correspondence, with its stream of petitions and memorials, stands as testimony to the influence Irishmen expected him to be able to wield.

Space does not allow a full discussion of the way in which Ormond used the immense quantity of patronage available to the viceroy. In any case it can be difficult to distinguish, from the host of supplicants, those who were his particular followers. He was confronted by as many as a hundred and fifty expectant faces at a levée in the autumn of 1710, when his return to Dublin Castle had been rumoured but not confirmed.[100] And by no means all of those who benefited from his goodwill had earned, or would requite, this favour. It was natural for the author of any begging letter, bread-and-butter acknowledgment, or unctuous compliment, to describe himself as one of the 'friends of the duke of Ormond', whether or not this was true. Nor was it invariably the case that those members of the Irish parliament and others who attended the public celebrations of Ormond's birthday, sometimes to the number of eighty or more, were particularly attached to him.[101] One must even be suspicious of the handful of parliamentary managers whom Chief Secretary South-

98 *H.C. 1690–1715*, iii, 954–5; v, 12–14, 119; *Hist. Ir. parl.*, iv, 97–8; vi, 35–6.

99 Patrick McNally, *Parties, patriots and undertakers: parliamentary politics in early Hanoverian Ireland* (Dublin, 1997), pp 90–95; and more generally, idem, 'Patronage and politics in Ireland, 1714–1727' (PhD thesis, Queen's University of Belfast, 1993).

100 — to [Charles, Lord Bruce], 22 Sept. 1710 (Wiltshire and Swindon History Centre, Ailesbury papers, 1300/1020).

101 Sir Richard Cox to Edward Southwell, 29 Apr. 1707 (B.L., Add. MS 38155, f. 27); same to same, 1 May 1708 (ibid., Add. MS 38156, f. 8); 'Members of Parliament present at dinner at the Bowling Green' 29 Apr. 1706 (ibid., Southwell papers, Eg. MS 917, f. 234); those present at the Bowling Green, 30 Apr. 1711 (ibid., ff 236–7); list of those who celebrated the duke of Ormond's birthday at the Tholsel, 6 Feb. 1712 (ibid., ff 244–5).

well summoned for pre-sessional consultations.[102] Those who were in Ormond's employ, or were indebted to him in some specific way, can be defined as his followers, but others may simply have been protesting friendship in the hope of preferment, as they would have offered themselves to any viceroy. A more useful test would be the observation of an individual's behaviour when Ormond was out of power, and here a few, like the Irish exchequer baron Robert Johnson or the master in chancery William Crowe, did continue an amicable correspondence after the duke was removed from office and seem genuinely to have regretted his deprivation.[103]

Sentiment of this kind seems to have entered more markedly into Ormond's political relationships as the years went by, and to have become increasingly important in holding together his 'interest'. History provided much of the foundation. Ormond's grandfather had advised him (somewhat obscurely) in 1685 that 'it doth not always happen that the posterity of parents who have been good and immediate friends continue to be so; but where it falls out to continue, there the friendship requires confirmation and increase by descent'.[104] Thus a significant number of Ormond's employees and clients came from families with a traditional attachment to the Butlers, such as the Ellises, Hartstonges, Southwells, Veseys, and Worths. In 1688 John Ellis was the first duke's private secretary, his brother William an office-holder in the palatinate. After the Revolution William went into Jacobite exile, but John stayed on in the second duke's service, while another brother, Welbore, was helped to the bishopric of Kildare by Ormond influence.[105] In the case of the Hartstonges, the first baronet, Sir Standish, had been attorney-general in Tipperary before securing a place on the exchequer bench; one son, also named Standish, held a post in the palatinate and was returned to the Irish House of Commons on the Ormond interest for Kilkenny city; a second, John, chaplain to the first duke, became archdeacon in Limerick, and then bishop of Ossory.[106] With the Veseys, son followed father directly. For John Vesey, eventually archbishop of Tuam, the ladder of ecclesiastical preferment had also originated with a chaplain's place, and

102 See for example Edward Southwell to Ormond, 21 Dec. 1703 (N.L.I., MS 991, p. 201). Six out of the ten M.P.s present may be described as personal followers of Ormond (Francis Bernard, Sir Richard Cox, William Crowe, Robert Fitzgerald, Robert Johnson and Southwell himself), while the other four were Tory politicians whose attachment to the duke was as the leader of their party and not as employer or patron (Stephen Ludlow, Robert Rochfort, Anderson Saunders and Henry Tenison).

103 For Johnson, see his letters to Ormonde, 26 Dec. 1706, 13, 19 Mar. 1706/7, 5 Apr. 1707 (H.M.C., *Ormonde* MSS, n.s., viii, 272, 290–92, 296); for Crowe, Sir Richard Cox to Portlock, 24 Aug. 1699 (N.L.I., MS 2,456, pp 435–6); Ormond to lords justices, 20 Oct. 1705 (N.L.I., MS 992, p. 250); Crowe to Ormond, 16 Jan. 1706/7 (H.M.C., *Ormonde* MSS, n.s., viii, 277–9).

104 Thomas Carte, *The life of James, duke of Ormond* ... (2nd ed., 6 vols, Oxford, 1851), v, 178–9.

105 A. P. W. Malcomson, *Archbishop Charles Agar: churchmanship and politics in Ireland, 1760–1810* (Dublin, 2002), pp 26–30. See *Oxf. D.N.B.*, xviii, 235–6, 261, 264–5; *D.I. B.*, iii, 606–608.

106 Ball, *Judges*, i, 357; Burtchaell, *Genealogical mems*, pp 92, 115–16; Barnard, 'Cork settlers', pp 342–3; Sir Standish Hartstonge to Ormond, 1 Nov. 1710 (N.L.I., MS 11,055/1). Thanking Ormond for securing a place for one of his children at Christ Church, Oxford, in 1699, John Vesey wrote, 'It is not enough, it seems, that I wear the marks of your most noble grandfather's favour. It is hereditary in your family to oblige from generation to generation' (Vesey to Ormond, 18 May 1699 (ibid., MS 2,456, p. 391)).

his son Thomas, John Hartstonge's successor at Ossory, began his career in the same capacity, among the second duke's chaplains. Often it was kinship or connexion with such families that brought new recruits into the Ormonds' service: marriage into the Ellis family may have drawn the Agars of Gowran into the Butler orbit;[107] marriage into the Hartstonges may have done the same for the Maudes;[108] while Sir Richard Cox found his way to Ormond's notice through the Southwells,[109] and William Worth seems to have brought into the duke's employment not only his nephew by blood, Edward Worth, but his nephew by marriage, Silvester Cross, and his protégé, Stephen Sweet.[110] There were other old retainers whose adherence to Catholicism, or involvement on the wrong side in the Jacobite war, made them unemployable or politically useless, but who cherished ancestral loyalty to the Butlers. Towards the end of Queen Anne's reign one or two began to creep back into public life. The baronet Sir Redmond Everard, distantly connected to Ormond by marriage, sloughed off his Catholic past to recover a seat in the Irish House of Commons, and a regular place at Ormond's dining table at Dublin Castle,[111] and in the 1713 election another name from the past was heard, when George Mathew also renounced his Catholic allegiance and was elected for County Tipperary. The devotion engendered in these families by length of service (though fractured in the case of William Worth by his summary dismissal as commissioner in 1705) was well expressed by the son of Archbishop Vesey, who reported to the duke in 1707 that his father was 'as steady in his obligations to your grace and family as in his principles, and I hope his sense of gratitude will always influence his whole family, who are not ashamed to own they owe what they have to the house of Ormond'.[112]

If a substantial number of Ormond's followers could claim a family attachment going back at least a generation, or a connexion to one of the Butler clients, there were others who were entirely new recruits: the County Cork lawyers Francis Bernard and Sir Richard Cox, for example, the English barrister Richard Nutley, or the private secretaries Kennedy and Portlock. But here again personal attraction and political sympathy were powerful factors. The second duke's good nature and charming manner were universally remarked by contemporaries.[113] Equally important was his reputation as a staunch upholder of Tory principles, which had survived support for the Prince of Orange at the Revolution, been revived by his

107 Burtchaell, *Genealogical mems*, pp 114–15; Malcomson, *Agar*, pp 26–30. A long-standing connexion with the Ellis family may also account for the recruitment of the Oxbridge dons Portlock and Watkins. Both had been at Westminster School with Welbore Ellis and Watkins was a friend of Welbore's brother John: John Welch (ed.), *The list of the Queen's scholars of St Peter's College, Westminster* ... (2nd ed., London, 1852), pp 189, 198, 202–203; *H.C. 1690–1715*, v, 810.
108 Burtchaell, *Genealogical mems*, pp 87–9, 104.
109 See above, p. 54.
110 Burtchaell, *Genealogical mems*, p. 103; Edward Worth to Stephen Sweet, [c. 1722] (P.R.O.N.I., D/2685/6/1).
111 *Burtchaell, Genealogical mems, pp* 109–10; bills of fare for Ormond at Dublin Castle, 28, 31 Aug. 1711 (formerly B.L., Loan 37/8).
112 Theodore Vesey to [Ormond], 29 July 1707 (N.L.I., MS 2,472, pp 267–8).
113 For examples, see *Memoirs of the secret service of John Macky* ... (London, 1733), p. 15; Swift, *Prose works*, ed. Davis et al., vii, 141; viii, 132–3.

public protest at being passed over for promotion in 1699, and confirmed by his accession to the Irish viceroyalty. During the intrigues and confusions of 1710–14 he even came to associate with those on the extreme, pro-Jacobite fringe of the English Tory party. Ormond's impeccable Tory credentials enabled him to capitalise on party enthusiasm in Ireland. All those who can be identified as his followers in Irish politics were Tories before 1714. Obviously there is something here of the chicken and the egg: no doubt some in the duke's employ felt that an expression of Tory prejudice would do them no harm. Nor were all Ormond's followers necessarily to be found among the hotter Tories. The infamous, quasi-Jacobite 'Swan Tripe Club' which met in Dublin in 1705 included two men who were close to him, Nutley and the chaplain John Hinton.[114] But the pro-Hanoverian element in the Irish Tory party was also well represented among his 'friends', in the persons of such active politicians as Francis Bernard, Sir Richard Cox, Thomas Medlycott and Edward Southwell.

Any attempt to quantify Ormond's political following in the Irish parliaments of King William and Queen Anne would be vulnerable to criticism on grounds of definition and evidence. Authoritative statistics are impossible to achieve. For one thing, we would have to know a great deal more about the details of the relationship between the duke and every individual. But by adopting certain basic criteria – employment in the household or estate, receipt of patronage in Ormond's gift, or successful nomination to a parliamentary seat – we can arrive at figures that suggest interesting general trends.[115] There were no direct dependants in the upper house, though a few lords (mostly bishops) would have had to acknowledge past obligations, or favours bestowed on their relations or connexions. In the Commons only six can be found in the parliament of 1692, but this number rose to nine in 1695, and then leapt to twenty-two in Queen Anne's first parliament, before falling back even more dramatically to four in 1713. Obviously the possession of the viceroyalty made an enormous difference. At the election of 1703 more than a score of Ormond's employees and clients were returned. Either borough patrons saw advantage in returning the viceroy's friends, or the successful candidates themselves had tried harder to find seats, knowing their patron would have a greater capacity to reward them, and wishing to make themselves more obviously useful.

Ormond's political following was thus very much larger when he enjoyed the privileges and powers that accompanied high office. The difference between the parliamentary session of 1711 (the last of the 1703 parliament), and the situation after the general election of 1713, when he was no longer viceroy, emphasises the point. It is clear that during the second duke's public career, which to all intents and purposes came to an end in 1715, the nature of his political 'connexion' was changing. The element of direct dependence was becoming less important; inevitably, as he drifted further and further into debt, and land was sold to raise money to satisfy creditors. As the number of his employees decreased, other kinds of relationship became more important. The resources of the Irish government, the army, and the various public

114 *The Swan Tripe-Club: a satyr on the high flyers* ... (London, 1710); John Barrett, *An essay on the earlier part of the life of Swift* ... (London, 1808), pp 107–23. Another member was the Dublin physician Edward Worth, a nephew of William (*Hist. Ir. parl.*, vi, 557–8).

115 For details, see Hayton, 'Dependence, clientage and affinity', pp 240–41.

bodies over which he presided, offered a means of boosting the income of his own employees and of attracting new followers on the basis of clientage. Finally, there was his position as a party leader, which drew Irish Tories to him through devotion to his person and his principles. Eventually Ormond's following dissolved into a kind of 'affinity' of like-minded High Church Tories, only a few of whom he employed, with others looking to him as a patron or holding to his interest out of respect for his family, his character, or his Toryism.

For a long time the weakness of Ormond's position was not apparent to contemporaries. The effects of the gradual disintegration of the once great estate were hidden because of the way in which commissioners, agents and collectors benefited personally from managing its decline, either by negotiating advantageous leases and purchases, or by acquiring new employment under the various arrangements that were made for the management of the property. In electoral terms, Ormond's influence seemed actually to be expanding in the early 1700s, whereas in reality previously dependent local interests, now matured into independence, were returning his clients in expectation of the benefits of ducal favour or out of party-political sympathy. Ormond's extraordinary success after 1702 in adding so many offices and dignities to the regimental commissions he had enjoyed in the 1690s meant that much more official patronage was at his disposal, while his easy assumption of the leadership of the Tory tendency in Ireland meant that he could mobilise party allegiance in his own cause. But behind the façade the duke's retinue was shrinking. With a smaller income, and less work to be done, he needed to employ far fewer people. Even without his Jacobite adventure and subsequent attainder he would have had to liquidate the Tipperary palatinate, using the machinery provided by the act of parliament in 1712, and eventually the icy fingers of retrenchment would have reached his overblown household establishment.

Keen observers could detect the reality in the 1713 parliament. Without access to the patronage provided by the viceroyalty, and no longer the unchallenged leader of the Irish Tories, following the recent emergence of Lord Anglesey as a formidable rival, Ormond made little impact on the Irish political scene during the upheavals of the winter of 1713/14. Indeed, his quondam followers did not all stand by their party: one disgruntled Tory reported that in the crucial Commons' divisions on the attempt to censure the High Tory lord chancellor, Sir Constantine Phipps, 'several of the duke of Ormond's pretended friends' voted with the Whig opposition.[116] The course of subsequent events is obscured by Ormond's fateful decision to flee to the Pretender, but it is instructive to note how few of his followers were prepared to make the leap with him. Induced to expect great things from Ormond's defection, the French authorities and even the ever-optimistic Jacobites were to be bitterly disappointed. 'We had sounded the duke's name high', recalled Lord Bolingbroke,

> His reputation and the opinion of his power were great. The French began to believe that he was able to form and head a party; that the troops would join him; that the nation would follow the signal whenever he drew his sword.... But when, in the midst

116 Mathew Forde to [Edward Southwell], 19 Dec. 1713 (B.L., Southwell papers, Add. MS 60583, f. 6).

> of all these bright ideas, they saw him arrive, almost literally alone, when, to excuse his coming, I was obliged to tell them that he could not stay, they sunk at once from their hopes.[117]

Only General Robert Echlin, Sir Redmond Everard and the English Tory Theophilus Oglethorpe eventually joined Ormond on the continent. Oglethorpe hailed from a staunchly Jacobite family, while both Echlin and Everard were almost bankrupt and, like Ormond himself, had little to lose but their debts.[118] Of those who stayed behind, Archibald Hutcheson has been labelled a Jacobite by some historians, on the basis of some murky intrigues in 1721–2, in which he may have represented the earl of Sunderland in discussions with Jacobite agents.[119] Richard Nutley, who remained in Ireland, his career beached by the Hanoverian succession, was probably Jacobite in his sympathies but not sufficiently committed to take any action.[120] Of the others, Francis Bernard, Thomas Medlycott and Thomas Pearce made peace with the new establishment: Bernard became prime serjeant in 1724 and two years later a judge of common pleas; Medlycott kept his place as an Irish revenue commissioner (in disgust, Ormond stripped him of his place as deputy steward of Westminster) and Pearce was made lieutenant-general of the forces on the Irish establishment.[121] But even more telling was the way in which many of Ormond's former adherents in his own counties of Kilkenny and Tipperary either dropped into decent obscurity, or began to arrange a new set of political relationships for themselves. Even in the 1715 general election Sir Henry Weymes was willing to compromise with political opponents in County Kilkenny, and Edward Worth joined forces with the Ponsonbys in Knocktopher.[122] It was not long before former Tories like the Agars were happy to call themselves Whigs.[123]

We must be careful about drawing too many conclusions from the disappearance of the former Ormond interest after 1715, for clearly the duke's flight and

117 'A letter to Sir William Wyndham' in *The works of … Henry St John, Lord Viscount Bolingbroke …* (8 vols, London, 1809), i, 58–9.

118 *H.C. 1690–1715*, iii, 955; v, 13–14; *Hist. Ir. parl.*, iv, 122; Tipperary S. Riding Co. Museum, Acc. 1985: 180, 191, 195, 206.

119 *H.C. 1715–54*, ii, 163–4; Eveline Cruickshanks, 'Lord North, Christopher Layer and the Atterbury Plot: 1720–23' in eadem and Jeremy Black (eds), *The Jacobite challenge* (Edinburgh, 1988), pp 93, 96; Eveline Cruickshanks, 'Lord Cowper, Lord Orrery, the duke of Wharton and Jacobitism' in *Albion*, xxvi (1994), p. 30; eadem, 'Charles Spencer, third Earl of Sunderland, and Jacobitism' in *E.H.R.*, cxiii (1998), 65–76; eadem and Howard Erskine-Hill, *The Atterbury Plot* (Basingstoke, 2004), pp 66, 73, 126, 136, 164, 209. But cf. Clyve Jones, '1720–3 and all that: a reply to Eveline Cruickshanks' in *Albion*, xxvi (1994), p. 43; idem, 'Evidence, interpretation and definitions in Jacobite historiography: a reply to Eveline Cruickshanks' in *E.H.R.*, cxiii (1998), pp 77–90.

120 Edmund Gibson to Bp Nicolson of Carlisle, 30 Oct. 1714 (Bodl., MS Add. A. 269, p. 36); Abp Lindsay of Armagh to [Arthur Charlett], 31 Jan. 1718/19 (ibid., MS Ballard 8, f. 113); Ball, *Judges*, ii, 72.

121 Ball, *Judges*, ii, 199; *H.C. 1690–1715*, iv, 792; v, 119; *H.C. 1715–54*, ii, 250–51; Charles Dalton, *George the First's army 1714–1727* (2 vols, London, 1910), i, 142–3.

122 Burtchaell, *Genealogical mems*, pp 97–8; Power, 'Parliamentary representation', pp 319, 325.

123 'Hist. Ir. parl.' project, notes on Kilkenny (P.R.O.N.I., ENV/5/HP/14/2); Malcomson, *Agar*, pp 93–5.

forfeiture would have been disastrous for the family no matter what the antecedents had been. But taking a long view, it is hard to imagine that Ormond would have been able to reconstruct his political connexion had he taken a different political line, as a 'Hanoverian Tory'. Leaving aside the fact that he was no great parliamentarian, the advantages that under Queen Anne had enabled him to enjoy an illusory eminence had now vanished. Patronage, and the prestige of party leadership, were weaker and more transitory determinants of political allegiance than traditional forms of magnate influence, the one depending on the enjoyment of high office or royal favour, the other on general circumstances that might suddenly alter. The loss of all his offices in 1714 was thus a crippling blow to Ormond, politically no less than financially, and the sharp decline of the Tory interest in Irish politics after 1715 meant that his ideological appeal would also have faded. With its protective carapace removed, the interior corruption of the Ormond estate, and with it the Ormond power, was at last open to the world.

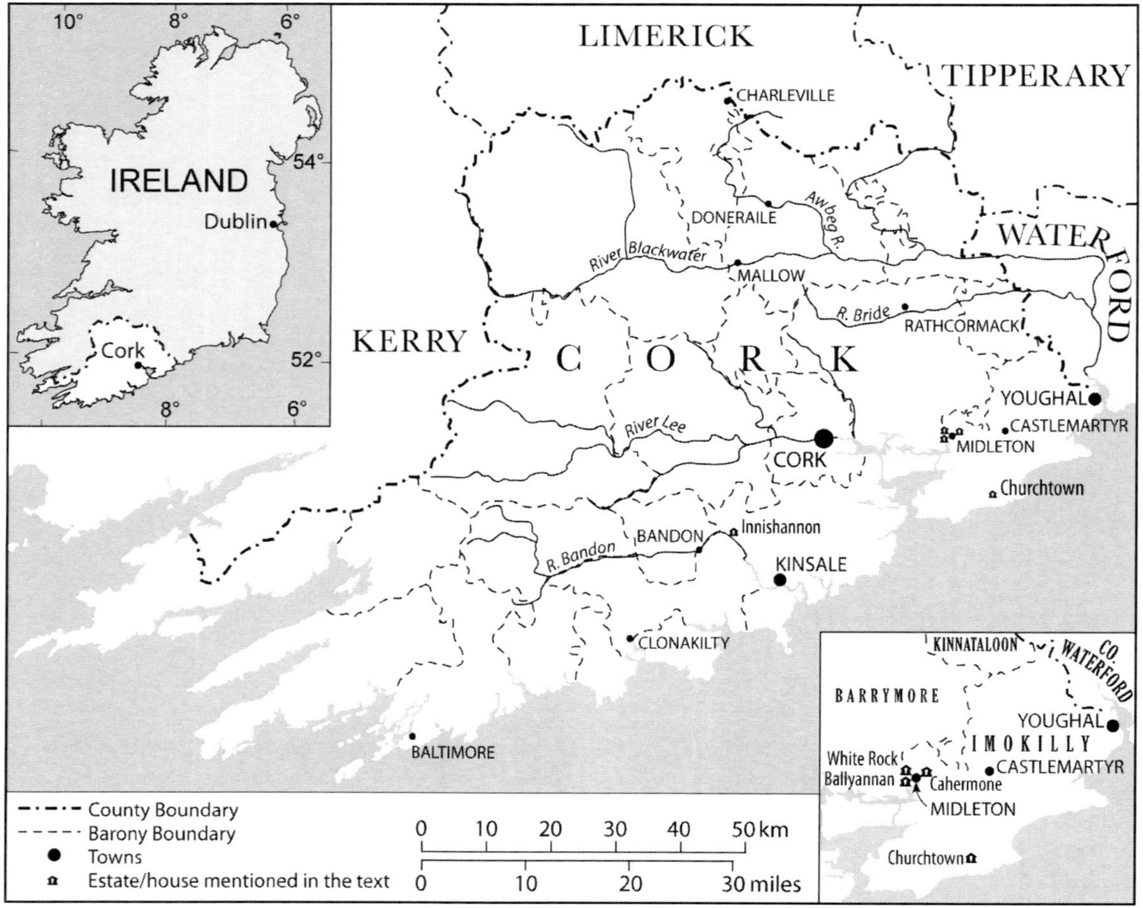

County Cork in the early eighteenth century

4

A presence in the country

The Brodricks and their 'interest'

A few miles to the south of the town of Midleton, in County Cork, near the shore of the Owenacurra estuary, may be found the remains of Ballyannan House, once the principal Irish residence of the Brodricks, in their time the greatest landed family in the district, and one of the most powerful political dynasties in Protestant Ireland. Alan Brodrick (c. 1655–1728) and his elder brother Thomas (1654–1730) emerged after the Williamite revolution as prominent members of the restored Irish parliament, at first alongside their father among the front rank of opposition speakers in the short-lived session of 1692; then, following the ministerial reconstruction undertaken by Lord Deputy Capell in 1694–5, in their own right as 'undertakers' for successive Whig governments.[1] Alan was made solicitor-general of Ireland in 1695, and elected to the chair of the Irish House of Commons in 1703. By this time he had become the undisputed chief of the Whig faction in Ireland.[2] Promotion to the judicial bench by the Whig administration in 1709 invited dismissal at the hands of the incoming Tory viceroy, Ormond, in 1711, but he returned to parliament in 1713 as Whig leader and once more as Commons Speaker. After the Hanoverian succession he was the obvious choice to be appointed lord chancellor of Ireland. However, from the woolsack he could no longer dominate his fellow Irish Whigs in quite the same way, and had to contend with the rivalry of the new Speaker, William Conolly. The guiding motif of Irish political history in the decade after 1714 was the struggle for ascendancy between these 'two great men'.[3] Ultimately Brodrick was the loser, and in 1725 he was obliged to resign the seals. By now ennobled as Viscount Midleton,

1 D. W. Hayton, *Ruling Ireland, 1685–1742: politics, politicians and parties* (Woodbridge, 2004), pp 44, 54–5, 61, 62, 64; C. I. McGrath, 'English ministers, Irish politicians and the making of a parliamentary settlement in Ireland, 1692–5' in *E.H.R.*, cxix (2004), pp 585–613; memorandum by Sir Richard Cox [,July 1695] (B.L., Southwell papers, Add. MS 38153, ff 12–13). For Alan Brodrick, see *Oxf. D.N.B.*, vii, 785–7; *D.I.B.*, i, 850–54 *H.C. 1715–54*, i, 489–90; *Hist. Ir. parl.*, iii, 266–9; for Thomas, *D.I.B.*, i, 858–9; *H.C. 1690–1715*, iii, 336–7; *H.C. 1715–54*, i, 491–2; *Hist. Ir. parl.*, iii, 272–3. Details of the genealogy and marital connexions of the family can be found in *Genealogical memoranda relating to the family of Brodrick* (London, 1872), pp 3–4, 7–8; J. J. Howard and F. A. Crisp (eds), *Visitation of England and Wales* ([London,] 1893–1921), Notes, vi, 9–14.

2 Hayton, *Ruling Ireland*, pp 89–90; C. I. McGrath, 'Alan Brodrick and the speakership of the Irish House of Commons, 1703–4' in James Kelly et al. (eds), *People, politics and power: essays on Irish history 1660–1850 in honour of James I. McGuire* (Dublin, 2009), pp 70–93.

3 The phrase was Sir Robert Walpole's (to the duke of Newcastle, 1 Sept. 1724 (B.L., Newcastle papers, Add. MS 32687, f. 54)).

The Brodrick family

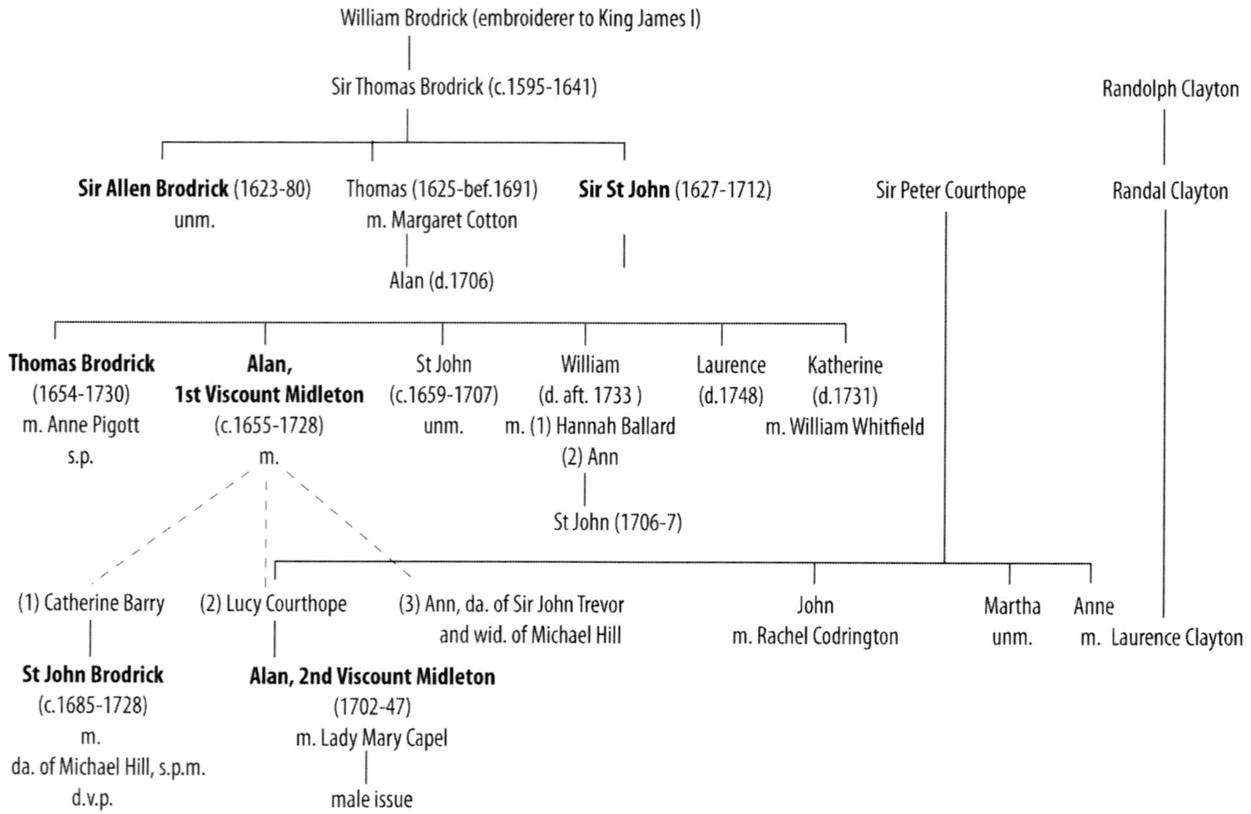

he took a back seat as his 'interest' was directed in the Irish parliament by his eldest son St John, in effect the leader of the opposition to Conolly's 'Castle party'.[4]

The family was then overtaken by a succession of dynastic disasters. In February 1728 St John died at Ballyannan, after a painful (and undiagnosed) illness aggravated rather than alleviated by the ministrations of physicians from Cork.[5] In August Midleton followed his son to the grave, and two years later Thomas Brodrick, who had made a parliamentary career at Westminster, died in England. Since Thomas had no surviving children, the headship of the family passed to Alan Brodrick's second son and namesake, who inherited the viscountcy but none of the drive or political acumen of his father. Leadership of the Brodrick 'interest' – the 'Munster squadron' as it was known[6] – passed instead to St John's friend Henry Boyle of Castlemartyr, a future Speaker and eventually earl of Shannon. In due course the Brodricks managed to recover some of their former status in Irish public life, largely through the efforts of Charles Brodrick (1761–1822), a younger son of the third viscount, who became Church of Ireland archbishop of Cashel after the Union, but they would never again be the force in Irish politics that they had been in the first decades of the eighteenth century.

Despite its idyllic waterside location, and the gentle beauty of the surrounding countryside, Ballyannan is a melancholy place for the historian; a hollow reminder of past greatness. Ballyannan wood is currently being developed as a nature reserve, but the house is in ruins, standing in farmland in which scarcely any traces of the Brodrick demesne may be recognised.[7] All this is in marked contrast to the fate of Castletown House in County Kildare, the principal country seat of Speaker Conolly, which has become a showpiece of the Irish heritage industry. Having been recovered by the Irish Georgian Society, it is managed by the Office of Public Works, which has begun a major project to restore the house and gardens to their former grandeur.

Truth to tell, there was always a sharp difference between the two houses and the ways in which their owners regarded them. Castletown, built in Conolly's lifetime as a demonstration of his wealth and power, was a fine example of the latest architectural style.[8] Within easy reach of Dublin, in an area – the Liffey valley – where

4 [Thomas Tickell] to Lord Carteret, 23 June 1727 (P.R.O.N.I., Tickell papers, T/2774, vol. iv, ff 91–4); Marmaduke Coghill to Edward Southwell, 8 Dec. 1727 (*Coghill letters*, p. 41). For St John, see *Hist. Ir. parl.*, iii, 270–72; *H.C. 1715–54*, i, 490–91.

5 Alan, 1st Viscount Midleton to his brother Thomas Brodrick, 23 Jan., 2, 24 Feb. 1727[/8] (S.H.C., Brodrick papers, 1248/7/195–6, 203–4, 209–10); Robert Bettesworth to Midleton, 30 Jan. 1727[/8] (ibid., 1248/7/199–200). For clarity and convenience, further references to family members in these notes will give Christian name only, with the prefix 'Sir' in the case of the first generation, Sir Allen and Sir St John; the suffix 'I' in the case of Sir St John's children, Alan (1st Viscount Midleton) and St John; and the suffix 'II' for the 1st Viscount's children, St John and Alan.

6 Hayton, *Ruling Ireland*, p. 113.

7 Denis Power et al., *Archaeological Inventory of County Cork*, ii: *East and south Cork* (Dublin, 1994), p. 233 and illustration opposite p. 244.

8 Patrick Walsh, *The making of the Irish Protestant ascendancy: the life of William Conolly, 1662–1729* (Woodbridge, 2010), ch. 9; T. C. Barnard, 'Mrs Conolly and Castletown 1720–1752' in William Nolan and Thomas McGrath (eds), *Kildare: history and society* ... (Dublin, 2006), pp 327–48; idem, *Improving Ireland? Projectors, prophets and profiteers, 1641–1786* (Dublin, 2008), pp 275–6, 281–5.

other members of the Dublin political élite were building houses in which they could happily rusticate while still being able to return at short notice to the capital, it served as a perfect theatre-set for the political house parties to which cronies and parliamentary supporters, and occasionally even viceroys, were invited.[9] Ballyannan, by contrast, sunk in the depths of provincial Ireland, was an old-fashioned fortified house. As far as can be deduced from surviving family papers, there was little in the way of architectural innovation, and only an intermittent engagement with the forms of conspicuous consumption – often dignified under the term 'improvement' – that preoccupied Conolly and his circle, who not only reconstructed and refurbished their mansions but emparked demesnes and transformed gardens according to fashionable taste.[10] The Ballyannan estate, and the family's other properties in the vicinity, served a different function, affording the Brodricks a physical presence in the county which provided the basis of their political support. In practical terms it also facilitated visits for financial or electoral purposes; when leases had to be renewed, or attention given to the affairs of the parliamentary borough of Midleton, which had been incorporated for the family and which they regarded as their own property.[11]

Castletown and Ballyannan may perhaps serve as emblematic of the contrasting approaches adopted by their owners to the demands of Irish political life in this period. The 'two great men' were very different in their backgrounds and career paths. Conolly was a nouveau riche attorney from County Donegal whose genealogy may well have been Catholic and Gaelic, and whose immediate forbears, if not the 'innkeepers' that contemporary snobs alleged, were at best no more than small-scale landowners: 'petty gentry', to use the English term.[12] Conolly became an attorney and, having made his fortune through astute land purchases and a fortunate marriage, enjoyed a highly successful political career as a 'man of business': an effective parliamentarian (if no orator), and an adept administrator with the intelligence to exploit to the full the patronage afforded by his place at the centre of the expanding Irish revenue bureaucracy. Although he acquired some property across the water (in Hampshire and in Wales) these were mere scraps in comparison to the vastness of his Irish estates.[13] He was firmly embedded in Irish Protestant society, so much so that he scarcely set foot outside the kingdom.[14] Indeed, he possessed few English friends and political allies, beyond the viceroys and chief secretaries whom he served and on whose good opinion he made a lasting impression. At the same time, although he was emphatically an Ulsterman, and satirised in

9 Walsh, *Making of the Irish Protestant ascendancy*, pp 182–3.

10 See below, ch. 6, and in general T. C. Barnard, *Making the grand figure: lives and possessions in Ireland, 1641–1770* (New Haven, Conn., & London, 2004); Finola O'Kane, *Landscape design in eighteenth-century Ireland: mixing foreign trees with the natives* (Cork, 2004).

11 Sir Robert Southwell to Sir John Perceval, 19 Mar. 1680/1 (H.M.C., *Egmont MSS*, ii, 104); Alan I to Thomas, 20 Apr. 1713 (S.H.C., 1248/3/111–112); analysis of electoral interests, 1713 (B.L., Southwell papers, Add. MS 34777, f. 24).

12 For Conolly, see *Oxf. D.N.B.*, xii, 986–88; *D.I.B.*, ii, 777–80; *Hist. Ir. parl.*, iii, 474–9; and esp. Walsh, *Making of the Irish Protestant ascendancy*.

13 Walsh, *Making of the Irish Protestant ascendancy*, pp 69, 76–7.

14 Ibid., pp 24, 27–8.

those terms,[15] his political 'interest' was not confined to a particular region. Because his electoral power-base was in the north-west, his supporters were sometimes described as a northern faction, but his own estates stretched across the country, from Donegal to Kildare, and his parliamentary lieutenants were by no means all northerners. Whatever their backgrounds, most had become habitués of the official world of Dublin, engrossed in business and public affairs. Their country residences, like Conolly's own mansion, were located for easy access to the capital; indeed, they tended to cluster within a short distance of Castletown.[16]

Alan Brodrick boasted a more exalted pedigree (admittedly over only a few generations), and was quick to object to the appointment of a person as socially inferior as Conolly alongside him as a lord justice in 1717.[17] He was also intimately acquainted with the English political scene, in which he had many contacts, some inherited and others forged on his own initiative. He and his brothers had been educated in England and the family possessed substantial estates there, to which they felt an attachment equal to, if not greater than, their affection for County Cork. Thomas, in particular, became an almost permanent absentee after c. 1710, spending much of his time in London or at Newmarket, where he could indulge his passion for horse-racing;[18] nor was he the only family member to be more or less permanently domiciled in England. The Brodricks thus fitted the definition of 'Anglo-Irish' much more closely than did Conolly (and others of his circle). The fact that both Alan and Thomas, and Alan's son St John, were elected to the Westminster as well as the Dublin parliament emphasises this contrast. Paradoxically, however, the family 'interest' in Ireland was much more regionally based than was Conolly's. Even though they spent more time away, residing in Dublin or in England, they were identified with the province of Munster, and with County Cork, and drew their core political support from relations, friends, and dependants there.

It was one of several apparent contradictions about them. They were clannish, operating in business and politics almost as a family enterprise; distant blood relations and extended marital connexions were cherished and sustained. But they were also quarrelsome and were frequently at odds with each other, usually over matters of finance or entitlement to property. None of the male members of the family was a 'country gentleman' in the classic sense, satisfied with a rural existence. Their natural environment was Dublin or Westminster, the courtroom, parliament-house, or council chamber. Yet they used the money they made through lawyers' fees or the profits of government office to purchase land. As landowners they were essentially *rentiers*; they made little effort to work their estates themselves or encourage local manufactures. But at the same time they were careful to insist on leasing to Protestant tenants who would undertake to carry out 'improvements'.

15 St John II to Alan I, 11 Mar. 1723/4, 14 Apr. 1724 (S.H.C., 1248/6/161–2, 7–8); D. W. Hayton, 'Two ballads on the County Westmeath by-election of 1723' in *Eighteenth-Century Ireland*, iv (1989), pp 26–9; Walsh, *Making of the Irish Protestant ascendancy*, p. 13.

16 See below, pp 130–31.

17 Alan I to Thomas, 7 Nov. 1717 (S.H.C., 1248/4/90–91).

18 He took a house in Newmarket in 1702 but otherwise shuttled between London and the family property at Wandsworth in Surrey (Alan I to Thomas, 6 Aug. 1702 (ibid., 1248/2/69–70)).

We know so much about the Brodricks because of the survival of a remarkable run of correspondence, mainly between Alan and his brother Thomas, but also with a third brother, St John, and between Alan and his sons, also called, confusingly, St John and Alan. The letters begin in the 1680s and end with the death of Alan, first Viscount Midleton, in 1728.[19] Much of what they have to say sheds light on the public affairs of Ireland and England, and this material has already been heavily used by historians. But the correspondence also provides evidence about domestic arrangements, personal relationships, and the ways in which generations of Brodricks maintained their landed and political 'interest' in Ireland and England.

I

The family had originated in Yorkshire, but migrated to Surrey when the first Viscount Midleton's great-grandfather was appointed embroiderer to James I. The embroiderer's son Thomas Brodrick, having been knighted by Charles I, made an advantageous marriage, into the Nicholas family of Wiltshire, which connected him with various important figures at the Caroline court. He became lieutenant-governor of the Tower of London but died in December 1641. Of his three surviving sons, one was an unobtrusive London merchant, but the other two, Allen (1623–80) and St John (1627–1711), achieved prominence.[20] Both secured knighthoods, like their father, and both established themselves in Ireland. Sir St John, the younger of the two, who was the father of Alan, first Viscount Midleton, served as provost marshal to Roger Boyle, Lord Broghill, later first earl of Orrery, during the Munster campaigns of the early 1650s, for which he was rewarded with a grant of Ballyannan and other property in the barony of Imokilly, County Cork, where Orrery had a substantial estate.[21] He remained Orrery's client throughout the Interregnum and well into the Restoration period, acting as overseer of his Irish property, and by the time of the Williamite revolution was recognised as one of the leaders of Irish Protestant opinion.[22] Sir Allen Brodrick's sympathies, on the other hand, were always Royalist. At the close of the civil wars he fled to France, where his

19 Ibid., 1248/1–9, passim. An edition of these letters is in preparation, under the editorship of Mr Michael Page of the Surrey History Centre, and the present author.

20 For Sir Allen, see *Oxf. D.N.B.*, vii, 784–5; *H.C. 1660–90*, i, 721–4; for Sir St John, *Hist. Ir. parl.*, iii, 270.

21 Barnard, *Irish Protestant ascents and descents 1641–1770* (Dublin, 2004), pp 68–9; Aidan Clarke, *Prelude to restoration in Ireland: the end of the Commonwealth, 1659–60* (Cambridge, 1999), pp 220–21.

22 T. C. Barnard, 'Political, material and mental culture of the Cork settlers c. 1650–1700' in Patrick O' Flanagan and C. G. Buttimer (eds), *Cork: history and society* (Dublin, 1993) p. 338; journal of Dean Rowland Davies, 24–30 Oct. 1689 (*Journal of the Very Rev. Rowland Davies ... dean of Ross*, ed. Richard Caulfield (Camden Soc., lxviii (1857), pp 57–58, 60); Sir Richard Bulkeley, *The proposal for sending back the nobility and gentry of Ireland, together with a vindication of the same, and an answer to the objections made against it, in a letter to a gentleman of Ireland* (London, 1690), pp 19–20; Sir St John Brodrick, *Sir St John Brodrick's vindication of himself, from the aspersions cast on him, in a pamphlet written by Sir Rich. Bulkely, entituled, The proposal for sending back the nobility and gentry of Ireland ...* ([London,] 1690).

mother's connexion with the Nicholas and Villiers families brought him in touch with leading figures in the Sealed Knot, and he was an active, though ineffectual conspirator. Returning to England with Charles II, he attached himself to Edward Hyde, earl of Clarendon, and was given a life patent as surveyor-general of Ireland. He also did well out of the Restoration land settlement in Ireland – helped by his appointment as a member of the court of claims – and secured the confiscated Irish lands of two regicides as well as managing the great estate (in County Cork) granted to the duke of York (the future James II). Since he never married, his death in 1680 resulted in his personal fortune passing to his brother's children.

The principal beneficiary in the next generation was Sir St John's eldest son, Thomas. By his uncle's will Thomas inherited the bulk of the property in England, centred on the manor of Wandsworth in Surrey, subject to a life interest in the property left to his father.[23] When he married (in 1673) the daughter of another Cork landowner, Alexander Pigott, of Innishannon, Sir St John settled on him the estate of Ballyannan, some parts of which were then leased back. The other five brothers received a much more modest provision, and had to make their own way in the world. With the exception of the youngest, Laurence, who became a clergyman (and a prebendary of Westminster) the principal means of doing so was the practice of the law. Alan, St John, and their younger brother William all received a legal training, Alan and St John at the Middle Temple and William at the Inner Temple. Alan and St John were working barristers, Alan in Ireland, St John in London, while William plied his profession for a time in Jamaica before returning to England, and eventually to Dublin.

This concentration of lawyers – accentuated even further if we consider that Thomas too received a university law degree, spent time at the Middle Temple, and at the beginning of his career seems to have practised law[24] – would have been exceptional in an English landed family of the period. Although young gentlemen would often keep chambers after a spell at university and in the process some would acquire a smattering of legal knowledge, in each generation only one son, perhaps two, would be put to the law in earnest. In Ireland the situation was different. The peculiarly contested nature of Irish landownership, the consequence of a century of confiscation and plantation, meant that ready access to legal expertise was vitally necessary for proprietors actively engaged in the acquisition and preservation of title. So the proportion of lawyers from landed families was higher in Ireland than in England even if the level of remuneration was substantially lower.[25] Alan Brodrick's income at the outset of his career amounted to no more than £120 a year, and even at the height of his reputation he probably received no more than £1,000 for profes-

23 Will of Sir Allen, 19 Apr. 1690 (T.N.A., Prob. 11/364, ff 132–3); 'The case of Thomas Brodrick' (S.H.C., Brodrick estate papers, G145/box 8/3).

24 Cf. *Hist.Ir.parl*,, iii, 272, which identifies him as a proctor in the court of arches and judge of common pleas for Munster in 1695.

25 T. C. Barnard, 'Lawyers and the law in later seventeenth-century Ireland' in *I.H.S.*, xxviii, no. 111 (May 1993), pp 256–82, and esp. pp 264–5, 274–7; Geoffrey Holmes, *Augustan England: professions, state and society 1680–1730* (London, 1982), ch. 5 and esp. pp 124–32, 144–6; David Lemmings, *Gentlemen and barristers: the inns of court and the English bar 1680–1730* (Oxford, 1990), ch. 1.

sional work.[26] This was a poor return in comparison with the more successful barristers in England, who were earning up to £2,000 a year in the 1660s and over £3,000 by the 1720s,[27] even allowing for the disparity in wealth between the propertied elites of the two kingdoms, a differential which presumably accounts for St John's decision to develop his practice in London.[28]

But there was more to be gained from a legal career than clients' fees. The law provided a range of profitable appointments, both local and national. Besides the £120 he earned by giving opinions and pleading cases, the young Alan Brodrick received £70 a year as recorder of Cork, and the rewards of his subsequent promotion up the ladder of Irish legal preferment were proportionately greater – to king's serjeant, solicitor- and attorney-general, chief justice of Queen's Bench and eventually lord chancellor. Even his unreliable younger brother William, professionally the least successful member of the family, was able to obtain some form of salaried employment, first as attorney-general for Jamaica, and eventually, after the Hanoverian succession, back in Ireland, as third serjeant.[29] And of course, the experience of advocacy was an excellent springboard for a successful parliamentary career. The contingent of lawyers among the membership of the early eighteenth-century Irish House of Commons has been estimated at between 12 to 15 per cent, including most of the prominent debaters and party leaders.[30]

In different ways, both Alan and St John prospered in the law – Alan through holding public office, St John as a well connected London barrister – while even the hapless William was able to keep his head above water with help from family and friends. Prosperity is more obvious to the historian in Alan's case. Aside from a few small purchases, St John's income was not translated into land – without a wife and children there was no compulsion to do so – and we only have an estimate of the value of his disposable assets, calculated after his death at about £10,000, though on what basis is unclear.[31] Alan, on the other hand, with two sons and a daughter to provide for (and for a time uncertainty as to whether his elder brother would leave an heir), did acquire a substantial portfolio of landed property, his Irish estates alone bringing in the region of £1,500 and £2,000 a year by the 1720s.[32] In his case,

26 Barnard, 'Lawyers and the law', pp 276–7.

27 Holmes, *Augustan Eng.*, p. 127; Lemmings, *Gentlemen and barristers*, pp 155–6.

28 In early eighteenth-century Ireland an income of £1,000 a year was certainly sufficient to denote a gentleman of 'quality'. The evidence for incomes and social status across England and Wales in this period is surveyed in T. C. Barnard, *A new anatomy of Ireland: the Irish Protestants, 1649–1770* (New Haven, Conn., & London, 2003), pp 57–64.

29 For William, see *Hist. Ir. parl.*, iii, 274–5; and for his tendency to exasperate his more successful siblings by irresolution and a weakness for gambling, see Sir St John to Thomas, 1 Nov. 1684 (S.H.C., 1248/1/220–21); Alan I to Thomas, 5, 9 May 1702, 16 July 1717, 25 Mar. 1719[/20] (ibid., 1248/2/61–2, 63–4; 1248/4/ 51–2, 230–31).

30 Barnard, 'lawyers and the law', pp 281–2. A contemporary list from 1695 marked 62 out of 300 members of the Irish House of Commons as lawyers, that is to say 20.6 per cent (B.L., Southwell papers, Add. MS 9715, ff 17–18). But even this excluded qualified lawyers like St John and Thomas Brodrick, who did not practise in Ireland, as well as attorneys like William Conolly.

31 Additional instructions to will of St John I, 2 Sept. 1707 (S.H.C., 1248/2/274–5); calculation by Alan I of the personalty of St John I at death, n.d. (ibid., 1248/2/286–7).

32 Rentals (ibid., G145/box 102/4).

of course, professional success had been combined with the additional, and very substantial, emoluments of office.[33]

Alan also benefited substantially from another important source of wealth in the early eighteenth century: marriage. He was married three times: first to Catherine, daughter of Redmond Barry of Rathcormac in County Cork; then in 1695 to Lucy Courthope, daughter of another local landowner Sir Peter Courthope, whose extensive estates lay to the west of Midleton; and finally in 1716 to Anne, daughter of the former Westminster Speaker Sir John Trevor, and widow of Michael Hill of Hillsborough, County Down. With Catherine he had a son, St John ('Senny'); with Lucy another son, Alan ('Nally'), and a daughter, Alice ('Allie', named after his mother and sister). Although both Lucy and Anne were heiresses, it was the Courthope marriage that proved the most lucrative of the three, for Lucy's brothers died childless, leaving the Courthope estates to be divided between herself and her sister Anne.

Since Thomas Brodrick did not produce a male heir who lived beyond infancy, the landed empire created by Sir Allen and Sir St John passed in due course to Alan's surviving son, and more or less intact, since there had been little erosion in order to provide for younger siblings, other than marriage portions for daughters. Alan's brother St John had died unmarried in 1707, bequeathing to Thomas (and thence to Alan's heirs) such landed property as he himself had inherited or purchased,[34] and although the younger brothers, William and Laurence, did each produce an heir, these children were not provided for out of their grandfather's or great-uncle's estates.

Two of Viscount Midleton's marriages produced sons: St John, by his first wife, and Alan, by his second. St John received the obligatory legal education and was called to the Irish bar in 1707.[35] A year later he succeeded his father as recorder of Cork, but made a disappointing lack of progress in the profession, especially after 1714, when more of his time was devoted to politics.[36] Unfortunately, he also spent most of his active political life in parliamentary opposition, which cost him money, and despite contracting a profitable marriage (the terms of which included the settlement of Irish property from both his father and his uncle Thomas), he dissipated his financial resources, and died in 1728 deeply in debt.[37] His half-brother, 'Nally', eventually the sole heir, was even less typical of a family whose approach to life had traditionally been businesslike and calculating. As a younger son, he was indulged rather than disciplined, being provided with a gentleman's education, complete with lengthy Grand Tour in the Netherlands, Germany and Italy, during which he purchased pictures for his uncle Thomas but seems to have gained nothing other

33 St John I was also steward of St Paul's (additional instructions to will, 2 Sept. 1700 (ibid., 1248/2, ff 274–5)).

34 Will, 2 Sept. 1700 (T.N.A., Prob. 11/495, ff 204–5).

35 Edward Keane et al. (eds), *King's Inns admissions papers* (Dublin, 1982), p. 54.

36 St John II to Alan I, 9 Aug. 1724 (S.H.C., 1248/6/49–50).

37 Same to same, 25 Aug. 1711, 6, 25 Aug. 1721 (ibid., 1248/5/67–8, 73–4); Jane Bulkeley to Jane Bonnell, 9 Apr. 1728 (N.L.I., Smythe of Barbavilla papers, MS 41,850/4). He had shown symptoms of extravagance in his early years, overspending his allowance at university (Alan I to St John I, 28 Sept. 1701 (S.H.C., 1248/2/27–8)).

than discrimination in his taste and polish in his manners.[38] Although his father had wanted him to study the law, he had neither the aptitude nor inclination.[39] After succeeding to the viscountcy in 1728 he waited until November 1733 before taking the oaths in the Irish House of Lords, and attended there for only another fortnight, making no impression whatsoever on proceedings.[40] Clearly, with his succession to the headship of the family, a phase in its history had come to an end.

II

This dynastic narrative, producing first a division and eventually a reuniting of the family estates and a recurrent need to make provision for younger sons and nephews, together with the physical separation of properties between Surrey and County Cork, created problems to which the Brodricks responded by a co-operative effort. This was informed by family pride, the kind of sentiment that induced the first Viscount Midleton, in drawing up his will, to acknowledge his brother Thomas as 'the head of my family and a great honour to it'. In 1720, when making provision for his widowed sister Katherine Whitfield, he explained his actions to Thomas in the following terms:[41]

> I have all along done what I have been able to do to support her and her family, nor is it sufficient ground for us to refuse doing so, although it be true that she threw herself away on a worthless and ungrateful man … but Christianity *as well as our own reputation* lay us under obligations to do something for her, and I desire you not to take it ill of me if I remind you that *as you are the head of the family, you will suffer most in reproach* if she wants …

A strong sense of family loyalty was also reflected in the compulsive recycling of Christian names, in the care with which Sir Allen arranged the descent of his lands to maintain the coherence of a large family estate, and the extent to which a concern for consolidation permeated other arrangements for the disposal of property: the will made by Alan and Thomas's brother St John, for example, which ensured that his own acquisitions would merge with the main line; and the inclusion of lands belonging to Thomas in 'Senny's' marriage settlement.[42] Perhaps the most striking

38 Thomas to Alan II, 6, 19 Nov. 1724, 4 Dec. [?1724] (S.H.C., 1248/6/82–3, 97, 100–101); Thomas and Martha Courthope to same, 22–23 Apr. 1725 (ibid., 1248/6/205–6); Alan II to Thomas, 4 May N.S. 1725 (ibid., 1248/6/219–20).

39 Alan I to Alan II, n.d. (ibid., 1248/9/140).

40 *L.J.Ire.*, iii, 242–50. Nor did he bother to seek election to the British parliament.

41 Will of Alan I, 19 Apr. 1726 (P. B. Eustace and Eilish Ellis (eds), *Registry of Deeds Dublin: abstracts of wills* (3 vols, Dublin, 1956–84), i, 167–8); Alan I to Thomas, 9 Dec. 1720 (S.H.C., 1248/4/369–70: emphasis added). Katherine's husband was an English clergyman, William Whitfield (1658–1717), vicar of St Giles Cripplegate, in London.

42 Thomas inherited the Wandsworth property from Sir Allen (plus his Irish lands), with remainder to Alan and his children (Sir Allen's will, 19 Apr. 1680 (T.N.A., Prob. 11/364, ff 132–3); St John's will, 2 Sept. 1700 (ibid., Prob. 11/495, ff 204–5); additional instructions, 2 Sept. 1700 (S.H.C., 1248/2/274–5)).

example of collective responsibility was the way in which family members undertook the management of estates for absentees. Thomas succeeded to Ballyannan when he married in 1673, but scarcely, if ever, lived there. He relied first on his brother Alan, who visited from Dublin intermittently in the 1680s and 1690s, and later, from the late 1710s, on his nephew St John, to whom he rented the property and who, for personal and political reasons, found it expedient to reside on an estate which he expected in due course to inherit.[43] The English properties were managed in a similar way. Wandsworth was looked after by the barrister St John in 1698–1701, whilst his father, Sir St John, attempted unsuccessfully to resettle in Ireland. In later years Thomas kept a close eye on the administration of Peper Harow, an estate near Godalming in Surrey, which Alan purchased in 1713.[44]

A powerful commitment to family, often manifesting itself in practical co-operation, extended to those with whom the Brodricks were linked by marriage. Alan maintained a close association with the Bettesworths of White Rock in County Cork who were 'cousins' of a sort. On account of this 'friendship and relation' he maintained 'Dick Bettesworth's son' Richard (1689–1741) at school, and eventually brought him in as M.P. for Midleton in 1727, while bestowing a sum of money on the daughter of another Bettesworth at her marriage. In return the elder Richard managed Alan's affairs for him in County Cork and provided accommodation for occasional visits.[45] Each of Alan's three wives brought with her a further set of connexions, the vitality of which he continued to recognise even when he had remarried. Long after Catherine Barry's death, for example, he still regarded his brother-in-law James Barry as his own 'brother' and James's sons as nephews, and sought to assist them where he could.[46] With the Courthopes, he took responsibility not only for Lucy's unmarried sister, Anne, but also her two widowed sisters-in-law, Martha ('Matty') and Rachel, for whom he provided a home at Peper Harow. In fact, the property had been bought in Martha's name, and she seems to have acted as chatelaine.[47] In correspondence they were all his 'sisters'. This ready acceptance of distant marital connexions as having equal force to ties of blood was reinforced

43 Alan I to Thomas, 28 Sept. 1701, 23 Dec. 1712, 16 Sept. 1718 (S.H.C., 1248/2/27–8, 1248/3/103–4, 1248/4/126–7).

44 Same to same, 20 Apr. 1713 (ibid., 1248/3/111–112); Thomas to Martha Courthope, 3 Mar. [1715] (ibid., 1248/5/382–3); same to Alan I, 11 June, 2 Aug. 1716, 22 Sept. 1721, 4 July 1722 (ibid., 1248/4/120–1, 122–23; 1248/5/87–8, 223–4).

45 Alan I to Thomas, 16 Apr. 1687, 8 July 1710, 15 Nov. 1712 (S.H.C., 1248/1/220, 1248/3/3–4, 95–6); John Benger to Alan I, 16 Oct. 1703 (ibid., G145/box 99); Alan I to St John I, 9 Nov. 1705 (ibid., 1248/2/229–30). For Richard Bettesworth, jr, see *Hist. Ir. parl.*, iii, 179–80.

46 Alan I to Thomas, 26 Apr. 1717 (S.H.C., 1248/4/13–14). He made his nephew 'Jemmy' Barry his purse-bearer as lord chancellor (same to same, 17 May 1725 (ibid., 1248/6/233–4)). See also same to same, 14 June 1717 (ibid., 1248/4/35–6), which shows him seeking to advance the career of his first wife's nephew, the clergyman John Matthews.

47 Articles of agreement for purchase of Peper Harow, 4 Aug. 1712 (S.H.C., 7360/1); vellum-bound book of documents relating to Peper Harow, 1712–13 (ibid., G145/box1); Thomas to Martha Courthope, 3 Mar. [1715] (ibid., 1248/5/382–3); same to Alan I, 22 Sept. 1721, 14 July 1722 (ibid., 1248/5/87–88, 225–6); Alan I to Thomas, 13 June 1723 (ibid., 1248/5/280–81); Thomas to Alan II, 25 Nov. 1725 (ibid., 1248/6/343–4). The will of St John I also included bequests to the two sisters-in-law (additional instructions to will, 2 Sept. 1707 (ibid., 1248/2/274–5)).

by the fact that such relationships sometimes extended over more than one generation. Three years after Alan married Lucy Courthope, for example, her sister Anne married Alan's cousin Laurence Clayton. Another double-link developed with the Hill family. In 1710 'Senny' married the daughter of Michael Hill. Six years later, after Michael Hill and Lucy Brodrick had both died, Alan married the widow. This was to prove an unsatisfactory alliance, for Mrs Hill had other daughters to provide for, which were a drain on the estate, and she was resented by her stepchildren.[48] But the Clayton marriage worked out well, despite a gritty process of negotiation over the division of the Courthope sisters' inheritance. 'Lory' was already a close friend, and the friendship not only survived these difficulties but in fact deepened as time went by.[49] From a 'cousin' he became Alan's 'brother Clayton'.[50]

A highly developed belief in the importance of family ties did not, however, exclude the possibility of conflict, and one of the many notable paradoxes about the Brodricks was that, for all their cohesiveness, they were prone – perhaps genetically predisposed – to quarrel. Whenever the complexities of wills, marriage settlements or other intra-familial arrangements induced a sense of thwarted entitlement, as they often did, resentment would be exacerbated by the angularity of temperament which all principals shared.[51] Sir St John, in old age, proved a particularly difficult customer. Wandsworth House remained his permanent residence until his death, but he occasionally visited County Cork[52] and in the late 1690s – for reasons none of his children could fathom – he decided to try once more to live in Ireland and decamped for a time to Cahermone, the neighbouring estate to Ballyannan. On his departure he did not leave Wandsworth in the care of Thomas, the heir apparent, but instead asked his third son St John to act as caretaker, possibly out of spite arising from some previous *contretemps*. At any rate, the arrangement became a further bone of contention between father and eldest son, and in addition effected a temporary rupture between the two brothers.[53] Thomas already held a long list of complaints against his father, over claims and counter-claims for 'rents and money', and there was soon one more grievance – perfectly gratuitous – when Sir St John built a wall around the Cahermone demesne that encroached on Ballyannan. By 1700 Thomas was 'expressing himself with great resentment', and Alan was seeking vainly to

48 Jane Bulkeley to Jane Bonnell, 9 Apr. 1728 (N.L.I., MS 41,580/4); Lady Midleton to same, 3 May 1730 (ibid., MS 41,580/3).

49 See, for example, Alan I to Thomas, 1 Mar. 1702/3, 26 Mar., 14 Aug. 1703 (S.H.C., 1248/2/82–3, 88–89, 105–6); Sir Richard Cox to Edward Southwell, 24 May 1707 (B.L., Southwell papers, Add. MS 38155, f. 49).

50 Alan I to St John II, 11 July 1704 (S.H.C.,1248/2/141–2). In 1720 Alan appealed to his brother Thomas to do what he could to prevent the ruinous fate he foresaw for Laurence Clayton's son Randal if he stayed in England and continued his foolish ways: 'your friendship for his father and the relation that is between you seem to call for your giving him some advice' (same to Thomas, 14 Dec. 1720 (ibid., 1248/4/375–6)).

51 'Ours is a melancholy family', Alan had written in 1683 (same to Sir St John, 9 Nov. 1683 (ibid., 1248/1/330–31)).

52 Sir St John to John Evelyn, 5 Apr. 1694 (B.L., Evelyn papers, Add. MS 15857, f. 74).

53 Alan I to Thomas, 25 Feb. 1699[/1700] (S.H.C., 1248/1/311–12).

mediate.[54] Worse still, the boundary disputes threatened to involve Alan as well, who was to inherit Cahermone.[55] And to complete the picture, brother St John was also on bad terms with his father over what he felt was the inadequate provision Sir St John had made for him.[56]

But before we assume that Sir St John was the only rogue elephant in the herd, we should note the aggrieved tone of Alan's complaints about his brother William's failure to show himself 'a considerate man';[57] Thomas's concern about his nephew St John's 'negligence' in paying rents that were due;[58] several harsh letters from Alan to 'Senny', one of which the recipient described as having been written in 'that severe, angry unkind manner, that I protest the bare reading of it puts me so far beside myself that I am not able to recollect my thoughts so as to write common sense';[59] recriminations from Thomas to Alan while young St John lay on his deathbed, virtually accusing him of treating his children unequally and favouring those of his second marriage;[60] and the second Viscount Midleton's lawsuit against his widowed stepmother in 1730, causing her to complain that the family 'are resolved to do everything they can to distress me'.[61] Alan, who had a lawyer's sense of proprietorial right as well as more than his fair share of *amour propre*, a quick temper, and a viper's tongue, also showed himself capable of falling out with members of the extended family. His long drawn-out negotiation with Laurence Clayton over the division of the Courthope estates had awkward moments,[62] and later he declared his determination to 'have done ... for ever' with his 'nephew' Redmond Barry when the young man failed to take his advice.[63] Even the Courthope widows could irritate if they became too demanding, and when Rachel asked Alan to intervene in a legal dispute with a nephew his response was unexpectedly, and unreasonably, sharp.[64]

Incidents of this kind were probably inevitable given conditions of proximity and mutual dependence, and their significance should not be exaggerated. In private, relations may have been edgy, but the Brodricks always took pains to present a

54 Same to same, 1, 8 Oct. 1700 (ibid., 1248/2/7–10). The bad blood remained for several years (same to same, 6 Jan. 1702/3, 12 June 1705 (ibid., 1248/2/78–9, 209–10)).
55 Sir St John to same, 1 Nov. 1684 (ibid., 1248/1/220–21); Alan I to same, 5 Sept. 1700 (ibid., 1248/2/5–6).
56 St John I to Alan I and Thomas, 22 Dec. 1698 (ibid., 1248/1/305–7); Alan I to Thomas, 8 Oct. 1700 (ibid., 1248/2/10).
57 Same to same, 16 July, 8 Aug. 1717 (ibid., 1248/4/51–2, 57–8)
58 Same to same, 16 Sept. 1718 (ibid., 1248/4/126–7)
59 St John II to Alan I, 6 Aug. 1721 (ibid., 1248/5/67–8). See also same to same, 25 Aug. 1721, 9 Aug. 1724 (ibid., 1248/5/73–4, 1248/6/49–50).
60 Thomas to Alan I, 5 Mar. 1727[/8] (ibid., 1248/7/215–16), Alan I to Thomas, 14 Mar. 1727[/8] (ibid., 1248/7/217–18). For evidence of Alan's grief at the death of his eldest son, see same to same, 14 Mar. 1727[/8] (ibid., 1248/7/ 217–18); Jane Bulkeley to Jane Bonnell, 9 Apr. 1728 (N.L.I., MS 41,580/4).
61 Lady Midleton to same, 3 May 1730 (ibid., MS 41,580/3).
62 Nicholas Greene to Alan I, 5 Feb. 1702[/3] (S.H.C., G145/box 98/1); detailed list of settlements (ibid., G145/box 102/5, pp 1–37, 49–55, 140–47).
63 Alan I to Thomas, 23 May, 27 June, 8, 16 July 1717 (ibid., 1248/4/29–30, 45–6, 47–8, 51–2).
64 Same to same, 8 Oct. 1720, 27 Sept., 12 Dec. 1725, 9 Mar. 1725[/6] (ibid., 1248/4/326–7, 1248/6/320–23, 345–6, 391–4); same to Rachel Courthope, 27 July, 21, 31 Aug. 1725 (N.L.I., Limerick (Stacpole) papers, MS 41,675/6).

united front to the world. This was vitally important to the management of their local 'interest' in County Cork, which was the enduring foundation of their political power. In national politics unity was not always so necessary. During the tortuous parliamentary politics of the period 1715–25, while Midleton carried on his struggle with Speaker Conolly from within Dublin Castle, presenting himself as a sincere servant of government, 'Senny' led the 'country' opposition in the Commons, obliging his father to explain to ministers that there were limits to paternal control over such a headstrong young man.[65] However, the Munster context made very different demands. What mattered there, above all else, was the reputation of the family.[66] Letters between Alan and Thomas, and between Alan and his sons, demonstrate hyper-sensitivity to potential danger, whether this arose from the impoliteness of a Barry connexion in not complying with electoral arrangements made for him,[67] or Sir St John's disregard for his neighbours as well as for his son in building his boundary wall around Cahermone, a *folie de grandeur* that produced 'mutterings' and raised the prospect that 'the country would present it and have it pulled down as a nuisance'.[68]

III

It was clearly vital for the family to be able to maintain a position at the apex of Cork society. Their particular strength lay in the north and east of the county, and they certainly concentrated their land purchases in that area, but aside from the closing years of Anne's reign, when opinion was polarised by party conflict and political alignments briefly reflected the geographical division between east and west (or north and south of the River Lee), the family 'interest' was not necessarily localised in the eastern baronies.[69] As a young man, Thomas Brodrick had given a great deal of his time and effort to county affairs. (Naturally enough, he took a particular interest in establishing horse-races at Youghal.[70]) After the Williamite revolution, he and his brothers were active in public life at a national rather than a provincial level. However, as lord chancellor in 1715, Alan Brodrick took care to ensure his own and his son's inclusion in the commission of the peace for County Cork, even though there was little prospect that either would serve, as well as the appointment of Thomas and 'Senny' to the commission of array, while he himself

65 Hayton, *Ruling Ireland*, pp 218–19. However, there is nothing in their private letters to suggest a difference of opinion between father and son, on principle or strategy, and in consequence Midleton's protests appear disingenuous.

66 Alan I to Thomas, 28 Dec 1699 (S.H.C., 1248/1/316–17).

67 See above, n. 63.

68 Alan I to Thomas, 5 Sept. 1700 (S.H.C., 1248/2/5–6).

69 Same to same, [c. 12 Jan. 1713/14] (ibid., 1248/3/155); Sir Richard Cox to Edward Southwell, 30 Jan. 1713/14 (B.L., Southwell papers, Add. MS 38157, f. 61); D. W. Hayton, 'Tories and Whigs in County Cork, 1714' in *Journal of the Cork Historical and Archaeological Society*, lxxx (1975), pp 84–8.

70 Barnard, 'Political, material and mental culture of the Cork settlers', p. 135.

assumed command (at least on paper) of a militia troop.[71] Subsequently the young St John, returning to reside for at least part of each year at Ballyannan, took his responsibilities seriously, offering the kind of hospitality that neighbours expected, and discharging his duties as a magistrate.[72] And of course considerable effort was always put into securing seats in parliament, for members of both the nuclear and extended family, partly as an end in itself, and partly as a demonstration of Brodrick ascendancy. In this respect pocket boroughs like Midleton were much less valuable than the more prestigious seats, for the county and for Cork city. Looking towards a likely general election in 1703, Alan Brodrick was anxious to make sure that the returns for county and city should be made first; Midleton had to be kept as insurance.[73] At every election between 1692 and 1728 a member of the family was chosen as knight of the shire, even though the costs incurred could be substantial, and were not confined to years in which elections actually took place.[74] Similar attention had also to be paid to the city, whose aldermen were conscious of their dignity. They complimented the Brodricks by choosing successive representatives of the family as their recorder, and Alan felt constrained not to abandon them until he had found a suitable replacement.[75] When he finally moved across to a county seat in 1713 it was to allow his eldest son to succeed him as one of the city M.P.s.

Maintaining a position on the *cursus honorum* of local government, and election as knight of the shire, served to confirm the importance of the Brodrick 'interest'. But the indispensable building blocks of that interest were still land and personal connexion. Both were prime considerations in the making of marriage alliances, a process dominated by strategic and financial calculations, and hedged about by a complex framework of property settlements. The marital history of the first Viscount Midleton forms a good illustration of the various purposes served by what was often, at least in part, a business transaction (though Alan's private correspondence shows a depth of feeling that would give the lie to any suggestion that money and land were the only considerations).[76] His first two wives were both from the gentry community of County Cork, and the landed inheritance that came with Lucy Courthope did a great deal to consolidate Brodrick dominance in the area around Midleton. Earlier, Thomas had also married into a Cork family, as had Sir St John, whose wife Alice was the daughter of Sir Randal Clayton of Mallow. Besides the acquisition of land, marrying within the county meant that the Brodricks thickened their network of

71 B.L., Egmont papers, Add. MS 46966, ff 161–3; N.A.I., M 2537, pp 304–5. According to H. F. Berry, 'Justices of the peace for County Cork, 1661–1800' in *Journal of the Cork Historical and Archaeological Society*, ser. 2, iii (1897), p. 60, Alan Brodrick was first appointed a J.P. for Co. Cork in 1682. Thomas's name does not appear on this list, but since it also omits St John's appointment in 1715 its reliability must be in doubt.

72 St John II to Alan I, 11 Aug. 1723 (S.H.C., 1248/5/287–8); Alan I to Thomas, 16 Dec. 1725 (ibid., 1248/6/347–50).

73 Same to same, 14 Aug. 1703 (ibid., 1248/2/105–6).

74 In 1714 St John II allegedly spent £500 on an election that did not take place (Sir John Perceval to Daniel Dering, 15 May 1714 (B.L., Egmont papers, Add. MS 47087, f. 71)).

75 Alan I to Thomas, 13 Apr. 1707 (S.H.C., 1248/2/258–9).

76 See in particular the outpouring of grief after the death of 'my dear Lucy' (same to St John I, 5 Jan. 1704/5 (ibid., 1248/2/161–2)).

local connexions. Alan's first marriage, to Catherine Barry, was especially useful in political terms, since her brother James and two nephews were all Irish M.P.s, James proving a staunch political ally.[77]

The same strategy that informed marriage arrangements was also visible in the family's approach to land purchase and management. They sought to accumulate property which would consolidate their physical presence in east Cork and its environs.[78] The most spectacular attempt ended in frustration, when a consortium of Cork landowners headed by Thomas failed in 1695 in a bid to acquire the forfeited Muskerry estate,[79] but Alan was able to buy property in the vicinity of Ballyannan, and in the neighbouring county of Waterford.[80] Ideally, to complete the effect, Ballyannan would need to have been completely refurbished and probably enlarged. This was what William Conolly achieved: in accumulating property he increased his rental income and the number of tenants obliged to him (and whom he could instruct at parliamentary elections), but he also built a great house as a symbol of his wealth, status, and power. The Brodricks took a different approach. To develop Ballyannan would involve spending money on a house in which (until the young St John arrived in the 1720s) they had no intention to reside. On the other hand, systematic exploitation of the possibilities for making and re-making leases had obvious attractions for a family preoccupied with maximising income and connexions.

It was yet another paradox that while the leases devised for the Brodricks' Irish tenants imposed a responsibility to carry out practical 'improvements' that would enhance the value of the land,[81] the major property remaining in the hands of the family was for many years resolutely unimproved. Following Thomas's abandonment of Ballyannan after the Williamite revolution the estate was neglected. On a brief visit with his wife in 1700, Alan was unhappy at what he saw.[82] The agent, William Spence, while perfectly civil in his manners, had become accustomed to taking liberties in his master's absence: he looked after the timber well enough and the horses (which were Thomas's prime concern[83]) but it was all too obvious that 'he makes haste to be rich'. He had overstocked the park with deer, and grazed large

77 Anderson Saunders to Edward Southwell, 18 Oct. 1707 (B.L., Add. MS 9715, f. 203); Sir Richard Cox to same, 24 Mar. 1713/14 (ibid., Add. MS 38157, f. 77).

78 For evidence that the family were constantly on the look-out for available land, see Nicholas Greene to Alan I, 28 Feb. 1720/1 (S.H.C., G145/box 98/1).

79 David Dickson, *Old world colony: Cork and south Munster 1630–1830* (Cork, 2005), p. 62; Walsh, *Making of the Irish Protestant ascendancy*, pp 45–6.

80 John Benger to Alan I, 16 Oct. 1703 (S.H.C., G145/box 99); memorandum on 'Glenane and Ballyfines' n.d. (ibid.); will of Alan I, 19 Apr. 1726 (Eustace & Ellis (eds), *Reg. deeds: abstracts of wills*, i, 167–8). See also Alan I to Thomas, 8, 13 May 1717 (S.H.C., 1248/4/21–2, 23–4) regarding a proposed purchase for St John II at Clonmel, on the borders of Counties Tipperary and Waterford.

81 Rentals (S.H.C., G145/box 102/4). See also Sir St John Brodrick, *Sir St John Brodrick's vindication of himself*, pp 22–23; St John I to Alan and Thomas, 27 Dec. 1698 (S.H.C., 1248/1/307); Nicholas Greene to Alan I, 9 Mar. 1720/1, 30 July 1723 (ibid., G145/box 98/1).

82 Alan I to Thomas, 5 Sept. 1700 (S.H.C., 1248/2/5–6).

83 For Alan's disapproval of horse-racing, which he regarded as 'an introduction to cheating, sharping, hypocrisy and lying', and a means by which gentlemen lost their credit and their fortunes, see same to Alan II, 10 Apr. 1718 (ibid., 1248/4/150–51).

numbers of his own cows there as well. At the same time the gardens were 'much out of order', and, as for the house itself, local people – presumably servants – were making free with the contents. Alan reported to his brother that he and Lucy

> took the freedom which you allowed of using your house and linen; and let me assure you that other people use your linen more than yourself or those you allow of; for Lucy observed, and so did I, that your napkins were in many places worn out and darned which she so lately bought new for you and your sheets also are used: your chairs are generally at the lodge and as soon as we turned our backs were carried there again and brought back when we returned.[84]

As long as the house remained unoccupied, things would not improve. In 1710 Alan reported that 'all things go strangely to ruin there', and following another short visit,

> I cannot but be concerned to see how you are abused and your estate encroached on by your tenants and others and you injured in another manner than anybody else would bear.... If it were not the loss of reputation as well as money I should be the less concerned; but really, permitting things of this nature must lessen you in the eyes of those who see things of this sort so little taken notice of. [85]

Although the house and gardens were evidently put back into repair when 'Senny' returned with his family in the 1720s, there is no indication from the surviving correspondence that anything more elaborate was attempted; and certainly nothing on the scale of Castletown or the other 'prodigy houses' of the period. No architect was engaged, nor any specialist in the decorative arts or the manipulation of landscape. After Senny's death his father wrote to Thomas 'of what he hath done at Ballyannan in making the place habitable, and beautifying it, and in planting and improving the land', but this was in the context of an appeal for the widow and her children to be allowed to remain in occupation.[86] The only member of the family to display enthusiasm for domestic 'improvements' was in fact Sir St John, who in his brief period of senile self-indulgence at Cahermone showed 'a fondness for buildings and projects' and contemplated reconstructing his gardens as well as enlarging his park.[87] 'Senny's' letters show an altogether different approach. He was not interested

84 Same to Thomas, 5 Sept. 1700 (ibid., 1248/2/5–6). See also same to same, 20 Apr. 1705 (ibid., 1248/2/193–4).

85 Same to same, 14 Nov. 1710, 29 May 1712 (ibid., 1248/3/31–2, 74–5). He was, however, casting stones from within the confines of a metaphorical glass-house, since his sometime residence in Fishamble Lane, Cork, of which he had made considerable use at the outset of his career, was, by 1721, in 'so dangerous and tottering a way that people are afraid to walk or pass' it (St John II to Alan I, 26 Mar., 9 Apr. 1721 (ibid., 1248/5/9–10, 204–5)).

86 Alan I to Thomas, 14 Mar. 1727[/8] (ibid., 1248/7/217–18).

87 Same to same, 25 Feb. 1699[/1700] (ibid., 1248/1/311–12); same to St John I, 4 Oct. 1701 (ibid., 1248/2/29–30). Sir St John evidently had a long standing interest in gardening (Laurence Clayton to St John II, 31 Aug. 1683 (ibid., 1248/1/183–4)). Other members of the family were interested in gardens for their produce, rather than appearance (Thomas to Alan I, 22 Sept. 1721 (ibid., 1248/5/87–8); Alan I to Thomas, 21 Sept. 1726 (ibid., 1248/6/310–11)).

in 'buildings and projects', but in making the estate pay.[88] Like his father, when he visited the estate in 1700 he looked closely at those elements which could make money, or, in the case of the deer park, could be turned to practical advantage in another way (through making compliments of venison to the local gentry[89]). When he travelled across to County Waterford to examine one of his father's purchases, he reported on the quality of the land, and the state of the timber.[90] And above all, he focused his attention on what could be obtained in rents.[91] This was perfectly characteristic of the family. Alan and his brothers each had a lawyer's eye for detail, and a determination to ensure they received their due. In one of his letters, Alan noted that he had been entering 'into my book' the particulars of the money he had in England and how it had been 'put out'.[92] Two of the most impressive documents in the family archive are conspectuses of the Irish estate that he drew up after he ceased to be lord chancellor.[93] They were intended for his younger son, to make him aware of his own entitlement and enable him to avoid being imposed upon.[94] Each consists of a vellum-covered book in which was set out not only the name and size of each parcel of land, but also its history and leasing arrangements. An enormous amount of time and care was put into the compilation, and the mentality behind it – cautious, suspicious, and ultimately self-reliant – is revealed by the warning included at the beginning of the second book:[95]

> I have known men who have lost their estates by the wickedness and breach of trust of their agents, who may discover some defect in the title and make ill use of the knowledge they get by being entrusted with the sight of the deeds, and often mislay or detain them till the client is obliged to pay them their exorbitant demands for the services they pretend to have done.

As far as the Brodricks were concerned, the principal value of landed property was the income to be drawn from it in terms of rent. In the 1690s they made it a policy to seek 'English Protestant tenants', but only because these were likely to be 'wealthy and excellent improvers' who would pay punctually.[96] But as well as the financial return on investment in land, there were potential gains in political terms. Obviously, these purchases created opportunities to reward friends and followers by the grant of leases. Rentals show that many of the tenants were themselves estab-

88 Thomas to Alan I, 18 Nov. 1721 (ibid., 1248/5/144–5); St John II to same, 11 Aug. 1723, 21, 29 Mar. 1724/5 (ibid., 1248/5/287–8, 1248/6/177–85, 189–90).

89 Alan I to Thomas, 14 Aug. 1703 (ibid., 1248/2/105–6); Philip Crofts to Sir John Perceval, 27 Sept. 1709 (B.L., Egmont papers, Add. MS 47025, ff 134–5).

90 St John II to Alan I, 23 Apr. 1723, 29 Mar. 1725 (S.H.C., 1248/5/271–2, 1248/6/189–90).

91 Same to same, 16 Mar. 1718[/19] (ibid., 1248/4/146–7).

92 Alan I to St John I, 9 Nov. 1705 (ibid., 1248/2/229–30).

93 Rentals (ibid., G145/box 102/4); list of settlements (ibid., G145/box 102/5). See also Alan I to Thomas, 23 Mar. 1713[/14], 5, 12 Apr., 9, 10, 16 July 1728 (ibid., 1248/3/170–71, 1248/7/221–7, 245–55).

94 List of settlements (ibid., G145/box 102/5)

95 Ibid.

96 St John I to Alan I and Thomas, 27 Dec. 1698 (ibid., 1248/1/307); St John II to Alan I, 29 Mar. 1725 (ibid., 1248/6/189–90).

lished landowners, presumably rack-renting to under-tenants who would farm the land, and that a significant proportion of these head tenants hailed from the upper ranks of the county gentry.[97] They included various Barrys and Bettesworths, including Standish Barry, 'a papist', but, as Alan wrote, 'the best of that kind I ever knew';[98] George Crofts of Churchtown, whose father had been an Irish M.P. in 1692; Robert Oliver of Castle Oliver, County Limerick, who sat for various constituencies (including his own county) from 1703 to 1727; and Bartholomew Purdon of Ballyclogh, a neighbour and relative of the Claytons,[99] who was a burgess of Midleton,[100] and represented several Cork boroughs between 1699 and his death in 1737.

IV

Their property and rental income, social position and personal connexions in County Cork provided the base from which the Brodricks could make their way in the world, and the financial and political capital with which their public careers could be launched. But what place did Midleton and its environs occupy in their minds? Alan and his brothers had been effectively brought up as Englishmen. They had been at school in England, and at university in Oxford rather than Dublin. Two brothers, St John and Laurence, made their entire careers in England. What is more, the family's roots were firmly set in England, more specifically in Surrey, and associations with that county retained their power. Wandsworth House was regarded as the ancestral seat, despite the fact that the estate belonging to the house was modest.[101] From the 1670s it became the principal residence first of Sir Allen, then his brother,[102] and eventually Thomas (it was there that he kept the pictures his nephew bought on his behalf).[103] All three asked to be buried there, as did Thomas's brother St John.[104] Such feelings were of a different order to those of other Irish Protestants who had inherited property in England; for example, William Conolly's close friend Marmaduke Coghill, who was descended from a Yorkshire gentry family and still owned Coghill Hall, at Knaresborough. He occasionally made the trek to

97 Rentals (ibid., G145/box 102/4); list of settlements (ibid., G145/box 102/5); Nathaniel Evans to Alan I, 25 Aug. 1727 (ibid., G145/box 98/1).

98 Alan I to Thomas, 11 Dec. 1719 (ibid., 1248/4/182–3).

99 Laurence Clayton to Alan I (ibid., 1248/2/303–4).

100 List of burgesses and freemen of Midleton, n.d. (ibid., G145/box 98/1).

101 'The case of Thomas Brodrick' (ibid., G145/8/3) asserted that a sale of the whole property, excluding the house, would not have raised £500.

102 For Sir St John, see for example, release of trust, 26 June 1688 (Centre for Buckinghamshire Studies, Dashwood papers, D–D/8/115); deed, 13 Oct. 1705 (S.H.C., G145/ box 95/1).

103 *The poll for knights of the shire for the county of Surrey, 1713* (London, 1713), p. 16; will of Thomas, 5 Aug. 1728 (T. N.A., Prob. 11/640, f. 97).

104 Will of Sir Allen, 19 Apr. 1680 (T.N.A., Prob. 11/364, ff 132–3); Owen Manning and William Bray, *The history and antiquities of the county of Surrey* … (3 vols, London, 1804–14), iii, 354; will of Thomas, 5 Aug. 1728 (T.N.A., Prob. 11/640, f. 97); *The registers of the parish of Wandsworth in the county of Surrey (1603–1787)*, trans. J. T. Squire (Lymington, 1889), p. 361; will of St John I, 2 Sept. 1700 (T.N.A., Prob. 11/495, ff 204–5).

Yorkshire, but only to check up on his agent,[105] and did not attempt to extend the estate, whereas the Brodricks did buy in Surrey. Although keeping chambers at the Middle Temple, St John invested in property near Reigate,[106] whilst Alan, as we have seen, acquired Peper Harow in 1713, and conceived of it as a house in which to live rather than a source of rental income; he even talked of retiring there, in preference to Cork.[107]

It is significant, too, that Alan chose to educate his sons in England. Both St John and Alan junior were sent to Eton (possibly an indication of upward mobility since Alan senior and Thomas had been educated in Surrey, at Kingston-upon-Thames) and thence to Cambridge. The reasons were made clear in a letter sent from Dublin to Thomas in 1717 when Alan was pondering what should be done with 'Nally', then coming to the end of his time at school.[108] 'Many here', he wrote,

> would persuade me to place him in this college, and give for reason that now there is a good provost and the education and discipline will not be the same as it was of late. This I own to be very true, but beside other reasons this weighs so with me as not to be capable I think of an answer: whoever proposes to come to anything considerable hereafter must make England the theatre he resolves to appear on: and this is so true that I see little fellows of this country by only spending some of their time there make themselves thought to be men of consequence, while others of real merit fare like our best clergymen and never rise by attending their cures.

The slight sourness of tone suggests ambivalence, and perhaps a tinge of regret that it was necessary to 'make England the theatre … to appear on', though Alan did not waver from the resolve that Nally should find his 'lot' across the water.[109] And so the young man followed his half-brother to Cambridge, where he was expected to collect acquaintances who in adulthood would become influential (as Senny's schoolfellows Townshend and Walpole had become).[110] The next step was to make a career in England, and it can have been no surprise when, later that same year, young St John tentatively asked permission to seek a parliamentary seat at Westminster. 'You must know', Alan informed his brother, 'he thinks getting into an English parliament would be the making of his fortune.' Since this ambition possessed Senny 'almost to madness', there was little point in standing in his way.[111] It took a while, but in 1721 he was returned at a by-election for Bere Alston in Devon.[112] In any case, however nervous he may have been at first of approaching his father, it was hardly likely that either Alan or Thomas would have tried to dissuade him. Although still an Irish M.P., for Midleton, Thomas was firmly settled in England, and spent his money not in Ireland but in attempting to secure his Westminster

105 *Coghill letters*, pp xiii, 56.
106 Will of St John I, 2 Sept. 1700 (T.N.A., Prob. 11/495, ff 204–5).
107 Alan I to Thomas, 12 June, 29 July 1720, 17 Nov. 1724, 12 Dec. 1725 (S.H.C., 1248/4/271–2, 292–3, 1248/6/92–5, 345–6).
108 Same to same, 27 July 1717 (ibid., 1248/4/53–4).
109 Thomas to Alan I, 9 Feb. 1724/5 (ibid., 1248/6/141–2).
110 Alan I to Alan II, 25 Feb. 1717/18 (ibid., 1248/4/114–115).
111 Same to Thomas, 22 Dec. 1717 (ibid., 1248/4/104–5).
112 St John II to Alan I, 16 Apr. 1721 (ibid., 1248/5/19–20).

seat in the notoriously venal borough of Stockbridge.[113] Alan too had succumbed to the lure of St Stephen's Chapel, having already joined his brother there in February 1717, having been chosen at a by-election for Midhurst in Sussex on interest of the duke of Somerset.[114]

This concentration of effort in England was to some extent a new departure, and the reasons were mixed. The family had always taken a genuine interest in the politics of their ancestral county, and the longer Thomas resided at Wandsworth the closer he became to the leading Whig families in Surrey, especially the Onslows of Clandon. The brothers had also been brought up to be acutely aware of the importance of having powerful connexions in England as a passport to political success in Ireland. Their uncle's relationship to the Hydes – and especially the Tory party chieftain Lord Rochester, viceroy of Ireland in 1700–1702 – was something they did not lose sight of even when party political differences stood in the way.[115] They also made their own friends, chiefly through helping to manage the grants King William made to his favourites of forfeited Jacobite estates in Ireland.[116] Later, the integration of the English and Irish party systems in Queen Anne's reign brought politicians in the two kingdoms into even greater proximity, and in the case of Thomas Brodrick drew him into the orbit of the Junto lord, Wharton, lord lieutenant in 1708–10.[117] It was almost a natural progression that Thomas should focus his energies in England when Sir St John's death in 1711 at last gave him untrammelled possession of Wandsworth. So in the Irish and English general elections of 1713 he did not seek re-election for County Cork, and instead obtained the seat in Stockbridge. Although he allowed himself to be chosen again at Midleton in 1715 to maintain the family interest, he had now, to all intents and purposes, abandoned the Dublin parliament.

Alan, on the other hand, did not seek a place at Westminster until pushed to do so by Irish political considerations, and used his voice and vote there in the hopes of repairing his position in Ireland. It soon became clear to him during the Irish parliamentary session of 1715–16 that he would need allies at court and in the ministry if he were to get the better of Conolly. The Speaker had impressed the lords justices, the duke of Grafton and Lord Galway, during the 1715–16 government, and through the two chief secretaries, Martin Bladen and Charles Delafaye, had the ear of the earl of Sunderland, briefly lord lieutenant himself in 1714–15 and now one of the leaders of the Whig ministry in Britain. By contrast, the contacts Alan and Thomas Brodrick had made in the years before 1714, men like Wharton and the other Junto lords, were of little use: either dead, or retired from active politics and supplanted by the rising generation.

113 Thomas to same, 6 Feb. 1719[/20] (ibid., 1248/4/214–15).

114 *H.C. 1715–54*, i, 336.

115 Sir Allen left bequests to Clarendon and Rochester (will, 19 Apr. 1680 (T.N.A., Prob. 11/364, ff 132–3)).

116 'Mr Brodrick's case' (B.L., Portland papers, Add. MS 70306); J. G. Simms, *The Williamite confiscation in Ireland 1690–1703* (London, 1956), pp 54, 127.

117 Sir Richard Cox to Edward Southwell, 26 Apr. 1709 (B.L., Add. 38156, f. 59).

Anxiety to make new friends in high places, or at least force himself on the attention of the mighty, probably accounts for Alan's election at Midhurst in 1717. In the British legislature his voice and vote would count, and in the last resort he could make trouble and give the ministers a more immediate reason to listen to him. But the strategy did not work.[118] He had been hopeful when the duke of Bolton was named as viceroy in 1717 but Bolton, too, seemed to fall under Conolly's spell. So in desperation – or so it was alleged[119] – he began an intrigue with the opposition Whigs, Walpole and Townshend. In the spring of 1719, whether for tactical reasons, or genuinely, out of principle, he rejected requests to support the administration's controversial Peerage Bill, refusing Lord Sunderland to his face,[120] and in the Irish parliamentary session that followed he watched as Senny inspired a cross-party onslaught against Sunderland's pet project for Ireland, the repeal of the sacramental test. Although Alan himself behaved with ostentatious loyalty to government in the heated debates over the assertion by the British House of Lords of their right to hear appeals from Ireland (arising from the case of *Annesley* v. *Sherlock*), this did not improve his position at court, and when the Irish parliamentary session of 1719 came to an end Sunderland determined that he should be dismissed from office. What saved him was not any influence he or his brother could bring to bear as Westminster M.P.s, but the gathering political crisis in both England and Ireland, and the caution urged by Walpole when he and Townshend became reconciled to the ministers. But if the Brodricks thought that they were now safe, and indeed were likely to benefit from the ending of the Whig Schism, they were disappointed. Bolton's replacement in the viceroyalty was none other than Grafton, who may have been a protégé of Walpole and Townshend but was also a good friend of Speaker Conolly. When Grafton came to Dublin Alan found himself once again left out of the viceregal inner cabinet. He then began another intrigue in England, this time with Lord Carteret, and made himself less helpful than he otherwise might have been in the next political storm to break in Dublin, over Wood's Halfpence. Again, Carteret's nomination to succeed Grafton in 1724 might have seemed likely to herald a sunrise in Alan's political fortunes, but there was to be another disappointment. Carteret, aware of the trap Walpole had laid in giving him the task of ending an impasse he had helped to engineer, trod carefully. Having at first tried to navigate between 'the two great men', he was obliged by the Brodricks' intransigence to come down on Conolly's side, and Alan was finally forced out of office.

This chain of events may help to explain the traces of bitterness in the manner in which Alan admitted the necessity of having his younger son educated at Cambridge and propelled towards a career in England, and also the exaggerated apprehension with which Senny sought paternal leave to apply for a seat at Westminster. At various times in his life Alan had expressed his doubts about the value of having

118 For what follows, see Hayton, *Ruling Ireland*, ch. 7.

119 No direct evidence survives in the correspondence, but since the Brodricks believed that the Irish postmaster-general, Isaac Manley, was opening their letters, they may well have decided to avoid any hint of self-incrimination.

120 Alan I to Thomas, 14 Dec. 1719 (William Coxe (ed.), *Memoirs of the life and administration of Sir Robert Walpole* (3 vols, London, 1798), ii, 173–4).

powerful English friends. When Thomas's involvement in the management of Irish forfeited estates threatened to expose the family to damaging criticism in Ireland Alan reminded his brother of previous warnings against too close an involvement with courtiers:[121]

> This with many other things convinces me that I told you right all along that acting an invidious part for great people was not the most prudent course to steer ... I am sure my uncle and father both suffered by it in their fortunes, and found cold returns of their services.

He now had further evidence to support this observation, and may well have spent his closing years ruminating on the truth of it. The tenor of his correspondence after 1725 suggests disillusionment with the English side of his family's Anglo-Irish identity, though the evidence is not conclusive. There was, at any rate a weariness with Westminster,[122] less talk of retiring to Peper Harow, and great effort expended on recording the family's Irish landholdings, as if in acknowledgment of the enduring importance of their power-base in Munster.

There may also have been a broader sense of disillusionment, arising from the way in which Irish governance appeared to be developing under the Hanoverians. Understanding the extent to which Alan Brodrick and his immediate family were Irish 'patriots', in the contemporary sense, is complicated by the demands made on them by political necessity. Shifts in their fortunes resulted in frequent switches of allegiance which in turn required them to go back on previously declared positions: from opposition to court in 1695, back to opposition in 1703–8, to court in 1708–10, opposition again 1710–14, and a kind of fence-straddling in 1714–24, culminating in a return to the political wilderness. In 1695, and again in 1707 and 1709, Alan and Thomas found themselves in difficulties when the governments they wished to serve presented them with the unpalatable task of subverting a constitutional principle they had formerly defended. In 1695 it was the vaunted 'sole right' of the Irish House of Commons to initiate money bills, though here they were saved by an ingenious compromise agreed with Lord Deputy Capell.[123] In 1707, under Pembroke's viceroyalty, it was their previous insistence that supply be granted annually that came back to haunt them, and in 1709 under Lord Wharton, the integrity of money bills produced in Ireland, which was threatened by the actions of the British Privy Council in making an amendment to the Commons' draft.[124] In each case, their enemies charged them with 'trimming' and the cynical abandonment of beliefs in pursuit of office. And after 1714 there would be worse accusations: in

121 Same to same, 28 Dec. 1699 (S.H.C., 1248/1/316–17).

122 Same to same, 14 Jan. 1726/7 (ibid., 1248/7/71–2); Alan I to Alan II, 4 July 1727 (ibid., 1248/7/75–6).

123 C. I. McGrath, *The making of the eighteenth-century Irish constitution: government, parliament and the revenue, 1692–1714* (Dublin, 2000), ch. 3; idem, 'English ministers, Irish politicians and the making of a parliamentary settlement'.

124 McGrath, *Making of the eighteenth-century Irish constitution*, pp 194–232; D. W. Hayton, 'Divisions in the Whig Junto in 1709: some Irish evidence' in *Bulletin of the Institute of Historical Research*, lv (1982), pp 213–21.

the controversy over the Lords' appellate jurisdiction Alan's freedom of manoeuvre was seriously constricted both by his exposed position as Dublin Castle's chief legal officer, and by the delicacy of his political position. Nonetheless, his consistent public advocacy of moderation led to him being stigmatised as a 'betrayer of his country'.[125]

The Brodricks as a family, and Alan in particular, were such combative politicians, and so alert to tactical advantage, that it is tempting to present them as entirely self-interested. But this may be unduly cynical.[126] They were certainly fond of stating principles (even if just as quick to compromise when circumstances required) and the discussion of public events in their correspondence was not always confined within a narrow framework of personal or factional gain. References to nationality in their letters conform to the pattern of others of their class: on the one hand, identification with an 'English Protestant' interest, while referring to Catholics as the 'Irish' and, at least as late as 1712, actively disavowing that notion that they themselves might be 'Irishmen'; on the other, a developing sense of the claims of the Irish 'nation', whatever that phrase might mean, to fair treatment under English government.[127] If a consistent thread may be detected in their thinking, it would seem to be an awareness of the inevitability of the English connexion, and fear that this might be endangered by the more extreme and excitable parliamentarians and authors who 'had the vanity to publish themselves' as 'patriots'.[128] But at the same time, there was a strong identification with Irish interests, most especially economic interests.

Moreover, for an Irish landed family there was much to be concerned about in the drift of English policy after 1714: the downgrading of the jurisdiction of the Irish parliament through the assumption by the British House of Lords of an appellate jurisdiction over Ireland, given brutal expression in the British Declaratory Act of 1720; the maintenance (and pressure for reinforcement) of discriminatory legislation against Irish exports to England and the English plantations overseas; the continued imposition on the Irish taxpayer of the British standing army; and the callous way in which Irish resources were used to pay English political debts (as for example in the dumping of English clergymen onto the Irish episcopal bench). Although he was tactfully quiet on the subject of the Declaratory Act, Thomas Brodrick was induced to intervene in a debate in the British House of Commons in February 1720 on the proposal to remove the drawback on hops exported to Ireland, an initiative he likened (with some exaggeration) to such notorious English measures as the Cattle Act of 1667, the Navigation Acts and the Woollen Act of 1699.[129] Not surprisingly, perhaps, it was the interests of Munster that most concerned the

125 Alan I to Thomas, 7 Feb. 1719[/20], 26 June 1720 (S.H.C., 1248/4/216–17, 285–6); D. W. Hayton, 'The Stanhope/Sunderland ministry and the repudiation of Irish parliamentary independence' in *E.H.R.*, cxiii (1998), p. 626.

126 S. J. Connolly, *Religion, law and power: the making of Protestant Ireland, 1660–1760* (Oxford, 1992), pp 86–91; idem, *Divided kingdom: Ireland 1630–1800* (Oxford, 2008), p. 215.

127 See above, ch. 2, and, for an example of concern for 'the nation' of Ireland, Alan I to Thomas, 17 July 1725 (S.H.C., 1248/6/271–2).

128 Same to same, 7 Feb. 1719[/20] (ibid., 1248/4/216–17).

129 Thomas to Alan I, 6 Feb. 1719[/20] (ibid., 1248/214–15).

family. In this respect the Woollen Act had been particularly provoking, striking at a staple of the provincial economy, and made more offensive by the fact that what was offered in compensation – encouragement for linen manufacture – was, to begin with, primarily of benefit to the north. In 1707 Thomas was being urged by his brother to take up at Westminster the question of protection for the remaining Irish export trade in woollen yarn, to prevent 'the inevitable ruin of the whole province of Munster'.[130] However, a decade later, when progress had been made in introducing linen to the south-west, Alan took a more generous line, conceding that whatever 'brings money into the kingdom, is a benefit to the whole'.[131]

In retrospect, the episode of Wood's Halfpence seems to have been the catalyst for the discovery (or rediscovery) of fervent 'patriotic' feelings. A few years earlier Alan Brodrick had been happy to join the hue and cry after the printer of Swift's *Proposal for the universal use of Irish manufacture* (1720), which at that time he doubtless regarded as irresponsible attention-seeking.[132] But by 1725 the wind had changed. His private letters burned with anger at the way 'the nation hath been treated in the matter of Mr Wood'.[133] The narrative of his behaviour in relation to the patent reveals the usual serpentine twists, dictated by political and personal considerations, as he balanced the necessity of maintaining ministerial confidence with the danger of unpopularity, and kept a close eye on the manoeuvres of his rivals. He also seems to have rewritten history after the event, asserting in letters to Thomas that what had cost him office was the 'mortal ... sin' of opposition to the halfpence.[134] Clearly the loss of the lord chancellorship had a radicalising effect, and this became even more pronounced as time went by. In 1727 he praised the honesty of St John's conduct in the Irish House of Commons in opposing 'the vile schemes ... to beggar the kingdom by Wood's money, and swelling the national debt'.[135] But before we assume that personal or family grievance was all that lay behind this change of tone, it is worth remembering the wider context, and in particular the sense of impending economic disaster that was enveloping Ireland in the late 1720s, with a succession of poor harvests, and evidence of actual starvation in the countryside. From Alan's correspondence we can glimpse his anxiety about the 'languishing condition' of the kingdom, which affected landed gentry as well as the ordinary people in its impact on the return of rents, a point that of course did not escape him.[136]

V

The Brodrick family may regarded as classically Anglo-Irish, in that they were an English family who had made their fortune in Ireland but retained strong links to England. Ancestral ties were reinforced by upbringing and education, and in several

130 Alan I to Thomas, 8 Feb. 1707 (ibid., 1248/2/254–5).
131 Same to same, 11 Dec. 1719 (ibid., 1248/4/182–3).
132 Irvin Ehrenpreis, *Swift: the man, his works, and the age* (3 vols, London, 1962–83), iii, 268.
133 Alan I to Thomas, 17 July 1725 (S.H.C., 1248/6/271–2).
134 Same to same, 3 Apr., 4 July 1725 (ibid., 1248/6/193–4, 259–66).
135 Same to same, 27 July 1727 (ibid., 1248/7/102–103).
136 Same to same, 30 Apr., 2, 18 May 1728 (ibid., 1248/7/ 231–6, 243–4)

instances by engagement in the legal profession, which demanded attendance at an English inn of court and introduced a broader range of English acquaintance. After c. 1680, and certainly after the revolution, successive generations of Brodricks spent most of their time away from County Cork. Sir St John's ill-fated spell at Cahermone in the period c. 1698–1701 was unusual, and his grandson's occupation of Ballyannan in the 1720s broke a long period of absence. At first Alan and Thomas had located themselves in the political world of Dublin, while their brother St John was in London, William in Jamaica and Lawrence in Oxfordshire. Ballyannan was sadly neglected. Thomas eventually returned to England on a permanent basis, and even Alan briefly considered retiring to the Surrey countryside. Yet the attractions of London life, and the allure of Newmarket, seem ultimately to have palled. Neither Thomas nor the younger St John made the impact at Westminster which had been hoped,[137] and Alan grew bitter in old age at the failure of his political career until he could hardly be bothered to seek re-election for Midhurst in 1727. In terms of landownership and electoral influence, the province of Munster had always provided the resources on which their public careers had been founded, and Alan's response to finding himself out of office in 1725 seems to have been to focus his attention back on the family's operations in County Cork.

To return to the contrast with which this essay began, between Ballyannan and Castletown, and between William Conolly and Alan Brodrick. By 1728, when Conolly had outlasted his great rival, it might be argued that he represented the future as far as Irish politics was concerned. Conolly was a social climber who had made his fortune at the expense of longer-established families who had fallen on hard times and had to sell off their estates. His rise to power had been accomplished through concentrating his efforts on the parliament and bureaucracy in Dublin rather than looking for a seat at Westminster and making alliances with English political families. As we shall see in a later chapter, the kind of 'patriotism' espoused by those who made up his immediate circle was 'constructive' rather than rhetorical. He and his friends lavished time and money on their houses and estates, which became political statements in themselves. By contrast, the Brodricks, as absentee rentiers, orientated primarily towards England, seemed to belong to a different age. What happened to the family interest after the deaths of Alan and Senny was a further reminder of the new realities of Anglo-Irish politics. While the second Viscount Midleton was content to live in English obscurity, his father's mantle as an Irish political leader passed to Henry Boyle, a cadet of the great planter family of the first earl of Cork. Boyle had been a loyal follower of Alan Brodrick,[138] and one of Senny's closest parliamentary colleagues.[139] Although he had also enjoyed (or suffered) an English education (at Westminster School and Oxford University) he did not take up the law and instead cultivated the character of a plain country gentleman. Combining the residual influence of the Brodricks in County Cork with

137 Thomas to Jane Bonnell, 'Sunday morning' (N.L.I., MS 41,580/2).

138 Alan I to Thomas, 20 Apr. 1713 (S.H.C., 1248/3/111–112); B.L., Add.MS 46966, ff 164–7; Sir Richard Cox to Edward Southwell, 24 Mar. 1713–14 (B.L., Add. MS 38157, f. 77); St John II to Henry Boyle, 16 Nov. 1714 (P.R.O.N.I., Shannon papers, D/2707/A/1/2/5).

139 St John II to Alan I, 23 May 1724 (S.H.C., 1248/6/27–8)

the more extensive electoral patronage of several absentee magnates from his own extended family – the earls of Burlington, Orrery and Shannon – he built up a local interest that came to surpass that of his first patron, and equipped him to succeed to the Commons Speakership in 1733 and become recognised as Dublin Castle's principal 'undertaker'. This in turn enabled him to ascend to the peerage in due course as earl of Shannon of the second creation.[140] Like the Brodricks, Boyle depended on a regional power-base, and he had learned from them how it was to be managed, but he must also have learned from watching William Conolly, and remained firmly rooted in his Irish and in his provincial environment.

140 For Boyle see *Oxf. D.N.B.*, vii, 79–81; *D.I.B.*, i, 718–20; *Hist. Ir. parl.*, iii, 241–6; Eoin Magennis, *The Irish political system, 1740–1765: the golden age of the undertakers* (Dublin, 2000), pp 23–9.

5

'Commonwealthman', unionist and king's servant

Henry Maxwell and the Whig imperative*

Henry Maxwell, squire of Finnebrogue, County Down, who successively represented three Ulster boroughs – Bangor, Killybegs and Donegal town – in the Irish House of Commons from 1698 until his death in 1730 (from the effects of an 'apoplectic fit'[1]), has attracted rather more scholarly attention than is usual for an early eighteenth-century Irish M.P. This is not because of his importance in the Irish parliament, or in Irish politics generally, though he was by no means an insignificant figure, but because of his political writing, and in particular the pamphlet published anonymously in 1703 arguing the merits of an incorporating Anglo-Irish union, *An essay towards an union of Ireland with England*.[2] This is a rare example of early eighteenth-century unionism, though by no means a straightforward statement of principle. As we shall see, Maxwell's intention in the pamphlet is susceptible to more than one interpretation; and it is equally impossible to construct a clear and unequivocal statement of unionist principles from his other published writings, or his speeches and votes in the House of Commons. If anything, his career illustrates the complexity of politics in early eighteenth-century Ireland, situated, as he was, within a matrix of sometimes conflicting influences. Most obviously, although he was undoubtedly a Whig, his family background within the established church in east Ulster disposed him to take a sour view of Presbyterian ambitions, and induced him to side with Tories in support of the maintenance of the sacramental test. But in addition his friendships and connexions with very different kinds of Whig politicians, in Ireland and in England, exposed him to a range of diverse and sometimes contradictory opinions on constitutional issues.

* Modified from 'Henry Maxwell, author of *An essay towards an union of Ireland with England* (1703)' in *Eighteenth-Century Ireland*, xxii (2007), pp 28–63.

1 Francis Burton to Jane Bonnell, 14 Feb. 1729/30 (N.L.I., Smythe of Barbavilla papers, MS 41,579/10).

2 For instance, Caroline Robbins, *The eighteenth-century commonwealthman* (Cambridge, Mass., 1959), ch. 5; Jim Smyth, 'Anglo-Irish discourse, c. 1656–1707: from Harrington to Fletcher' in *Bullán*, ii (1995), pp 17–34; idem, '"No remedy more proper": Anglo-Irish unionism before 1707' in Brendan Bradshaw and Peter Roberts (eds), *British consciousness and identity: the making of Britain 1533–1707* (Cambridge, 1998), pp 315–18; D. W. Hayton, 'Ideas of union in Anglo-Irish political discourse, 1692–1720: meaning and use' in D. George Boyce, Robert Eccleshall and Vincent Geoghegan (eds), *Political discourse in seventeenth- and eighteenth-century Ireland* (Basingstoke, 2001), pp 142–68. See also *D.I.B.*, vi, 442–4.

I

Maxwell was born in 1669 into a clerical family, the only (or only surviving) son of Robert Maxwell, dean of Armagh, and his Scottish wife Isabella.[3] Having entered Trinity College, Dublin, in 1683, he took his bachelor's degree in 1688, an unusual attainment for a young gentleman with a landed inheritance before him, and possibly an indication that he was intended for a profession, either the church or the law. At any rate he entered the Middle Temple in 1693, after surviving the traumas of the Williamite revolution, but by this time could have had few thoughts of a legal career since he left without being called to the bar.[4] While in London he seems to have made contact with a group of English Whigs attached to the third earl of Shaftesbury, philosopher-grandson of the founder of the English Whig party. In their regard for libertarian principles, Shaftesbury and his friends saw themselves as 'real' or 'true' Whigs; historians have labelled them 'Country Whigs'. They included pamphleteers and political commentators, like the members of the so-called 'Grecian Tavern' circle, who in the 1690s sat at the feet of the veteran republican Henry Neville, and organised the press campaign against the standing army; and also back-bench members of the Whig party in the English House of Commons, who on occasion broke with the rest of their party and voted for reforming measures such as place bills. Also operating in this 'Country Whig' milieu were Maxwell's fellow countrymen Robert Molesworth and John Toland, both of whom have been identified, in Caroline Robbins's pioneering study of the transmission of civic republican theory from civil war England to revolutionary America, as belonging to a distinct group of Irish 'commonwealthmen'. Robbins included Maxwell in this circle, though without supporting evidence beyond his authorship of several pamphlets, including the *Essay*.

Henry Maxwell's principal connexion with the Shaftesbury circle was the young army officer James Stanhope, with whom he corresponded after his return to Dublin.[5] In later years Stanhope would become secretary of state and chief minister to George I but in his political youth he was an enthusiastic 'Country Whig', a supporter of 'place' legislation at Westminster, for example, even when his party leaders, the so-called Whig Junto, disapproved.[6] Maxwell remained on close terms with him

3 For what follows, see also *Hist. Ir. parl.*, v, 222–3. As the author notes, the Blackwood pedigrees (P.R.O.N.I., MIC/315/8/43) give his mother's identity as Jane, daughter of Robert Chichester.

4 He wrote later, in a pamphlet of 1721, 'As for law terms, I will studiously avoid them, as being little acquainted with them myself, as I presume will be most of my readers' (Henry Maxwell, *Reasons offer'd for erecting a bank in Ireland; in a letter to Hercules Rowley, esq* (1st ed., Dublin, 1721), pp 5–6.

5 Maxwell to Stanhope, 23 Nov. 1703, 25 Mar. 1705, 24 Feb. 1709/10, 6 Dec. 1713 [*recte* Jan. 1714] (Centre for Kentish Studies, Stanhope papers, U1590/O141/11, printed in *Eighteenth-Cent. Ire.*, xxii 2007), pp 50–63).

6 [Stanhope] to [Sir John Cropley], 17, 24 Feb. 1705/6 (T.N.A., Shaftesbury papers, PRO 30/24/20/112, 113); Cropley to Stanhope, 19 Feb. 1705/6, 26 Mar. 1706 (Centre for Kentish Studies, U1590/C9/31). Robert Molesworth was also a member of Shaftesbury's circle: *H.C. 1690–1715*, iv, 832–3; *Letters from ... the late earl of Shaftesbury to Robert Molesworth ...* [, ed. John Toland] (London, 1721).

until at least 1714, the date of the last surviving letter from Maxwell in Stanhope's private papers. A mutual friend also mentioned in the correspondence was Sir George Markham, a Lincolnshire baronet of a refined and scholarly disposition (and a non-practising barrister of the Middle Temple), who was also associated with Shaftesbury (and Robert Molesworth), through the 'new Junta for architecture'.[7] Even more intriguingly, he was at least an occasional visitor in the late 1690s to the Grecian Tavern, where we know he supped with 'commonwealthmen' such as Toland and John Trenchard,[8] and, it is tempting to speculate, might have encountered Maxwell too.

Maxwell's first appearance in Irish politics came at a by-election in 1698 for Bangor, County Down, at which he was returned on his family's interest. This by-election was the second in quick succession for the borough. The Tory and former Speaker Sir Richard Levinge had previously been chosen, but Bangor was no more than an insurance policy for him; he had also been chosen for Longford, for which he opted to sit. The second writ for Bangor was issued on 20 October and nine days later Maxwell took his seat in the chamber, a rapid sequence of events that suggests an unopposed return.[9] Within a fortnight he was named along with Alderman Edward Singleton of Drogheda to bring in 'heads of a bill' (a draft prepared in the Irish parliament for submission to the Irish and English privy councils, in accordance with Poynings' Law) to regulate the butchery trade.[10] Maxwell introduced the heads on 19 November, and although Singleton chaired the committee to which they were referred, both men were subsequently ordered to carry the successful heads to the lord lieutenant and it was Maxwell who reported back to the House on the success of their errand.[11] Maxwell was included on three other committees in this session, suggesting precocity. One, to prepare heads of a bill to create a paper office in Ireland, involved other M.P.s from Ulster, including two men with whom he would be associated in later years, Samuel Dopping (also the son of a clergyman), who sat for Armagh, and Edmund Francis Stafford, from Staffordstown, County Antrim.[12]

Having made a modest impact in his first session, Maxwell had to wait four years before he was in a position to develop his parliamentary career. The crises over the English Woollen and Forfeitures Resumption Acts deterred the ministry from calling another Irish parliament until 1703. Unfortunately we know nothing of Maxwell's reaction to the turmoil that followed the passage of these acts. It seems highly probable, given his later political connexions, and some observations in his published writings, that he was sympathetic to the campaign of county addresses in 1701, the so-called 'national remonstrance' against the forfeitures resumption,

7 *H.C. 1690–1715*, iv, 759–60; Edward McParland, 'Edward Lovett Pearce and the new junta for architecture', in Toby Barnard and Jane Clark (eds), *Lord Burlington: architecture, art and life* (London, 1995), pp 151–65.

8 James Brydges's diary, 12 Feb. 1698 (Huntington Library, Stowe MS 26/1).

9 *C.J.Ire.* (2nd ed.), ii, 783, 797, 807.

10 Ibid., 826. Years later Singleton's son, Henry, would be Maxwell's colleague in the parliamentary faction headed by Speaker William Conolly.

11 Ibid., 826, 834, 842, 844.

12 Ibid., 834, 859, 865.

but no address from County Down has come to light. Once parliament resumed, however, he quickly provided evidence of his partisan loyalties.

Re-elected for Bangor in 1703, again without opposition so far as we can tell, he was nominated to several committees on private legislation and petitions – which if nothing else indicates regular attendance – and piloted through the Commons a bill designed to provide for a general naturalisation of 'Protestant strangers', and to encourage the immigration of Huguenots and other Protestant refugees.[13] At first glance such a measure may not seem to have party-political overtones, but ever since 1692 the recruitment of the Protestant interest had been a priority for those in the Irish parliament who called themselves Whigs; indeed, a bill 'for the encouragement of Protestant strangers' was attempted in 1697 by the archetypal Irish 'commonwealthman' or 'Country' Whig, Robert Molesworth.[14] Along similar lines was Maxwell's support for the Commons general 'representation' of economic and constitutional grievances – including the forfeitures resumption – which blamed Ireland's economic ills on the failure to summon frequent parliaments, and called for either the restoration of 'a full enjoyment of our constitution' or a union with England.[15] This was the work of associates of the Speaker, Alan Brodrick, the leader of the Irish Whigs, and the committee that prepared the text was chaired by Molesworth.[16] According to Brodrick, it was Maxwell who made the motion to print the representation, which divided the House on party lines. He was followed in the debate by, among others, William Conolly and Samuel Dopping.[17]

But Maxwell's Whiggism, in the classical, or at least in the English, sense of the term, had its limits. English Whigs were (and had always been) resolute defenders of the civil rights of Protestant Dissenters, partly from libertarian motives and partly from the perceived necessity to unite the Protestant communities against the threat of 'popery', as represented by the Jacobite Pretender and the French king. These sentiments were far from being universal among Irish Whigs. Whereas the English Whig party always contained a strong Dissenting element, Irish Whiggery was distinctively Anglican. Moreover, in Ireland Protestant Dissent meant chiefly Presbyterianism, and the concentration of Scottish Presbyterians in Ulster presented a different aspect to the diverse and geographically dispersed communities of English Nonconformists.

Maxwell's views were made clear in a debate in October 1703 in the committee of supply, when the 'Country' opposition to which he belonged launched an attack on the pension list in the civil establishment, with a view to pruning the more objectionable cases – English absentees, political opponents and the like. Maxwell spoke early in the debate in favour of 'going to particulars in order to take off the charge'.[18]

13 Ibid., iii, 31, 37, 46, 101, 196.
14 *H.C. 1690–1715*, iv, 830.
15 *C.J.Ire.* (2nd ed.), iii, 65–7.
16 Edward Southwell to earl of Nottingham, 30 Sept., 23 Oct. 1703 (N.L.I., MS 991, pp 135–8, 154–6); same to same, 9, 15, 23, 25 Oct. 1703 (*C.S.P., dom.*, 1703–4, pp 149–50, 156, 170, 174).
17 Alan to Thomas Brodrick, 11 Feb. 1703/4 (S.H.C., Brodrick papers, 1248/2/123–4).
18 D. W. Hayton, 'A debate in the Irish House of Commons in 1703: a whiff of Tory grapeshot' in *Parliamentary History*, x (1991), p. 159.

The Court party, supporting the Tory lord lieutenant, Ormond, then turned the tables on the Whigs and picked out for particular condemnation the *regium donum*, the pension of £1,200 a year paid to the General Synod of Ulster for distribution to Presbyterian ministers. This initiative raised a storm of invective from both Tories and Whigs, directed against Presbyterians. Maxwell, who declared himself 'alway[s] a churchman', gave it as his opinion that 'Dissenters ought to be content with not being persecuted'; it was 'not prudent to give them encouragem[en]t'.[19] Other 'Country' stalwarts followed suit, notably the two Armagh M.P.s, Samuel Dopping and Marmaduke Coghill, both of whom, like Maxwell, had ecclesiastical connexions. Indeed, in notes of the debate kept by Speaker Brodrick, few if any Whigs were recorded as speaking in favour of the *regium donum*, except perhaps William Conolly (though the words attributed to him are ambiguous).[20]

The picture that emerges of Maxwell's political attitudes at this early stage in his parliamentary career suggests three main elements: a commitment to the Whig cause, in so far as this meant preserving a strong Protestant interest in Ireland; the outlook of a 'Country' oppositionist, comprising concern for parliamentary liberties, the economic well-being of Ireland, and a belief in the necessity (and extreme unlikelihood) of uncorrupt government; and the prejudices of an Irish Anglican, particularly against the Presbyterians of his native Ulster. All three elements were clearly visible in succeeding sessions of parliament, as his prominence in the Commons increased further (if we may judge by the number of times his name appears in the *Journals* and in accounts of debates).[21]

First, his Whig allegiance. Letters from Alan Brodrick during the following session, in 1705, show Maxwell once more acting with the Whig opposition to Ormond's government, over the supply and against the release from custody of the disgraced vice-treasurer Sir William Robinson.[22] In a parliamentary list compiled in 1706 he was placed among the opposition.[23] In the 1707 session, after Ormond's replacement by the moderate Lord Pembroke, he participated in a partisan initiative led by Alan Brodrick and William Conolly to embarrass Tories on the Irish privy council.[24] Then in 1709 he moved with the rest of his party to support the Whig viceroy, Wharton, being listed among those who voted for the returned money bill despite alterations made by the British privy council, a litmus test of support for Wharton's administration.[25] He was also named to two politically significant committees to prepare addresses of thanks: to the Queen for a monetary donation to finance the ministry's

19 Ibid., p. 161.

20 Ibid.

21 In 1705 Maxwell was named to nine select committees and reported from one of them; in 1707 he was named to twenty-one, reporting from three: *C.J.Ire.* (2nd ed.), iii, 229, 240, 251, 304, 311, 321, 327–8, 344, 345, 365, 366–7, 371, 374, 378, 384–5, 388, 414, 418, 419, 420, 431,449, 450, 454, 455, 464, 465, 495, 509, 511, 518.

22 Alan to St John Brodrick, 24 Mar 1704/5, 7 June 1705 (S.H.C., 1248/2/183–4, 207–8).

23 'A list of the present House of Commons in Ireland, 1706' (B.L., Southwell papers, Add. MS 9715, ff 150–1).

24 *C.J.Ire.* (2nd ed.), iii, 543.

25 'Dublin [12] Augt. 1709, list of those who spoke pro and con in the money bill' (B.L., Add. MS 34777, f. 67).

scheme for assisting Palatine immigration into Ireland; and to the viceroy for the benefits his administration had supposedly brought to the country.[26]

Second, there was Maxwell's adherence to Whig constitutional principles. In 1705 he moved for a bill to regulate the qualification of M.P.s (presumably along the lines of the landed qualification bills introduced by English 'Country party' activists);[27] and in 1707 he went further than his Whig colleagues in denouncing the Irish privy council for interfering with the 'heads' that parliament had prepared for transmission to England, attempting unsuccessfully to bring in a motion that Speaker Brodrick, for one, found too extreme.[28]

Finally, Maxwell's objections to the extension of legislative privilege to Presbyterians were rehearsed once more during the 1707 session when Pembroke half-heartedly sought a repeal of the sacramental test clause in the 1704 Popery Act and Maxwell was one of several Ulster Whigs who expressed abhorrence of the proposal.[29] Potentially the most significant point about this episode is the identity of the two 'Country' or Whig Members cited as having joined him in denouncing Presbyterian claims: Samuel Dopping and Edmund Francis Stafford. They have already been encountered in Maxwell's company, and their co-operation on this occasion may have meant more than simply a shared aversion to repeal.[30]

Dopping is the more interesting of the two. He again appeared alongside Maxwell later in the 1707 session, speaking in favour of a privilege bill, together with some other prominent Whigs, including the lawyer and future judge William Whitshed. A contemporary account of this debate noted that the issue was 'not a party business', with Speaker Brodrick joining Tories in opposition to the bill, but made an intriguing reference to Whitshed and his 'new friends'.[31] Both Dopping and Whitshed were noted at this time as M.P.s who had previously voted with the Whigs but were now 'beginning to differ from them very often'; in Dopping's case explicitly on a point of principle – as he saw it, Brodrick's betrayal of conscience in abandoning a former insistence on annual supply bills.[32] It is tempting to place Maxwell in this group; certainly the surviving evidence of his parliamentary connexions points in

26 *C.J.Ire.* (2nd ed.), iii, 685, 689.

27 Alan to St John Brodrick, 6 Mar. 1704/5 (S.H.C., 1248/2/176–7).

28 Richard Stewart to [Edward Southwell], 18 Nov. 1707 (B.L., Southwell papers, Add. MS 9712, ff 82–4); account of parliamentary proceedings, 25 Nov. 1707 (ibid., Add. MS 9715, f. 229).

29 Anderson Saunders to Edward Southwell, 10 July 1707 (Leicestershire, Leicester and Rutland Record Office, Finch papers, box 4950, bdle 22). Maxwell's loyalty to the church did not extend to defending the High Church party in convocation; indeed, he supported moves in 1705 to censure the lower house of the Irish convocation for trespassing on parliamentary privilege, although, as Alan Brodrick noted, at one point he and some other M.P.s wavered sufficiently to suggest offering the convocation more time to make its apology – possibly in response to a Tory stratagem of raising the issue of Presbyterian demands for repeal of the test (Alan to St John Brodrick, 14 Mar. 1704/5 (S.H.C., 1248/2/180–2)).

30 Stafford was a trustee of the marriage settlement in 1713 between Maxwell and his second wife, Dorothy Brice: draft of marriage settlement (P.R.O.N.I., Perceval-Maxwell papers, D/1556/16/3/1).

31 Account of proceedings in the Irish House of Commons, 21 Oct. 1707 (B.L., Add. MS 9715, f. 208).

32 Robert Johnson to Ormond, 14 Oct. 1707 (H.M.C., *Ormonde MSS*, n.s. viii, 312); Robert to [Hugh Howard], 18 Sept. 1707 (N.L.I., Wicklow papers, MS 38,597/24); C. I. McGrath, *The*

that direction. He may have continued in the same company at the start of the following session, when Dopping was said to be at the head of a 'flying party', as Chief Secretary Addison put it, probably thinking of the so-called 'Country' or 'whimsical' Whigs at Westminster: 'a set of Members that ... seem ambitious of copying after gentlemen in the English House of Commons with regard to freedom and independence from all parties'.[33] If so, Maxwell's vote in favour of the money bill in August 1709, after it had been amended by the British Privy Council, would have marked a break with these 'Country' Members, since Dopping, for one, voted against the altered bill.

Another hint of Maxwell's devotion to principle over party faction comes from the sobriquet that seems to have been applied to him quite early on in his Commons career. In a mock library list, circulated in April 1704, he was lampooned as a quixotic figure: 'The renowned actions of the knight of the sorrowful face. By Mr Maxwell.'[34] Nearly a decade later, Lord Abercorn called him 'our Don Dismallo, or the knight of the sorrowful countenance'.[35] This could of course be a reference to a saturnine appearance, or a haughty or gloomy manner, or all three, and the young Cork baronet Sir John Perceval, for one, explained it as deriving from the fact that Maxwell was 'so ugly'.[36] But it is just possible that it may also have referred to a penchant for tilting at constitutional windmills, a kind of absurd, patriotic chivalry.[37]

At some point, however, perhaps in 1709 or 1710, the trajectory of Maxwell's political career shifted. He did not abandon his party principles, but seems to have placed more emphasis on the importance of keeping government in safe Whig hands than in pursuing constitutional notions, and thus became more reliable in managerial terms. In particular he seems to have attached himself firmly to the faction headed by William Conolly, the formidable *arriviste* who after the Hanoverian succession would occupy the chair of the Irish House of Commons from 1715 until shortly before his death in 1729. Conolly, as Speaker and *de facto* first commissioner of the Irish revenue board, became the leading court 'undertaker' in Parliament. Moreover, in public at least, he was sympathetic to the repeal of the sacramental test.[38] When young, Maxwell might well have found difficulty in accommodating himself to these political attitudes. Yet after 1715 he was to become such a close follower of Conolly that he could be derided by political enemies as 'the Speaker's echo'.[39]

making of the eighteenth-century Irish constitution: government, parliament and the revenue, 1692–1714 (Dublin, 2000), pp 198–209.

33 Addison to Ld Somers, 12 Aug. 1709 (*The letters of Joseph Addison*, ed. Walter Graham (Oxford, 1941) p. 177); same to earl of Godolphin, 21 May 1709 (ibid., p. 169); Geoffrey Holmes, *British politics in the age of Anne* (London, 1967), pp 221–3, 340–1.

34 Alan to Thomas Brodrick, 15 Apr. 1704 (S.H.C., 1248/2/132–3).

35 Abercorn to [Edward Southwell], 5 Jan. 1713/14 (P.R.O.N.I., Abercorn papers, D/623/A/3/12).

36 'An Irish parliamentary diary from the reign of Queen Anne', ed. D. W. Hayton, in *Analecta Hibernica*, no. 30 (1982), p. 139.

37 The 1704 lampoon may have been known to Swift, who applied the same nickname to Lord Nottingham – 'Dismal' – perhaps for similar reasons.

38 D. W. Hayton, *Ruling Ireland, 1685–1742: politics, politicians and parties* (Woodbridge, 2004), p. 197.

39 Ld Brodrick to Thomas Brodrick, 10 June 1716 (S.H.C., 1248 /3/386–7). It is worth noting, however, that, unlike some other political lieutenants of the Speaker (Marmaduke Coghill, Thomas

The association is not easy to explain, and the answer may well lie in a better understanding of Conolly's personality, rather than Maxwell's. It is not even possible to chart the chronology exactly. It may be that the two men had always been friends: as early as 1703 Maxwell had asked Stanhope to intercede on Conolly's behalf should a complaint be made against his friend in the English parliament arising from dealings over Irish forfeited estates.[40] Later, Conolly had been responsible for Maxwell's election to Parliament in 1713, for the pocket borough of Killybegs, and in the following winter Maxwell had spent some time as Conolly's house-guest at Castletown, his estate in County Kildare.[41] However, there seems still to have been a little distance between them, for in August 1714 Maxwell, uncertain as to where he could find a seat in George I's first House of Commons, wrote to Archbishop King of Dublin to intercede with Conolly for the continuance of his favour.[42] Eventually he was returned for Donegal, another of Conolly's boroughs, but not before he had received a rebuke for an action that Conolly interpreted as a slight. Evidently Maxwell had first canvassed unsuccessfully in his own county, and when he did eventually ask for Conolly's help found himself upbraided for not having done so from the first.[43]

Maxwell's behaviour in the Irish House of Commons offers other clues. As we have seen, it was in the middle of the 1709 session that he seems to have broken with Dopping's 'flying squadron', in voting for the amended money bill. His appearances in the *Journals* also tail off half-way through this session, after he had played a significant part, alongside two High Church Tories, John Cliffe and Abel Ram, in promoting a bill 'for the more effectual instructing Irish papists in English, and in the principles of the Church of Ireland'.[44] He is not mentioned at all in the proceedings of the 1711 session, which could well mean that he did not attend, but was back for the short-lived parliament of November–December 1713. Oddly, his name was absent from the division lists over the Speakership and the politically contentious chairmanship of the committee of privileges and elections.[45] In fact, he had been present almost from the first day of the session, speaking consistently on the opposition side, subsequently served on a number of committees, and acted as a teller on the Whig side in a division on the nomination of a Commons chaplain.[46] Perhaps most important, he was named to the committee of 18 December to draft an address for the removal of the Tory lord chancellor, Sir Constantine Phipps, a committee

Marlay and Thomas Trotter), Maxwell received no bequest, however small, in his patron's will (T.N.A., Prob. 11/636, ff 90–92). This was a (lack of) distinction shared with, among others, Sir Ralph Gore and Henry Singleton, and presumably marks a border between personal and political friendship.

40 Maxwell to Stanhope, 23 Nov. 1703 (*Eighteenth-Cent. Ire.*, xxii (2007), pp 51–3).

41 Thomas Knox to Alexander Murray, 28 Apr.1711 (P.R.O.N.I., Murray of Broughton papers, D/2860/4/21); same to Conolly, 16, 22 Nov. 1713 (ibid., Castletown papers, T/2825/C/5/19–20); Maxwell to Stanhope, 6 Dec. [1714] (*Eighteenth-Cent. Ire.*, xxii (2007), pp 58–63).

42 Maxwell to King, 14 Aug. 1714 (T.C.D., Lyons (King) collection, MS 1995–2008/1505).

43 Conolly to [Maxwell], 11 Oct. 1715 (P.R.O.N.I., D/1556/16/4/2).

44 *C.J.Ire.* (2nd ed.), iii, 716, 740, 751.

45 B.L., Add. MS 34777, ff 90–91.

46 'Irish parl. diary from reign of Anne', ed. Hayton, p. 126; *C.J.Ire.* (2nd ed.), iii, 949.

whose chairman was Conolly.[47] And Maxwell was included among the opposition leaders summoned by the viceroy to Dublin Castle after the adjournment in January 1714 in a vain attempt to secure agreement on a compromise that would have facilitated the recall of parliament.[48]

II

When George I's Irish parliament met, in November 1715, party distinctions were complicated by the appearance of separate factions organised around personalities, and it was soon apparent that Maxwell was a faithful adherent of the new Speaker, William Conolly. The 1715 election had resulted in so great a Whig majority in the Commons that Whig politicians seeking personal advantage were no longer inhibited by concern for the security of their party. The 'Court' grouping under Conolly's leadership found itself opposed by an alliance of unreconstructed Tories and malcontent Whigs headed by St John Brodrick, son of the former Speaker Alan, who himself had been raised to the peerage (as Baron Brodrick) and made lord chancellor. Until his eventual resignation in 1725 Alan Brodrick sought to present himself as a loyal minister of the crown, and his son as wilful and disobedient, but in practice the Brodrick family and their dependants worked together to try and undermine Conolly's position. For the next decade Irish parliamentary politics resolved into a struggle for power between chancellor and Speaker. Though Maxwell does not figure in Conolly's own letters he is named in the correspondence of the Brodrick family as one of the Speaker's principal lieutenants,[49] alongside Sir Ralph Gore, Isaac Manley, Thomas Marlay and former Tories like Marmaduke Coghill, Henry Singleton, Thomas Trotter and Agmondisham Vesey, who also felt able to give their loyalty to Conolly despite differences on the Presbyterian issue.[50]

Maxwell was now an extremely prominent M.P., figuring very frequently in the record of Commons proceedings. In the 1715/16 session he served on the committee of accounts, and on nearly twenty select committees, including three to draft heads of bills.[51] As a staunch Whig, he played a full part in the pursuit of the previous Tory administration. He chaired the committee of the whole house on the state of the nation, which investigated allegations of the abuse of power by Lord Chancellor Phipps, and was also named to committees dealing with complaints from urban corporations at interference by the privy council in local elections.[52] One action that was out of kilter with his previous parliamentary record was his appointment on

47 *C.J.Ire.* (2nd ed.), iii, 993. Maxwell was said to have made an earlier motion for a parliamentary censure against Phipps, on 10 Dec., which failed (Joshua Dawson to Edward Southwell, 15 Dec. 1713 (B.L., Southwell papers, Add. MS 60583)).

48 Abercorn to [Edward Southwell], 5 Jan. 1713/14 (P.R.O.N.I., D/623/A/3/12); Alan to Thomas Brodrick, 5 Jan. 1714 (S.H.C., 1248/3/151–2).

49 Ld Brodrick to Thomas Brodrick, 5 Apr. 1716 (S.H.C., 1248/3/352–5); and below, p. 128.

50 See below, pp 128–9.

51 *C.J.Ire.* (2nd ed.), iv, 15, 18, 19, 28, 29, 33, 38, 68, 118, 121, 133, 162, 226, 229, 232, 235, 236, 243, 249, 253, 263, 271, 273.

52 Ibid., 39, 41, 45, 61, 162, 226, 229, 243.

17 December 1715, together with Sir Gustavus Hume, to draw up heads of a bill to exempt from the penalties of the law those Protestant Dissenters who had served in the militia while unqualified.[53] This was certainly a modification of the hard line he had previously taken over the test, but may be partly explained by his attachment to Conolly, who himself favoured legislative relief to Dissenters, and was in this respect doing the bidding of the English ministry.[54] It may also derive from the fact that Maxwell's prime concern at this time was the threat from popery, which demanded measures to unite the Protestant interest against possible Jacobite invasion. After all, the bill was a minimal concession and did retain the test intact.[55]

Maxwell was a little less busy in the 1717 session, omitted from the major standing committees appointed at the outset, and serving on only a dozen select committees, none of them drafting committees for heads of bills.[56] In the following session, in 1719, his name does not occur at all in the *Journals*, which presumably indicates non-attendance. Ill-health would be one explanation; another might be an unwillingness to become involved in what promised to be a full-scale battle over another government proposal to repeal the test, which the Brodrick faction united with surviving Tories to frustrate. Maxwell was a significant absentee from the gathering of privy councillors and Commons managers summoned to Dublin Castle by the viceroy before the session 'to sound their sense how far they would go in favour of the Dissenters'.[57] Whether or not he chose discretion, or was genuinely indisposed, he escaped potential embarrassment as someone who had repeatedly put himself on record as condemning repeal.

After the failure of its repeal scheme, the Stanhope-Sunderland administration in England at first decided on a drastic solution to what they saw as the problem of managing the Irish Parliament, by removing Brodrick, now Lord Midleton, from the lord chancellorship. They were thwarted, however, by an alteration in the balance of power in English politics, which forced a reunion between the two principal Whig groupings – the followers of Stanhope and Sunderland, and the opposition faction headed by Walpole and Townshend. One result of this rapprochement was that the Brodricks secured some protection, at least in the short term. Whether Conolly or Midleton would gain the upper hand now depended on a trial of strength between the two men and their friends in the Irish parliament.

53 Ibid., 133. See S. J. Connolly, *Religion, law and power: the making of Protestant Ireland, 1660–1760* (Oxford, 1992), p. 165.

54 See Hayton, *Ruling Ireland*, pp 225–6; Bp Synge to [Abp Wake], 14 Feb. 1715[/16] (Christ Church, Arch W. Epist. xii).

55 One might interpret Maxwell's continued support for the encouragement of Protestant immigration after 1715 (for which see below, pp 120–21) as further evidence that he had modified his previous position, given that by the middle of Anne's reign the propensity of Huguenot and Palatine refugees to maintain separation from the established church had provoked Tories and High Churchmen to stigmatise them as Dissenters. On the other hand, it would be understandable if, while nurturing a peculiar hostility towards Ulster Presbyterians, because of the local context, he had at the same time been capable of taking a different view of other elements of the Dissenting population.

56 *C.J.Ire.* (2nd ed.), iv, 318, 321, 325, 326, 383, 384, 386, 399, 431, 433, 470, 471, 473.

57 T.N.A., SP 63/377/175.

Maxwell's contribution to the ensuing power-struggle fixed the political role he had been developing since 1714, as one of the Speaker's henchmen. He was present on the very first day of the 1721–2 session, being named to the 'grand' committee of privileges and elections,[58] was then nominated in second place to the committee of accounts, and served in almost every one of the committees preparing addresses to king or viceroy.[59] He also took a vocal part in parliamentary deliberations on the establishment of a national bank. Here, however, the necessity of following the dictates of faction resulted in an unseemly zig-zagging that compromised his public reputation. The original proposals for a bank in the summer of 1720 had met with the Speaker's approval, involving as they did several of his closest followers, like Sir Ralph Gore, Viscount Boyne, and Brabazon Ponsonby.[60] That the Brodricks also backed the project did not seem to concern him. In this situation Maxwell not only subscribed funds himself[61] but in 1721 published two pamphlets in support of the bank, making the case on economic grounds, and taking pains to reassure those fearful of the social and constitutional implications.[62] Yet when the Commons debated the issue in September he 'spoke earnestly against it, protesting [that] ... it would ruin the kingdom', and cited the precedent of the South Sea Bubble, the relevance of which he had previously disparaged in print.[63] Three weeks later, in a committee of the whole House, he joined the Speaker in voting for the bank, in a division in which supporters of Conolly and Midleton appeared on the same side.[64]

The reasons for this double volte-face are not easy to identify but must be located in the changing priorities and tactics of the Speaker. There were further shifts to come. Firm opposition to the bank in the House of Lords seems now to have convinced Conolly of the unwisdom of persevering with the project, despite the fact that the lord lieutenant, Grafton, was committed to it. The next stage in his serpentine campaign was to try to put an end to the controversy. By early November, according to Midleton, Conolly had made promises to the enemies of the bank

58 *C.J.Ire*. (2nd ed.), iv, 697.

59 Ibid., 696, 710, 719, 860.

60 R. E. Burns, *Irish parliamentary politics in the eighteenth century* (2 vols, Washington, D.C., 1989–90), i, 120–23.

61 *List of subscribers to the Bank of Ireland* [?1721] (Marsh's Library, MS Z.1.1.13, no. 59). Conolly's name does not appear on this list, but it does include three other members of his party: Isaac Manley, Thomas Marlay and Agmondisham Vesey.

62 Henry Maxwell, *Reasons offer'd for erecting a bank in Ireland; in a letter to Hercules Rowley, esq* (1st and 2nd eds, Dublin 1721); idem, *Mr Maxwell's second letter to Mr Rowley; wherein the objections against the bank are answer'd* (Dublin, 1721).

63 Sir Richard Levinge to Edward Southwell, 25 Sept. 1721 (Sir Richard G.A. Levinge, *Jottings for the history of the Levinge family* (Dublin, 1873), pp 64–5); *Mr Maxwell's second letter* ..., pp 14, 17, 21. Ironically, in the first of his pamphlets in favour of the bank, Maxwell, blissfully unaware of what was in store, had appealed to his audience to confirm 'whether I have not always been ready to own that I had altered my opinion, when upon a debate I was convinced that I had been in a mistake' (*Reasons offer'd for erecting a bank in Ireland* ..., p. 3).

64 'The names of the voters for and against the Bank, 14 Oct. 1721, in the House of Commons' (S.H.C., 1248/5/105–6, transcribed in Joseph Griffin, 'Parliamentary politics in Ireland during the reign of George I' (MA thesis, National University of Ireland (University College, Dublin), 1977), pp 190–3)).

that he 'would put himself at the head of them'.[65] By this stratagem he presumably hoped to ingratiate himself with the viceroy as the protector of government, while at the same time exposing the Brodricks to unpopularity as the chief advocates of a dangerous scheme. Again according to Midleton, Maxwell was one of the 'humble attendants' of the Speaker sent to talk to the Members who were against the bank.[66] Under this pressure, the chancellor himself reversed his position and voted against the bill in the Lords.[67]

There was then a final twist. After the bill to establish a bank had been dropped, the Commons passed two resolutions against the principle of 'establishing a public bank' in Ireland, the first that it could find no safe foundation for such an institution, and the second that setting up a public bank would be 'of the most dangerous and fatal consequence to His Majesty's service, and the trade and liberties of this nation'. Whether this was perceived as going too far, or an implicit criticism of the viceroy, Conolly's followers now transferred themselves, almost to a man, into the pro-bank lobby. In the decisive division, on the first of the two resolutions, Maxwell not only voted with the minority but acted as a teller.[68]

The unpleasant experience of repeatedly revoking, and re-revoking, publicly expressed views evidently sharpened the edge of Maxwell's animosity towards the Brodricks. It was with a mixture of grim humour and self-righteous disgust that Midleton reported gossip from the Castletown Christmas festivities, attended by the lord lieutenant, at which Maxwell 'in his cups said ... that he would have a slap at the chancellor'.[69] When parliament resumed the means were revealed. Maxwell complained about a bill having been amended at the Irish privy council, and moved for a committee to investigate the changes the council had made to parliament's heads before engrossing them. When this committee was appointed, Maxwell was given the chair.[70] Such a defence of the Irish legislature would be of a piece with Maxwell's previous 'patriotic' engagement over constitutional grievances, but Midleton was in no doubt that in this instance it was a stunt aimed principally at himself, and attributed it to the imbroglio over the bank, claiming that Maxwell had 'lost his wits since his elaborate [?noise] about the bank did not convince men'.[71]

Succeeding sessions confirmed Maxwell's importance in the Speaker's faction, which, following the arrival of Lord Carteret in 1724 and the resolution of the crisis over Wood's Halfpence, secured itself as the party of government. A simple calculus of his prominence in the Commons would be the number of times that his name was mentioned in the *Journals*. In the 1723–4 session he brought in two sets of heads of bills and was named to fourteen select committees, reporting from

65 Midleton to Thomas Brodrick, 9 Nov. 1721 (S.H.C., 1248/5/129–30).

66 Ibid. See also Griffin, 'Parlty politics', pp 105–07.

67 Burns, *Irish parlty politics*, i, 129–30.

68 *C.J.Ire.* (2nd ed.), iv, 832; 'A list of those that voted for the bank' (Rosse papers (the earl of Rosse, Birr Castle, Birr, Co. Offaly), B/1/1/6).

69 Midleton to Thomas Brodrick, 5 Jan. 1721[/2] (S.H.C., 1248/5/165–6).

70 Ibid.; same to same, 10 Jan. 1721[/2] (ibid., 1248/5/171–3).

71 Same to same, 10 Jan. 1721[/2] (ibid.).

six of them (presumably as chairman);[72] in 1725–6 he presented one set of heads and served on seventeen select committees, reporting from five;[73] while in 1727–8, when a namesake, John Maxwell, was also in the House, making some identification difficult, he was certainly appointed to seven select committees, reporting from three, and in addition may have been the 'Mr Maxwell' who presented one set of heads, and was nominated to seven more select committees.[74] Even more significant, perhaps, is his regular appearance in the major committees named at the beginning of each session: privileges and elections, public accounts, and the drafting committees for the loyal addresses. In 1725 and 1727 Maxwell's name was among the first three listed in the address and privileges committees; and in the 1725–6 session he chaired the committee drafting the address of thanks to the viceroy at the end of the session.[75] Fragments of other evidence confirm this circumstantial account: papers in his personal archive relating to government expenditure, and to parliamentary precedents on money bills, which indicate an interest, and presumably involvement, in the preparation of supply legislation;[76] an invitation to a private dinner at Dublin Castle with Carteret in 1726; and evidence that he acted as a 'whip' for local Ulster M.P.s whose attendance was required in crucial divisions.[77]

By the close of his parliamentary career Maxwell, having started out as a self-consciously principled M.P., had become an exemplar of ministerial reliability. But in this later incarnation he was not simply a Castle hack, attending Conolly's Castletown congresses and doing what he was told in the Commons in return for a share in power and place. For one thing, Maxwell did not hold office himself – apart from allowing the government to appoint him an Irish privy councillor in 1727 – and there is little evidence that he attempted to use government patronage to provide for others, although he did bring his influence to bear, in conjunction with other local M.P.s, to advance the concerns of his county.[78] Furthermore, the record of his parliamentary activity shows that he retained at least some of the concerns that had marked his first years in the Commons. Ostensibly, one such was the issue of government interference in Irish legislation. He was appointed again in January 1724 and December 1727 to committees to compare bills returned from Whitehall with what had been transmitted, but bearing in mind the episode in 1722 it may be safer to say

72 *C.J.Ire.* (2nd ed.), v, 12, 18, 28, 31, 99, 132, 134, 137, 138, 139, 140, 145, 148, 149, 154, 156, 164, 172, 189, 190, 206, 207, 208, 209, 212.

73 Ibid., 238, 240, 243, 249, 254, 256, 269, 275, 277, 279, 284, 285, 289, 347, 348, 349, 354, 355, 358, 363, 366, 367, 384, 388, 400, 405.

74 Ibid., 428, 446, 447, 449, 450, 455, 461, 517, 528, 529, 543, 561, 570, 572, 573, 574, 585, 596, 614, 620.

75 Ibid., 238, 239, 249, 384, 388, 405, 428, 429, 445.

76 P.R.O.N.I., D/1556/16/4/13, 18. He had been primed to speak for the money bill in 1729 should the ministry's tactic of depending on ostensibly 'independent' back-benchers have failed to carry the day (Marmaduke Coghill to Edward Southwell, 20 Dec. 1729 (*Coghill letters*, p. 80)).

77 John Plukenett to Maxwell, 28 Feb. 1725[/6] (P.R.O.N.I., D/1556/16/4/17); Samuel Waring to Maxwell, 12 Feb. 1725/6 (ibid., D/1556/16/4/15).

78 Thomas Medlycott to Maxwell, n.d. (ibid., D/1556/16/4/20). Maxwell was approached in 1725 by a lowly customs employee at Dungarvan for help in promotion from boatman to riding officer, but I have found no evidence that he subsequently intervened with the revenue board on the boatman's behalf: Hugh Floyd to Maxwell, 25 Nov. 1725 (ibid., D/1556/16/14/12).

that on these occasions he was holding a watching brief for the Castle rather than nurturing resentment at restrictions on legislative autonomy.[79] The initiatives with which he himself became involved demonstrate above all a continuing concern with the maintenance of the Protestant interest in Ireland, and the development of the Irish economy, subjects which he saw as intimately linked. His surviving private correspondence shows him seeking out information from local office-holders about the relative numbers of Protestant and Catholic inhabitants,[80] and in the Commons he was involved in preparing heads in 1721 'to prevent the further growth of popery', in 1725 to encourage Protestant charity schools, and in 1726 to oblige Catholics to educate their children as Protestants and to prevent 'occasional conformity' by Catholic converts.[81] He was also heavily involved in legislation to foster economic 'improvement', and here, although he took charge of the 1721–2 bill for the encouragement of tillage, the main subject of his interest was manufacture: in 1721–2 the regulation of malting; in 1723–4 the facilitation of export sales of beef and dairy products; in 1725–6, the prevention of smuggled imports of East Indian silks, and the encouragement of crape making.[82] Predictably, for a member from east Ulster, he was most often involved with initiatives relating to the linen industry: in 1721–2 he served on select committees to inspect the condition of linen manufacturing, and to report on a petition from Drogheda on the mayor's seizure of linen yarn; and in 1723–4 he chaired a second committee of inquiry into the industry and took the resulting bill through all the stages in the Commons, a sequence repeated in the following two sessions.[83]

III

Situated within this biography are Maxwell's various published writings. The first to be attributed to him, *Anguis in herba* … (snake in the grass) published in London early in 1702, which took its title from a quotation from Virgil referring to an imminent and unforeseen danger, was intended to demonstrate the foolishness of making peace with Louis XIV of France, the supposed would-be universal monarch, who would not keep the terms of any treaty that was not in his interest.[84] It was a closely textured account of recent European history, designed to bolster support for a resumption of hostilities in order to avoid the disastrous consequences of the joining together of the realms of France and Spain under the Bourbons: 'War is an

79 *C.J.Ire.* (2nd ed.), v, 189, 450. See below, p 000.

80 James Forth to Maxwell, 5 Dec. 1724 (P.R.O.N.I., D/1556/16/4/3); John Disney to Forth, 19 Jan. 1724[/5] (ibid., D/1556/16/4/5); list of houses inhabited by Protestants and Roman Catholics in Athlone (ibid., D/1556/16/4/4).

81 *C.J.Ire.* (2nd ed.), iv, 729; v, 342, 363.

82 *Ibid.*, iv, 699, 709, 718, 732 772; v, 132, 139, 140, 154, 156, 240, 269, 349, 358, 363, 366; drafts of heads of bill to regulate the weighing and packing of butter [c. 1723] (P.R.O.N.I., D/1556/16/4/9–10).

83 *C.J.Ire.* (2nd ed.), iv, 704, 849; v, 99, 134, 149, 154, 157, 207, 209, 240, 277, 367, 449, 517, 528, 543, 572, 573, 585, 620, 623. Cf. ibid., iii, 119.

84 *Anguis in herba: or the fatal consequences of a treaty with France* … (London, 1702).

evil, which is always hateful for the mischiefs it brings with it, yet 'tis sometimes not only eligible, but necessary for the greater miseries it averts. If this were ever the case of a nation, it is that of England at this time.'[85] Nothing in the pamphlet referred directly to domestic politics, though it is obvious that those who were opposed to war – the more extreme wing of the Tory parliamentary opposition in England – had to be regarded as at best misguided and at worst willing collaborators in the destruction of the liberties of Europe. This was standard Whig polemic, when the party had returned to power in England following a general election in which they had sought to stigmatise their opponents as closet Jacobites in the pay of the French.[86]

As a justification for England's participation in the War of the Spanish Succession it was sufficiently successful, and politically useful, to be reprinted twice, in 1707 and 1711, on the latter occasion to counter growing Tory propaganda against the continuance of hostilities, not least Swift's *Conduct of the allies*.... There was nothing to suggest that it was specifically the work of an Irish Protestant – indeed it was written explicitly from an English point of view – nor does it have much connexion with Maxwell's other writings, except perhaps in a passage in which the author drew attention to the damaging effect a union of France and Spain would have on the cloth manufacture of England, by giving French weavers unrestricted access to Spanish wool.[87] Emphasis on the likely losses to trade and shipping, and damage to the prospects of employment for the poor, reflect the preoccupations of his later pamphlets.

The *Essay towards an union* ... was published in London in 1703 (by late November according to Maxwell himself in his letter to Stanhope, so presumably written no later than the beginning of the Irish parliamentary session of 1703–4), and reprinted in Dublin the following year. In it Maxwell pressed for a union of England and Ireland, on the same integrationist model as the sixteenth-century union between England and Wales, so that Ireland should be 'made into the nature of a county of England'.[88] One context for the pamphlet was obviously the contemporary debate over an Anglo-Scottish union, recently renewed both at a parliamentary level and in print. With some Scottish writers making the case for a federal union, Maxwell's proposal – written for an English audience in the guise of an English author – promising equal taxation and the retention of an English majority in a united legislature, was obviously attractive. An even more important context was the crisis in Anglo-Irish relations following the assertion by the English parliament in 1698–1700 of its right to legislate on Irish affairs, over woollen exports and forfeited estates. The controversy over the forfeitures, and in particular over the 'national remonstrance', had resulted in accusations of an Irish campaign for independence, a smear politicians in Dublin were desperate to repudiate. The Irish parliament was to meet in the autumn of 1703, for the first time since 1699. Those Whigs, like Conolly, who had organised the remonstrance, and now found themselves in opposition to the Tory

85 Ibid., p. 56.

86 Henry Horwitz, *Parliament, policy and politics in the reign of William III* (Manchester, 1977), pp 295–300.

87 *Anguis in herba* ..., p. 65.

88 *Essay* ... (Dublin ed., 1704), pp 12, 35.

viceroy, Ormond, still hoped to make political capital from the constitutional difficulties between the two kingdoms, yet without giving their enemies the opportunity to brand them as separatists; hence the Commons 'representation' (which Maxwell moved should be printed), complaining of Ireland's treatment at the hands of the English but pressing for union rather than autonomy. It was precisely this approach that Maxwell's *Essay* ... had already espoused.

Maxwell began with an acknowledgment that the right of the English to legislate for Ireland could not be disputed, 'it being sufficient for those of that nation [the Irish] to know, that this is a power which England claims, and is able to vindicate'.[89] But it was in the interest of England to exercise its power with care. The reasons why Ireland should be indulged formed the core of his case. There was, first of all, the indirect threat to English liberties, involving Maxwell in 'commonwealth Whig' rhetoric. Without union, the only means of governing Ireland, other than by federal or classically colonial constitutional relationships which would leave Ireland free to govern itself, were, first, 'an unequal league', with the Irish deprived of English liberties, an arrangement which had already encouraged Charles I, his sons, and Oliver Cromwell to develop 'ambitious designs' at home; and second, the use of a standing army.[90] Maxwell's other arguments were more practical: a more tender policy would nurture the innate loyalty of Irish Protestants, who (unlike the Scots) were 'naturally the offspring of the people of England', and by allowing the Irish economy to develop, would strengthen the kingdom against Jacobite disaffection.[91] Union, to his mind, presented the best and easiest method of ensuring these happy consequences, and the final two thirds of the text were taken up with reassuring English readers that they would indeed reap economic benefits from the arrangement: that the Irish economy would remain subservient to the English, Irish manufactures would not undercut English competitors, there would be no outflow of capital or population from England to Ireland, and London would retain its dominance as a commercial centre.

> For ... the trade and communication of those kingdoms being as free and easy as between any two parts of the same country, it will naturally and necessarily follow that the business and trade of Ireland will be diverted from foreign nations, and chiefly confined to England. So that England will not only regain that part of the Irish trade which it has lost, and is likely to do more and more, but will likewise put itself into a more full and absolute possession of the Irish trade than ever it had, or can have, under any other circumstances than those of an union.[92]

It is not always easy to distinguish the substantive arguments advanced in this pamphlet from the devices of rhetoric. In order to appeal to his English audience, and to defend his fellow countrymen, Maxwell was obliged to accept that there should be severe limitations on Irish legislative autonomy. Undoubtedly his comments about threats to liberty and a standing army might also have been tailored to his

89 Ibid., p. 3.
90 Ibid., pp 4–6.
91 Ibid., pp 8–11, 12.
92 Ibid., p. 35.

readers' prejudices, given that those who had recently shown themselves the fiercest advocates of English legislative supremacy were also those who had taken the lead in denouncing a standing army under King William.[93] Furthermore the entire thrust of the pamphlet is suspiciously close to the political strategy adopted in the 1703–4 session of the Irish Parliament by the Whig opposition of which he was a member. However, there remains a significant difference between a pamphlet crafted so as to raise a major issue before English public opinion, and a more narrowly conceived parliamentary campaign in Dublin, intended to embarrass a viceroy, whose protagonists required for purposes of self-protection a patina of deference to the English connexion. There seems little reason to doubt Maxwell's sincerity in proposing a union, which would have fitted with his sense of ethnic and religious connexion with England, as against Scotland and the Ulster Scots Presbyterian communities whom he disliked; and his genuine concern for the liberty of the subject. Nor was his acceptance of Irish legislative dependence necessarily feigned. In his publications it was always treated as unproblematic. His parliamentary objections to the *operation* of Poynings' Law – when not merely tactical, as in 1721–2 – were perfectly reconcilable with an acknowledgment of its ultimate justification.

One of the most striking aspects of the *Essay* is the amount of space given over to the subject of trade and industry, and an emphasis on the danger that economic depression would result in Ireland's depopulation, which would pave the way for a Jacobite and popish restoration. These were themes that recurred in Maxwell's last forays into print, eighteen years later, the two pamphlets on the bank in 1721. Both were in the form of open letters to his second wife's uncle by marriage, Hercules Rowley (1679–1742), M.P. for County Londonderry, who was publicly sceptical of the bank project and concerned at the damage it might do to the Irish body politic.[94] The burden of the two pamphlets was to reassure readers that the bank could not endanger the economy of Ireland or the liberties of Irishmen. On the contrary, Maxwell argued that it was the only means for the kingdom to achieve prosperity. Much of what he had to say depended on the belief that the bank would lower interest, and he developed a detailed analysis of the relationship of interest rates to agricultural and industrial production, trade and land values. In doing so he was careful to answer the objections (characteristic not only of a Tory but of a 'Country' or 'real' Whig point of view) that Ireland would be susceptible to financial 'bubbles', or that a sinister 'monied interest' would be created to rival the landed.[95] More positively, he concentrated on the likely benefits accruing to trade and manufacture, especially to the linen industry.[96] These would in turn bring political gains, through

93 Hayton, *Ruling Ireland*, pp 71–80.

94 See above, n. 62. Both were answered: Hercules Rowley, *An answer to a book intitl'd, Reasons offer'd for erecting a bank in Ireland, in a letter to Henry Maxwell, esq.* (Cork, 1721; 2nd ed., Dublin, 1721); idem, *An answer to Mr Maxwell's second letter to Mr Rowley, concerning the bank* (Dublin, 1721). For a detailed discussion of the published debates on the bank, see Michael Ryder, 'The Bank of Ireland, 1721: land, credit and dependency', in *Hist. Jn.*, xxv (1985), pp 557–82.

95 Maxwell, *Reasons offer'd for erecting a bank in Ireland* ... (1st ed.), pp 8, 28–9; *Mr Maxwell's second letter* ..., pp 4–5, 19.

96 *Reasons offer'd for erecting a bank in Ireland* ... (1st ed.), pp 30–32, 41, 46–7, 49, 52–3, 57–9, 61; *Mr Maxwell's second letter* ..., p. 23.

reversing the decline in Ireland's population.[97] While Maxwell never explicitly stated that he expected an increase in *Protestant* inhabitants, this is what he meant: his account of Ireland's recent economic history lauded the supposed population increase that had occurred after the Revolution through the arrival of Huguenots and other foreign Protestants, before depression had set in after 1715. The implication was that the process could be renewed.[98] This takes us back to some of his earliest preoccupations in parliament, and it should be noted that precisely the same recommendations can be found in the writings of Robert Molesworth, with whom Maxwell had been associated at the start of his political career, but who was now plying his 'patriotism' in opposition.[99]

Implicit in Maxwell's arguments was an understanding of the Anglo-Irish relationship that was both realistic and optimistic. He began his first pamphlet on the bank with an acknowledgment of Ireland's subordination, and a plea that his fellow countrymen adopt a similarly pragmatic attitude:[100]

> ... the circumstances of Ireland, by reason of her dependence, are such, that she cannot always obtain the advantages she aims at, when she would, nor in the manner she desires; yet I have constantly observ'd, that we have thought it our wisdom, rather to take a part, than refuse the whole, and, in favours granted, rather to accept them in the manner they would be granted in, than refuse them, because we could not have them in the manner we desired.

Later he turned again to the fact of Ireland's dependence, this time its economic subordination, and the continued draining of money and resources to England. He did not presume to suggest that this situation would change[101] – it was in the nature of Anglo-Irish governance – but pressed the view that once Ireland's manufactures had developed, these 'drains' would be an advantage to the country, tending to increase land values and promote 'improvements'. They would not harm the economy and would be a motive for the English to 'encourage Ireland to increase in all those trades and manufactures, that do not directly interfere with its own'.[102] The constitutional limitations on Irish autonomy might be galling; they might in the

97 *Reasons offer'd for erecting a bank in Ireland* ... (1st ed.), pp 11, 12, 36–7, 39–41, 42, 45, 47, 52, 54, 59; *Mr Maxwell's second letter* ..., p. 23.

98 *Reasons offer'd for erecting a bank in Ireland* ... (1st ed.), pp 14, 21, 23, 40, 48. He did not, however, mention the Scots who had come to Ulster in large numbers in the 1690s.

99 Molesworth has been much studied. The details of his life and career are conveniently summarised in the biographical entries in *Oxf. D.N.B.*, xxxviii, 530–32, and *H.C. 1690–1715*, iv, 826–35. His pamphlet *Some considerations for the promoting of agriculture, and employing the poor* (Dublin, 1723), shares many of Maxwell's preoccupations, and discussion of the relationship of governance to economic improvement is also to be found in his most famous work, *An account of Denmark, as it was in the year 1692* (London, 1694). For example, Maxwell's discussion of the damaging economic effects of the prevalence of holy days in Catholic countries (*Reasons offer'd for erecting a bank in Ireland* ... (1st ed.), p. 57) is a distant echo of Molesworth, *Account of Denmark*, p. 254.

100 *Reasons offer'd for erecting a bank* ... (1st ed.), p. 4.

101 'England does not want the assistance of a bank, either to cramp our trade, or increase our dependance, when she thinks fit to do so' (*Mr Maxwell's second letter* ..., p. 9).

102 *Reasons offer'd for erecting a bank* ... (1st ed.), pp 18, 19–20, 22, 24, 61–2.

past have produced evil effects; but they were not to be challenged, and might even be made to work for Ireland's benefit. Indeed, at some points in his *Second letter* ... he seemed prepared to defend the current constitutional arrangements. For one thing, rule by the English Parliament was still rule by a parliament and not by an arbitrary monarchy, and now the danger of a pro-Jacobite Tory administration had passed, no one could believe that English M.P.s, however hard they might 'bear upon' Ireland, would allow a monarch to act arbitrarily.[103] Second, the elaborate scrutinising process which Irish legislation had to undergo at the hands of the Irish and British privy councils was in itself a defence against the malicious acts of a faction in Dublin, in this case the putative 'monied interest' whose power Rowley professed to fear: 'how can any reasonable men believe', wrote Maxwell, 'that these men ... could pass a bill through both Houses of Parliament, and thro' both Privy Councils of England and Ireland, that would be detrimental or ruinous to the kingdom, and enable them to set up an *imperium in imperio*'.[104]

IV

The most salient aspect of Maxwell's public personality was the strength of his commitment to Whig ideals and prejudices, and to the Irish Whig faction, during the heyday of party conflict in Queen Anne's reign. In the parliamentary sessions of 1703–5 he was firmly attached to the Whig opposition headed by Speaker Brodrick against the Tory ministry of the duke of Ormond; in 1710, after a possible flirtation with Whitshed's 'flying squadron' he returned to the Whig fold, concerned that a premature peace would negate the advantages achieved by Marlborough's victories and suspicious that the Irish Tory administration headed by Sir Constantine Phipps was secretly paving the way for the Pretender. His Whig loyalty was even strong enough to qualify his enmity to Protestant Dissenters. In 1705, while still opposed to any relaxation of the sacramental test, he distinguished himself from the 'high flyers' in parliament and convocation and lined up alongside those moderates who preferred a gentle deferral of Presbyterian demands to a brutal snub.[105] In 1714 he wrote of the necessity for unity among Protestants of the 'British interest' against the greater threat from popery – again showing an obsession with demography, and the gross imbalance between Protestant and Catholic populations in Ireland, but reassuring himself in the case of Protestant Nonconformity that, although numerous, Dissenters were socially inferior and barely represented among the landed classes.[106] This helps to explain the modification that has already been noted in his attitude to Dissent after 1714.

It would be easy to view Maxwell's political career after 1714 as an instance of a common trope of eighteenth-century political commentary: youthful idealism giving way to the comforts of office. Undoubtedly there are instances of intellec-

103 *Mr Maxwell's second letter* ..., pp 18, 19, 20.

104 Ibid., p. 17.

105 See above, n. 29.

106 Maxwell to Stanhope, 6 Dec. [1714] (*Eighteenth-Cent. Ire.*, xxii (2007), p. 58).

tual about-turns and cynical short-termism, most obviously in his somersaults over the bank project in 1721. Yet strong threads of consistency are visible; principally, his anxiety for the maintenance of the Protestant interest in Ireland against any return of a popish government, and a wish to promote Ireland's economic development, itself a means of strengthening the Revolution settlement. Commitment to the maintenance of the Hanoverian succession and the British connexion could easily have persuaded him to compromise some principles for the greater good. Fear of what he saw as the Jacobite tendency of Irish Tories even induced him to countenance concessions to Dissenters in the cause of Protestant unity. To someone of this cast of mind, the factious mischief-making of the Brodricks and their Tory allies after 1715 would probably have seemed not only morally reprehensible but politically dangerous, and unswerving support for the Castle a necessary guarantee of stability.

An examination of Maxwell's political activities and writings adds to our understanding of the nature of Protestant Irish political life and thought in the decades after the Glorious Revolution, but does so by blurring sharp lines. His biography suggests that simple definitions such as 'Whig', 'Country Whig', or even 'Church Whig' all require subtle qualification. His early writings would characterise him as an Irish variation on an English theme, illustrating the influence and limitations of Whig ideology among Irish Protestants. But after the triumph of Whiggery in Ireland in 1714 he was able to modify 'patriotic' ideals to accommodate the realities of Castle politics under Conolly. This does not necessarily indicate moral frailty, or even a capacity for self-delusion (though he may have been prone to both), but an underlying coherence of belief, adapted to changing circumstances. His acceptance of the restricted constitutional space in which Irish politicians were obliged to operate, and emphasis on economic improvement as the panacea for his country's ills, were consistent with the underlying political priority that stares out from both his actions and his words: the defence of the Protestant establishment.

6

'Paltry underlings of state'?

The character and aspirations of the 'Castle' party, 1715–32*

In his writings, both public and private, Jonathan Swift voiced a low opinion of politicians. 'I have conversed in some freedom with more ministers of state of all parties than usually happens to men of my level,' he boasted to Alexander Pope in 1721,

> And I confess, in their capacity as ministers, I look upon them as a race of people whose acquaintance no man would court, otherwise than upon the score of vanity or ambition. The first quickly wears off (and is the vice of low minds, for a man of spirit is too proud to be vain) and the other was not my case. Besides, having never received more than one small favour, I was under no necessity of being a slave to men in power, but chose my friends for their personal merit, without examining how far their notions agreed with the politics then in vogue.[1]

Certainly he had little regard for those in power in Ireland during the long years of his Dublin exile. When they do figure in his satire, they appear as selfish and corrupt, 'paltry underlings of state'; at best feeble and ineffective defenders of their country's interests, and at worst willing collaborators in its reduction to a state of slavery. Needless to say, this is not how Irish politicians saw themselves, nor how they were represented by their admirers. Clergymen preaching panegyrics, friends or family members preparing inscriptions to adorn commemorative monuments, authors offering tribute (often in the form of flattering dedications); all took a very different view, emphasising disinterested public service and genuine patriotism.[2] Not surprisingly, perhaps, posterity has tended to favour the satirist; the sharpness of

* This chapter has drawn upon material from '"Paltry underlings of state"? The character and aspirations of the "Castle" party, 1715–32', in Claude Rawson (ed.), *Politics and literature in England and Ireland in the age of Swift* (2010) © Cambridge University Press, reproduced with permission.

1 Swift to Pope, 10 Jan. 1721 (*The correspondence of Jonathan Swift*, ed. Harold Williams (5 vols, Oxford, 1963), ii, 370.

2 See, for example, the dedications to Speaker Conolly in James Sterling, *The rival generals: a tragedy. As it was acted act the Theatre Royal, in Dublin* ... (London, 1722), p. iv, and John Browne, *An essay on trade in general; and on that of Ireland in particular* (Dublin, 1728); James Sterling, *A funeral poem on the death of the right honourable William Conolly* ... (Dublin, 1729); the brief ode to Conolly's memory included in *Tunbrigalia: or, Tunbridge miscellanies, for the year 1730* (London, 1730), p. 12; the dedication to Lord Chancellor Midleton in [David Bindon,] *Some reasons, shewing the necessity the people of Ireland are under, for continuing to refuse* Mr *Wood's coinage* (Dublin, 1724); p. 4; and the monumental inscriptions to Coghill and Conolly, quoted below, p. 148.

Swift's wit and the power of his prose has exerted such an influence over the popular understanding of the way Ireland was governed in the early eighteenth century that his characterisation of those Irishmen who managed the Irish parliament for English viceroys and ministers – the 'undertakers' – has achieved widespread acceptance.

This essay seeks to uncover the mentality and ideology of the Irishmen who acted as parliamentary managers and under-managers for Dublin Castle at the time when Swift was writing some of his sharpest attacks on the way Ireland was being governed. It was a period that saw the affirmation of the power of the Westminster parliament to legislate for Ireland in the British Declaratory Act of 1720, the defeat of the project to establish an Irish national bank in 1721, the attempted enforcement of Wood's Halfpence in 1723–5, and a serious crisis for Irish agriculture in the late 1720s, provoking a radical reassessment of strategies for economic regeneration. Testing the prejudices of the dean against what can be discovered of the motivations and thought-processes of those who suffered at his pen offers a different perspective on the constitutional and political relationship of Ireland and Britain, and on the intellectual framework in which Irish politicians and administrators operated. These individuals certainly grew fat from office (in some cases literally as well as metaphorically), and enjoyed privilege, patronage, and a modicum of power, but they also carried a public responsibility and considered writers like Swift to be at best irritating, and at worst dangerously subversive.

I

It might be argued that in the period 1715–26 there were two distinct '[Dublin] Castle parties' as rival magnates struggled for dominance: on the one hand the followers of the Speaker (and first commissioner of the revenue) William Conolly, and on the other a faction headed in the Commons by St John Brodrick but owing ultimate allegiance to St John's father Alan, first Viscount Midleton, who had been appointed lord chancellor on the Hanoverian succession.[3] In the party battles of Queen Anne's reign the two had fought side by side, but they now became bitter rivals. Tory losses at the Irish general election of 1715 had left Whigs in an overwhelming majority in the Commons, and a block creation of coronation peerages ensured that Tories in the upper house would also be outnumbered. Now the Whigs were free to quarrel among themselves. Midleton, although the undisputed leader of the party before 1714, found that his elevation to the woolsack was a political mistake, since the House of Lords was less important than the Commons. Conolly had the more valuable managerial role, as well as greater resources of patronage in the revenue. He capitalised on his advantages, and tried to make himself indispensable to government by doing whatever he was asked, while the Brodricks responded to perceived slights by flirting with opposition.

3 For what follows see Patrick McNally, *Parties, patriots and undertakers: parliamentary politics in early Hanoverian Ireland* (Dublin, 1997), pp 120–36; D. W. Hayton, *Ruling Ireland, 1685–1742: politics, politicians and parties* (Woodbridge, 2004), pp 217–35.

For present purposes, Conolly's faction has been taken as constituting the 'Castle party' even though the lord chancellor remained in office until 1725. While Midleton himself took a strong line in public in defence of executive power and the maintenance of English constitutional supremacy, his son led the family 'interest' in the Commons on rather a different course, joining the rump of Tories in defending the sacramental test, championing the rights of the Irish House of Lords against English encroachment, and denouncing Wood's Halfpence. Conolly and his followers, by contrast, were disposed to do whatever successive lords justices and lords lieutenant wanted, except in extreme cases, where the effort would have made them intolerably unpopular. After Midleton's resignation Conolly was bound even more closely to government, and was obliged to defend publicly policies with which he personally disagreed. After his death in 1729 his political heir, Sir Ralph Gore, went the same way, expressing reservations about some viceregal decisions in private but remaining loyal in parliament and steering the administration through the dangerous parliamentary sessions of 1729–32 without conceding to opposition outrage at the economic crisis gripping the country.

The task of identifying all the members of Conolly's 'Castle party' would be beyond the available evidence; we have relatively few parliamentary lists for the period, and Conolly's own private papers are disappointingly uncommunicative. Moreover, one would have to accept that personal and factional allegiances shifted over time, and that those on the fringes of either of the main political 'connexions' might well have voted in different ways over different issues. What can be done, however, is to identify the leading figures, through correspondence, both friendly and hostile, a few printed commentaries and satires,[4] and to a lesser extent, through the *Journals* of the two houses of the Irish parliament, which list committees and those who reported from them, tellers in divisions, and the members responsible for introducing legislation. The parliamentary evidence has to be used carefully, but it can tie in particular individuals for whom other indirect evidence survives (and even more important, it can tell us something about the priorities of those involved). It also helps to pinpoint those among Conolly's supporters who were the more active in parliament, and it is the active members of the faction, not obscure or passive dependants, who form the real objects of interest.

The strength of Conolly's party lay in the Commons, which in practice was the more important of the two houses, for it was there that the vital business of the session was transacted, the preparation of the 'heads' of bills granting the time-limited taxes 'additional' to the crown's 'hereditary' revenues, without which government could not function. Even though, according to Poynings' Law, bills proper were prepared by the Irish privy council and, after scrutiny in England, were returned for approval or rejection (but not amendment) by the Irish parliament, the two houses of the Irish parliament had developed a practice which permitted them a share in the framing of statute by drafting 'heads' that were sent to the council to be turned into form. Each set of 'heads' went through only one house, and drafting heads of money bills

4 For example, D. W. Hayton, 'Two ballads on the County Westmeath election of 1723' in *Eighteenth-Century Ireland*, iv (1989), pp 7–30, esp. pp 17–18, 28–9.

was accepted as the province of the Commons.[5] By the 1720s, in fact, most public legislation was taking its rise in the lower house, and the constitutional role of the House of Lords was being eroded.[6] Moreover, it was becoming easier for government to control the Lords: the smaller membership, the poverty of many peers, and the presence of a sizable cohort of bishops depending on the court for preferment, would create a standing ministerial majority once the remnant of High Church irreconcilables on the episcopal bench died off.[7] By the mid-1720s, therefore, Conolly could safely concentrate his energies on the management of the lower house. However, it was still unwise to ignore the Lords, as was evident from the heated debates in 1717 and 1719 over the vexed question of the appellate jurisdiction, and Conolly needed friends there to take care of his and the Castle's interests. Major-General Gustavus Hamilton, a veteran of the Jacobite war, who was created Lord Hamilton in 1715 and Viscount Boyne two years later, was his principal spokesman in the upper house until dying in 1723,[8] to be succeeded in this role by the churchman Theophilus Bolton, successively bishop of Clonfert (1722) and Elphin (1724), and archbishop of Cashel (1730), who along with his successor at Clonfert (and eventually Cashel) Arthur Price, owed his advancement to Conolly's influence.[9]

At the head of Conolly's troops in the Commons stood the Speaker's henchman Sir Ralph Gore, who served as chancellor of the exchequer and chairman of the committees of supply and ways and means from 1717, until he himself succeeded to the Speakership.[10] According to Alan Brodrick he was simply 'a creature' of Conolly, one who 'hath a spirit low enough not to disdain being thought a dependant'.[11] Gore had not been in the first flight of Whig party politicians in

5 See in particular C. I. McGrath, *The making of the eighteenth-century Irish constitution: government, parliament and the revenue, 1692–1714* (Dublin, 2000), ch. 3; idem, 'English ministers, Irish politicians and the making of a parliamentary settlement in Ireland, 1692–5' in *E.H.R.*, cxix (2004), pp 585–613; John Bergin, 'Irish legislative procedure after the Williamite revolution: the operation of Poynings' Law, 1692–1705' (PhD thesis, University College Dublin, 2005); James Kelly, *Poynings' Law and the making of law in Ireland, 1660–1800: monitoring the constitution* (Dublin, 2007), ch. 2.

6 Hayton, *Ruling Ireland*, pp 108–9; Kelly, *Poynings' Law*, pp 134, 204. Cf. F. G. James, *Lords of the ascendancy: the Irish House of Lords and its members, 1600–1800* (Blackrock, Co. Dublin, 1995), pp 75–8, 83–6.

7 F. G. James, *Ireland in the empire, 1688–1770: a history of Ireland from the Williamite wars to the eve of the American Revolution* (Cambridge, Mass., 1973), pp 95–7; idem, *Lords of the ascendancy*, pp 78–9; R. E. Burns, *Irish parliamentary politics in the eighteenth century* (2 vols, Washington D.C., 1989–90), i, 18; McNally, *Parties, patriots and undertakers*, pp 52–4.

8 See the biographical entries in *Hist. Ir. parl.*, iv, 333–4, and *Oxf. D.N.B.*, xxiv, 809–10.

9 Abp Boulter of Armagh to Ld Carteret, 7 Mar. 1726[/7] (*Letters written by his excellency Hugh Boulter, ...* (2 vols, Oxford, 1769–70), i, 146); Conolly to Thomas Clutterbuck, 2 Jan., 17/18 Feb. 1726[/7] (I.A.A., Conolly papers, A/3/43, 46); Francis Burton to Jane Bonnell, 19 Jan. 1729/30 (N.L.I., Smythe of Barbavilla papers, MS 41,579/10). For Bolton see *Oxf. D.N.B.*, vi, 495–6; for Price, ibid., xlv, 281–2.

10 For Gore's importance, see Henry Rose to Maurice Crosbie, 25 June 1720 (N.L.I., Talbot-Crosbie papers, P.C. 188).

11 Ld Brodrick to Thomas Brodrick, 14 June 1717 (S.H.C., Brodrick papers, 1248/4/35–6). For Gore, see *Hist.Ir. parl.*, iv, 284–6; *Oxf. D.N.B.*, xxii, 985.

Queen Anne's reign,[12] but he was reliable and well-connected, and backed by a covey of Gore cousins and other relations. In George I's first Parliament his closest lieutenant was probably the County Down squire Henry Maxwell.[13] Less prominent at the outset of the period, but in due course making themselves indispensable, were the portly canon lawyer and inveterate committee-man Marmaduke Coghill, who after Conolly's retirement succeeded to the key position of first commissioner of the revenue;[14] Coghill's fellow civilian Thomas Trotter, who eventually joined him in the revenue;[15] and the barristers Thomas Marlay (solicitor-general in 1720, and eventually chief baron of the Exchequer)[16] and Henry Singleton (prime serjeant in 1726 and later master of the rolls).[17] Less prominent in debate, but still useful politically, were 'Ben' Parry, registrar of deeds and a regular attender at the Irish privy council;[18] his fellow councillor, the egregious Richard Tighe (pilloried by Swift as 'Dick Fitzbaker');[19] Tighe's kinsman Henry Sandford, who was also brother-in-law to the earl of Kildare;[20] Isaac Manley, the postmaster-general notorious for prying into the mails;[21] Henry Rose from County Limerick, another barrister and future judge, who at first enlisted with the Brodricks but then changed sides;[22] Agmondisham Vesey, son of the former archbishop of Tuam, and ambitious for office;[23] Major (later Lieutenant)-General Owen Wynne, said to be one of Conolly's 'bosom friends';[24] Brabazon Ponsonby, still a relatively junior figure though ultimately, as first earl of Bessborough, to become an 'undertaker' in his own right;[25] and a cluster of minor treasury, exchequer and customs officials, headed by Theophilus Clements, the teller

12 He was not included among the Whig leaders invited to Dublin Castle in January 1714 by the viceroy, Shrewsbury, to explore the opportunities for a compromise settlement of political differences that would permit a resumption of the parliamentary session (Ld Abercorn to [Edward Southwell], 5 Jan. 1713/14 (P.R.O.N.I., Abercorn papers, D/623/A/3/12)).

13 During the parliamentary session of 1715–16 Lord Chancellor Brodrick referred to Gore and Maxwell as 'the Speaker's two confidants' (Ld Brodrick to Thomas Brodrick, 5 Apr. 1716 (S.H.C., 1248/3/352–5)). For Maxwell, see above, ch. 5.

14 *Coghill letters*, pp xi–xxii. See also *Hist. Ir. parl.*, iii, 442–5; *Oxf. D.N.B.*, xii, 411–12.

15 *Hist.Ir. parl.*, vi, 443–4.

16 Ibid., v, 191–3. Marlay was recommended by Conolly for a place on the judicial bench in 1720 (rough note by Conolly on legal promotions (I.A.A., Conolly papers, A/3/15A–B)).

17 *Hist.Ir. parl.*, vi, 276–7; *Oxf. D.N.B.*, l, 787–8.

18 *Hist. Ir. parl.* vi, 21–2. See also Sir Richard Levinge to Edward Southwell, 17 Oct. 1721 (Sir Richard G. A. Levinge, *Jottings for history of the Levinge family* (Dublin, 1873), p. 65).

19 *Hist. Ir. parl.*, vi, 395–7; *Swift: poetical works*, ed. Herbert Davis (London, 1967), pp 339–46, 247–51, 605–6; Jonathan Swift and Thomas Sheridan, *The Intelligencer*, ed. James Woolley (Oxford, 1992), pp 100–114, 130–34.

20 *Hist. Ir. parl.*, vi, 233–4; Hayton, 'Co. Westmeath election ballads', p. 29; Midleton to Thomas Brodrick, 21 Oct. 1723 (S.H.C., 1248/5/323–4).

21 *Hist. Ir. parl.*, v, 190–91; Swift to Charles Ford, 27 Nov., 31 Dec. 1724 (*Swift corr.*, ed. Williams, ii, 42, 46); St John Brodrick to Midleton, 11, 21 Jan. 1723[/4] (S.H.C., 1248/5/358–9, 368–9).

22 *Hist. Ir. parl.*, vi, 188–90; Charles Delafaye to —, 4 May 1716 (T.N.A., SP 63/374/219); rough note by Conolly on legal promotions (I.A.A., Conolly papers, A/3/15A–B).

23 *Hist. Ir. parl.*, vi., 468–9; Midleton to Thomas Brodrick, 30 Sept. 1717, 11 Nov. 1721 (S.H.C., 12548/4/73–4, 1248/5/136–7).

24 *Hist. Ir. parl.*, vi, 562–3; Midleton to Thomas Brodrick, 11 Nov. 1721, 21 Oct. 1723 (S.H.C., 1248/5/136–7, 323–4).

25 *Hist. Ir. parl.*, vi, 79–81.

of the exchequer, and including Clements's son Nathaniel and Luke Gardiner, who became deputy vice-treasurer in 1733.[26] These were the men closest to Conolly, who attended his house-parties, were consulted about parliamentary strategy and tactics, and formed a roster of pro-government debaters in parliament.

II

The first point to be made about Conolly's circle is that their party political backgrounds were highly varied. There were dyed-in-the-wool Whigs, like Conolly himself, Henry Maxwell, a man who enjoyed close friendships with leading members of the Whig party in England,[27] Theophilus Clements, who had the reputation among fellow Whigs of having been 'honest in the worst of times',[28] and Isaac Manley, whose first recorded political statement was to have joined the Monmouth rebellion in 1685.[29] But Conolly also picked up a significant number of ex-Tories in the dark days for Irish Toryism after 1714,[30] notably Coghill,[31] Singleton[32] and Vesey.[33] Even Bishop Bolton, though a protégé of the politically Whiggish Archbishop King of Dublin, seemed more at home with the Tories in the early years of the Hanoverian regime.[34] All had political pasts to live down. But with the exception of Vesey, who

26 Ibid., ii, 433–4, 425–30; iv, 257–60; A. P. W. Malcomson, *Nathaniel Clements: government and the governing elite in Ireland, 1725–75* (Dublin, 2005), chs 1–2, 5; Theophilus Clements to Conolly, 29 July 1727 (I.A.A., Conolly papers, A/3/49).

27 See above, p. 105.

28 Charles Delafaye to earl of Sunderland, 24 Jan. 1715/16 (B.L., Blenheim papers, Add. MS 61640, f. 80).

29 George Roberts, *The life, progresses and rebellion of James, duke of Monmouth* (2 vols, London, 1844), i, 262; ii, 51, 260; Bp Godwin of Kilmore to [Abp Wake of Canterbury], 9 June. 1716 (Christ Church, Oxford, Wake papers, Arch. W. Epist. xii); Hayton, 'Co. Westmeath election ballads', p. 28; Jane Bulkeley to Jane Bonnell, 9 Dec. [?1721] (N.L.I., Smythe of Barbavilla papers, MS 41580/3), referring to Manley as one of Conolly's 'creatures', and 'is said to be one of them that is a cat's claw, to do things that he has no mind to appear in himself'.

30 The flexibility of Conolly's attitude to former political enemies may also be visible in his admission as a freeman of Galway in 1722, alongside the ex-Tory George Staunton, as part of a resurgence of the Staunton-led Tory interest in the city (Galway corporation minute, 28 Aug. 1722 (National University of Ireland, Galway, Hardiman Library, Galway corporation records, minute book F, p. 103)).

31 Coghill was described in 1716 as 'a Tory more by dependence than principle' (Bp Godwin to [Abp Wake], 27 Feb. 1715/16 (Christ Church, Arch. W. Epist. xii)) and in 1729 as a 'moderate' (Arthur Hill to Boyle, 15 Apr. 1729 (P.R.O.N.I., D/2707/A/1/2/39)).

32 In 1729 he was said to stand at the head of 'a brigade of Tories' (Arthur Hill to Henry Boyle, 15 Apr. 1729 (P.R.O.N.I., D/2707/A/1/2/39)), and as late as 1738 was still being 'represented as a warm Tory' by those who wished to prejudice the English ministry against his claims to preferment (William Richardson to Bp Howard of Elphin, 4 Jan. 1738 (N.L.I., Wicklow papers, MS 38,597/11)).

33 Thomas Trotter, as a civil lawyer and consistory court judge, and the son-in-law of a Tory M.P., Abel Ram, may well have been a Tory by political inclination, but had not sat in the Irish parliament before 1715 and it is impossible to confirm this supposition.

34 Bp Godwin to [Abp Wake], 31 Oct. 1716 (Christ Church, Arch W. Epist. xii).

turned his coat sharply as soon as his father died in 1716,[35] they were all Tories of a moderate hue: none could be linked with the excesses of the Irish administration of 1711–14.[36] Conolly – like Sir Robert Walpole – preferred to shine in the company of cronies, and appears not to have admitted to his inner circle those who bridled at inferiority. Equally important, perhaps, is that Conolly had known a number of his recruits for some time. His association with Coghill went back at least to 1701,[37] and it was probably Coghill who had enlisted Singleton and Trotter, the latter as early as 1713.[38] Maxwell had been on terms of close friendship with Conolly by 1703, and in the 1713 election both he and Benjamin Parry had been elected to the Commons for Conolly's boroughs with Gore also involved in campaigning.[39]

Second, Conolly's was unlike other Irish parliamentary factions in the period in that it was not primarily based on family or regional connexions, although these can be detected and in some cases were important. His party contained some substantial family groups – the much ramified Gores, for example, who at one time could boast nine representatives in the Irish House of Commons, and the Ponsonbys in County Kilkenny – but these groups were linked to the Speaker through friendship and patronage rather than blood ties or marriage. By contrast the Brodrick faction, which Brodrick's ultimate political successor, Henry Boyle inherited and developed during the 1730s, was based on a network of brothers, brothers-in-law and cousins (the Boyles rivalling the Gores as the most extended of Irish landed families).[40] Nor was Conolly's party in essence a regional connexion, like the St Georges in Connacht in Queen Anne's reign, or the Cork or Munster 'squadron' commanded by Brodrick, and later Boyle.[41] Because Conolly was himself from the north-west, with substantial electoral patronage deriving from his extensive land acquisitions in Counties Donegal and Londonderry, and because one or two of his key supporters, notably Gore and Maxwell, also hailed from the north (though far apart geographically) his party was sometimes identified with the province of Ulster, but this characterisation was artificial. If anything, it would be more appropriately identified with the capital and its environs. In terms of residence, rather than county of origin, men

35 Ld Brodrick to Thomas Brodrick, 5 Apr. 1716 (S.H.C., 1248/4/352–5) ranked Vesey with the Tories in 1716 parliament, but during 1717 Conolly described him as having acted the part of an 'honest man' in the Commons then and in the preceding sessions (Conolly to Charles Delafaye, 8 Aug. 1717 (T.N.A., SP 63/375/152)).

36 Coghill, Singleton, and Vesey may still have been reckoned as sympathetic to the Tory interest on the questions relating to the established church, as all three were included early in the 1719 session on what appears to be a lobbying list of M.P.s – the vast majority recognisable as Tories from Queen Anne's reign – in relation to the proposed repeal of the sacramental test (I.A.A., Conolly papers, A/3/9B).

37 Coghill had been involved with Conolly in organising the so-called 'national remonstrance' against the English Forfeitures Resumption Act (*C.J.*, xiii, 718; Patrick Walsh, *The making of the Irish Protestant ascendancy: the life of William Conolly, 1662–1729* (Woodbridge, 2010), p. 56).

38 Memorandum by Trotter about election matters [1713] (I.A.A., Conolly papers A/3/2A–B).

39 See above, p. 111.

40 See above, ch. 4.

41 Robert Johnson to Ormond, 2 Aug. 1707 (H.M.C., *Ormonde* MSS, new ser., viii, 307); Richard Stewart to [Edward Southwell], 18 Nov. 1707 (B.L., Southwell papers, Add. MS 9712, f. 82); above, ch. 4.

like the Clementses, Coghill, Gardiner, Manley, Marley, Tighe, and Trotter, inhabited the official world of Dublin. And when they built new country seats they often did so within easy reach of the capital: Viscount Boyne, for example, moved from his ancestral estates in the north to set himself up at Stackallan in County Meath; Henry Singleton resided across the road from Coghill in Drumcondra, just north of Dublin, Marlay at Celbridge Abbey, close to Conolly's own rural base at Castletown, Vesey down the road at Lucan (Conolly called him 'my neighbour in the country'[42]) and Ponsonby at Bishop's Court, at Straffan, also in Kildare, 'so near' Castletown 'that he can be there on an hour's warning'.[43]

What, then, did distinguish them as a group and hold them together? Most obviously Conolly's friendship and patronage. All benefited from the Speaker's ability to find jobs in government for themselves, their relations and friends. But beyond this basic currency of political obligation were strong personal connexions to the Speaker and each other. Their presence can be traced in Conolly's correspondence, and some, though not all, appear as beneficiaries in his will.[44] They can also be traced in each other's social circles, corresponding and visiting,[45] sharing in financial transactions or the purchase of land,[46] acting together in marriage settlements,[47] and ultimately being named as executors, trustees and beneficiaries in each other's wills.[48] Some – the lawyers – worked together in a professional capacity. Marlay, Rose and Singleton were barristers, and eventually judges; Coghill and Trotter both held degrees in civil law and practised in the ecclesiastical courts; while Conolly himself had made his money in the humbler capacity of an attorney. Others, like Luke Gardiner, had begun their careers in the law (or, in the case of Henry Maxwell, had attended an inn of court, though never called to the bar) but now occupied places in the Castle bureaucracy. What we have, therefore, is a close-knit group

42 Conolly to Delafaye, 8 Aug. 1717 (T.N.A., SP 63/375/172).

43 Midleton to Thomas Brodrick, 9 Mar. 1723[/4] (S.H.C., 1248/5/384–5).

44 T.N.A., Prob. 11/636, ff 90–92. There are bequests to his 'good friends' Bishops Theophilus Bolton and Arthur Price, and to Coghill, Marlay and Trotter (the first two also executors (cf. Thomas Pearson to Jane Bonnell, 16 Mar. 1729[/30] (N.L.I., MS 41,580/24)).

45 See e.g. Agmondisham Vesey to Sir Thomas Vesey, bp of Ossory, 11 Apr. 1727 (N.L.I., De Vesci papers, MS 38,876/2).

46 See, for example, deed relating to mortgage on lands in Denbighshire, held by Marmaduke Coghill and Agmondisham Vesey, 1705 (N.L.I., De Vesci papers, MS 38,745/5); mortgage between Thomas Carter et al. and Thomas Meredith, Marmaduke Coghill, Thomas Marlay et al., 8 Aug. 1720 (N.L.I., Wicklow papers, MS 38,369/19); assignment of lands to Brabazon Ponsonby and Luke Gardiner, 24 Aug. 1728 (N.L.I., Gardiner papers, MS 36502/8); exemplification of common recovery, 28 Nov. 1729 (again involving Gardiner and Ponsonby) (Nottinghamshire Archives, Staunton papers, DD/5/9/20).

47 For example, marriage settlement of Thomas Carter, jr, and Mary Claxton, 10 Oct. 1719 (N.L.I., Wicklow papers, MS 38,613/14).

48 Coghill's, with a bequest to Henry Singleton is at T.N.A., Prob. 11/695, ff 223–30; Singleton's, with a bequest to Thomas Marlay, is at N.A.I., 999/431, and abstracted in P. B. Eustace and Eilish Ellis (eds), *Registry of Deeds, Dublin: abstracts of wills* (3 vols, Dublin, 1954–84), ii, 124; the wills of Gore's widow and General Wynne, witnessed by Nathaniel Clements, are at ibid., i, 282, 240. See also ibid., 217 (will of James Topham, for which Coghill and Marlay were trustees), 238 (will of Thomas Pearson, M.P., Conolly's brother-in-law, who named Marlay and Trotter among the beneficiaries, together with 'my niece Coghill').

of Dublin-based men of business – lawyers, government functionaries, professional politicians with well remunerated sinecures; men from a variety of party political backgrounds linked by friendship and the patronage of the most powerful politician in Ireland. Their backgrounds are relatively easy to delineate, but what can be said about their view of themselves and of the function and purpose of government?

III

One possible answer comes from the American historian Reed Browning's work on the political thought of the Walpolean Court Whigs.[49] Browning claimed to have identified an 'ideology' of Court Whiggery that, as he put it, bore the 'impress' of Ciceronian ideas of law and government; that is to say an ideology which looked for guidance to Cicero's *De officiis*, and in contrast to the 'Catonic' vision of Country Whigs demonstrated the possibility of exercising virtue in government. Whether or not one accepts these arguments, they are not automatically transferable to Conolly's clique, other than to remind us, perhaps, that there can be more to office-holding than venality, and more to the exercise of power than self-interest. The political cultures of England and Ireland in the first half of the eighteenth century, though similar in many respects, were also crucially different. Irish Protestant gentlemen studied the same classical texts as their English counterparts, their libraries included many of the same works of history and political theory, they shared many of the same assumptions and preoccupations, but with one exception. For an Irish politician the public interest that he might claim to serve was the interest of Ireland, and the common perception was that the principal threat to that interest came not so much from the overbalancing of the constitution or the spread of corruption in any general sense but specifically from the oppressive nature of English government. The Anglo-Irish connexion, in other words, posed a political question that Browning's 'Ciceronians' did not have to consider.

The effort to discover whether Conolly's followers possessed a shared political outlook that was anything more than a form of collective opportunism is not greatly helped by the source materials. Browning was able to concentrate on prominent individuals who had each published reflections on the nature of politics in which they attempted to rationalise and justify their own behaviour. Of the Irish Castle party headed by Conolly, only Henry Maxwell left any published work, and all of it focused on specific rather than general issues. None of his colleagues, not even the most verbose, was given to philosophical reflection on the vocation of office-holding. Only Conolly and Coghill are represented by substantial surviving collections of private correspondence, and these discuss practical matters rather than the nature of politics – in itself, perhaps an indication of priorities. What can be traced in the letters is a prevailing impatience with what Conolly, Coghill, and their friends perceived as factious and self-serving opposition. Coghill's letters express a

49 Reed Browning, *Political and constitutional ideas of the court Whigs* (Baton Rouge, La. & London, 1982).

mild contempt for those in parliament who 'played the patriot', whether established politicians striking a pose for popularity, or country gentlemen whose starry-eyed sincerity was the transient product of youth and inexperience;[50] and irritation at the effusions of the popular press, which he regarded as ill-timed and unhelpful. On one occasion he criticised Swift for 'making that division amongst us that must do mischief ... whereas the happiness of this country must subsist by the good agreement and harmony amongst us all, whether English or Irish Protestants'.[51] He was particularly exercised by the publication in 1731 of *Some observations on the present state of Ireland ...*, by the young County Cork 'patriot', Sir Richard Cox, at a crucial stage in negotiations between the 'Irish lobby' at Westminster and the Walpole administration. Just as Coghill's friend Lord Perceval was hoping to persuade English M.P.s of the willingness of the Irish 'political nation' to cooperate with the British parliament, Cox declaimed against the mercantilist protectionism with which Westminster had malevolently restricted Irish trading freedoms, and revived the spectre of Irish claims to legislative autonomy. Not surprisingly, Coghill described it as a 'cursed pamphlet', whose outbursts of anti-English sentiment were 'most scandalous and wicked'.[52]

What these references perhaps indicate is a perennial sense of managerial world-weariness, rather than any explicit ideal of public service. On the positive side it could be lauded as 'moderation': a rational, and at the same time sophisticated, even cosmopolitan, awareness of what was possible in the real world; the product of experience, whose horizons were broader than the parochialism of Dublin politics. Thus Coghill was described by one embattled supporter of the 'English interest' in the House of Lords as 'a fast friend to the present government ... as moderate in the Irish interest as most who are born here', and Benjamin Parry by another as 'truly honest and steady to the English interest ... has good sense, and the advantage of seeing the world abroad have given him a right turn, and cleared him of all narrow national partialities'.[53] Negatively, it might appear as a mere reflex action of deference to the powerful and resentment at troublemakers asking awkward questions. As Midleton observed sarcastically of Henry Singleton, he displayed 'constant goodwill and affection to those in power under King George I'.[54] However, it may be possible to dig a little more deeply if we focus on the principal issues agitating Irish politics in the first decades of the eighteenth century: the nature of the Anglo-Irish constitutional relationship, and the possibilities for the economic and social 'improvement' of the kingdom.

The constitutional dependence of Ireland was determined by the essential nature of power-relations between the two kingdoms, and the identification of the ruling propertied elite in Ireland with the maintenance of English rule, an identification reinforced by the events of the Glorious Revolution and its aftermath. The country

50 Coghill to Edward Southwell, 8 Dec. 1727 (*Coghill letters*, pp 40–41).
51 Coghill to Southwell, 18 June 1728 (ibid., p. 55).
52 Coghill to Ld Perceval, 14 Apr. 1731 (ibid., pp 111–12).
53 Bp Godwin to [Abp Wake], 6 July 1720 (Christ Church Arch. W. Epist. xiii, no. 184); Bp Evans of Meath to [same], 24 Dec. [1716] (ibid., Arch W. Epist. xii).
54 Midleton to Thomas Brodrick, 10 Jan. 1721[/2] (S.H.C., 1248/5/170–3).

was ruled by a viceroy nominated by the monarch, which in theory deprived the Irish political classes of the capacity of influencing through their parliament the choice of their own government. In practice, however, since Lord Capell's tenure of the lord deputyship in the 1694–6, government had been carried on through negotiation between the viceroy and his Irish political managers, whose qualification for office lay in the support they could claim in the Irish parliament. Three significant constitutional issues remained unresolved, however. First, the legislative process was still determined by Poynings' Law, which gave a supervisory role to the Irish and British privy councils. Second, the British parliament had assumed a power to legislate for Ireland, on both public and private matters, a power exercised frequently in the period 1690–1707, though more sporadically thereafter, and given statutory expression in the Declaratory Act passed at Westminster in 1720. And finally the British House of Lords had asserted an appellate jurisdiction over Irish cases, above and beyond that of the Irish House of Lords, a claim also restated in the Declaratory Act.

While some political writers and a handful of the more obsessive or excitable back-benchers in the Irish parliament attacked these arrangements as contravening the political rights of Irishmen (or Englishmen living in Ireland), what was far more characteristic of Irish Protestant opinion in the so-called 'age of Molyneux and Swift' was the acceptance of constitutional restraints in pursuit of the greater good the English connexion was assumed to bring. From time to time in the Irish House of Commons members would denounce Poynings' Law, but with a few exceptions these complaints were directed at interference by the Irish rather than by the British privy council, and derived from the more immediate political motive of embarrassing either the ruling parliamentary clique or particular councillors. The admittedly frequent interventions by the British privy council were seldom directed at popular measures, and only very rarely at the holiest of holies, a money bill. Amendments at Whitehall were often necessary corrections to bills which had been poorly drafted and, even when deletions were made or provisions inserted that had real political significance in Ireland, these were not necessarily unpopular, the best example being the sacramental test clause added to the 1704 Popery Act, excluding Dissenters from crown and municipal office, which was welcomed by a clear majority in both houses of the Irish parliament.[55] Nor, it must be said, was Westminster's power to legislate for Ireland always disputed. Such English statutes as the act of 1689 settling the crown of Ireland on William and Mary, and the Act of Settlement of 1701, were welcomed by Irish Protestants; and even such an enthusiastic 'patriot' as Archbishop King of Dublin was prepared to avail himself of the opportunity to secure a private act at Westminster, since the more cumbersome nature of the Irish legislative process made it both easier and cheaper to do business of this kind in England.[56]

55 J. G. Simms, 'The making of a penal law (2 Anne, c.6), 1703–4' in *I.H.S.*, xii, no. 46 (Sept. 1960), pp 105–18; Edward Southwell to earl of Nottingham, 26 Feb. 1703/4 (*C.S.P.*, *dom.*, 1703–4, pp 542–4).

56 Philip O'Regan, *Archbishop William King of Dublin (1650–1729) and the constitution in church and state* (Dublin, 2000), pp 150–51; King to Robert King, 22 Nov. 1705 (T.C.D., Lyons (King) papers, MS 1995–2008/1181).

Some English acts were bitterly resented, especially the Woollen Act of 1699 and the Forfeitures Resumption Act of 1700, but in each case parliamentary opposition in Ireland focused on the effects rather than the principle. Members of the House of Lords were also agitated about the trumping of their appellate jurisdiction at Westminster. The long-running controversy over the case of *Annesley* v. *Sherlock*, which focused attention on the issue, resulted in the commitment to custody of Irish judges perceived as collaborating in English trespass on Irish judicial preserves.[57] Nevertheless, the passage of the Declaratory Act, which reaffirmed English jurisdictional authority over Ireland, produced no parliamentary response. It may well be that some of the published comment on *Annesley* v. *Sherlock*, and the parliamentary speeches of some of the more committed 'patriots', had come dangerously close to challenging what one peer called the '*arcana imperii*' – the constitutional connexion between Britain and Ireland.[58] Whatever the reason, Conolly's own view of the controversy was cool to the point of being dismissive. As English ministers fretted that the Declaratory Act would inflame patriotic sensibilities and discussed how to postpone the session, he wrote that

> really my humble opinion is that the House of Lords will be in a better temper, for as to the point of jurisdiction, that is over and determined, and cannot be returned or repeated, and sure no wise or thinking man will or can stir further in it, especially when they consider they may risk future parliaments and do the nation more mischief than they can ever do them good ... And further, why should this resentment reach the House of Commons, who never concerned themselves in the Lords' jurisdiction or had anything to do with that matter, but many of them to my knowledge used all their endeavours not to have the Lords commit my lord chief baron and the rest ...[59]

The points Conolly was making are typical of references to be found in the correspondence of his associates on such constitutional issues, that is to say, first, it was pointless to resist the fact of English constitutional domination since this was built into the nature of the relationship between the two kingdoms; second, those who agreed with him were 'wise and thinking men' and by implication those who disagreed were foolish and blindly reactive; and third, to achieve the good of the nation required a pragmatic approach. Nothing very exciting here, intellectually, but indicative of an attempt to rationalise a position that others satirised as merely passive and self-serving.

[57] Isolde Victory, 'The making of the 1720 Declaratory Act' in Gerard O'Brien (ed.), *Parliament, politics and people: essays in eighteenth-century Irish history* (Blackrock, Co. Dublin, 1989), pp 14–19; O'Regan, *Abp King*, pp 263–74; D. W. Hayton, 'The Stanhope/Sunderland ministry and the repudiation of Irish parliamentary independence' in *E.H.R.*, cxiii (1998), pp 612–13.

[58] Ld Perceval to Charles Dering, 5 Mar. 1719/20 (B.L., Egmont papers, Add. MS 47029, ff 22–5). See also [John Toland,] *Reasons most humbly offer'd to the hon[ourable] House of Commons, why the bill sent down to them from the most hon[ourable] House of Lords, entituled, An act for the better securing the dependency of the kingdom of Ireland, upon the crown of Great Britain, should not pass into a law* (London, 1720), pp 12–13. The debates are discussed in Victory, 'Making of the Declaratory Act', pp 17–22, 26–8; Hayton, 'Repudiation of Irish parliamentary independence', pp 615–20.

[59] Conolly to duke of Grafton, 29 Aug. 1720 (I.A.A., Conolly papers, A/3/15A–B).

It was not always possible to maintain this complacent attitude, however. Conolly and other members of his party occasionally found it politically necessary or convenient to make a public defence of Irish interests. As a lord justice, and revenue commissioner, Conolly was placed in an extremely difficult position by the furore against Wood's Halfpence, and, rather than be outflanked, was obliged to withhold the active assistance that English ministers sought from him.[60] Three years earlier, he and his closest associates had played an even more devious game in relation to the project to establish an Irish national bank. This was originally a non-party, or cross-party scheme, to promote the economic welfare of the kingdom, in which Viscount Boyne, Sir Ralph Gore, and Henry Sandford had been 'managers', Theophilus Clements, Gardiner, Manley, Marlay, Maxwell, Parry, Ponsonby, Rose, Vesey and Wynne early investors, and Maxwell a public advocate, but it ran into trouble during its progress through the Irish parliament.[61] The role played by Conolly's party in the ensuing debates is difficult to explain, as he and his followers switched from supporting the bank to opposing it on patriotic grounds, and then back to supporting it again, but it is likely that he was seeking to balance the attractions of popularity with the desirability of wrong-footing the Brodricks.[62] The same, rather desperate, opportunism gave rise in the same session to a malicious motion from Henry Maxwell against the operation of Poynings' Law, which was specifically intended as an attack on Midleton's actions in the Irish privy council.[63]

Much earlier in his career, Conolly himself had taken up a frankly confrontational position over one instance of English parliamentary interference in Irish affairs: the Forfeitures Resumption Act of 1700. Here he had a particular axe to grind, having made a fortune himself through dealing in forfeited estates, as a purchaser and manager.[64] The resumption was presented in England as an assault by the 'Country Party' on court corruption, but the implications in Ireland were very different, for the forfeited Jacobite estates granted by King William to Whig politicians and royal favourites had been sold or leased to Irish Protestants, and to rescind the grants would have resulted in serious financial consequences for a significant section of the Irish landed classes. A key element of the political crusade against the act in Ireland was the so-called 'national remonstrance', a series of county addresses to the King, in the organisation of which Conolly took the lead, aided by two men who were to later to be closely associated with him in government, Gustavus Hamilton and

60 Albert Goodwin, 'Wood's halfpence', in *E.H.R.*, li (1936), repr. in Rosalind Mitchison (arr.), *Essays in eighteenth-century history* (London, 1966), pp 122–3; Hayton, *Ruling Ireland*, pp 233–4.

61 James Macartney et al. to Ld Perceval, 2 June 1720 (B.L., Add. MS 47029, ff 32–3); *List of subscribers to the Bank of Ireland* [?1721] (Marsh's Library, MS Z.1.1.13, no. 59); Henry Maxwell, *Reasons offer'd for erecting a bank in Ireland; in a letter to Hercules Rowley, esq.* (1st & 2nd eds, Dublin 1721); idem, *Mr Maxwell's second letter to Mr Rowley; wherein the objections against the bank are answer'd* (Dublin, 1721). On the controversy over the Bank, see in general Michael Ryder, 'The Bank of Ireland, 1721: land, credit and dependency' in *Hist.Jn.*, xxv (1982), pp 557–82.

62 See above, pp 114–15.

63 Midleton to Thomas Brodrick, 5, 10 Jan. 1721[/2] (S.H.C., 1248/5/165–6, 171–3).

64 Walsh, *Making of the Irish Protestant ascendancy*, ch. 3.

Marmaduke Coghill.[65] Clearly the issue was of vital importance to Conolly personally, but it is important to note that the addresses did not actually challenge the right of the English parliament to legislate for Ireland, even though the signatories were caricatured by their English opponents as aiming at 'independency', a charge they vigorously denied.[66]

The only member of Conolly's faction who expressed public views on the nature of the Anglo-Irish constitutional relationship was Henry Maxwell.[67] As we have seen in the preceding chapter, Maxwell had cultivated in his younger days a number of interesting contacts in England, including the future chief minister James Stanhope, then an independent-minded back-bencher, and through Stanhope the circle of 'Country Whigs' surrounding the third earl of Shaftesbury. He wrote two political pamphlets in the early 1700s, one calling for war against the great tyrant Louis XIV, and the other, in 1703, recommending a union of England and Ireland, some of the arguments of which were redolent of the 'classical republican' rhetoric in recent English tracts against a standing army.[68] Maxwell also spoke in the Irish parliament in favour of regular sessions and against the operation of Poynings' Law. It would be tempting to see the trajectory of his career in terms of the gradual evaporation of youthful principle (as might be said of Stanhope), and a superficial reading of the evidence would support this interpretation. However, it is possible to trace a consistent thread in Maxwell's understanding of the Anglo-Irish political connexion. His objections to the Poynings' Law procedure were not to English conciliar superintendence but to the involvement of the Irish privy council in drafting bills of their own and amending the 'heads' sent up from the Commons, in a way that made the council almost a third partner in the legislative process. Second, Maxwell's appeal for an Anglo-Irish union in 1703 – one of the objectives of which was to defend the Irish Protestant elite from the charge levelled against supporters of the remonstrance, of seeking independence from England – far from releasing Ireland from the suffocating embrace of its sister kingdom, would in practice have tightened English control over Irish affairs, since the English majority in a united parliament would have been empowered to legislate for Ireland without the need for a statutory instrument. Later, in the two pamphlets he wrote in 1721 in support of a national bank, Maxwell acknowledged Ireland's constitutional subordination as an unchallengeable fact of political life, and argued that English supervision was a guarantee of Ireland's freedom from the machinations of its own vested interests.[69] He explained

65 J. G. Simms, *The Williamite confiscation in Ireland, 1690–1703* (London, 1956), pp 125–6; Hayton, *Ruling Ireland*, pp 82–3; Walsh, *Making of the Irish Protestant ascendancy*, pp 56–7.

66 Hayton, *Ruling Ireland*, p. 80; idem, 'Ideas of union in Anglo-Irish political discourse: meaning and use' in D. G. Boyce et al., *Political discourse in seventeenth- and eighteenth-century Ireland* (Basingstoke, 2001), pp 150–51.

67 For what follows, see above, pp 117–22.

68 *Anguis in herba: or the fatal consequences of a treaty with France* … (London, 1702); *An essay towards an union of Ireland with England* (London, repr. Dublin, 1703).

69 Maxwell, *Reasons offer'd for erecting a bank* … (1st ed.), p. 4; idem, *Mr Maxwell's second letter* …, pp 9, 17, 18, 19, 20.

publicly the virtues of a pragmatic constitutionalism in the same terms as Conolly had done privately:[70]

> the circumstances of Ireland, by reason of her dependence, are such, that she cannot always obtain the advantages she aims at, when she would, nor in the manner she desires; yet I have constantly observ'd, that we have thought it our wisdom, rather to take a part, than refuse the whole, and, in favours granted, rather to accept them in the manner they would be granted in, than refuse them, because we could not have them in the manner we desired.

IV

A cynic might well have said, of course, that the advantages arising from the English connexion to Maxwell himself, his political chieftain and their friends, were considerable, in the shape of jobs, pensions and opportunities to turn political power into profit. None the less, it is clear from the correspondence of other members of the Conolly connexion, notably Coghill, writing in the early 1730s, that there was genuine belief in the constructive possibilities of the existing constitutional system. Between 1729 and 1731 Coghill, now a revenue commissioner, worked in close co-operation with Viscount Perceval (the future Lord Egmont), to persuade the English parliament to remove the duty on imported Irish yarn, open more ports to receive Irish wool and woollen products, and remove some of the restrictions on colonial trade in the earlier Navigation Acts, in return for a pledge from the Irish parliament to restrain the illicit trade to France.[71] Coghill relied not only on Perceval's friendship with Sir Robert Walpole, and his own contacts among English politicians, but his belief that English M.P.s would accept that that the English and Irish economies could and should be mutually supportive. Sadly for him, few of them did.

Economic issues figured prominently in Coghill's correspondence from the late 1720s onwards, and not only while he held office as a revenue commissioner, when he might have been expected to take an official interest in the promotion of trade. Although not himself possessed of large estates and thus of the opportunity for direct participation in economic enterprise, he took a particular interest in the 'improvement of Ireland', reading and disseminating the literature on the subject, collecting information on trade patterns, and communicating these to friends in England who he thought were able to shape policy.[72] His circle of correspondents included many of the leading figures involved in promoting agricultural and technical innovation and settling new industries: Thomas Prior (whom he was said to have employed[73])

70 *Reasons offer'd for erecting a bank* … (1st ed.), p. 4.

71 Coghill to Perceval, 5 Apr. 1729, 14 Feb., 5 Mar. 1729/30, 25 Jan., 23 Feb., 4, 12, 23 Mar. 1730/1, 30 Mar., 14 Apr., 4 May 1731 (*Coghill letters*, pp 65–7, 90, 92–4, 104–12, 114–15); Perceval to Coghill, 19 Apr. 1729, 6 May 1730 (B.L., Egmont papers, Add. MS 47032, ff 110, 178–9). H.M.C., *Egmont diary*, i, 31, 48–9, 156, 159, 161–6; James, *Ireland in the empire*, pp 156–7.

72 *Coghill letters*, pp xvii–xviii.

73 James Smyth to William Smyth, 23 Dec. 1729 (N.L.I., MS 41,582/7). See also below, p. 194.

and James Hamilton, Lord Limerick, both stalwarts of the Dublin Society, the pamphleteer David Bindon, and two absentee landowners who despite residing in England took a great interest in the 'improvement' of their estates, Viscount Perceval, and Edward Southwell.[74] Coghill himself served for many years on the Linen Board, which had been established by act of parliament in 1711 for the promotion of the linen manufacture, and from 1729 on the Navigation Board, a similar statutory body that granted public money for developing economic infrastructure. He was also closely involved in the management of a number of charitable enterprises, including schools, hospitals and the Dublin workhouse, which took the notion of 'improvement' beyond economic progress to encompass broader social objectives, alleviating poverty and inculcating in the Irish population a form of English civility which in the minds of many enthusiasts was also intimately connected with the promotion of Protestant piety.[75]

Almost all the other prominent members of Conolly's party were involved in schemes for the 'improvement' of Ireland, through their own efforts, through belonging to voluntary organisations or government bodies, or promoting legislative initiatives. In 1723 Henry Maxwell – whose writings had recommended increased Protestant settlement in Ireland for just this purpose[76] – was included by Bishop Francis Hutchinson among a small number of exemplary 'improvers'.[77] Together with Richard Tighe, Maxwell was among the subscribers to John Laurence's A *new system of agriculture* (1727).[78] He may also be linked (as may Henry Rose), through tellerships and committees in the House of Commons, with Arthur Dobbs, author of the *Essay on the trade and improvement of Ireland* (1728, 1730), someone who was also a favourite of William Conolly,[79] and through Dobbs with public advocates of 'improvement', including Coghill's friends Prior and Bindon. These were the men who provided the ideas and energy behind the foundation in June 1731 of the Dublin Society, itself both a symbol and instrument of the cause of improvement,[80]

74 For Prior see below, pp 193–7; for Hamilton, *Hist. Ir. parl.*, iv, 342–4; for Bindon, ibid., iii, 180. For Coghill's connexions with Bindon, Hamilton, and Prior, see Coghill to Edward Southwell, 4 Feb. 1728[/9], to Ld Perceval, 4, 12 Mar. 1730/1, 14 Apr.1731 (*Coghill letters*, pp 60, 106, 108, 112); and for his correspondence with Perceval and Edward Southwell, ibid., passim.

75 *Coghill letters*, p. xix.

76 See above, pp 120–21.

77 Francis Hutchinson, *A letter to a Member of Parliament, concerning the imploying and providing for the poor* (Dublin, 1723), p. 6.

78 John Laurence, *A new system of agriculture, being a complete body of husbandry and gardening* ... (Dublin, 1727), subscription list.

79 *C.J.Ire.* (4th ed.), ii, 613; iv, 34; James Smyth to William Smyth, 11 Dec. 1727 (N.L.I., MS 41,582/5). On Dobbs, see Desmond Clarke, *Arthur Dobbs esquire 1689–1765* ... (Chapel Hill, N.C., 1957); Caroline Robbins, *The eighteenth-century commonwealthman* (Cambridge, Mass., 1959), pp 149–52; *Oxf. D.N.B.*, xvi, 340–42. Note that Dobbs's *An essay on the trade and improvement of Ireland* (Dublin, 1729), pp 69–72, echoes Maxwell's earlier pamphlet in arguing for the advantage to England of a British-Irish union (Robbins, *Eighteenth-century commonwealthman*, p. 149).

80 On the establishment and early history of the society, see Terence de Vere White, *The story of the Royal Dublin Society* (Tralee, [1955]), chs 1–3; Clarke, *Arthur Dobbs*, ch. 4; T. C. Barnard, *Making the grand figure: lives and possessions in Ireland, 1641–1770* (New Haven, Conn., & London, 2004), p. 198; idem, 'The Dublin Society and other improving societies, 1731–5' in James Kelly and M. J. Powell (eds), *Clubs and societies in eighteenth-century Ireland* (Dublin, 2010), pp 53–88.

and several members of the Castle party were among the members admitted in its first year. Archbishop Bolton and Bishop Price joined in September 1731, Luke Gardiner, Isaac Manley and Henry Rose in November, Richard Tighe in December, and Benjamin Parry in the following March. Others may also have been admitted but their membership was not formally recorded in the minutes.[81] Of course, not everyone joined such societies for entirely serious purposes, and elements of sociability and snobbery became even more pronounced when the new viceroy, Dorset, gave the society his patronage in December 1731, but the records of meetings exude an earnestness in the cause of national improvement, and occasionally we encounter specific evidence of agricultural or industrial activity, as in March 1732 when barrels of a new compost were distributed to members, including Marmaduke Coghill.[82]

Membership of the various statutory bodies charged with supervising schemes for the economic and social 'improvement' of Ireland provides less clear proof of commitment to the cause, since the overall number of nominees in each case was high, and prominent dignitaries, clerical and lay, could expect to be named. But the cumulative evidence is suggestive. The board established to oversee the development of the linen manufacture by an Irish act of 1711 (9 Anne, c. 3 [Ire.]) included Conolly, Coghill, Gustavus Hamilton and Henry Sandford among its more than seventy original members. They were later joined by Bolton, Gardiner, Gore, Marlay, Ponsonby, Rose, Singleton, and Trotter.[83] The Dublin workhouse, when reorganised by statute in 1727/8 (1 Geo. II, c. 27 [Ire.]), included among its trustees Conolly, Gore, Marlay, and Singleton *ex officio*, and by name Bolton, Nathaniel and Theophilus Clements, Coghill, Manley, Maxwell, Parry, Ponsonby, Rose, Tighe, Vesey, and Wynne.[84] And finally the Navigation Board, established to administer the funding raised by the Navigation or Tillage, Act of 1729–30 (3 Geo. II, c. 3 [Ire.]), a portmanteau measure pushed forward by the ministry as essential to the regeneration of the Irish economy, which comprehended the draining of bogs, the promotion of tillage, and the building of canals,[85] included among its over ninety nominated members a squadron of familiar faces: Bolton, Coghill, Gardiner, Gore, Marlay, Maxwell, Parry, Ponsonby, Rose, Sandford, Singleton, Tighe, Trotter, Vesey, and Wynne.[86] How many of these individuals attended meetings is generally unknown,

81 Dublin Society minutes, 16 Sept., 11, 18, 25 Nov., 4 Dec. 1731, 2 Mar. 1731[/2] (R.D.S., society minute book 1, ff 4, 16–18, 23, 48). *Hist. Ir. parl.* also records 'information taken from the *Almanacs*' to the effect that Coghill, Marlay, Singleton and Trotter were 'foundation members' of the society, while noting that this evidence is 'not necessarily reliable' (i, 11; iii, 445; v, 192; vi, 277, 443).

82 Dublin Soc. min., 23 Mar. 1731[/2] (R.D.S., soc. min.bk 1, f. 51).

83 *Precedents and abstracts from the journals of the trustees of the linen and hempen manufactures of Ireland* (Dublin, 1784), pp 2, 60, 67, 101, 117, 131.

84 *The statutes at large, passed in the parliaments held in Ireland* ... (20 vols, Dublin, 1786–1801), v, 314–15.

85 See Ld Carteret to Edward Southwell, 8 Jan., 9 Feb. 1729/30 (B.L., Southwell papers, Add. 38016, ff 19, 23); and also the covering letter with the 'transmiss' of the bill sent by Carteret and Irish privy council (the signatories including Bolton, Coghill and Maxwell) to the British privy council, 3 Jan. 1729 (B.L., Hardwicke papers, Add. MS 36138, ff 116–17).

86 *Statutes at large ... Ireland* ..., v, 342–3. For Bolton's particular practical interest in schemes to drain bogland, see Edward McParland, *Public architecture in Ireland, 1680–1760* (New Haven, Conn., & London, 2002), p. 25.

but Coghill's own correspondence shows that he, for one, did involve himself in the work of the Navigation Board,[87] while a signed order of the workhouse governors in 1729 bears the names of Manley, Sandford, and Tighe;[88] and the records of the Linen Board show that Bolton, Coghill, Gardiner, Gore, Marlay, Ponsonby, Rose, Sandford, Singleton, and Trotter were all at one time or another active members.[89]

In parliament Henry Maxwell had a particularly strong record of sponsoring legislation to foster economic development. Between 1715 and his death in 1730 he was involved in the preparation, introduction and progress of bills for harbour construction, the improvement of tillage, the reduction of interest charged on loans (a nostrum advanced by various apostles of economic improvement[90]), the safeguarding of fisheries, the employment of the poor, the facilitation of exports of beef and dairy products, the protection of the woollen industry, the encouragement of tanning and of the manufacture of 'Bologna crape', and, almost on an annual basis, measures to improve the quality of linen.[91] But he was far from unusual in this regard among the leading lights of the Castle party. Agmondisham Vesey and Henry Rose were particularly active. They helped Maxwell draft tillage bills, bills for reducing interest, and for regulating the sale of butter, and were also prominent in the legislative campaign for improving Ireland's roads. Vesey took a leading role in the promotion of measures for the development of mining, and Rose in preparing bills setting the poor to work.[92] Thomas Marlay, too, was frequently given responsi-

87 Coghill to Edward Southwell, 7 May 1730 (*Coghill letters*, pp 101–2). The charter establishing the Incorporated Society for Promoting English Protestant Working Schools in Ireland, in 1733, the 'charter schools', included, besides the great officers in church and state, Coghill, Manley, Sandford, Tighe, Trotter and Wynne (*A copy of his majesty's royal charter, for erecting English Protestant schools in the kingdom of Ireland* ... (Dublin, 1733)), but I am inclined to put little weight on this, since, although Conolly himself left money in his will to establish a charity school, none of Conolly's close supporters had previously been involved with the foundation or maintenance of such institutions: see below, ch. 7; Edward Synge, *Methods of erecting, supporting and governing charity-schools: with an account of the charity-schools in Ireland; and some observations thereon* ... (3rd ed., Dublin, 1721).

88 *By-laws, rules and orders, for the better regulating of hackney-coaches ... within the city of Dublin ... made by the governors of the workhouse of the city of Dublin* (Dublin, 1729), p. 18.

89 *Precedents and abstracts*, pp 23, 55, 77, 83, 97, 101, 117, 131, 139. Ponsonby applied for a grant from the board in 1725 to set up a bleach yard; Theophilus Clements in 1726 for encouragement for a spinning school (ibid., pp 73, 79).

90 See, e.g., John Browne, *Seasonable remarks on trade. With some reflections on the advantages that might accrue to Great Britain* ... (Dublin, 1728), p. 63; idem, *A reply to the observer on Seasonable remarks* (Dublin, 1728), p. 18; David Bindon, *A scheme for supplying industrious men with money to carry on their trades, and for better providing for the poor of Ireland* (Dublin, 1729), pp 6–7, 9, 12–14, 21–2; Prior, *List of absentees*, p. 19; Arthur Dobbs, *An essay on the trade and improvement of Ireland, part II* (Dublin, 1731), pp 19–20.

91 *C.J.Ire.* (4th ed.), iii, 14, 38, 130, 133, 252, 253, 296–7, 317, 332, 348, 349, 350–51, 400, 407, 418, 426, 434, 480, 484, 523, 545; drafts of heads of bill to regulate the weighing and packing of butter [c. 1723] (P.R.O.N.I., Perceval-Maxwell papers, D/1556/16/4/9–10); above, pp 116–17.

92 *C.J.Ire.* (4th ed.), iii, 14, 127, 328,407, 416, 434, 612, 616–17; iv, 12, 15, 34. In Rose's case, we have direct confirmation of his interest in spreading tillage and protecting Irish industry. In 1731, looking forward to the new parliamentary session, he informed a correspondent in County Kerry (where his own parliamentary seat lay) that he favoured a prohibition on the importing of French brandy, since 'our own spirits, extracted from malt etc., will bring in a much greater revenue, and

bility for such legislation, as might only have been expected from someone who was a senior law officer for ten years, as solicitor-general 1720–7 and attorney-general 1727–30. From 1717, when he was named to a drafting committee on heads of a bill for the employment of the poor, he was involved in the preparation and discussion of legislation on improving roads, planting and preserving timber, encouraging tillage, and regulating the Dublin workhouse.[93] Coghill worked on bills for the planting of timber, the manufacture and sale of dairy products, the promotion of the leather industry, and the repair of highways.[94] Trotter chaired the committee appointed to examine the petition of a paper-maker for financial sponsorship by parliament, and was also involved in a timber planting bill, and in various legislative attempts to deal with poverty.[95] Richard Tighe led a Commons inquiry into the possibility of manufacturing gunpowder in Ireland and worked on bills for tillage, timber, roads, and the problem of the idle poor.[96] Sir Ralph Gore chaired the committee in 1715–16 preparing heads of a bill to preserve the salmon fishery, and was involved in measures to regulate the linen industry and the improvement of Dublin harbour.[97] Henry Singleton took prime responsibility in 1729 for the legislation establishing the Navigation Board, and also participated in the drafting of heads of bills for the regulation of the Dublin workhouse, and the construction of roads.[98] Benjamin Parry was involved in managing several linen bills and the Dublin harbour bill;[99] Isaac Manley in bills for reducing the interest of money, and employing the poor;[100] and Henry Sandford in bills for the employment of the poor and establishing the Dublin–Kinnegad turnpike.[101] The 'Castle party' was also identified with the parliamentary campaign to improve the education of poor children in the Protestant religion and in 'habits of industry'. When leave was granted in 1723 for heads for a bill to amend the act relating to free schools, the M.P.s named were Trotter, Marlay, Coghill, and Singleton, and a similar bill in 1725 included Trotter, Coghill, and Maxwell on the drafting committee, with Maxwell in the chair.[102]

It is worth pointing out Conolly himself – though singled out for praise by Thomas Prior in his *List of absentees* ..., published in 1729, as a landlord who lived in Ireland and kept his wealth in the country[103] – did not have a reputation for the energetic

at the same time consume our corn, and increase the tillage, and, as the French trade is grown very pernicious I could also wish that a further duty might be laid on claret, and white wine. This would hinder it from being so common as it is, and such whose purses could not come at it would be contented with their own manufacture.' (Henry Rose to Sir Maurice Crosbie, 23 Sept. 1731 (N.L. I., Talbot-Crosbie papers, P.C. 188).

93 *C.J.Ire.* (4th ed.), iii, 133, 206, 252, 315, 480, 519.

94 Ibid., 252, 337–8, 449–50, 484.

95 Ibid., 227, 315, 406, 434, 437, 519.

96 Ibid., 185, 252, 315, 326, 327, 348.

97 Ibid., 38, 144, 525.

98 Ibid., 490, 599, 613.

99 Ibid., 39, 92–4, 144, 525.

100 Ibid., 268, 407, 434.

101 Ibid., 315; ibid., iv, 12.

102 Ibid., iii, 349, 425.

103 Thomas Prior, *A list of the absentees of Ireland, and the yearly value of their estates and incomes spent abroad* ... (Dublin, 1729), p. 35. He was of course a multiple internal absentee.

exploitation of his property, and for most of his career left management to stewards and agents, his eyes turned to rental income rather than agricultural productivity.[104] However, he did engage more directly in the last years of his life, when bad harvests plunged the economy into crisis. The effects were felt most keenly in north-west Ulster, where Conolly owned large tracts of land, and where miserable economic conditions resulted in mass emigration, mainly of Presbyterians, to north America. His agent Robert McCausland kept him informed of the condition of the tenantry, and although he did not take McCausland's advice and recommend the introduction of a law to prevent emigration he did what he could to advance charitable efforts for the relief of distress.[105]

If it existed at all, Conolly's public commitment to 'improvement' took a more personal form. While not giving much attention to the economic progress of his estates, he was prepared to pay, and on a lavish scale, for the building of a new house, in the latest architectural fashion, at Castletown in County Kildare. Conolly's Palladian mansion, designed by the young Edward Lovett Pearce, decorated with plaster ceilings by Italian craftsmen, decked out with fine furnishings, and surrounded by formal gardens, staged the house parties which were his, and Ireland's, equivalent of the congresses held by Walpole at Houghton.[106] Clearly the building of Castletown was meant in part as a political statement. It has been linked with the building of the new Parliament House in Dublin between 1729 and 1731, also designed by Pearce, which was much more obviously an assertion of patriotic self-respect.[107] But whether the kind of conspicuous consumption that Castletown represented can properly be classified with more constructive investment in agricultural or industrial development is an open question. Some historians think it should be, and discussions of the vogue for 'improvement' in eighteenth-century Ireland have included under that general heading the construction of new houses, importation of English and continental luxuries, emparking of demesnes, and horticultural experimentation.[108] In this respect it is worth noting that Conolly's example was followed, or perhaps in some case anticipated, by most of his close friends: Marmaduke Coghill left the house outside Dublin that he had inherited, Belvedere House, in the hands of his friend Henry Singleton, and built a new mansion across the road, Drumcondra House, which may also have been the work of Pearce, with a sumptuous interior

104 Patrick Walsh, 'The career of William Conolly, 1689–1729' (PhD thesis, T.C.D., 2007), chs 1, 8.

105 Ibid., ch. 6.

106 Maurice Craig and the Knight of Glin, 'Castletown, Co. Kildare' in *Country Life*, clxv (1969), pp 722–6, 798–802; the Knight of Glin and John Cornforth, 'Castletown, Co. Kildare' in ibid., pp 882–5; Barnard, *Making the grand figure*, pp 91–3; Finola O'Kane, *Landscape design in eighteenth-century Ireland: mixing foreign trees with the natives* (Cork, 2004), pp 48–55; Mary Jones to Jane Bonnell, 13 Jan.[?1727] (N.L.I., Smythe of Barbavilla papers, MS 41,577/1).

107 Edward McParland, 'Building the Parliament House in Dublin' in *Parliamentary History*, xxi (2002), pp 131–40; idem, *Public architecture in Ireland*, ch. 7.

108 L. J. Proudfoot, 'Landownership and improvement, c. 1700 to 1845' in idem and William Nolan (eds), *Down: history and society* ... (Dublin, 1997), pp 214–18; Andrew Sneddon, 'Bishop Francis Hutchinson (1660–1739): a case study in the eighteenth-century culture of improvement' in *I.H.S.*, xxxv, no. 139 (May 2007), pp 308–9; idem, *Witchcraft and Whigs: the life of Bishop Francis Hutchinson, 1660–1739* (Manchester, 2008), ch. 8.

and extensive pleasure grounds.[109] Singleton in turn began to remodel Belvedere in his retirement. He was 'very busy adding to his house and altering his gardens', as Mrs Delany observed: 'like a conceited connoisseur', he was 'doing strange things, building an absurd room, turning fine wild evergreens out of his garden, and planting twigs'.[110] Elsewhere Theophilus Bolton may have engaged Edward Lovett Pearce to build the new episcopal palace at Cashel, on which he is alleged to have spent £3,600; Arthur Price, while rector of Celbridge, possibly employed the surveyor-general Thomas Burgh (architect of the new library at Trinity College) to build Oakly Park; Lord Boyne erected a new house at Stackallan, while in the same county, Thomas Trotter had the renowned Irish architect Richard Castle create for him a mansion on his ancestral estate at Duleek, and Brabazon Ponsonby employed another rising star, Francis Bindon, to produce plans for Bessborough House in County Kilkenny.[111] Luke Gardiner, the vice-treasurer, developed several squares and streets on the north side of Dublin city, a process which his protégé and successor, Nathaniel Clements, a very junior member of the Castle faction under Conolly and his immediate successors, carried forward, before reconstructing the house in Phoenix Park which he occupied by virtue of holding the office of ranger of the park.[112]

V

Of course, none of this effectively distinguishes the members of the Castle party from the general run of eighteenth-century Irish country gentlemen. Conolly's and Coghill's new houses and gardens could be matched by the embellishments to architecture and landscape undertaken by political opponents, such as Viscount Molesworth.[113] Nor was a concern for economic 'improvement' to be found only in the ranks of the Castle party. There were opposition 'patriots' as well as government officials in the Dublin Society, and, to give only one example, Maxwell's advocacy of the further settlement in Ireland of colonies of foreign Protestants with manufacturing expertise, echoed Molesworth.[114] But what is significant about the commitment to improvement to be found in Conolly's party is that it was presented as an expression of their 'patriotism' and used to distinguish this more conservative brand from what they saw as the factiousness of their opponents.

109 F. E. Ball, *A history of the County Dublin* (6 parts, Dublin, 1902–20), pt 6, p. 171; T. U. Sadleir and P. L. Dickinson, *Georgian mansions in Ireland* … (Dublin 1915), pp 65, 67; Rolf Loeber, *A biographical dictionary of architects in Ireland 1600–1720* (London, 1981), p. 54; McParland, *Public architecture in Ireland*, p. 12; Barnard, *Making the grand figure*, p. 174.

110 *Letters from Georgian Ireland: the correspondence of Mary Delany, 1731–68*, ed Angélique Day (Belfast, 1991), p. 44.

111 Barnard, *Making the grand figure*, pp 54, 173, 182, 202–3; Mark Bence-Jones, *Burke's guide to country houses*, i: *Ireland* (London, 1978), pp 41, 113, 226, 264. For a more sceptical view of Bolton's responsibility for building at Cashel, see A. P. W. Malcomson, *Archbishop Charles Agar: churchmanship and politics in Ireland, 1760–1810* (Dublin, 2002), pp 334–8, 340, 342–50.

112 Malcomson, *Nathaniel Clements*, pp 202–4; McParland, *Public architecture*, pp 145–59.

113 O'Kane, *Landscape design in 18th-cent. Ireland*, ch. 1.

114 Maxwell, *Reasons offer'd for erecting a bank in Ireland* … (1st ed.), pp 14, 21, 23, 40, 48.

The elaborate arrangements for Conolly's funeral in 1729, organised by his widow, included the distribution of seven hundred Irish linen scarves among the mourners, an ostentatious gesture intended to emphasise the Speaker's commitment to Irish industry.[115] In making these arrangements Mrs Conolly was not only expressing her own well-known concern for the encouragement of Irish manufacture,[116] but also staking a claim for her deceased husband's credentials as a representative of Irish 'patriotism' in what was contested ground between government and opposition. Each side claimed a commitment to the interests of Ireland, but went about proving their sincerity in different ways. 'Country' members put forward votes and resolutions aimed at preserving the rights and privileges of the Irish parliament, exposing corruption and incompetence in government, or, in some cases, seeking to embarrass the viceroy by engineering a crisis in Anglo-Irish relations.[117] This was what Bishop Bolton called 'peevish patriotism', espoused by those who 'set up for popularity'.[118] For the Castle party, on the other hand, patriotic pretensions could be established by supporting constructive measures for the development of the Irish economy, and for the improvement of Irish society, within the existing constitutional framework.

The obvious question is whether this kind of pragmatic, economic-oriented patriotism constituted a genuine aspiration or merely a posture. The evident concern shown by ministerialist Whigs for fostering improvement on their own property, for passing legislation to nurture Irish manufactures and improve infrastructure, and their connexion with bodies like the Dublin Society and the Linen and Navigation Boards, provides one answer.[119] Another is suggested by the complexities of the relationships within government, between Irish politicians and English appointees. When Conolly fell seriously ill in 1728, and the end of his political career was in sight, he was lauded by one of his lieutenants for the way in which he had been able to represent the native-born political elite on the commission of lords justices; it was vital, the argument ran, that his replacement be an Irishman and one similarly committed to advancing national interests.[120] Gore, his successor, was said to have encountered difficulties with his English colleagues on the commission, who neither knew nor cared for Ireland as much as he did.[121] Admittedly, the sharpest differences that occurred between lords justices, and indeed more generally between men like

115 Francis Burton to Jane Bonnell, 19 Nov. 1729 (N.L.I., MS 41,579/9).

116 In 1721 she had bought 'seven stuff suits of clothes' to give away 'for the encouragement of the poor weavers' (Jane Bulkeley to Jane Bonnell, 4 Apr. 1721 (ibid., MS 41,580/3).

117 McNally, *Parties, patriots and undertakers*, pp 185–91.

118 Bp Bolton to [Ld Carteret], 16 July 1728 (P.R.O.N.I., Massereene–Foster papers, D/562/92). Cf. Philip Perceval to Lord Perceval, 1 Feb. 1725/6 (B.L., Add. MS 47031, ff 93–4); Abp Boulter to [duke of Newcastle], 23 Oct. 1729 (T.N.A., SP 63/391/184–5); Carteret to Edward Southwell, 26 Feb. 1729/30 (B.L., Add. MS 38016, ff 25–6).

119 In this connexion it is instructive to note the thesis proposed in James Livesey, 'The Dublin Society in eighteenth-century Irish political thought' in *Hist. Jn.*, xlvii (2004), pp 615–40, that the intellectual principles underlying the establishment of the Dublin Society (with which Conolly's faction had close links) represented a new departure in Irish 'patriotism', away from the old obsession with the Anglo-Irish constitutional nexus, and towards a programme of social reformation.

120 Coghill to Edward Southwell, 13 June 1728 (*Coghill letters*, p. 53). See also Coghill to Edward Southwell, jr, 22 Feb. 1732[/3] (ibid., p. 120).

121 Coghill to Edward Southwell, jr, 31 Mar. 1733 (ibid., p. 124).

Conolly and Gore and agents of the 'English interest' like Primate Boulter and Lord Chancellor Wyndham, concerned recommendations to office. When responding to vacancies in the judiciary, or the Church of Ireland episcopate, Conolly invariably pushed forward Irishmen – and invariably his own loyal supporters – while Boulter at first argued the advantages of reminding the Irish of their subordinate status by bringing in Englishmen, who would be more likely to stand loyal to government in any crisis in Anglo-Irish relations, such as had occurred over Wood's patent.[122] This was indeed 'patriotism' of a sort, even if it was in Conolly's personal interest to recommend his friends and dependants. In the revenue commission he took a similar line, appointing Irishmen to posts in the customs and excise ostensibly on grounds of knowledge and experience, and with an explicit objective of increasing the professionalism and efficiency of collection, though with the additional benefit to himself of expanding the reserve of obligation among Irish political families.[123] But not all the battles fought by Conolly and Gore with their English colleagues were over patronage. Others concerned matters of policy, often economic policy – whether to revalue the currency, for example, or to prevent the export of corn in times of distress.[124] Over the course of their careers in government the two Speakers could claim a number of successes in struggles which were hidden from the public gaze and from which they derived no political capital. It would have probably have surprised back-bench 'patriots' that staunch courtiers like Bolton and Coghill should be accused by Archbishop Boulter, the prime spokesman for the 'English interest' in the Dublin government, of being unreasonably 'patriotic' and thus unreliable.[125]

No amount of searching will reveal a clearly and expressly articulated 'ideology' among the governing elite in early Hanoverian Ireland. Unlike Browning's selection of Court Whigs, Conolly and his friends did not reflect upon – at least not in writing – the difficulties of reconciling virtue with the exercise of power. One obvious place to look for evidence of the way in which the concept of public duty was understood, epitaphs on funerary monuments, also yields a poor return, except for the tributes paid by Mrs Conolly to the memory of the Speaker, and Marmaduke Coghill's sister to her deceased brother, to which we shall return. What can be identified, however, is the social context which the Castle party inhabited, and the mentality which they seem to have shared and which shaped their political attitudes. Much of this is perfectly unexceptional for men of their class and time: acceptance of the constitutional arrangements under which Irish government operated – given the absence of a practicable alternative – and a concern for the social and economic improvement of the kingdom. But for those charged with the business of administration and the making of law, such commonplaces might easily be elevated into points of prin-

122 McNally, *Parties, patriots and undertakers*, pp 168–73; Hayton, *Ruling Ireland*, p. 249; Walsh, 'Career of Conolly', ch. 7.

123 Walsh, *Making of the Irish Protestant ascendancy*, ch. 7.

124 Abp Boulter to Carteret, 14 Dec. 1728, 25 Apr. 1730 (*Boulter letters*, i, 268; ii, 3–4); Boulter to duke of Dorset, 22 July 1732 (ibid., ii, 78–80).

125 Boulter to Bp Gibson of London, 25 Apr. 1727 (ibid., i, 157); Boulter to Newcastle, 20 Feb. 1728[/9] (ibid., 283).

ciple, especially when contrasted with the more extreme rhetoric of 'patriots' within parliament and popular pamphleteers outside it.

It was an attitude that Swift professed to regard as bogus. In a memorable passage in the Drapier's *Letter to the whole people of Ireland*, he parodied ministerial patriotism in describing how the myrmidons of the Castle would in all likelihood seek to persuade Irish M.P.s to accept the ruinous coinage minted by the rascal Wood.

> Depending persons would have been told, in plain terms, that it was a service expected from them, under the pain of public business being put into more complying hands. Others would be allured by promises ... It would perhaps have been hinted ... that gentlemen ought to consider whether it were prudent or safe to disgust England. They would be desired to think of some good bills for encouraging of trade, and setting the poor to work; some further acts against popery ... Perhaps a seasonable report of some invasion would have been spread ... and we should have been told, that this was no time to create differences, when the kingdom was in danger.[126]

The stinging force of this passage comes from the wicked accuracy with which it imitated the case usually made by parliamentary 'undertakers' and their assistants in order to convince M.P.s of the necessity of accepting unpopular measures. When in due course such arguments were put forward, readers would infer what the dean wished them to infer, namely that the Castle spokesmen were hacks serving a turn rather than patriots serving their country. This does not, of course, mean that we should take Swift's public denunciations at face value; indeed, he may not himself have taken an entirely negative view of Conolly's 'Castle' party. While he roundly condemned Tighe, Clements and Vesey in print, and sneered at Speaker Conolly in private correspondence,[127] Swift enjoyed good relations with Coghill, regarded Price as 'honest and good natured', eventually came to appreciate the merits of Bolton, and always held a high opinion of Henry Singleton, whom he described as 'one of the first among the worthiest persons in this kingdom' and named an executor of his will.[128]

Some of Conolly's followers may have conformed to the caricature of Dublin lawyers and officials on the make; second-rate political figures who were emulating their patron in making fortunes from a privileged access to power. But amidst the

126 *The Drapier's letters and other works 1724–1725*, ed. Harold Williams, in *The prose works of Jonathan Swift*, ed. Herbert Davis et al. (16 vols, Oxford, 1939–74), x, p. 76. See also the *Humble address to both Houses of Parliament* ... with its reference to 'certain bold undertakers of weak judgment, and strong ambition, who seek to find their accounts in the ruin of the nation, by securing or advancing themselves' (ibid., pp 145–6) and its further condemnation of corrupt office-holders (ibid., p. 147). I am grateful to my colleague, Professor S. J. Connolly, for reminding me of the passage in the *Letter to the whole people of Ireland*, which is quoted at greater length in his *Divided kingdom: Ireland 1630–1800* (Oxford, 2008), p. 238.

127 Swift to John Gay and the duchess of Queensberry, 28 Aug. 1731 (*Swift Corr.*, ed. Williams, iii, 428). See also Swift, *Drapier's letters*, ed. Davis, p. 8.

128 Swift to Abp King of Dublin, 2 Mar. 1716/17 (*Swift Corr.*, ed. Williams, iii, 255); Swift to Knightley Chetwode, [Dec. 1723] (ibid., 424–5); Swift to Charles Ford, 2 Apr. 1724 (ibid., iii, 10); Swift to Carteret, [17 Apr. 1725] (ibid., iii, 58); Swift to John Barber, 1 Mar. 1734/5 (ibid., iv, 300); Thomas Sheridan to Swift, 23 June 1735 (ibid., 355).

flaunting of wealth they do seem to have prided themselves on the possession of a genuine concern for the improvement of their country, and a coherent and realistic strategy for achieving it. This self-belief is expressed in the words of the monument to Speaker Conolly, in Kildraught church near Castletown, which eulogised his devotion both to crown and kingdom. 'As a subject he was loyal; as a citizen, patriotic.' 'He served his country without forgetting his duty to his king, and served his king without forgetting what was due to his country.'[129] It appears even more floridly in the inscription placed by Hester Coghill under the oversized statue of her brother Marmaduke in the church built from the ample profits accrued from his two decades in high office.[130] Whether or not it accurately represents his character is immaterial; what is important is the terms in which Hester couched her eulogy, and which may stand as an epitome of the political pretensions of her brother and his friends:

> his experience of the true interest of his prince and of his country, and his strict attention and invincible regard to both, qualified him equally to discharge his trust as a counsellor and servant of the crown and a representative of the subject ... his universal benevolence, endeared by the most engaging and affable behaviour, and associated with the greatest zeal and abilities, distinguished him in every scene and period of life as the friend of mankind, and caused his death to be lamented as a national loss.

129 Quoted in C. I. Graham, 'The right honourable William Conolly, Speaker of the Irish House of Commons' in *Journal of the County Kildare Archaeological Society*, iii (1899–1902), pp 113–14.
130 Homan Potterton, *Irish church monuments 1570–1880* (Belfast, 1975), pp 76–7; Ball, *Hist. Co. Dublin*, pt 6, pp 173–4.

7

Creating industrious Protestants

Charity schools and the enterprise of religious and social reformation*

Of the many questions that might be asked about the course of the Protestant Reformation in early modern Ireland, one of the most popular, and in the long run probably the most important, is also the simplest: why, over several centuries, did proponents of the reformed religion not win over the hearts and minds of a majority of Irish men and women? Was it a failure of means, or of will, on the part of the reformers? Indeed, can it be properly described as a failure at all? For historians of the sixteenth and early seventeenth centuries, these have been matters of vigorous debate. Little consideration has been given, however, to the most promising of the opportunities missed by the established church, that brief dawn in the aftermath of the Glorious Revolution when the Catholic political interest in Ireland lay broken and, to all intents and purposes, impotent. Surveying the prostration of their enemies, and secure in their own power, some Protestant politicians and churchmen confidently predicted the fatal decline of popery on the island. Yet, despite the enactment of a succession of statutes to restrict or banish Catholic parish clergy and religious, and to encourage conversion, popery did not wither but survived to flourish again.

Once upon a time, conventional wisdom explained this disappointment in terms of Protestant complacency and weakness: an Irish parliament of hard-faced landowners was cynically contriving penal laws with the entirely secular aim of preserving their own monopoly of property and power; a Church of Ireland establishment, materially poor and spiritually torpid, was unable and unwilling to rise above the mundane. Just how far this contemptuous view – ultimately derived, one suspects, from the anti-clericalism of eighteenth-century caricaturists – diverged from the reality has been demonstrated by the careful research of scholars like J. C. Beckett, T. C. Barnard and S. J. Connolly. In rehabilitating conscientious bishops and parish incumbents from ritualised condemnation, they have also emphasised the positive contribution made by the established clergy to the 'improvement' of Ireland.[1] Indeed, it is now possible to identify a powerful reformist strain in the

* Originally published as 'Did Protestantism fail in eighteenth-century Ireland? Charity schools and the enterprise of religious and social reformation, c. 1690–1730' in Alan Ford, J. I. McGuire and Kenneth Milne (eds), *As by law established: the Church of Ireland since the Reformation* (Dublin, 1995), pp 166–86, 268–75.

1 See especially T. C. Barnard, 'Improving clergymen, 1660–1760' in Alan Ford et al. (eds), *As by law established: the Church of Ireland since the Reformation* (Dublin, 1995), pp 136–51; idem,

early eighteenth-century church, present in clergy and laity alike, and manifest in stricter episcopal visitations, in the revival of convocation, the formation of voluntary societies for reforming manners and propagating the gospel, and the foundation of charity schools to teach the children of the poor the rudiments of learning and true Christianity.[2] No longer somnolent, the Church of Ireland appears active and vigorous, though still underfinanced and undermanned; and even the members of the Irish parliament seem to have been capable of genuine concern for the promotion of Protestantism, alongside more worldly objectives.

With such a picture in mind, to talk of a 'second Reformation' occurring in this period does not seem fanciful. But such a notion throws into sharper relief the basic problem of the church's failure to capitalise on its political advantages in the generation after the Williamite victory. Why was this 'second Reformation' no more successful than the first in accomplishing the conversion of the natives? That question, implicit in much general writing on early eighteenth-century church history, has still to be formally addressed: to adapt the conceit favoured by some early modernists, it has been neither '*bien posée*' nor '*mal posée*' but '*ne posée jamais*'.[3]

Once the question is asked, at least some of the answers must be sought in the nature and the context of the reforming 'movement' that gives the history of the Church of Ireland in the early eighteenth century its distinctive tone. This description of the various initiatives for ecclesiastical and spiritual renewal promoted by clergy and laity is a construction of historians rather than a contemporary usage, but it is not an unreasonable imposition, given the common purposes that are discernible, and the involvement of an identifiable cohort of individuals. In the minds of these activists, the different strands in the 'reforming' programme – an improvement in the quality of the clergy, the provision of new facilities for the instruction of their flocks, and a stricter enforcement of moral discipline in society at large, especially among the poor – were interwoven. The pious laymen and women who endowed

'"Almoners of Providence": the clergy, 1647 to c. 1780' in idem and W. G. Neely (eds), *The clergy of the Church of Ireland 1000–2000: messengers, watchmen and stewards* (Dublin, 2006), pp 78–105; S. J. Connolly, *Religion, law and power: the making of Protestant Ireland, 1660–1760* (Oxford, 1992), chs 5–6; idem, 'Reformers and highflyers : the post-Revolution church' in Ford et al. (eds), *As by law established*, pp 152–65. See also J. C. Beckett, 'The government and the Church of Ireland under William III and Anne' in *I.H.S.*, ii, no. 7 (Mar. 1941), pp 280–302; idem, 'William King's administration of the diocese of Derry, 1691–1703' in ibid., iv, no. 14 (Sept. 1944), pp 164–80; M. E. Gilmore, 'Anthony Dopping and the Church of Ireland, 1685–1695' (MA thesis, Queen's University Belfast, 1988).

2 Beckett, 'Government & Church of Ire.'; idem, 'William King's administration of dioc. of Derry'; Gilmore, 'Dopping & Church of Ire.', chs 6–7, T. C. Barnard, 'Reforming Irish manners: the religious societies in Dublin during the 1690s' in *Hist. Jn.*, xxxv (1992), pp 805–38; idem, 'Protestants and the Irish language, c.1675–1725' in *Journal of Ecclesiastical History*, xliv (1993), pp 243–72; Connolly, 'Reformers and highflyers'; *Scholar bishop: the recollections and diary of Narcissus Marsh, 1638–1696*, ed. Raymond Gillespie (Cork, 2003), pp 9–11; D. W. Hayton, 'Bishops as legislators: Marsh and his contemporaries' in Muriel McCarthy and Ann Simmons (eds), *Marsh's Library: a mirror on the world* (Dublin, 2009), pp 62–87.

3 Nicholas Canny, 'Why the Reformation failed in Ireland: *une question mal posée*' in *Journal of Ecclesiastical History*, xxx (1979), pp 423–50; Karl Bottigheimer, 'The failure of the Reformation in Ireland: *une question bien posée*' in ibid., xxxvi (1985), pp 196–207.

churches, libraries, schools, hospitals, and workhouses also endorsed proposals for legislation that would have suppressed blasphemy, profane swearing, drunkenness, and the breaking of the Sabbath, while many of the bishops and parsons who campaigned for reforms within the church were also patrons of 'reformation of manners' societies and charity schools. They drew much of their inspiration from England, where a campaign for spiritual renewal, begun by 'voluntary societies' of laymen, had extended in the last decade of the seventeenth century into a national campaign for the 'reformation of manners' through the use of the secular and ecclesiastical courts to punish offenders, and, more constructively, through educating the poor and their offspring in workhouses and charity schools.[4]

The importance of these enthusiasts was disproportionate to their numbers, and in discussing Irish Protestant approaches to proselytism in this period a peculiar significance attaches to their scale of priorities. This is not to say that they shared anything approaching a manifesto. There is a risk in throwing men and measures together in this way, and especially in the adoption of the word 'movement', which implies the existence of a publicly defined party with a co-ordinated programme. Although the proponents of ecclesiastical and social reform displayed many similarities of outlook and intention, and often collaborated in their various enterprises, objectives differed according to circumstances. To understand the workings of the 'second Reformation' of the early eighteenth century we must take into account not only the common concerns of the reformers, but the differences, in personality and local context, that influenced the direction of their efforts.

Nowhere, perhaps, is this degree of differentiation more apparent, and more important, than in the educational initiatives to which they devoted so much time and effort. Of all their schemes, the foundation of schools for needy children appeared the most promising. The prospect of cultivating basic literacy, useful skills, industrious habits, and above all knowledge and understanding of right religion, and thereby transforming hapless waifs into model Christians, touched every impulse in the reforming mind. Not only was education always a popular charitable endeavour, in due course it became the reformers' prime concern.[5] In England, the energies

4 The literature on this subject has reached formidable proportions. Contrary to appearances, what follows is a select bibliography: G. V. Portus, '*Caritas Anglicana*' (London, 1912); D. W. R. Bahlman, *The moral revolution of 1688* (New Haven, Conn., 1957); Eamon Duffy, 'Primitive Christianity revived: religious renewal in Augustan England' in Derek Baker (ed.), *Renaissance and renewal* (Studies in Church History, xiv, Oxford, 1977), pp 287–300; A. G. Craig, 'The movement for the reformation of manners, 1688–1715' (PhD thesis, University of Edinburgh, 1980); Tina Isaacs, 'Moral crime, moral reform and the state in early eighteenth-century England: a study of piety and politics' (PhD thesis, University of Rochester, N.Y. , 1979); eadem, 'The Anglican hierarchy and the reformation of manners, 1688–1738', in *Journal of Ecclesiastical History*, xxxiii (1982), pp 391–411; C. M. Rose, 'Religion, politics and charity in Augustan London, c. 1680–c. 1720' (PhD thesis, University of Cambridge, 1989); R. B. Shoemaker, 'Reforming the city: the reformation of manners campaign in London, 1690–1738' in Lee Davison et al. (eds), *Stilling the grumbling hive: the response to social and economic problems in England, 1689–1750* (Stroud, 1991), pp 99–120; Tony Claydon, *William III and the godly revolution* (Cambridge, 1996); Faramerz Dabhoiwala, 'Sex and societies for moral reform, 1688–1800' in *Journal of British Studies*, xlvi (2007), 290–319.

5 On charity schools in general the standard work is still M. G. Jones, *The charity school movement: a study of eighteenth-century Puritanism in action* (Cambridge, 1938), though some of

that had originally sparked efforts to improve public morals were redirected into the multiplication of charity schools. The Society for Promoting Christian Knowledge (S.P.C.K.), founded in London in 1698/9 with a broad strategy for the spiritual regeneration of the English people, had within a decade narrowed its efforts and become indentified solely as a purveyor of charitable education.[6]

This observation applies equally in Ireland, where the movement for 'moral reformation' took much the same course. At first it advanced on a wide front: in the early 1690s, with the formation of 'voluntary societies' in which devout young men gathered to pray, sing psalms and mutually encourage repentance; then with a brief campaign for the 'reformation of manners', led by magistrates and assisted by societies on the English model and also with the emergence of a didactic approach to poor relief, manifest in the apprenticing of poor children and a scheme to erect a workhouse in Dublin, started in 1705.[7] Bishops and clergy were heavily involved from the outset, and in Queen Anne's reign the church participated in a body, through convocation, whose members were specifically charged with finding means for 'the reformation of manners'.[8] At the same time, a new generation of schools was coming into existence, through the efforts of the very people responsible for other elements in the reforming strategy.[9]

The first school established in Ireland after the Glorious Revolution was in Dublin in 1695, in the parish of St Audoen. A year later another was founded in neighbouring St John's, and in 1698 Bishop Nathaniel Foy of Waterford opened the subject to public debate in a sermon before the Irish House of Lords in which he urged renewed application to bringing a Protestant education to the children of the natives.[10] Early progress was slow: an account of charity schools published in London

her interpretations have been persuasively revised in Craig Rose, 'Evangelical philanthropy and Anglican revival: the charity schools of Augustan London, 1698–1740' in *London Journal*, xvi (1991), pp 35–65; idem, '"Seminarys of faction and rebellion": Jacobites, Whigs and the London charity schools, 1716–1725' in *Hist. Jn.*, xxxiv (1991), pp 831–55.

6 Edmund McClure (ed.), *A chapter in English church history: being the minutes of the Society for Promoting Christian Knowledge ...1698–1704* (London, 1888), pp 1–4; Bahlman, *Moral Revolution of 1688*, pp 37–9, 43–6, 54–5, 70–72, 76–7; Isaacs, 'Anglican hierarchy & reformation of manners', pp 392–7; Joan Simon, 'From charity school to workhouse in the 1720s: the SPCK and Mr Marriott's solution' in *History of Education*, xvii (1988), pp 113–29.

7 Barnard, 'Reforming Irish manners'; David Dickson, 'In search of the old Irish poor law' in Rosalind Mitchison and Peter Roebuck (eds), *Economy and society in Scotland and Ireland 1500–1939* (Edinburgh, 1988), pp 113–19. See also Rowena Dudley, 'The Dublin parishes and the poor, 1660–1740' in *Archivium Hibernicum*, liii (1999), pp 80–94.

8 List of standing committees of lower house of convocation, 11 Jan. 1703/4 (T.C.D, MS 668/1, f. 1); *Records of Convocation*, ed. Gerald Bray (20 vols, Woodbridge, 2006), xvii, pt 1, pp 100, 105, 106, 186, 215.

9 On Irish charity schools, see *Twelfth and thirteenth reports of the Board of Education in Ireland* (Parliamentary Papers, 1813–14), v, 279–323; Timothy Corcoran, *State policy in Irish education* (Dublin, 1916), pp 96–7, 102; Jones, *Charity school movement*, pp 214–32; Seán Ó Coindealbháin, 'Schools and schooling in Cork city 1700–1831' in *Journal of the Cork Historical and Archaeological Society*, ser. 2, xlviii (1943), pp 44–8; Michael Quane, 'Aspects of education in Ireland 1695–1795' in ibid., lxxiii (1968), pp 120–28; Peadar McCann, 'Cork city's eighteenth-century charity schools: origins and early history' in ibid., lxxxiv (1979), pp 102–11.

10 *Methods of erecting, supporting and governing charity schools: with an account of the charity schools*

in 1706, underestimating slightly, listed only three for Ireland (all in Dublin) as compared with nearly 270 in England and Wales.[11] But momentum was growing, and by 1712 the number had risen to nineteen.[12] In the following decade, while other reforming initiatives faltered – agitation for the reformation of manners died away, the Dublin workhouse ran into difficulties, and convocation self-destructed in an explosion of partisan recrimination[13] – charity schools proliferated. It is possible to trace some 180 foundations by c. 1720,[14] each the product of a personal or parochial initiative, but after 1717 coming under the umbrella of a national society based in Dublin (and meeting in St John's church). Little evidence survives of the activities of the 'Society for Promoting Christian Knowledge in Ireland by the Method of Charity Schools' but it was clearly modelled on the S.P.C.K. in England and sought close connexions with the parent society.[15] There was some variation between schools in form and function. A few – Lady Orkney's, for example, at Midleton in County Cork, Lord Weymouth's foundation at Carrickmacross, in County Monaghan, and the small academy which Francis Annesley hoped to build at Castlewellan in County Down – even though originating in the reforming enthusiasm of the patron, were each intended to provide the equivalent of a grammar-school education for the sons of lesser gentry and 'strong farmers'.[16] But the vast majority followed the pattern of English charity schools: small institutions, usually with no more than two dozen inmates, administered by landlords themselves or by parochial authorities, maintained by voluntary subscription, and offering a scanty curriculum in which a Protestant catechism and a Protestant work-ethic predominated,

Despite Bishop Foy's clarion call, these charity schools did not for the most part seek to spread Protestantism among the native Catholics. Instead (and here they differed sharply from their successors, the 'charter schools' established from 1734 under royal imprimatur by the 'Incorporated Society') they gave their attention to

in Ireland (2nd ed., Dublin, 1719); St John's churchwarden's account books 1660–1711 (R.C.B., P328/6/1, pp 182, 195); Nathaniel Foy, *A sermon preach'd in Christ's Church, Dublin, on the 23d of October 1698 … before the House of Lords* (Dublin, 1698).

11 *An account of charity schools lately erected in England, Ireland, and Wales* (London, 1706), p. 19.

12 *An account of charity schools in Great Britain and Ireland* (new ed., 1712), p. 59.

13 Barnard, 'Reforming Irish manners', pp 819–20, 832–4; Dickson, 'In search of the old Irish poor law', p. 151; Connolly, ' Reformers & highflyers', pp 155–64.

14 Precise enumeration is impossible, as evidence for the existence of schools is patchy to say the least, and, in the case of over-optimistic lists given by pamphleteers seeking to attract contributions, manifestly unreliable. An attempt to construct a list is made in D. W. Hayton, 'Did Protestantism fail in eighteenth-century Ireland? Charity schools and the enterprise of religious and social reformation, c. 1690–1730', in Ford et al. (eds), *As by law established*, pp 183–6.

15 S.P.C.K. minute book 8, pp 93, 109 (S.P.C.K. Archives, now in Cambridge University Library); Henry Maule to Robert Stearne, 8 Oct., 12 Nov., 1717 (ibid., Abstract Letter Book (henceforth A.L.B.) 8, items 5390, 5445); *Methods of erecting, supporting and governing charity schools in Ireland* (2nd ed., Dublin, 1719), p. 4; Jones, *Charity school movement*, p. 227.

16 Michael Quane, 'Midleton school, County Cork' in *Journal of the Royal Society of Antiquaries of Ireland*, lxxxii (1952), pp 1–27; idem, 'Viscount Weymouth's grammar school, Carrickmacross' in ibid., lxxxvi (1956), pp 26–51; indenture by Ld Weymouth, 20 Apr. 1711 (P.R.O.N.I., Armagh diocesan registry papers, DIO/4/8/11/1); statutes and constitutions for the grammar school at Carrickmacross, 1711 (P.R.O.N.I., DIO/4/8/11/2); Francis Annesley to Abp King, 21 June 1704 (T.C.D., Lyons (King) collection, MS 1995–2008/1091).

the weaker brethren in the Protestant community. To judge by the terms of their endowments, very few schools were designed to cater solely or even chiefly for Catholics. Some were allowed to admit children of Catholic parents only in the absence of suitable Protestant candidates;[17] most were expected to enrol Protestant children first. Of the way things worked out in practice, we know very little. Registers survive for three schools: Bishop Foy's own school in Waterford, St John's in Dublin and the Green Coat School in Cork.[18] In the case of Foy's school a record was made of the denominational affiliation of its pupils, which shows that of the fifty children admitted in the first intake in 1711 only one was of Catholic parentage on both sides, and eight more were the offspring of mixed marriages (usually a Catholic father and a Protestant mother). Thirty-seven pupils came from solidly Church of Ireland families. These proportions were maintained over the next two decades. The registers of the St John's school and the Green Coat School do not specify religious denomination, but there is a paucity of obviously native Irish or Old English Catholic surnames among the pupils, which suggests a similar composition.[19]

Without evidence to the contrary, it seems reasonable to assume that most schools were in practice as in theory instruments for the redemption of lapsed Protestants rather than a means to open the eyes of ungodly papists. Moreover, as we shall see, even those which did hope to make converts often had other ends in view, namely the imposition of a firmer social discipline and the training of a more productive work-force. That these schools should have failed to make inroads into the Catholic allegiance of the majority of the population should come as no surprise, therefore, since this was not their purpose. What we need to know is why, in the favourable political climate of the early eighteenth century, the active element in the Church of Ireland community should have responded in such an introverted manner to the opportunities offered by the political defeat of popery. How it was that, until the establishment of the charter schools, educational reform was not explicitly identified with proselytism; until, in other words, the most auspicious moment was passed?

Charity schools were not of course the only means by which children might be instructed in the Protestant faith. Previous generations of benefactors, whether great

17 *Methods of erecting ... charity schools in Ireland*, p. 7.

18 Register of Bishop Foy's school (consulted when in private possession; now R.C.B., MS 523); St John's charity school accounts (R.C.B., P328/12/1); Green Coat Hospital school minute book (parish church of St Ann Shandon, Cork).

19 The first twenty children to attend the school in St John's included a Butler and a Wall, but the remaining surnames seem to be English in origin. Of the forty children who comprised the first intake of the Green Coat School, only five possessed recognisably Irish Catholic surnames: Lewis Creague, Bridget Duggan, Jeremy Leary, Edward Murphy and John Roche. Such evidence should, however, be treated with extreme caution; the inclusion in the Foy school register of a number of Protestant children with similar names demonstrates the unwisdom of assigning religious affiliation on this basis. Allegedly there were charity schools in Cork that took both Protestant and Catholic pupils, but the immediate precursor of the Green Coat School, Edward Worth's Blue Coat Hospital, established in 1699, took only Protestant boys: *Pietas Corcagiensis; or, A view of the Green Coat Hospital* (Cork, 1721), p. 29; *12th & 13th repts of the Board of Education*, v, 303; McCann, 'Cork city's eighteenth-century charity schools', pp 110–11. It may be significant that the library of the Green Coat School (a catalogue of which is appended to *Pietas Corcagiensis*) held very few items in the Irish language.

landowners like Richard Boyle, first earl of Cork, or philanthropists like the pious merchant Erasmus Smith, had left a legacy of privately endowed schools for the children of the poor (of which the Blue Coat School in Dublin was the most famous), and 'classical' schools such as Swift's alma mater at Kilkenny. More important in this context, however, are the schools established under statute in the sixteenth and early seventeenth centuries in order to foster the spread of the Reformation: the parish schools which the parliament of Henry VIII required to be established throughout the kingdom, to bring the native Irish to civility by teaching their children the English language as well as approved theology; the diocesan grammar schools planned by the Elizabethan regime; and the 'free schools of royal foundation', on the English grammar-school model, projected as part of the Ulster Plantation.[20] Together, these various institutions represented an official alternative to the voluntary endeavours of charity schools. In particular, the network of parochial education ought to have answered the ends for which the charity schools were contrived. By the end of the seventeenth century, however, it was badly in need of an overhaul. Episcopal visitations tell a sorry tale. In the diocese of Dromore in east Ulster there were more parishes without a schoolmaster than with one.[21] Elsewhere, the diocese of Limerick contained only seven parish schoolmasters; Derry a mere five, two of whom doubled as parish clerks; Raphoe in the north-west five, all of whom were parish clerks; while in Clogher, in mid-Ulster, twenty parishes had no school, ten had masters who were non-resident, and in a further four the function of schoolmaster and parish clerk was combined.[22]

Alongside the voluntary contribution made by the founders of charity schools the period also witnessed attempts to revive the parochial school system. In visitation charges, reforming bishops set the tone. Narcissus Marsh of Dublin (and later Armagh) emphasised the statutory duty of parish incumbents to ensure that children under their care were properly catechised, while Anthony Dopping of Meath set out a detailed programme for the fulfilment of the ambitions behind the Henrician act, which would have involved the imposition of legal penalties on Catholic parents who failed to send their children to be catechised, the suppression of rival Catholic schools, and the sending out of 'missionary preachers … in the Irish tongue'.[23] The lower house of Convocation in 1711 also recommended increasing the number of parochial schools as part of a package of measures designed to assist the conver-

20 Catherine Murray, 'English schools in Ireland in the seventeenth and eighteenth centuries' (MA thesis Queen's University Belfast, 1954), pp 1–7, 22, 27; Michael Quane, 'The diocesan schools 1570–1870' in *Journal of the Cork Historical and Archaeological Society*, ser. 2, lxvi (1961), pp 26–49; T. C. Barnard, *Cromwellian Ireland: English government and reform in Ireland 1649–1660* (Oxford, 1975), pp 186–9.

21 Dromore visitation, 1694 (P.R.O.N.I., DIO/4/5/3/21).

22 Clogher visitation, 1700 (ibid., DIO/4/5/3/27); Raphoe visitation, 1692 (N.L.I., Smythe of Barbavilla papers, MS 41,575/6); Limerick visitation, 1698 (R.C.B., D13/1/1); Derry visitation, 1691 (ibid., Leslie papers, 61/6/8).

23 *The charge given by Narcissus, lord archbishop of Dublin to the clergy of the province of Leinster … 1694* (Dublin, 1694); state of the diocese of Meath, 1693 (P.R.O.N.I., DIO/4/28/2/1); Philip Loupès, 'Bishop Dopping's visitation of the diocese of Meath, 1693' in *Studia Hibernica*, xxiv (1988), pp 127–51, esp. pp 148–9.

sion of the Catholic population.[24] The Irish parliament took heed: a statute of 1696 reinforced the obligation on parish incumbents to ensure that schools were kept, and further legislation in 1718 and 1721 facilitated landed endowments for the purpose.[25] With more rigorous episcopal supervision this produced an increase in the number of parochial schoolmasters (though whether the standard of teaching improved is another matter).[26] At the same time, parliament enacted measures to prohibit Catholic education, at home as well as abroad, in private as well as in public.[27]

Space does not permit an extended treatment of this 'official' strategy, but two points must be made. First, that it attracted the attention of a wide variety of Protestants, both clerical and lay, without producing a sustained rush of excitement. The willingness of parliament to pass enabling legislation, and of ecclesiastical authorities to enforce the law, testifies to a consensus in favour of a functioning parochial education system. Even keen reformers, despite their evangelical ethos, could see the practical value in an element of compulsion, despite the absence of any expression of philanthropic virtue, since they also suffered from the general unease at the thought of a populace ignorant of basic doctrine and failing to observe the outward forms of religion.[28] So much is clear from the willingness of members of the 'Society for Promoting Christian Knowledge in Ireland ...' to subscribe for the printing and distribution of great quantities of Bibles (in English),[29] and from the prominent part played by one reforming bishop, Edward Synge, in framing the 1718 Act and in pressing for further attention to the parochial schools (albeit in the context of Protestant plantation).[30] The second point is that support for parochial schools was still

24 *Recs of Convocation*, ed. Bray, xvii, pt 1, pp 392–4.

25 Murray, 'English schools in Ireland', pp 11–13. Without the support of a landed endowment some parish schoolmasters would have to rely on the contributions that the vestry could levy on parish inhabitants: see, for example, vestry minutes of the parish of Culdaff and Clonea, Co. Donegal, 3 June 1696 (P.R.O.N.I., D/803/1, p. 13).

26 For evidence of increasing numbers of parochial schoolmasters, compare the visitations of Derry in 1691 and 1718 (R.C.B., Leslie papers, 61/6/8), which show a rise from six to 43, and the series of visitations of Limerick from 1698 to 1714 (ibid., D134/1/2–3, 9–15), where the expansion is less dramatic but still substantial, from seven in 1698 to an average of 18 in 1708–14. Direct evidence of episcopal involvement is perhaps best illustrated in Bishop Ashe's diocese of Clogher: ibid., D1/7/1–D1/72/4, passim; P.R.O.N.I., Clogher diocesan records, DIO/2/9/11–1095, passim.

27 Corcoran, *State policy in Irish education*, pp 93–6, 103–8; J. J. Auchmuty, *Irish education: a historical survey* (Dublin, 1937), pp 54–5; P. J. Dowling, *The hedge schools of Ireland* (Cork [, 1968]), pp 223–31.

28 One keen advocate of charity schools did, however, denounce the parochial system as doomed to failure because of the omission of any positive inducement to Catholic parents to submit their offspring to be taught. Offers to clothe and apprentice children were, he felt, the only way to attract pupils (Edward Nicholson to S.P.C.K., 30 Aug. 1715 (S.P.C.K. Archives, A.L.B. 6, item 4450)).

29 Thomas Prior to Sir John Rawdon, 20 Jan. 1718[/19] (HA 15566); Bp Evans of Meath to Abp Wake of Canterbury, 5 Feb. 1718[/19] (Christ Church, Oxford, Wake papers, Arch. W. Epist. xiii, (unfol.)).

30 Synge to Abp Wake, 28 Dec. 1717, 13 Nov. 1718 (Christ Church, Arch. W. Epist. xiii), 31 July 1718 (ibid., Arch. W. Epist. xii, f. 296); Thomas Prior to Sir John Rawdon, 27 June 1719 (HA 15581); Edward Synge, *A brief account of the laws now in force in Ireland for encouraging the residence*

by no means unanimous. Some sceptics remained, who regretted any discouragement to the exercise of what they considered a clergyman's proper duty of catechism, and feared that the appointment of a parish schoolmaster would be exploited by lazy and unscrupulous incumbents as a chance to engage a curate on the cheap.[31] Such arguments weighed heavily with the most powerful personality in the Church of Ireland hierarchy, William King, successively bishop of Derry (1690–1703) and archbishop of Dublin (1703–29). While not unremittingly hostile to improving educational opportunity (he was, for example, an energetic and highly valued governor of the Dublin Blue Coat School[32]), King was at best a lukewarm supporter of parochial education, and a consistent if discreet opponent of charity schools, as indeed of all voluntary initiatives that derogated from the authority of the establishment.[33]

Mention of Bishop King, however, points up the more important distinction between committed 'reformers' and the main body of Augustan churchmen, who might be happy enough to endorse the idea of parochial catechising but were sceptical of, or indifferent to, any more extensive educational provision. King was no Laodicean, indeed, he was one of the most conscientious episcopal administrators of his day. But his private writings reveal little of the intense spiritual anxiety to be found in Marsh's diary,[34] or in the sermons of Bishop Edward Wetenhall of Cork, who wrote in 1694 of that surpassing 'charity to the souls of men' which consisted in labouring 'to instruct them, who are ignorant of God and their duty'.[35] The difference was not in firmness of their resolve but in the nature of their understanding. For reformers, the church stood at a moment of crisis and of opportunity. Their zeal took them beyond the common acceptance of the value of education, towards a belief that teaching the children of the poor was a sacred duty, by which they might return a depraved people to the path of virtue, and come closer to realising the kingdom of God on earth. The message comes through loudly in a tract published in

of the parochial clergy and erecting English schools (Dublin, 1723). In this pamphlet Synge not only proposed further plantation but reminded landlords of their responsibility to introduce Protestant under-tenants on their estates, even where this might result in financial loss.

31 E.H. to Provost Huntington, 18 Feb. 1691/2 (T.C.D., college muniments, TCD/MUN/P/1/562); Bp Vigors of Ferns to same, 26 Feb. 1691/2 (ibid., TCD/MUN/P/1/564). Bishop Thomas Lindsay of Killaloe (a future primate) seems to have been unhelpful to parish schools in his diocese in 1703 (earl of Inchiquin to Sir Donough O'Brien, 29 June 1703 (*The Inchiquin manuscripts*, ed. John Ainsworth (Dublin, 1961), p. 76)). For an example of the way in which a curacy and a schoolmaster's place might be combined to make one reasonable salary, see Dean Ralph Lambert to Edward Southwell, 28 Nov. 1712 (B.L., Southwell papers, Add. MS 21131, f. 18).

32 Sir Frederick R. Falkiner, *The foundation of the hospital and free-school of King Charles II, Oxmantown, Dublin* (Dublin, 1906), pp 127, 153–5, 157.

33 King to Bp Edward Smyth of Down and Connor, 12 Apr. 1698 (T.C.D., King letterbooks, MS 750/1, pp 209–10); same to Bp Hartstonge of Ossory, 4 May 1698 (ibid., p. 222); same to Abp Vesey of Tuam, 30 Jan. 1704[/5] (ibid., MS 750/3/1); same to Abp Wake, 21 Sept., 21 Nov. 1717 (ibid., MSS 750/11/2/303–5, 750/11/3/11–14). The Welshman John Evans, bishop of Meath, expressed doubts about the mental stability of charity school enthusiasts (Evans to Abp Wake, 5 Feb. 1718[/19] (Christ Church, Arch. W. Epist. xiii)).

34 Typescript copy of Marsh's diary 1690–6 (Marsh's Library, MS Z2.2.3b), now published as *Scholar bishop*, ed. Gillespie.

35 Edward Wetenhall, *Be ye also ready: a method and order of practice* (London, 1694), esp. pp 161–5.

1695 by Samuel Foley, bishop of Down and Connor, who, in pressing on Protestant parents in his diocese the importance of properly educating their sons and daughters in the tenets of reformed religion, spoke in almost millenarian terms of the prospect thereby to 'reform the world, and ... make the next a godly and happy age'.[36]

This outlook was shared by many of the busiest and most influential sponsors of charity schools, to whom the education of poor children was one of a range of measures necessary to revivify the church and propagate 'true piety' in the population at large. Archbishop Marsh 'set himself heartily to promote religion' by all means at hand. In Dublin, besides encouraging the 'voluntary societies' and the public campaign for the reformation of manners, he 'endowed a weekly lecture ... worth £40 a year' and 'caused abundance of good books for the common people to be printed and dispersed'.[37] His protégé, Nathaniel Foy, who as a Dublin curate in the 1680s had endorsed schemes to put out poor boys as apprentices, set an example of piety in his bishopric of Waterford that included the strenuous enforcement of Sabbath observance as well as his own foundation of a charity school.[38] St George Ashe, provost of Trinity College before becoming bishop of Clogher, was a vociferous supporter of the societies for the reformation of manners and of charity schools.[39] So too was Bishop Peter Browne of Cork (yet another former Trinity provost), who preached powerfully in 1698 in commendation of the 'visible piety' of the reformation of manners societies, and in his *Humble proposal for parochial reformation* urged clergy and parish officers to 'go incessantly from house to house, to instruct, admonish and earnestly exhort those whom God has entrusted to their care'.[40] Another keen exponent of parochial education, Edward Synge, acknowledged the intellectual influence of the Trinity professor of Hebrew, Benedict Scroggs, a patron of the voluntary societies in the 1690s;[41] while Dr Henry Nicholson, builder of three charity schools in and around Castle Baldwin in County Sligo, shared with a number of English reformers

[36] Samuel Foley, *An exhortation to the inhabitants of Down and Connor concerning the religious education of their children* (Dublin, 1695), esp. pp 3, 6–8, 16, 20, 22–4, 26.

[37] Barnard, 'Reforming Irish manners', pp 810–12; James Bonnell to John Strype, 4 Jan. 1694/5, 6 May 1695, 6 May 1696, 26 May 1697 (Cambridge University Library, Baumgartner papers, Add. MS 1, ff 115, 117–18, 121–2, 123–4); *Scholar bishop*, ed. Gillespie, pp 9–10, 41; *The remembrances of Elizabeth Freke, 1671–1714*, ed. R. A. Anselment (Camden Soc., ser. 5, xviii, Cambridge, 2001), pp 205–6; *An account of the societies for the reformation of manners, in England and Ireland* (3rd ed., London, 1700), list of subscribers.

[38] *Scholar bishop*, ed. Gillespie, p. 37; vestry accounts of the parish of St Bride, St Michael le Pole and St Stephen, Dublin, 10 Apr., 6 Dec. 1683, Apr. 1685, Apr. 1698 (T.C.D., MS 1476); Bp Foy to Bp King, 28 Apr. 1693 (ibid., MS 1995–2008/268); *Account of societies for reformation of manners*, list of subscribers.

[39] St George Ashe, *Two sermons preached at Tunbridge Wells* (London, 1714); idem, *A sermon preached to the societies for the reformation of manners, at St Mary-le-Bow on Monday, December the 31st, MDCCXVI* (London, 1717).

[40] Peter Browne, *A sermon preached at St Bride's church, Dublin, April 17, 1698 ...* (Dublin, 1698); R. W. Jackson, *Peter Browne, devotional writer of the eighteenth century* (Dublin, 1963), pp 8–11.

[41] Synge to Bp Wake, 4 May 1709 (Christ Church, Arch. W. Epist. xvii, f. 208); *Methods of erecting ... charity schools ...*, p. 21; Benedict Scroggs, *A sermon preached before the religious societies in the city of Dublin on the 29th of Septemb. 1695* (Dublin, 1695). For Scroggs (c. 1658–96), a prebendary of St John's, Dublin, see G. D. Burtchaell and T. U. Sadleir, *Alumni Dublinenses* (Dublin, 1935), p. 740.

a fascination with the so-called 'French prophets', the refugee Camisard preachers who had caused a sensation in pious London society.[42]

The same general commitment to a variety of reforming initiatives was also visible among lay enthusiasts for charity schools. Those Dublin parish vestries in which the 'reformation of manners' had germinated and constructive programmes for poor relief had been pioneered also took the lead in setting up schools.[43] Among individual philanthropists, pride of place must go to William Handcock, who as recorder of Dublin led the magisterial attack on 'immorality' in the capital, and whose son endowed a school on his Westmeath estate.[44] Others included two English absentee peers, who were both early members of the S.P.C.K.: Lord Weymouth, founder of the Carrickmacross school, and Lord Digby, who set up two schools on his Irish properties in King's County.[45] A man renowned for his strong religious convictions, Digby was also a public supporter of reformation of manners societies,[46] as was Thomas Watson Wentworth, heir not only to broad acres in Yorkshire but to a substantial estate in County Wicklow on which a school was situated.[47] Among resident landlords of a reforming bent we may count the first Lord Egmont, whose charity school in County Cork was the first in a series of philanthropic endeavours, culminating in his membership of the Georgia Society;[48] and Lord Lanesborough, who maintained schools in Counties Leitrim and Longford, while helping to establish the Dublin workhouse on a model devised by reformers in Bristol.[49] His countess, a niece of Bishop Compton of London, and patroness in her own right of a school at Buttevant in County Cork, was a woman of exceptional piety even among the female philan-

42 Hillel Schwartz, *The French prophets* (Berkeley & Los Angeles, Calif., 1980), pp 124, 133, 328.

43 See the records of the following parishes: St Bride, vestry accounts 1663–1702 (R.C.B., P327/4/1, ff 98–9, 101–102, 105–107); St Catherine and St James, vestry book 1693–1730 (ibid., P117/5/2, pp 182, 219, 256, 268); St John, churchwardens' account books 1660–1711 (ibid., P328/6/1, pp 173, 178, 182, 195); St Mary, vestry minute book 1699–1739 (ibid., P277/7/1, pp 78, 105, 148, 192–4).

44 Dublin corporation 'Monday book' 1658–1712 (Dublin City Library and Archive, Dublin city archives, MR/18, p. 1340A); John Dunton, *The Dublin scuffle*, ed. Andrew Carpenter (Dublin, 2000), p. 232; Barnard, 'Reforming Irish manners', pp 816–17; *12th & 13th repts of the Board of Education*, v, 317.

45 Weymouth was also a contributor to the Dublin workhouse (Weymouth to Mr Fitch, 8 Mar. 1705/6 (Longleat House, Thynne papers, 179, f. 127).

46 For Digby, see Howard Erskine-Hill, *The social milieu of Alexander Pope: lives, example and the poetic response* (New Haven, Conn., 1975), ch. 5; *H.C. 1690–1715*, iii, 877–81.

47 *Methods of erecting … charity schools …*, p. 356; Abp King to Francis Annesley, 3 July 1714 (T.C.D., MS 750/4, f. 176); D. W. Hayton, 'Moral reform and Country politics in the late seventeenth-century House of Commons', in *Past and Present*, no. 128 (1990), pp 64–5.

48 B.L., Egmont papers, Add. MSS 47056, 47126–30, 47136, 47204–93, passim; *The journal of the earl of Egmont: abstract of the trustees' proceedings for establishing the colony of Georgia 1732–1738* (Athens, Ga., 1962); *Oxf. D.N.B.*, xliii, 657–8.

49 Alderman John Page to [?Abp King], 26 Jan. 1705[?/6] (Marsh's Lib., MS Z3.1.1/cxlvii); Abp King to ld mayor of Dublin, 20 Feb. 1704[/5] (T.C.D., MS 750/3/1, p. 98); notebook of extracts on religious subjects (N.L.I., Lane papers, MS 8645/1); 'Abstract of the account from the corporation of the poor at Bristol for the use of the Irish corporation for the poor in Dublin …' (ibid.); Hayton, 'Moral reform & Country politics', pp 67–8; *Bristol corporation of the poor: selected records 1696–1834*, ed. E. E. Butcher (Bristol Record Society publications, ii, Bristol, 1932).

thropists of her day. Warnings delivered by no less a personage than Archbishop King of the dangers posed by her excessive devotion to religious observances, to the neglect of the normal requirements of human society, attest to the symptoms of a serious case of reforming fever.[50]

This was an outlook profoundly influenced by the writings and the example of continental Protestant pietism, and in particular by the Lutheran theologians Philip Spener and August Francke, who at Halle in Prussia had founded a charity school which served as a prototype for schools in England and Ireland.[51] Francke's published account of the experiment, *Pietas Hallensis*, was the essential text of the reforming movement, reprinted several times by the S.P.C.K. for distribution among its members, one of whom, a Gloucestershire parson, reported that to read it 'made my very heart leap with joy'.[52] The S.P.C.K. was the most important channel through which the current of German pietistic enthusiasm flowed into England and Ireland, though continental ideas had already made some impact in London through the leadership supplied by men like Anthony Horneck in the formation of the 'voluntary societies' in London in the 1670s.[53] In Ireland, Marsh and his fellow bishops played a major role, alongside a handful of lay enthusiasts: the Irish accountant-general James Bonnell, a priest manqué at the centre of a circle of Dublin reformers, including Bishops Dopping, Foley and Wetenhall;[54] Sir Robert King, another friend of Bonnell's and an admirer of Horneck;[55] the eccentric baronet Sir Richard Bulkeley, a man with an appetite for theological novelty in any form;[56]

50 King to Lady Lanesborough, 9 Aug., 25 Sept. 1702 (T.C.D., Lyons (King) collection, MSS 1995–2008/1459/2, pp 63–4, 101); same to Capt. Fox, 29 June 1708 (ibid., King letterbks, MS 750/3/2).

51 On the influence of German pietism, see in general F. E. Stoeffler, *German pietism during the eighteenth century* (Leiden, 1973), esp. pp 71–87; W. R. Ward, 'The relations of enlightenment and religious revival in central Europe and the English-speaking world' in Derek Baker (ed.), *Reform and Reformation* (Studies in Church History, Subsidia, ii, Oxford, 1979), pp 281–305; W. R. Ward, 'Power and piety: the origins of the evangelical revival in the eighteenth century' in *Bulletin of the John Rylands Library*, lxiii (1980), pp 231–52; D. L. Brunner, *Halle pietists in England: Anthony William Boehm and the Society for Promoting Christian Knowledge* (Göttingen, 1993).

52 Maurice Wheeler to Bp Wake, 6 Apr. 1706 (Christ Church, Arch. W. Epist. xxiii, item 157).

53 For Horneck see Duffy, 'Primitive Christianity revived', pp 290–1; John Spurr, 'The church, the societies and the moral revolution of 1688' in John Walsh et al. (eds), *The Church of England, c. 1689–c. 1873: from toleration to tractarianism* (Cambridge, 1993), pp 127–42; S. T. Kisker, *Foundation for revival: Anthony Horneck the religious societies, and the construction of an Anglican pietism* (Lanham, Md., 2008); *Oxf. D.N.B.*, xxviii, 155–6.

54 For Bonnell, see William Hamilton, *The life and character of James Bonnell* (Dublin, 1703), esp. pp xv–xvii, 21, 206, 227; Edward Wetenhall, *Of the intermediate state of blessed souls: a sermon preached at the funeral of James Bonnell April 29, 1699* (Dublin 1703), esp. pp 1, 30–31; Barnard, 'Reforming Irish manners', pp 818–19; *D.I.B.*, i, 649–51.

55 Hamilton, *Life of Bonnell*, p. 253; Edward Nicholson, *The death-bed repentance fully considered* (Dublin, 1712), pp 64–7; *A vindication of Sir Robert King's designs and actions* (Dublin, 1699).

56 Abp King to Bulkeley, 8 Jan. 1707[/8] (T.C.D., MS 750/3/2, pp 177–8); Schwartz, *French prophets*, pp 53, 65, 70, 79, 86–7, 96–8, 112–19, 131–3, 219, 224, 241, 257, 272–7; Barnard, 'Reforming Irish manners', p. 818; *Hist. Ir. parl.*, v, 29; *D.I.B.*, i, 979–80.

and Abel Ram of Ramsfort, County Wexford, son of the Dublin goldsmith who had been chairman of the board of governors of the Blue Coat School.[57]

In the early years of the S.P.C.K., when it was struggling to gain a foothold in Ireland but could not overcome the surreptitious hostility of Archbishop King and the counter-attractions of the Irish convocation as an alternative vehicle for ecclesiastical reform, Ram and Bulkeley served as its Irish correspondents, together with Bishop Edward Smyth of Down and Connor (and unofficially Bishop Ashe of Clogher, who was in contact with the society but was not a subscriber).[58] Some progress was made in 1710–12 as a result of the endeavours of the Irish clergyman John Richardson to drum up interest in a project to translate into the Irish language the New Testament, book of common prayer and an Anglican catechism. This appealed to members of the S.P.C.K., who were already involved in similar schemes to assist the conversion of native speakers in Wales.[59] The society acquired another active Irish correspondent in the person of Brigadier Robert Stearne, and in a sermon at St Clement Dane's in Westminster Bishop Ashe repeated Nathaniel Foy's call for a campaign to convert the Catholic Irish by means of charity schools.[60] Education also figured briefly on the agenda of the Irish convocation in 1711, as Bishop Wetenhall led a petition to the lord lieutenant, the duke of Ormond, for a charter to establish a society in Ireland for this purpose.[61] But the association of the S.P.C.K. and its correspondents with Richardson backfired, as the question of whether to appeal to Irish-speakers in their own tongue, or to insist on the teaching of the English language as a prerequisite for conversion, became yet another point at issue between the factions in Irish ecclesiastical politics. 'High Churchmen' (that is to say those sympathetic to the Tory party in the state) distrusted Richardson on personal grounds, because he was patronised by Archbishop King and King's Whiggish friends, and damned his translations along with his connexions. At the same time, those who were arguing that charity schools represented the most effective means of promoting Christian knowledge in the population at large regarded his ideas as likely to waste valuable resources, and seem to have kept him at arm's length.[62]

57 Barnard, 'Reforming Irish manners', pp 817–18; Falkiner, *Hospital & free-school of Charles II*, p. 108; *D.I.B.*, viii, 385–6.

58 McClure, *Chapter in Eng. church hist.*, pp 37, 91, 211, 221–3; W. O. B. Allen and Edmund McClure, *Two hundred years: a history of the S.P.C.K.* (London, 1888), p. 39; W. A. Bultmann and P. A. Bultmann, 'The roots of Anglican humanitarianism: a study of the membership of the S.P.C.K. and S.P.G., 1699–1720' in *Historical Magazine of the Protestant Episcopal Church*, xxxiii (1964), p. 18.

59 Richard Mant, *History of the Church of Ireland* (2 vols, London, 1840), ii, 223–30; Allen & McClure, *Two hundred years*, p. 204; *Correspondence and minutes of the S.P.C.K. relating to Wales, 1695–1740* (University of Wales Board of Celtic Studies, History and Law Series, x, Cardiff, 1952), pp 47–50, 277; Connolly, *Religion, law & power*, pp 299–300; Barnard, 'Protestants & Irish language', pp 254–60.

60 S.P.C.K. min. bk 5, pp 183, 186, 256 (S.P.C.K. Archives); T. J. Johnston et al., *A history of the Church of Ireland* (Dublin, 1953), pp 238–9.

61 Sir Charles S. King (ed.), *A great archbishop of Dublin: William King D.D.* ... (London, 1906), pp 296–8. See also *Recs of Convocation*, ed. Bray, xvii, pt 1, pp 392–3.

62 Edward Nicholson to S.P.C.K., 30 Aug. 1715 (S.P.C.K. Archives, A.L.B. 6, item 4450); Henry Maule to Mr Shute (ibid., A.L.B. 7, item 5227); same to S.P.C.K., 12, 26 Aug. 1717 (ibid., A.L.B. 8, item 5355). See also Barnard, 'Protestants & Irish language', pp 261–5.

It was the demise of convocation in the new political climate obtaining after the Hanoverian succession that eventually spurred the clergy to embrace voluntarism. Abel Ram, still a torchbearer for the S.P.C.K., tried in vain to start up an Irish equivalent of the society in 1716, with the backing of the equally zealous Archdeacon Thomas Walls of Achonry (a friend of Swift),[63] but it was another (and even more dynamic) figure, Henry Maule, a Cork-based clergyman later to be dean and then bishop of Cloyne, who succeeded where Ram and others had failed. Admitted as a corresponding member of the S.P.C.K. in 1715, Maule rapidly recruited more Irish members for the society, bringing together enthusiasts who had previously operated in isolation.[64] His first plan was to exploit the influence of the S.P.C.K. to secure a viceregal recommendation to the Irish parliament for the establishment of a national fund for charity schools. Political pressure was only able to obtain a statute specifically to assist the Green Coat School that Maule himself had created in Cork. However, the momentum generated by the parliamentary campaign produced the 'Society for Promoting Christian Knowledge in Ireland …', which met for the first time in October 1717 and took up the challenge of co-ordinating and publicising the work of the schools.[65] The most striking instance of German pietist influence on the Irish charity school movement dates from this period of close co-operation between the S.P.C.K. in London and the new offshoot in Dublin,[66] the publication in 1721 of a manifesto, and in effect a charitable appeal, on behalf of the Green Coat School, composed by Maule and entitled *Pietas Corcagiensis* in imitation of the Halle original. It described the school and its library (which contained, among other improving works, the recently published *Life* of James Bonnell) as a 'nursery of religion', intended to counteract the 'seminary of vice' to be found in the surrounding urban squalor. Maule promised his readers that in return for charitable contributions they could expect 'an increase of all goodness' in the city of Cork.[67]

The fact that Halle pietism provided the intellectual underpinning for reforming activities, in Ireland no less than in England, had significant implications for the potential of charity schools as instruments for the conversion of the natives.[68] The pietist emphasis was on quality, if necessary at the expense of quantity. Their aim was to recover the purity and thus the power of the 'primitive' church. Such an ideal was not to be imposed from above; the programme had to begin at ground level with initiatives conceived on a small scale. Evangelism found its most effective medium through personal contact, in which exhortation and example figured strongly.[69] In the case of the charity schools, their very existence might almost be enough. The

63 Henry Maule to Mr Jennings, 6 Sept. 1716 (S.P.C.K. Archives, A.L.B. 7, item 4904).

64 S.P.C.K. min. bk 7, pp 26, 38, 196 and unpaginated section at back (S.P.C.K. Archives).

65 Ibid., pp 41, 46–7; min. bk 8, pp 61–2, 76–7, 86–7, 93, 100, 109; Maule to Mr Shute, 16 Apr. 1717 (S.P.C.K. archs, A.L.B. 7, item 5277); same to Robert Stearne, 8 Oct., 12 Nov. 1717 (ibid., A.L.B. 8, items 5390, 5545).

66 W. K. Lowther Clarke, *A history of the S.P.C.K.* (London, 1959), p. 219.

67 *Pietas Corcagiensis*, pp 5, 7–8, 22, 39–43, 52.

68 Rose, 'Evangelical philanthropy', p. 35; idem, 'The origin and ideals of the SPCK 1695–1716' in Walsh et al. (eds), *Church of England*, pp 172–90.

69 Rose, 'Evangelical philanthropy', p. 42. For an Irish example, see Scroggs, *A sermon* …, pp 31, 50, 62–3.

extensive publicity given to benefactors, and the high profile insisted upon for the pupils in the collective worship of their parishes (attendance *en bloc*, and in uniform, at all Sunday services, after a formal procession to church behind the schoolmaster or mistress) seem to indicate that the schools were to be seen as public embodiments, or demonstrations, of Christian virtue.[70] Individually, a true convert could proselytise by example. Pupils who understood clearly and then acted upon what they had imbibed were to be the salt which would save the ignorant and reprobate. Instances in which childish piety had opened parental eyes and won over hearts were thus especially cherished in the promotional literature that the advocates of the schools put forth.[71]

To those of a 'reforming' stamp, a strengthening of Protestant spirituality represented the most effective bulwark not only against vice and irreligion but against a resurgent Roman Catholicism. There was a pronounced element of defensiveness here, which might seem surprising in view of the political condition of post-Revolution Ireland, but is more comprehensible when placed in a European context. The members of the S.P.C.K., and the continental theologians from whom the society took its inspiration, were by no means 'soft' on popery.[72] In essence they were intent on paring the forces of the Reformation to a sharper point. Their evangelical emphasis had originated in anxiety at what appeared to be the forward march of Counter-Reformation Catholicism in Europe. In Ireland, as in England, those who belonged to the 'reforming' tendency were convinced that, through the sceptical writings of rationalist freethinkers, and the indifference, ignorance, and moral decline of the bulk of the Protestant population, the reformed religion was steadily losing ground, its poorer adherents even beginning to adopt native Irish manners and native Irish superstitions.[73] The contemporary definition of anti-Catholic legislation, as bills 'to prevent the further growth of popery', although in retrospect it may appear an affectation, was sincerely meant. The priority was therefore to haul in backsliders from the Church of Ireland community, so that progress might be made from a solid foundation.[74] There was obviously little or no room for the methods of bribery and intimidation through which those who framed the 'popery laws' hoped to stimulate defections. James Bonnell, for one, denounced any forcing of Catholic consciences as 'a pretty device for lazy Christians to make use of'.[75] Nor indeed was the reforming

70 *Methods of erecting … charity schools*, pp 9–11, 18; *Pietas Corcagiensis*, pp 26–7, 31; Green Coat School min. bk, p. 28, unpaginated sections *sub* 26 July, 6 Aug., 15 Dec. 1718, accounts July 1716.

71 For example, *Methods of erecting … charity schools …*, p. 41; *Pietas Corcagiensis*, p. 34.

72 In regard to Ireland, the S.P.C.K. itself was explicitly conversionist in its approach, continuing to support Richardson's proposals for translation despite opposition from Maule and the society's other correspondents (S.P.C.K. min. bk 8, pp 66, 169, 191).

73 Edward Nicholson, *A method of charity schools recommended* (Dublin, 1712), p. 42; *Printed proceedings of the Society for Promoting Charity Schools* ([Dublin,] 1725) (Marsh's Lib., Ms Z1.1.13, item, 97); *The true way to render Ireland happy and secure … in a letter to the right honourable Robert Molesworth* (Dublin, 1698), pp 9–10, 16–17; Eamon Duffy, '"Poor Protestant flies": conversions to Catholicism in early eighteenth-century England' in Derek Baker (ed.), *Religious motivation* (Studies in Church History, xv, Oxford, 1978), pp 289–304.

74 Rose, 'Evangelical philanthropy', pp 43–5.

75 Hamilton, *Life of Bonnell*, pp 238–9.

approach in its purest form consonant with any policy of wholesale conversion that would pollute the ranks of the godly with the mercenary or lukewarm.

Continental pietism was not, however, the only intellectual influence on the reformers. Sixteenth- and seventeenth-century Puritanism (if historians are still permitted to use that term) was another. Many of those involved in the charity school movement hailed from families that had been active in the godly cause under the Commonwealth and Protectorate, particularly in the ranks of the more conservative Presbyterians. Some remained distinctively Calvinist in their theology.[76] Among Irish enthusiasts, such traces can be found in the background of Sir Richard Bulkeley, whose father was said to have attended Nonconformist conventicles in the Restoration period,[77] and in the early life of James Bonnell, a Cambridge pupil of the Dissenting divine Edmund Calamy.[78] Nor was the contribution of Presbyterianism to the 'second Reformation' merely historical. In England Protestant Nonconformists played a major part in the reformation of manners and in devising projects for setting the poor to work (an operation in which the Calvinist abhorrence of 'idleness' found institutional expression). In Scotland, too, Presbyterians set up their own reformation of manners societies, and a Society for Promoting Christian Knowledge in emulation of the English original;[79] while in Ireland it was openly admitted by loyal Anglicans that Protestant Dissenters set an enviable pace in the reformation of manners, and they may also be credited with giving a lead in the practice of badging the poor.[80]

Although some would (mistakenly) see Calvinism as offering little stimulus to proselytism, in so far as belief in a predestined salvation for the elect should have removed any grain of urgency, early eighteenth-century evidence points in the opposite direction: the work of the Scottish S.P.C.K., for example, whose schools were specifically intended for the children of popish clansmen, as part of the hoped-for pacification of the Highlands.[81] Furthermore, it was the authoritarian side of the reformers' activities, epitomised by the societies for the reformation of manners, which was derived most obviously from the 'Puritan' past, and indeed from the Presbyterian present. Moral regulation, especially the enforcement of Sabbath

76 Hayton, 'Moral reform & Country politics', pp 74–6.

77 Barnard, 'Reforming Irish manners', p. 818.

78 Hamilton, *Life of Bonnell*, p. 13.

79 'A narrative by Sir David Hume of Crossrig …', 11 Aug. 1702 (National Records of Scotland, Hume of Marchmont papers, GD 158/57); *An account of the rise, constitution and management of the Society in Scotland for Promoting Christian Knowledge* (2nd ed., Edinburgh, 1720).

80 James Bonnell to John Strype, 25 Jan. 1698[?/9] (Cambridge Univ. Lib., Add. MS 1, ff 126–7); Browne, *A sermon preached … April 17. 1698*, p. 11; Barnard, 'Reforming Irish manners'; Dickson, 'In search of the old Irish poor law', p. 151. For Scottish precedents, see Rosalind Mitchison, 'The making of the old Scottish poor law' in *Past and Present*, no. 63 (1974), pp 62–80.

81 John Mason, *A history of Scottish experiments in rural education* (London, 1935), ch. 1; Jones, *Charity school movement*, pp 176–214, 377–83; John Mason, 'Scottish charity schools of the eighteenth century' in *Scottish Historical Review*, xxxiii (1954), pp 1–13; D. J. Withrington, 'Education and society in the eighteenth century' in N. T. Phillipson and Rosalind Mitchison (eds), *Scotland in the age of improvement* (Edinburgh, 1970), pp 169–99; C. W. J. Withers, 'Education and Anglicization: the policy of the SSPCK towards the education of the Highlander, 1709–1825' in *Scottish Studies*, xxvii (1982), pp 37–47.

observance, reflected the aspirations of both the mid-seventeenth-century English Commonwealth and the contemporary Scottish kirk. Within the charity schools, Calvinist influence may be seen most clearly in a determination to eradicate 'idleness' and to substitute economically useful and morally uplifting 'habits of industry', which suggests a tendency towards social engineering rather than the nurturing of apostolic spirituality,[82] a wish to dictate modes of behaviour to those whose misfortunes placed them at the disposal of the pious. And in so far as 'moral reform' sought to impose standards on society as a whole it must be viewed as the polar opposite of the pietist approach; concerned with the aggregate rather than the individual, with external behaviour rather than with the life of the spirit.

There is enough here to suggest that 'Puritan' influences ran counter to the introspection and defensiveness that was otherwise characteristic of reformers. But Calvinism also introduced another element into the equation, an enhanced awareness of the force of divine Providence in guiding the destiny of the Protestant community. Providentialism was not exclusively Calvinist,[83] but it was reinforced by the 'covenant theology' which viewed English, Scottish and/or Irish Protestants as an 'elect nation' with a special relationship to the Almighty, and a special purpose on earth in carrying out His wishes. It would not be an exaggeration to say that it provided the keystone of the reformers' programme, since it gave meaning to their analysis of the 'moral crisis' supposedly confronting society, and primed them with an imperative for action.[84] A belief in the existence of this 'moral crisis' united reformers of all kinds: clergymen alarmed at the slackening in popular religious observance and angry at the publication of heretical tracts; godly laymen outraged by the spread of vice; those who saw the increasing evidence of poverty and crime as signs of a breakdown in social order. Sermons and pamphlets of the period bristle with jeremiads against the rising tide of immorality, profanity and irreligion that threatened catastrophe in the form of Providential judgment.[85] For Irish Protestants to neglect their public duty was for the 'elect nation' to forget its covenant, a failure that would bring down the wrath of the God who had upheld them in the dark days of King James's reign, and who might well inflict the return of a popish king as condign punishment.

The pervasive fear of Providential judgment naturally focused the attention of reformers on the task of redeeming the Protestant people in the eyes of God,

[82] See, for example, Foley, *An exhortation*, pp 7–8, 26.

[83] The Providentialist element in Restoration Anglicanism is discussed in John Spurr, '"Virtue, religion and government": the Anglican uses of Providence' in Tim Harris et al. (eds), *The politics of religion in Restoration England* (Cambridge, 1990), pp 29–47.

[84] Craig Rose, ' Providence, Protestant union and godly reformation in the 1690s' in *Transactions of the Royal Historical Society*, ser. 6, iii (1993), pp 151–69.

[85] See, for example, Wetenhall, *Be ye also ready*, pp 91–2; John Stearne, *A sermon on the prayer of Moses* (Dublin, 1695), pp 23–4; *A discourse concerning prophane swearing and cursing* (Dublin, 1697), p. 27; Browne, *A sermon preached … April 17. 1698*, p.11; Alexander Sinclare, *A sermon preach'd before the societies for reformation of manners in Dublin, April the 11th, 1699* (Dublin, 1699), p. 7; William Hamilton, *Discourse concerning zeal against immorality and prophaneness* (Dublin, 1700), pp 28–9; St George Ashe, *A sermon preached to the societies for reformation of manners, at St Mary-le-Bow, on … December the 31st, 1716* (London, 1717), pp 30–31.

through a reformation of manners and a revival of true piety, rather than attempting the conversion of Catholics. Even in Dublin, where 'immoralities' of all sorts were assumed to be rife in conditions of economic distress,[86] the positive measures taken to educate the poor away from idleness, drink, gambling, prostitution or violent crime were restricted to a minute proportion of the inhabitants, distinguished by their adherence to the established church. Of the twenty-six charity schools in the capital, only two, both attached to St Patrick's cathedral, were specifically directed towards the offspring of the Catholic poor.[87]

Hitherto, in seeking to explain why Irish charity schools should have concentrated their efforts on Protestant children, I have been arguing from generalisations. At this point it will be useful to turn back, and to qualify the general argument, in order to confirm assertions of the importance attaching to individual character and local context. Some qualifications have already been hinted at; for example, in discussing the 'moral crisis' with which reformers believed themselves to be confronted, but which could be pictured in various forms, as constituting a challenge to orthodox Christian doctrine, public virtue, or social order. Although pietist enthusiasm and 'Puritan' prejudice could each furnish a broadly similar outlook, there was room for differences of emphasis. These differences were even more pronounced outside reforming circles, among those whom the promoters of charity schools sought to interest in their projects.

The advantages that were advertised as likely to accrue from the endowment of a charity school related either to the preservation of public order or to the achievement of economic progress. Both would naturally emerge as a consequence of the inculcation of civic virtue, which would render children not only amenable to moral discipline but (according to a favourite 'Puritan' text) 'useful in their own time', and thus provide 'a constant supply of useful men both in church and state'.[88] To landed proprietors and local merchants there was a more direct attraction in the prospect of the development of new manufactures, with pupils being taught to spin and weave, and set to productive work in the classroom. As much as anything else, Lord Egmont's school in County Cork was a means of regenerating an estate ravaged during the Jacobite wars.[89] The decision to board the pupils was taken with a view to squeezing as much work out of them as possible, and not, as Egmont argued retrospectively, to keep them from reverting to the bad habits and ill principles of their parents.[90] The most obvious examples of industrial schools were those sponsored by the Linen Board, but in practice these were indistinguishable from schools erected

86 David Dickson, 'The place of Dublin in the eighteenth-century Irish economy' in T. M. Devine and David Dickson (eds), *Ireland and Scotland 1600–1850: parallels and contrasts in economic and social development* (Edinburgh, 1983), pp 177–9.

87 *Methods of erecting ... charity schools ...*, pp 24–5.

88 St George Ashe, *A sermon preached in the Trinity-College chappell before the university of Dublin January the 9th 1693–4* (Dublin, 1694), p. 15.

89 Ld Perceval to Berkeley Taylor, 22 Feb., 15 Mar., 2, 6 Sept., 1715 (B.L., Add. MS 46966, ff 27, 47, 97, 102); same to same, 17 Mar. 1715/16 (ibid., Add. MS 46967, f. 40). Similar circumstances obtained in relation to the school founded by Mrs Catherine O'Brien at Corofin, Co. Clare (*Inchiquin* MSS, ed. Ainsworth, pp 39, 108, 116, 136, 145, 148).

90 Ld Perceval to Berkeley Taylor, 20 Dec. 1715 (B.L., Add. MS 46966, f. 137); to same, 15 Nov.,

by a landowner like Sir John Rawdon, with the intention of training boys to the techniques of linen production, after which they would be given parcels of land on his estate to 'carry on the trade'. [91] And if manufacture proved impracticable, there was the inducement of breeding a new generation of husbandmen and gardeners to cultivate the land according to English practice, and honest servants to fill what was considered a serious gap in the labour market.[92] Besides future prosperity, the schools offered the hope of a better-behaved populace and thus a more stable society. At their most basic they would be 'shops for morals' (to adopt a phrase of Charles Dickens), in which the precepts of *The whole duty of man* might be instilled[93] alongside an appreciation of the merits of the established constitution in church and state. Readers of pamphlets canvassing the merits of charitable giving knew well enough how to decode statements about

> the Christian and useful education of poor children tending not only to the good of themselves, both in soul and body, but also to the preservation of others from the numerous evils they might be exposed to, from such children's not being instructed in the duties of religion and civil life.[94]

Such considerations naturally helped to determine whether a school aimed at taking in Catholic children as well as, or even instead of, Protestants. Where economic motives were uppermost, those in authority would generally be less concerned with denominational affiliation, though there may be an additional distinction between those absentee landlords who assumed that they would be able to make their tenantry exclusively Protestant, and residents who knew the reality and were prepared to countenance leases to Catholics willing and able to pay. A

26 Dec. 1718 (ibid., Add. MS 46969, ff 96, 107); to same, 25 June, 30 Sept., 24 Oct. 1720 (ibid., Add. MS 46970, ff 62, 77, 96).

91 *Methods of erecting ... charity schools ...*, p. 30. For a similar school in Kilkenny city, established by the 2nd duke of Ormond, the corporation, and other local landowning and commercial interests, in order to stimulate linen manufacture, see 'Manufactory of Kilkenny paper' (N.L.I., Ormond papers, MS 11,070); Kilkenny corporation minute book 1690–1717, p. 151 (N.L.I., microfilm P.5136). On the Linen Board schools, see Jones, *Charity school movement*, p. 225; H. D. Gribbon, 'The Irish Linen Board, 1711–1828' in L. M. Cullen and T. C. Smout (eds), *Comparative aspects of Scottish and Irish economic and social history 1600–1900* (Edinburgh, [1977]), pp 82–4; and for some individual examples, *Methods of erecting ... charity schools ...*, pp 21–2, 31 (Killough, Co. Down; Abbeyleix, Queen's Co.); will of Henry Turner, 16 Mar. 1705 (P.R.O.N.I., Castleward papers, D/2092/1/2, letterbook 2, p. 8) and John Stevenson, *Two centuries of life in Down* (Belfast, 1920), pp 209–10 (Bangor, Co. Down). For Rawdon, see below, ch. 8.

92 Edward Nicholson, *A method of charity schools recommended* (Dublin, 1712), p. 44; *Printed proceedings of the Society for Promoting Charity Schools*; *Some few letters selected, from an account of work-houses and charity schools for employment of the poor in England, with a preface to excite some such application of our charity in Ireland* (Dublin, 1728), pp v–vii; *Methods of erecting ... charity schools ...*, pp 38–40.

93 Quane, 'Viscount Weymouth's grammar school', p. 32; *Methods of erecting ... charity schools ...*, p. 34; Green Coat School min. bk, 28 Nov. 1720. See also *A letter from a member of the Incorporated Society in Dublin* ([Dublin, 1733]), p. 11; Isaacs, 'Moral crime, moral reform & the state', p. 38.

94 *Methods of erecting, supporting and governing charity schools: with an account of the charity schools in Ireland* (2nd ed., Dublin, 1719), p. 3.

stranger to Ireland, like the young Yorkshire squire Thomas Watson Wentworth, was more likely to insist that his school be filled with Protestant children in the same way that he expected his estate to be settled with Protestant tenants.[95] Someone like Egmont, who had lived in Ireland, would take in willing workers wherever he could find them, and whatever their religious proclivities.[96]

Anxiety over the maintenance of social and political order could affect the admissions policy of a school much more directly. Whether it did would depend on the extent to which the forces of disorder were given a sectarian identification. In Dublin, and possibly in other large conurbations, this tended not to be the case unless some particular political issue had arisen. Despite a recent influx of Catholics, the population of the capital was still substantially Protestant,[97] and run-of-the-mill crime was not assumed to be the province of a Catholic under-class. Rural Ireland was different. Protestants might be scarce, sectarian relations strained, and anti-social behaviour of any kind on the part of local Catholics assumed by the propertied residents to have a religious, and therefore a political, undertone. A striking feature of the geographical pattern of charity school foundations is the cluster recorded in counties affected by the 'houghing' outbreak of 1711–13, in the north midlands and in Connacht.[98] The benefactor of one such school, at Hollymount in County Mayo, was Archbishop John Vesey of Tuam.[99] Vesey was interested in church reform and given to preaching a strongly Providential theology, but he was also deeply perturbed by the activities of the houghers, and inclined to see their attacks on livestock as harbingers of a Jacobite uprising.[100] The coincidence of his political fright and educational benefaction is highly suggestive. The connexion is even firmer in the case of that indefatigable publicist for charity schools, the septuagenarian Sligo clergyman Edward Nicholson, whose boast was that he had endowed a charity school place for every year of his age.[101] One of his pamphlets promised that charity schools would save Irish society from 'idleness, debauchery, villainy, and, at last, unavoidable rebellion', for without the guidance given by the schools children

95 Abp King to Francis Annesley, 3 July 1714 (T.C.D., MS 750/4, f. 176); *An account of charity schools lately erected in Great Britain and Ireland* (London, 1709), p. 44. For other examples, see lease by earl of Athlone to Thomas Twigg, 24 June 1698 (N.L.I., Baker papers, D.27192); Thomas Prior to Sir John Rawdon, 20 June 1719 (HA 15579).

96 Ld Perceval to Berkeley Taylor, 28 Feb. 1718/19 (B.L., Add. MS 46970, f. 28); *Methods of erecting … charity schools …*, p. 16. Some absentees also adopted this approach (Ld Weymouth to Mr Mainwaring, 17 Aug. 1705 (Longleat, Thynne papers, 179, ff 124–5)).

97 Dickson, 'Place of Dublin in 18th-cent. Ir. economy', p. 183.

98 S. J. Connolly, 'The houghers: agrarian protest in early eighteenth-century Connacht' in C. H. E. Philpin (ed.), *Nationalism and popular protest in Ireland* (Cambridge, 1987), pp 139–62.

99 Nicholson, *Method of charity schools*, p. 39.

100 John Vesey, *Sermon preach'd to the Protestants of Ireland in and about the City of London … October 23. 1689* (London, 1689); Abp Vesey's donations to Dublin workhouse, 1706–7 (N.L.I., De Vesci papers, MS 38,817); Nicholson, *Method of charity schools*, dedication; Vesey to Joshua Dawson, 22 Jan. 1711/12 (T.N.A., SP 63/367, f. 276); Dawson to Vesey, 12 Feb. 1711/12 (Bodl., MS Eng. Hist. b. 125, f. 120); Hayton, 'Bishops as legislators'.

101 *The methods used for erecting charity schools in Great Britain and Ireland* (London, 1715), p. 28.

would degenerate into 'vagabonds, sturdy beggars, thieves, robbers, highwaymen, rapparees or tories, houghers, murderers and rebels'.[102]

Behind this analysis lay a traditional theme of English policy: the achievement of security through the Anglicisation of Gaelic society. The identification of Protestantism with 'Englishness' and thus with the necessary virtues of loyalty, 'civility', and a capacity for economic improvement, was bound to resonate in public discourse in a period of insecurity and post-war reconstruction. Politicians no less than churchmen hoped for a numerical reinforcement of the Protestant interest, either by further plantation or by the conversion of the native Irish.[103] The theme was too important to be ignored, and it ran like a thread through the texture of charity school sermons. Bishop Foy's address to the Irish House of Lords in 1698 provides an extreme example, preaching a mission 'to reduce ... the Irish nation' to Protestant, Anglicised civility, analogous to the mission of St Paul to 'the pagans'.[104] In general, however, it was a secondary consideration, an argument to catch contributions rather than an essential internal dynamic. The response of Henry Maule and his friends to John Richardson's translation proposals reveals the true priorities of the charity school lobby. They were obliged to accept the desirability of conversion as an objective, but would have no truck with this particular means, and were content to argue from patently unrealistic estimates of the spread of the English language (Nicholson declaring at one point that the children of the native Irish now spoke English 'universally'[105]) so long as they could preserve their own control over the financial resources of Protestant philanthropy. More typical than Foy's sermon were the remarks of Archbishop Synge, some twenty years later: although concerned to advertise charity schools as potent weapons in the ongoing war against popery, he placed greater stress on redeeming the sinful than on enlightening the superstitious, and extolled as the most effective instrument of conversion the giving of a good example by worthy Protestants.[106]

Nonetheless, the power of the conventional argument about Anglicisation cannot be passed over lightly. It was present in educational discourse throughout this period, and indeed became increasingly visible in the latter stages of the charity school movement, until reaching an apogee with the inauguration of the charter schools. While aspirations for economic improvement and a residual concern with effecting some form of social control were certainly present in the ethos of the 'Incorporated Society', it was much more openly directed towards proselytism than the 'Society for Promoting Christian Knowledge in Ireland ...', which it replaced. What is interesting is the changing balance between the long-term requirements of governance and social policy, and the various theological imperatives, material

102 Nicholson, *Method of charity schools*, pp 25–6, 28, 34–7. Even Nicholson did not advocate that schools should admit only Catholics, preferring the proportions to be fifty-fifty.

103 For a prominent example, [Sir Richard Cox,] *An essay for the conversion of the Irish* (Dublin, 1698). Cox himself founded a charity school on his estate at Dunmanway, Co. Cork.

104 Foy, *A sermon preach'd ... the 23d of October 1698*.

105 Nicholson to S.P.C.K., 30 Aug. 1715 (S.P.C.K. Archives, A.L.B. 6, item 4450). See also Barnard, 'Protestants & Irish language', pp 261–5.

106 Edward Synge, *The reward of converting sinners from the errors of their ways* (Dublin, 1719).

ambitions and other personal motives that lay behind the craze for charity schools. The scales dipped or rose according to local circumstances, and also responded to shifts in the general political climate which influenced ways in which Irish Protestants conceptualised the threat from popery.

To take geography first. The most obvious difference was between country and town, or rather what was imagined as a bandit-infested countryside where all disorder appeared as potential rebellion, and the urban slums where epidemics of poverty and crime were non-denominational. The latter was true in Dublin and Cork, especially, and possibly also in such other towns as Drogheda and Kilkenny, which saw attempts to put into execution the laws against 'immorality'.[107] But rural conditions varied too; Protestants in Counties Roscommon or Sligo, who felt themselves to be isolated and vulnerable, would place a higher premium on the rule of law than landowners in more intensively planted areas, whose prime concern was the recovery of rental values following civil war and economic recession.[108] And Anglican landlords in Ulster, like the earl of Abercorn in Counties Donegal and Tyrone, Sir John Staples in County Londonderry, or the Rawdons in Down, might see their chief interest as fortifying the established church against the incursions of Presbyterians, whose academies were the subject of Anglican resentment both in convocation and parliament. Bishop Wetenhall's petition to the lord lieutenant in 1711 requesting encouragement for charity schools was in part a reaction to the possibility that Catholics might be converted to Presbyterianism, while a prominent Irish Tory, Arthur Annesley, earl of Anglesey, lauded the English charity schools specifically because they were weaning Dissenting families back to the Church of England.[109]

Just as important as local context to understanding the different purposes for which schools were founded is an appreciation of the shifts that occurred in public attitudes in response to perceptions of political and social change. For while each charity school depended for its existence on some personal or parochial initiative, the overall pattern was influenced by such things as fashion, publicity, organisational back-up, and the encouragement afforded by those in authority, in church and state. And the power of fashion, the impact of ideas, and the morale of the campaigners were in turn affected by external conditions, more especially the public consciousness of the state of Catholicism in Ireland. If a graph could be constructed to plot

[107] Barnard, 'Reforming Irish manners', p. 815; *Council book of the corporation of Drogheda*, i: *From the year 1649 to 1734*, ed. Thomas Gogarty (Drogheda, 1915), pp 243, 245–6, 250, 267, 270, 320, 327; Kilkenny corp. min. bk 1690–1717, p. 136 (N.L.I., mic. P.5136).

[108] Lord Weymouth was keen that his schoolmaster in Carrickmacross should make converts of the more prominent members of the local Catholic community, and encouraged him to pay particular attention to the MacMahons, the 'ancient proprietors' of the barony of Ferny (Weymouth to Mr Carver, 18 Sept. 1708 (Longleat, Thynne papers, 179, ff 125–6)).

[109] King (ed.), *A great archbishop*, p. 297; Arthur Annesley to Arthur Charlett, 12 Apr. 1705 (Bodl., MS Ballard 10, ff 167–8). See also *A representation of the present state of religion* (Dublin, 1712), pp 12–13; Thomas Prior to Sir John Rawdon, 20 Jan. 1718[/19] (HA 15566); James Bonnell to John Strype, 22 Sept. 1692 (Cambridge, Univ. Lib., Add. MS 1, ff 100–101), for the idea that the foundation of 'a seminary or college of divines at Derry' would be 'the best bulwark for the church against Scotland and the growth of kirkism'.

the changing intensity of Protestant fears of popery in the first half of the eighteenth century it would resolve into a jagged line of peaks and troughs, the peaks coinciding with political crises. The correlation is not so obvious in the early years of King William's reign, when anxiety engendered by events in Europe was offset by confidence in the destruction of the Catholic interest at home.[110] (In this respect the priorities set by charity school enthusiasts and other 'reformers' are a better guide to the state of Protestant opinion than the varying level of parliamentary commitment to penal legislation, which could be distorted by party-political tactics.) More dramatic effects, however, were produced by the prolonged crisis over the Protestant succession, ushered in by the Jacobite invasion scare of 1708, fuelled by the antics of the Irish Tory administration of 1711–14, and only relieved by the safe accession of a Hanoverian monarch, followed by the defeat of the Jacobite rebellion in England and Scotland.

At the same time, the more forward-thinking members of the Protestant community were coming to realise that the popery laws, upon whose efficacy the Irish parliament had placed so much reliance, were failing in their avowed purpose of extirpating the Catholic religion. Beyond making life hazardous and uncomfortable for the Catholic clergy, they had in fact accomplished little of substance; indeed, it was assumed that many of the entries on the so-called 'convert rolls' represented conversions in name only.[111] In response, Protestants either looked for more statutes, – to strengthen penalties and close loopholes – or turned to the ways of persuasion. Anti-Catholic tracts were printed; Anglican clerics preached on the theme; and efforts were made to refurbish the methods of proselytism, notably in the field of education, with renewed interest in the parochial schools. Gathering speed, with a renewed emphasis in polemical literature on the persecutions endured by continental Protestants, the interest in conversion moved towards a culmination in the charter schools.

Some attempt may be made to trace in outline the effect of these changes on the charity school movement. The function of the earliest schools had been to recall poor Protestant children to their religion and to instil in them the virtues of hard work and obedience, while the conversion of Catholics was left to the implementation of laws and the working of self-interest, bolstered by individual persuasion and pious example. With the additional inducement of economic profit the foundation of schools became briefly a fashionable pursuit for conscientious philanthropists and improving landlords. The intrusion of a stronger conversionist element may

110 See *The true way to render Ireland happy and secure*, p. 13: ''tis generally thought [the Irish Catholics] are so subdued there is no danger of their disturbing us for the time to come'.

111 *Representation of the present state of religion*, pp 19–22; Bp Synge to Bp Wake, 13 Apr. 1715 (Christ Church, Arch. W. Epist. xii, f. 7); Abp King to Henry Maule, 24 Aug. 1722 (T.C.D., MS 750/7/186–7); same to Wake, 12 July 1727 (ibid., MS 750/8/231–2); *An humble proposal for obtaining His Majesty's royal charter to incorporate a society for promoting Christian knowledge among the poor natives of the kingdom of Ireland* (Dublin, 1730), pp 4–5. See also T. P. Power, 'Converts' in idem and Kevin Whelan (eds), *Endurance and emergence: Catholics in Ireland in the eighteenth century* (Blackrock, Co. Dublin, 1990), pp 101–27; and more generally, Michael Brown, Charles Ivar McGrath and Thomas Power (eds), *Converts and conversion in Ireland, 1650–1850* (Dublin, 2005).

be dated to around 1711–12, as convocation addressed the theme, Edward Nicholson's pamphlets presented charity schools as the most effective solution to the acute problem of disorder in the Irish countryside, and the S.P.C.K. showed a belated interest in bringing Ireland into its sphere of operations. Together, these developments restored the traditional religio-political perspective of English policy, and, significantly, they coincided with the gathering political storm over the succession. Less obviously, perhaps, the ultimate resolution of that crisis robbed the charity school movement of some of its impetus. But disillusionment with the effectiveness of the popery laws kept alive a popular interest in the political and social uses of education, and in 1734 the charity schools were in a sense reborn, with a different order of objectives: proselytism first, and moral reformation, social discipline and economic reconstruction accorded subsidiary roles.

The charter schools not only represented a change of direction. They marked a new beginning, for the majority of schools established since 1695 seem to have been in desperate straits by the mid-1720s.[112] Testamentary bequests were still being made to inaugurate new schools or sustain existing foundations, but Lord Orrery spoke for many potential benefactors in 1725 in declaring the very idea of a charity school to be impracticable.[113] While a handful continued in their original form for a long and useful life, notably Bishop Foy's school in Waterford, and the Green Coat School in Cork, the remainder were taken over and re-established as charter schools, or disappeared entirely.

The reasons for this failure were many and various, often deriving from the particular circumstances of individual schools: the wilting enthusiasm of a patron, the incompetence of a schoolmaster, or a failure to offer sufficient material inducements to parents. Some more general reasons may be adduced. Covert opposition from Archbishop King and others within the Church of Ireland hierarchy retarded early progress by presenting convocation as an alternative instrument of ecclesiastical and moral reform, and even after 1715 King managed to hinder the search for official backing, retailing Whig slurs that the S.P.C.K. schoolmasters in England were indoctrinating their pupils in high-flying Tory principles.[114] Among laymen the vogue for setting up schools waned, as the trumpeted economic advantages failed to materialise. Landlords came to appreciate a truth that Archbishop King had long since grasped, that the schools were training a workforce for an economy which was as yet insufficiently developed to make use of it.[115] And as arguments about public order focused once more on potential Catholic insurgency instead of the late

112 *Printed proceedings of the Society for Promoting Charity Schools*. For evidence of the difficulties experienced by individual schools, see Thomas Prior to Sir John Rawdon, 11 July 1719 (HA 15583); Berkeley Taylor to Ld Perceval, 3 June, 19 July,. 18 Aug. 1720 (B.L., Add. MS 46971, ff 59, 63, 68); Perceval to Taylor, 25 June, 24 Oct. 1720 (ibid., ff 62, 96); Taylor to Perceval, 4 May 1721 (ibid., Add. MS 46972, f. 56); Perceval's diary, May 1721 (ibid., f. i); earl of Orrery to Brettridge Badham, 3 Apr., 18 June 1725 (N.L.I., Orrery papers, MS 4177, items, 47, 53).

113 Orrery to Badham, 3 Apr., 18 June 1725 (N.L.I., MS 4177, items, 47, 53).

114 Abp King to Abp Wake, 212 Sept. 1717 (T.C.D., MS 750/11/2/303–5); Rose, '"Seminarys of faction and rebellion"'. Bishop Evans of Meath made the same suggestion about the Dublin schools (Evans to S.P.C.K., 2 Aug. 1717 (S.P.C.K. Archives, A.L.B. 8, item 5307)).

115 Abp King to Abp Wake, 212 Sept. 1717 (T.C.D., MS 750/11/2/303–5).

seventeenth-century obsession with public immorality, there was a recognition that localised experiments were inadequate to the scale of the problem, and that what was needed was some kind of national programme with official approval.

The 'reforming' ethos that informed the foundation of charity schools had been inspired by a highly vocal and influential minority, who in the first decades of the eighteenth century had set the Church of Ireland's public agenda. Their theology disposed them to pay more attention to the degraded condition, as they saw it, of the Protestant minority than the recalcitrance of the Catholic majority, and in their educational schemes they were primarily concerned to save the souls of fellow Protestants and in doing so avert an adverse judgment of Providence. In this they were no different to their counterparts in England. But the peculiarities of the Irish situation naturally magnified the other benefits that schools were thought to provide; social, economic, and ultimately political. In the long run policy prevailed over enthusiasm. To ask what might have happened had it not done so from the start opens up intriguing possibilities, but on reflection must ultimately be as futile as any other exercise in counter-factual speculation, since enthusiasm rather than policy was in essence what the 'second Reformation' of the early eighteenth century was all about.

The Rawdon family

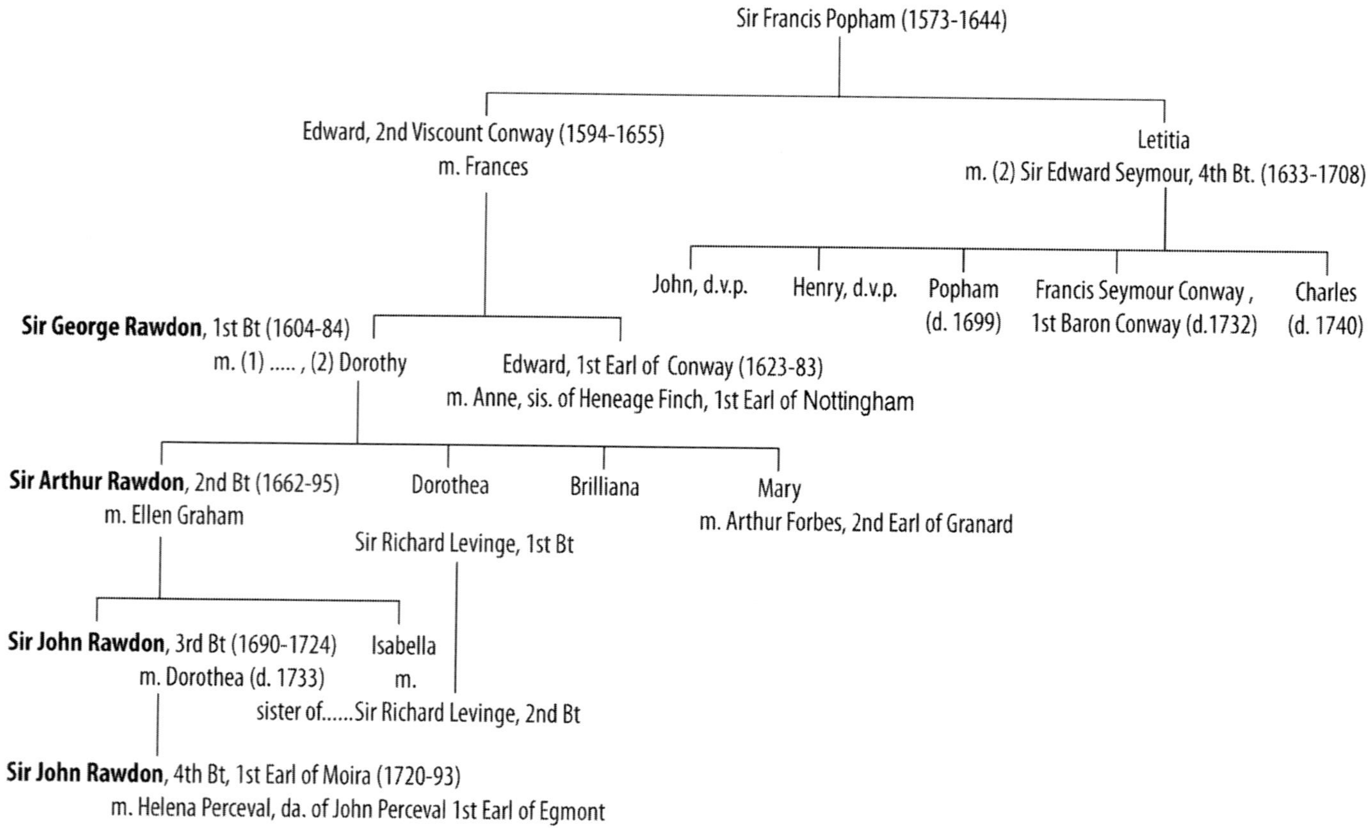

8

A question of upbringing

Thomas Prior, Sir John Rawdon, 3rd Bt, and the mentality and ideology of 'improvement'

Although historians of eighteenth-century Ireland are aware of the association between the Irish economic writer Thomas Prior (1681–1751), the founder of the Dublin Society, and the Rawdon family of Moira, County Down, the connexion has only been remarked upon by scholars working on the Rawdons, and in particular by those interested in the life of John Rawdon, first earl of Moira, the pious, philanthropic intellectual (and husband of the blue-stocking Elizabeth), to whom Prior acted as a mentor.[1] Biographers of Prior have focused instead on his connexion with Bishop Berkeley.[2] But Prior's primary working relationship, at least until the mid-1720s, was with the Rawdons. Not only did he receive his first employment from them, he was also a family friend, and for a time lived in the Rawdon household. He was particularly close to Lord Moira's father, Sir John Rawdon, 3rd Bt (1690–1723), whose relatively short life and limited involvement in public affairs have largely sequestered him from the attentions of posterity, but whose character and interests foreshadowed the achievements of his son.

The nature and extent of Prior's involvement with the affairs of the third baronet are documented in his letters to his employer, the bulk of which repose in the Irish section of the Hastings collection at the Huntington Library in California. Consideration of this relationship offers a different perspective on Prior's association with the Rawdon family, suggesting that in the long term intellectual exchange between agent and landlord may have been reciprocal, instead of the unilateral influence attributed to Prior by students of the life and career of Lord Moira. There may also be a broader significance in tracing Prior's early experience of estate management and his domestic situation in the Rawdon household, since the interests of the family touched on various aspects of one of the organising principles of Prior's thought: the idea of 'improvement'.

Much has been written on the enthusiasm for 'improving' Ireland in the early modern period.[3] As a result, we now have a much keener appreciation of the impor-

1 Compare the entries in *D.I.B.* for Prior (xviii, 307–9) and John Rawdon, first earl of Moira (viii, 395–6).

2 For Prior see also *Oxf. D.N.B.*, xlv, 423; Desmond Clarke, *Thomas Prior, 1681–1751, founder of the Royal Dublin Society* (Dublin, 1951); Teddy Fennelly, *Thomas Prior: his life, times, and legacy* (Port Laoise, 2001). There is a brief notice in Caroline Robbins, *The eighteenth-century commonwealthman* (Cambridge, Mass., 1959), p. 159.

3 See especially the contributions of T. C. Barnard: 'Gardening, diet and "improvement" in later

tance of the idea of 'improvement' in the ethos of the governing class, and the extent to which this could permeate political, religious, social and cultural life. However, the very fact that subscription to the cause of 'improvement' appears to have been so general sometimes threatens to deprive the term of specific meaning. There is a danger that historians, having discovered in the consensual assumption that Ireland required to be 'improved' a salient aspect of the mentality of the propertied and intellectual elite, might overplay the point, until commitment to 'improvement' becomes a catch-all explanation for any and every development in political and social thought.[4]

Some intellectual rigour has been injected into the subject in the specific area of political ideas. Without question, 'improvement' formed a central theme of public debate in the period c. 1720–50. Anxiety over the economic and social condition of Ireland – the backwardness of agriculture and manufacture, the chaotic and inadequate system of currency, and what was perceived as endemic poverty, manifested in a visible increase in the numbers of beggars in both town and countryside – animated Swift and other pamphleteers in the 1720s. It was brought to a head in 1727–9 by a series of bad harvests leading to subsistence crises and large-scale emigration, especially of Ulster Presbyterians to north America.[5] Some 'patriots', especially among the parliamentary opposition, revived the grievance of British interference in Irish trade. Others, including economic writers like Prior and pragmatic government politicians and administrators in Dublin Castle, concentrated on proposals for the regeneration of the Irish economy from within.[6] Prior's most famous work, his *List of the absentees of Ireland …* (1729), emphasised the need to conserve the resources of Ireland to promote Irish manufactures, while the Dublin Society, founded on his initiative in 1731, embodied this kind of practical 'patriotism' by providing a forum for the discussion and development of new ideas in agriculture and industry.[7] The Dublin Society has been identified by James Livesey, in an important article, as representing a new political ideology, in which former differences over religious and constitutional principle were to be put aside, and a new form of civil society

seventeenth-century Ireland' in *Journal of Garden History*, x (1990), pp 71–85; idem, 'Improving clergymen, 1660–1760' in Alan Ford, J. I. McGuire and Kenneth Milne (eds), *As by law established: the Church of Ireland since the Reformation* (Dublin, 1995), pp 136–51; idem, *Improving Ireland? Projectors, prophets and profiteers, 1641–1786* (Dublin, 2008).

4 Scepticism has already been expressed in T. C. Barnard, 'The artistic and cultural activities of the Caldwells of Castle Caldwell, 1750–1783' in *Irish Architectural and Decorative Studies*, x (2007), pp 96–8; idem, 'The Dublin Society and other improving societies, 1731–88' in James Kelly and M. J. Powell (eds), *Clubs and societies in eighteenth-century Ireland* (Dublin, 2010), pp 53–88.

5 James Kelly, 'Jonathan Swift and the Irish economy in the 1720s' in *Eighteenth-Century Ireland*, vi (1991), pp 7–31; Patrick Kelly, 'The politics of political economy in mid-eighteenth-century Ireland' in S. J. Connolly (ed.), *Political ideas in eighteenth-century Ireland* (Dublin, 2000), pp 105–29.

6 See above, ch. 6.

7 Thomas Prior, *A list of the absentees of Ireland, and the yearly value of their estates and incomes spent abroad …* (Dublin, 1729). On the establishment and early history of the society, see Terence de Vere White, *The story of the Royal Dublin Society* (Tralee, [1955]), chs 1–3; Desmond Clarke, *Arthur Dobbs esquire 1689–1765 …* (Chapel Hill, N.C., 1957), ch. 4.

created on the basis of a shared commitment to natural philosophy and economic development.[8]

On the other hand, we should not forget that, as Andrew Sneddon has observed, the idea of 'improvement' was protean.[9] It could encompass a number of very different things, ranging from the traditional concerns of English-inspired reform programmes from the mid-sixteenth century onwards – the moral and social reformation of the native Irish and the introduction of proper standards of 'civility'– to the simple concerns of domestic economy – making an estate more profitable, more comfortable, and even (in terms of exterior design and interior furnishing) more fashionable. In each case, a justification can be constructed for regarding these activities as aspects of the more general 'improvement' of Ireland. Making Ireland 'English' (or indeed 'British') involved not only educating the inhabitants in the ways of a civil society, but also creating a commercialised and sustainable market economy, through efficient agriculture, the intensive exploitation of natural resources, the encouragement of manufactures, and the development of a recognisable infrastructure of towns, roads and waterways. Religion was central to this project, since Protestantism cemented loyalty and was also thought to encourage 'habits of industry'. In a private context, the creation of a country estate, with grand house, emparkment, demesne and even pleasure gardens, could also contribute to the process of Anglicisation and 'social improvement', by introducing into Ireland significant features of the English landscape. Similarly, the importation of exotic plants or luxury goods might be thought to constitute one marker of the transition to a 'modern' economy, and in an individual to distinguish a more refined taste.

There are, however, difficulties in lumping together these various phenomena under a single heading, since each is susceptible to an alternative explanation. For a landlord local economic development might be a matter of urgent financial necessity; the spread of Protestantism a manifestation of a strong personal religious commitment; the construction or refurbishment of a country house and the creation of an elaborate garden a form of conspicuous consumption. Moreover, the ultimate effects of some 'improving' activities counteracted the intention of others: the importation of foreign luxuries, for example, undercut the development of domestic industries, so that in this respect the general mentality of 'improvement' (conflating personal and national) might be in conflict with the specific ideology of 'improvement' as articulated by economic writers.

A study of the relationship between Thomas Prior and the Rawdons in the period leading up to the publication of the *List of absentees* ... and the foundation of the Dublin Society, serves three purposes. In a limited way it helps to understand the development of Prior's ideas through exposure of the context in which he was

8 James Livesey, 'The Dublin Society in eighteenth-century Irish political thought' in *Hist. Jn.*, xlvii (2004), pp 615–40. See also idem, *Civil society and empire: Ireland and Scotland in the eighteenth-century Atlantic world* (New Haven, Conn., & London, 2009), ch. 2, esp. pp 57–62.

9 Andrew Sneddon, 'Legislating for economic development: Irish fisheries as a case study in the limitations of "improvement"', in D. W. Hayton, James Kelly and John Bergin (eds), *The eighteenth-century composite state: representative institutions in Ireland and Europe, 1689–1800* (Basingstoke, 2010), p. 136.

operating at the outset of his career. It also enables an exploration of the interrelationship between the different facets of 'improvement' – religious, personal, social and economic – since, as we shall see, the Rawdons and their rather unusual agent demonstrated a concern with each. And finally, Sir John Rawdon's peculiar political background supplies clues to a connexion between the advocates of 'improvement' and a group of constructive 'patriots' within government in the 1720s and early 1730s, who may have played a role in the transmission of these ideas to the new generation represented by the first earl of Moira.

The Rawdon family were by origin minor Yorkshire gentry. Sir John Rawdon's grandfather George, the first baronet, had made his fortune through the patronage of the Conway family, as secretary to the first and second Viscounts Conway, and finally through marriage to the sister, and only surviving sibling, of the third viscount and first earl.[10] The Conways were absentee English landlords of an extensive Irish estate centred on Lisburn Castle in County Antrim, and after the Restoration Rawdon took on the management of these Irish properties[11] (with a room of his own in the castle[12]). In so doing he established himself as a significant local figure in his own right, developing estates at Brookhill near Lisburn, which he held on a long lease from Lord Conway,[13] and Moira, which he owned. Later, when the Rawdons had become embroiled in a lawsuit with the earl of Conway's successors, the history of Sir George's stewardship came under scrutiny. Opinions differed as to whether he or Conway had benefited more from the arrangement. Rawdon's supporters contended that his management had rescued the estate from dereliction. Debts amounting to about £34,000 had been cleared, the annual return substantially increased, and the town of Lisburn not only preserved from ruin during the rising of 1641, but extensively 'improved': it became a significant market town, a parliamentary borough (in 1662), and a diocesan centre (with its parish church upgraded to cathedral status). Rawdon instigated, and indeed undertook at his own expense, an extensive programme of building, including the construction of a market house.[14] His detractors, on the other hand, alleged that Rawdon owed the expansion of his own estate entirely to his connexion with Conway; an exaggeration, since it ignored Rawdon's enterprise on his own behalf, and his acquisition of lands from the Cromwellian confiscations.[15] Presumably the arrangement proved mutually beneficial. Certainly by the time of his death in 1684 Rawdon had become a substantial landed proprietor, with estates in Counties Antrim, Down, and Wicklow, as well as his small ancestral seat of Rawdon Hall in Yorkshire; and in the will he made the previous year he

[10] *Oxf. D.N.B.*, xlvi, 140–41.

[11] Sir Standish Hartstonge to Lady Graham, 6 Dec. 1683 (HA 14962).

[12] Inventory of the goods in 'Lisburne House', 2 Oct. 1692 (Edward Berwick, *The Rawdon papers* ... (London, 1819), p. 411).

[13] Thomas Prior to Sir John Rawdon, 3 Mar. 1718[/19] (HA 15572).

[14] John Coghill to Sir George Rawdon, 6 Oct. 1683 (HA14286); 'E.B.' to 'a gentleman of Lisburn', 7 Jan. 1683[/4] (HA 13907); copy of will of Sir George Rawdon, 19 Oct. 1683, with codicil, 30 July 1684 (HA 15697); and in general Raymond Gillespie, 'George Rawdon's Lisburn' in *Lisburn Historical Society Journal*, viii (1991), pp 32–6.

[15] *The case of the right honourable Francis ... Lord Conway, in answer to the case of Sir John Rawdon Bart* ... [Dublin, ?1705], p. 3.

provided from his personalty marriage portions of £2,000 for each of his unmarried daughters, Dorothy and Brilliana. He was also in the first rank of Irish society: a privy councillor and sometime member of the Irish parliament. In family terms, besides the cachet of having himself married into a leading Anglo-Irish aristocratic family, he had subsequently married a daughter to the earl of Granard and his son to an heiress who was granddaughter both to a Scottish peer, Lord Menteith, and to the former archbishop of Armagh, John Bramhall.

Arthur, who succeeded to the title and estates, seemed to have a brilliant future.[16] He expected to inherit not only his father's property but that of Lord Conway, whose 'darling' he had been.[17] However, these golden prospects turned to dust. His patrimony was depleted by the necessary provision that had to be made for Sir George's other dependants – the Yorkshire property, for example, was appropriated for the maintenance of his two unmarried sisters – and the estate was burdened with substantial debts.[18] Allegedly 'there was not one sixpence of ready money left' towards the payment of legacies and funeral expenses, and the only valuable goods – plate and farm stock – raised less than £100.[19] Matters were made worse by the near impossibility of obtaining rents from Irish tenants: the poverty of the country and the scarcity of ready money had been recurrent themes in estate correspondence from the early 1680s onwards, and in May 1688 Sir Arthur Rawdon had written from Moira that 'I believe no country was ever so poor, nor is there any prospect of amendment'.[20] The depredations of rival forces during the Williamite war caused the condition of the Ulster economy to deteriorate further.[21] The new baronet found himself in financial difficulties and in 1695 persuaded his sisters to execute a deed which placed in the hands of trustees those properties on which their portions were secured, with priority given to the settlement of creditors' claims.[22] Just before his death a bill was introduced into the Irish parliament to permit the sale of property to meet debts, only for it to be respited by the English privy council.[23]

All this was bad enough, but the real blow suffered by Sir Arthur had been in his great expectations from the Conway connexion. He had been treated by the earl as heir presumptive.[24] However, in August 1683, when Conway lay mortally ill at his English seat, Ragley Hall, he was prevailed upon to revise his will, leaving his third wife Ursula £15,000 and the use of his estates in England and Ireland for

16 *D.I.B*, viii, 391–2.

17 Henry More to Sir George Rawdon, 18 Oct. 1683 (HA 15374).

18 'Mrs Dorothy Rawdon's case' (HA 15698; there is another copy in Marsh's Library, MS Z.1.13). As early as 1668 Sir George Rawdon settled his estate on trustees, partly in order to facilitate the payment of his debts (copy of Rawdon's will (HA 15697)).

19 'Mrs Dorothy Rawdon's case' (HA 15698).

20 Rawdon to Hans Sloane, 10 May 1688 (B.L., Sloane MS 4036, ff 34–5).

21 The house at Moira, for example, was plundered by Jacobite forces (Arthur O'Lavery to Sir Arthur Rawdon, [?19] Oct. 1691 (N.L.I., MS 117, f. 126)).

22 See e.g. Thomas Stanhope to [Sir Arthur Rawdon], 5 Oct. 1687 (HA 15897); Thomas Dance to same, 25 Dec. 1694 (HA 14621); state of Sir John Rawdon's case [c. 1711] (HA 15703); Nicholas Canny, 'The formation of the Irish mind: religion, politics and Gaelic Irish literature' in *Past and Present*, no. 95 (May 1982), p. 115.

23 *L.J.Ire.*, ii, 310, 312.

24 George Gore to [?Dorothy] Rawdon, 5 Mar.1705 (HA 14803).

her lifetime, but more importantly adopting as his next heirs the sons of his cousin Letitia (*née* Popham), second wife of the prominent English parliamentarian Edward Seymour (from 1688, Sir Edward, 4th Bt). The first heir was to be Seymour's second son, Popham Seymour, with remainders to Popham's brothers, Francis and Charles. There was no mention of Sir George or Arthur. The only – inadequate – compensation was the bequest of £2,000 each to Arthur's sisters Dorothy and Brilliana.[25] The Rawdons were convinced that Conway had not been *compos mentis* when the new will had been drawn up,[26] and that the affair had been a contrivance of Edward Seymour, who had been present as a witness.[27] Sir Arthur immediately went to law, but having lost expensively in two Irish courts, king's bench and chancery (an outcome he and his friends ascribed to judicial corruption, and the improper use of influence by Seymour's friends in the Irish government),[28] he abandoned the suit in 1687, settling for the legacies to his sisters, only half of which was paid.[29]

Between Sir Arthur's death in 1695 and the point at which John, his only son, attained his majority in 1711, the financial position of the family improved considerably. According to Sir John's panegyrist, his distant cousin George Wilkins (rector of nearby Blaris parish), he had been 'born to a large estate' and was 'master of a good inheritance'.[30] He certainly behaved as if he were comfortably off, instructing Prior in the refurbishment of his home, replanting of his garden, and purchase of books, plate and other luxury items.[31] Much of the credit must go to his mother, Helen, who had managed her son's affairs during his minority, dying in 1710 just before he came of age. Even though she was assisted by friends and family, hers had been a formidable task. She was hard-pressed by her husband's creditors,[32] and efforts to squeeze rent from the tenantry were frustrated by the crisis in the Irish rural economy.[33] Ultimately, it seems, she must have used her own very substantial inheritance, derived from the estate of Archbishop Bramhall, which had been settled on her by her mother, to pay off the debts.[34]

25 Copy of will of Edward, earl of Conway, 9 Aug. 1683 (HA 14572; abstract at H.M.C., *Hastings MSS*, i, 321–2). He died on 11 Aug., and the will was proved the same day. See also *Conway letters* ..., ed. Marjorie Hope Nicholson (New Haven, Conn., 1930), p. 469.

26 Lady Graham to Sir George Rawdon, 12 Sept. 1683 (HA14825); John Coghill to same, 6 Oct. 1683 (HA 14286); Edmond Ellis to Arthur Rawdon, 9 Feb. 1683[/4] (HA14653).

27 See e.g. Arthur Rawdon to Nicholas Turke, 20 Oct. 1683 (HA15605).

28 Petition of Arthur Rawdon, 24 May 1684 (*C.S.P.*, *dom.*, 1684–5, p. 31); Thomas Stanhope to [Sir Arthur Rawdon], 24 Nov. 1684, 27 Jan., 5 Feb. 1684[/5] (HA 15849, 15858–9); David Campbell to same, 31 Jan. 1684[/5] (HA 14148)

29 *The case of the right honourable Francis ... Lord Conway ...*, p. 1.

30 George Wilkins, A *sermon preached at Magheralin on the occasion of the death of Sir John Rawdon, Bart., late of Moyrah in the county of Down ...* (Dublin, 1725), p. 20. See also Canny, 'Formation of the Irish mind', pp 115–16.

31 See below, pp 183–4.

32 See, for example, A. Walter to Lady Rawdon, 9 July 1696 (HA 15968), Alan Brodrick to same, 6 June 1702 (HA 14090); Brilliana Rawdon to Alan Brodrick, 12 Nov. 1702 (HA15611), reporting the visit of one importunate creditor who had 'threatened my sister in so insolent and rude a manner that I don't know what such a fellow may do if the law will in the least allow it'.

33 Thomas Stanhope to Lady Rawdon, 12 Aug. 1704 (HA 15900).

34 Lady Isabella Graham to Lord Menteith, 29 Mar. 1683[/4] (HA 14828); 'Mrs Dorothy Rawdon's case' (HA 15698); list of 'Dublin debts settled' [n.d.] (HA 15701); Berwick, *Rawdon papers*, p. 3.

Lady Rawdon also faced continuing legal (and political) challenges as she strove to secure her son's rights. The prolonged struggle over the Conway will had left a residue of bitterness and a sense of unfinished business. Fearful that their Irish tenants would find a pretext to withhold rents, the Seymours brought a private bill into the Irish parliament in March 1705 that would have ratified the chancery judgment upholding the will.[35] They were frustrated in this initiative by neat footwork from Lady Rawdon's supporters, so turned instead to Westminster and brought a similar bill into the English House of Lords.[36] This passed into law, though opposition in the Commons produced an additional proviso (of doubtful value) saving Sir John Rawdon's right to contest the will at some point in the future.[37] Unexpected difficulties then arose with Lady Rawdon's sister-in-law Dorothy. Although very supportive of her nephew's rights in the contest with the Conways, she was anxious about her own position, and in particular the integrity of the arrangement she and Brilliana had entered into in 1695, to place in the hands of trustees the lands on which their portion and maintenance were secured. Thus at her request the Irish parliament passed a private act in 1709 to protect her entitlement.[38] Because of the risk that it might prove a precedent for others to undermine the 1695 trust, Lady Rawdon felt obliged to submit a petition against the bill on behalf of her son,[39] and after her death Sir John organised, through his legal advisers, the introduction of another private bill to explain his aunt's act, which failed to reach the statute book despite two attempts (in 1710 and 1711). Legal opinion differed as to whether it was necessary, however, and since neither Brilliana nor Dorothy married, the financial pressure did not materialise.

Thanks largely to his mother, therefore, Sir John Rawdon entered into possession of his inheritance without the financial worries that had plagued his father. Nevertheless, the experiences of his minority must have left an impression. Troubles with creditors, the uncertainties caused by legal action, and a sense of embattlement with powerful outside forces, seem to have toughened his approach to estate management and made him cautious of political entanglements. Less obviously, perhaps, the financial constraints under which his father and mother had laboured, and the decline of the Rawdons from the high local standing that his grandfather had achieved, may have engrained in him the resolve to recover this lost prestige by 'making a grand figure'.[40] Certainly elsewhere in his family circle a severe view was taken of the failure of landed proprietors to maintain the economic and social position commensurate with their status.[41] Thus we find Sir John taking a close

35 *C.J.Ire.* (2nd ed.), iii, 275.

36 Dorothy Rawdon to Brilliana Rawdon, 29 Sept. 1705 (HA 15632); *L.J.*, xviii, 63.

37 *L.J.*, xviii, 82, 85, 126, 130–31; *C.J.*, xv, 139–40, 180–81, 184; Brilliana Rawdon to Hans Sloane, 19 Feb. 1705/6 (B.L., Sloane MS 4040, f. 133).

38 *C.J.Ire.* (2nd ed.), iii, 640.

39 Ibid., 681.

40 On this theme, see T. C. Barnard, *Making the grand figure: lives and possessions in Ireland, 1641–1770* (New Haven, Conn., & London, 2004).

41 Dorothy Rawdon to Sir John Rawdon, 6 July [?1722] (HA 15638): 'my Lord Drogheda has sold all his estate but £800 p.a. to Lord Hillsborough. How poor a figure a nobleman makes that reduces himself to such circumstances, that he has not so much as a claim to compassion.'

interest in the recovery of rents and renewal of leases, on occasion sometimes a little too aggressively for local gentry opinion,[42] and maximising the profitability of his estate.[43] The effect can be seen in the increased net income from the property, which rose from approximately £3,100 p.a. in 1717 to almost £4,000 at his death.[44] He was also determined to reside, so the house at Moira was redecorated and restocked, the garden and demesne developed, and trees planted.[45]

The condition of the Irish economy in the early eighteenth century dictated a more constructive approach to the management of a landed interest: there was no point in pressing tenants beyond their ability to pay. So, in common with other neighbouring landowners, Sir John Rawdon sought to increase economic capacity through the encouragement of manufacture, specifically the production of linen. The establishment of the Linen Board in 1711 offered the possibility of grants, and Sir John was able to obtain funding to set up 'spinning schools' on his property, for which he purchased flax and spinning wheels (at a cost of £12), and employed a 'mistress' (at £6 a year) to teach girls the requisite skills.[46] He was also willing to prefer tenants who would take up weaving.[47] The results were disappointing, however, because of the low price linen commanded.[48]

While the determination shown by Sir John in restoring the fabric of his estate and the reputation of the Rawdons may be explained at least in part as a reaction to recent vicissitudes, the way in which he went about the task was strongly reminiscent of his predecessors. In important respects his interests and activities followed family precedent. An obvious example is his promotion of the linen industry, which his grandfather had pioneered. Already by the mid-seventeenth century linen was being made locally, and Sir George Rawdon had tried to improve its quality by importing better raw materials.[49] In other respects, too, Sir George set a pattern as an aggressive and 'improving' landlord, at least in the early stages of his career, intent not only on expanding his holdings through purchase, but on developing their economic potential. Besides his work in Lisburn on behalf of the Conways, he was responsible for the establishment of market towns at Moira and Ballynahinch, and enjoyed a considerable reputation as a builder of roads. Some of the schemes he explored were technologically advanced, including, for example, bringing piped water to Lisburn.[50] His son Arthur does not seem to have had the funds, nor perhaps

42 Prior to Sir John Rawdon, 7 Feb. 1718[/19], 20, 22 27 June, 11 July 1719 (HA 15568, 15579–81, 15583)

43 Same to same, 4, 28 Apr., 20 June 1719 (HA 15575, 15577, 15579).

44 Rentals of Sir John Rawdon's estate, 1717–1724 (P.R,.O.N.I., Granard papers, T/3765/L/2/19/1–6).

45 Prior to Sir John Rawdon, 12 Feb. 1718[/19], 20, 27 June 1719 (HA 15569,15579, 15581).

46 Same to same, 6, 11 July 1719 (HA 15582–3)

47 Same to same, 11 July 1719 (HA 15583).

48 Same to same, 11 July 1719 (HA 15583).

49 Sir George Rawdon to Conway, 6 Apr. 1667 (*C.S.P.*, *Ire.*, 1666–9, p. 34)1.

50 *Oxf. D.N.B.*, xlvi,140–41; Rawdon to Conway 4 July 1665 (*C.S.P.*, *Ire.*, 1663–5, pp 602–3); Gillespie, 'George Rawdon's Lisburn'.

quite the inclination, for large-scale enterprises,[51] although he took notice of practical inventions with a potential industrial application.[52] He did, however, develop his own particular interest, which might be described as 'improvement' of a kind, even if its effects were felt (and were intended to be felt, at least in the first instance) only within the Rawdons' own demesne.

To posterity Sir Arthur's reputation lies in his contribution to the development of the formal and botanical garden in Ireland. He may have been schooled in the appreciation of horticulture by his father, or have simply been influenced by his surroundings at Lisburn Castle, where elaborate formal gardens had been established. At any rate, he constructed at Moira an extended pleasure garden with a variety of features – walks, vistas, canals, even a maze – and stocked with exotic specimens. The inspiration came from his correspondence with Hans Sloane, who had visited Jamaica in 1687 in the retinue of the governor, Lord Albemarle. On receiving reports of Sloane's discoveries, Rawdon requested seeds, gave the Oxford botanist William Sherard employment in his household, and sent his own gardener, James Harlow, to the Caribbean to collect plants, at a cost that he could hardly afford.[53] The garden languished for a time after his death, as his widow did not maintain an establishment at Moira, but the family interest in acquiring botanical curiosities did not subside. His sister Brilliana continued to write to Sloane to the same purpose.[54] In due course Sir John followed suit.[55] When re-establishing himself at Moira he imported a tulip tree and other exotic plants and seeds, some of which were obtained for him by his aunts Brilliana and Dorothy, who shared their deceased brother's botanical interests.[56] Both brother and sister were acquainted with the chemist William Maple, whose efforts to establish a 'physic garden' in Dublin, at Trinity College, were assisted by Sir John with gifts of plants.[57]

51 He was, however, a devotee of horse-racing and tried – at some financial cost – to establish a racecourse on his land at Ballynahinch: Rawdon to Lord Conway, 19 Aug. 1682 (*C.S.P.*, *dom.*, 1682, p. 349); Thomas Stanhope to Sir Arthur Rawdon, 27 Feb., 1, 6 Mar. 1685/6 (HA 15587–9)).

52 For example, Hans Sloane informed him in 1687 of a new wind-powered water-pump he had observed in the docks at Portsmouth (Sloane to Rawdon, 10 Sept. 1687 (HA 15790)).

53 Charles Smith, *The ancient and present state of the county of Down* (Dublin, 1744), p. 103; C. H. Lett, 'Botanists of the north of Ireland' in *The Irish Naturalist*, xxii, no. 2 (Feb. 1913), p. 21; E. St J. Brooks, *Sir Hans Sloane: the great collector and his circle* (London, 1954), pp 130–4; E. C. Nelson, 'Sir Arthur Rawdon (1662–1695) of Moira: his life and letters, family and friends, and his Jamaican plants' in *Proceedings and Reports of the Belfast Natural History and Philosophical Society*, ser. 2, x (1977–82), pp 30–52; Patrick Bowe and Keith Lamb, *A history of gardening in Ireland* (Dublin, 1995), p. 24; *Oxf. D.N.B.*, l, 278–80.

54 Brilliana Rawdon to Sloane, 26 Sept. 1703 (B.L., Sloane MS 4039, f. 190).

55 Brooks, *Sloane*, p. 134.

56 Brilliana Rawdon to Sloane, 26 Sept. 1703 (B.L., Sloane MS 4039, f. 190); Prior to Sir John Rawdon, 12 Feb. 1718[/19] (HA 15569); Dorothy Rawdon to same, 6 July [?1722] (HA 15638). On one occasion Sloane sent the family a microscope (Brooks, *Sloane*, p. 134).

57 Dorothy Rawdon to Sir John Rawdon, 6 July [?1722] (HA 15638). For Maple see *D.I.B.*, vi, 354–5. It may only be coincidence that Maple resided in Fishamble Street, Dublin, where the Rawdons owned property (*C.J.Ire.* (2nd ed.), v, 23; copy of will of Sir George Rawdon, 19 Oct. 1683, with codicil 30 July 1684 (HA 15697)). In fact, the tenant of the property was Alderman Robert Curtis (rental of Rawdon estate, 1724 (P.R.O.N.I., T/3765/L/2/19/6)). Maple was later

Sir Arthur Rawdon and his father had been men of wide interests. While not bibliomanes on the scale of their distant connexion the English politician Robert Harley, they had each acquired and read books with discrimination.[58] Sir John showed a similar interest in improving his mind. In London in the winter of 1718–19 he purchased a range of printed matter – books, 'papers and pamphlets' – both scholarly and entertaining, and despatched them to Ireland to add to the collection in his Dublin house, which was to be sent north to found a library at Moira.[59] Nothing is known of his education (which was presumably undertaken at home), and little of his reading habits, other than his acquisition in 1718 of 'Mr Hutchinson's book'[60], and 'the book relating to Dr Bently'[61] and possession of lengthy runs of the *Mercator* and the *British Merchant*,[62] but as a young man he had kept up his father's correspondence with scholars and men of science like Sloane,[63] and an interest in antiquarian learning is also suggested by the fact that he subscribed to a published account of the archaeological and historical remains on Anglesey.[64]

Another powerful family trait was the profession of genuine religious sentiment and the commitment to living a virtuous and useful life. Dorothy, the first Lady Rawdon, is said to have been devout – she was praised as such in her husband's will[65] – and fragments of correspondence suggest that Sir George was similarly inclined.[66] When making his will, he advised his two daughters to attend to the advice of their cousin Joseph Wilkins, dean of Clogher, whom they were to take as their 'spiritual guide', in order 'that God may bless them and provide for the fatherless, so as they may live comfortably in his faith and fear'. The archbishop of Dublin, Francis Marsh, was joined with Wilkins as an 'overseer' of the will, presumably to provide further counsel.[67] Little is known of the intermediate generation, but the same pious disposition was visible in Sir John Rawdon, at least if we are to judge from the funeral

among the founder-members of the Dublin Society: de Vere White, *R. Dublin Soc.*, p. 10, speculated fruitlessly on the origin of his connexion with Prior, which now becomes clear.

58 Henry More to Lady Conway, [1674] (*Conway letters* ..., ed. Nicholson, p. 388); David Campbell to Sir Arthur Rawdon, 31 Jan. 1684[/5] (HA 14148).

59 Prior to Sir John Rawdon, 26 Aug. 1718, 16 Dec. 1718, 27 Jan. 1718[/19], 27 June 1719 (HA 15564–5, 15567, 15581).

60 Possibly Francis Hutchinson, *The life of the most reverend father in God John Tillotson, archbishop of Canterbury* ... (London, 1717); or idem, *A defence of the compassionate address to papists. Being an answer to the queries of a papist, relating to that address* ... (London, 1718); or idem, *An historical essay concerning witchcraft* ... (London, 1718).

61 Most probably Joseph Craven, *Two letters to the reverend Dr Bentley, Master of Trinity College in Cambridge, concerning his intended edition of the Greek testament* ... (London [1717]).

62 Prior to Sir John Rawdon, 16 Dec. 1718, 27 Jan. 1718[/19] (HA 15565, 15567).

63 Brooks, *Sloane*, p. 134.

64 Henry Rowlands, *Mona antiqua restaurata: an archaeological discourse on the antiquities, natural and historical, of the isle of Anglesey* (Dublin, 1723).

65 Copy of will of Sir George Rawdon, 19 Oct. 1683, with codicil, 30 July 1684 (HA 15697); Berwick, *Rawdon papers*, p. 280.

66 For example, Sir George Rawdon to Arthur Rawdon, 17 Dec. 1683 (HA15694). During the 1650s Rawdon had provided a home for Jeremy Taylor, the Laudian devotional writer, former royal chaplain and future bishop of Down: T. C. Barnard, *Cromwellian Ireland: English government and reform in Ireland 1649–1660* (Oxford, 1975), p. 151.

67 Copy of will of Sir George Rawdon, 19 Oct. 1683, with codicil, 30 July 1684 (HA 15697).

sermon preached by George Wilkins. Naturally, some of the conventional praise is to be discounted, but there is enough detail about the subject's life to suggest familiarity. According to Wilkins, the 'honour of God' was 'the chief leading principle' in Sir John's character: he was first and foremost 'a person of true seriousness and earnest devotion in … public worship'.[68] Concern with the provision of pastoral care for his tenants, reflected in the building of a new parish church at Moira, presumably reflected this.[69] The detailed provisions of his own will, which unfortunately remain obscure, might well reinforce this picture, since their benevolent intentions were praised by Swift in the same breath as others leaving money to church and poor.[70] Sir John's widow, who took as her second husband Charles Cobbe, bishop of Dromore and eventually archbishop of Dublin, seems to have been of a similar temper.[71]

In this period strong religious feeling was often accompanied by a particular outlook on social questions, in particular poverty and its consequences, which implied a concern with improving the condition of the lower orders. The charitable impulse to poor relief was customarily moderated towards an emphasis on providing opportunities for the poor to help themselves. The Rawdons were no exception. Sir George Rawdon and his wife Dorothy were much given to charitable work with the poor,[72] and in his will Sir George recommended the same course of action to his son, but with a caveat: [73] he urged Arthur,

> when he shall come to possess my estate, that he be always very charitable, and relieve the poor constantly, to have that he purposes in his heart to give, still in readiness to distribute himself cheerfully and piously as occasion shall be offered, to such as he believes to be in most need, rather than to wandering idle beggars, the quantum whereof yearly I think not necessary to determine, but intend to leave such a stock of money for him with a trusty friend for his first year's charity, as may give him an example for after times to imitate, or rather exceed as it shall please God to bless and increase his stock …

This attitude resurfaced in later generations. According to Wilkins's eulogy, Sir John was a man of great compassion, who was always ready to do good 'in employing the poor in works of improvement', but 'he did not care to encourage strolling beggars,

68 Wilkins, *A sermon preached at Magheralin …*, p. 14.

69 Prior to Sir John Rawdon, 20, 22, 27 June 1719 (HA 15579–81); Smith, *Ancient and present state of … Down*, p. 104.

70 Swift wrote that in April 1724 Rawdon was one of three 'fools' who had recently died and made 'wise' wills, the others being Bishop John Evans of Meath and Theophilus Butler, first Lord Newtownbutler (Swift to Charles Ford, 2 Apr. 1724 (*The correspondence of Jonathan Swift*, ed. Harold Williams (5 vols, Oxford, 1963–5), iii, 11)). An abstract of the will is printed in P. B. Eustace and Eilish Ellis (eds). *Registry of Deeds, Dublin: abstracts of wills* (3 vols, Dublin, 1954–84), i, 126.

71 Gabriel James Maturin, *A sermon preach'd at the funeral of Lady Dorothy Rawdon, in the parish church of Moyrah, September the 18th, 1733* (Dublin, 1733); Alec Cobbe, 'The Cobbe family of Hampshire and Ireland' in Alastair Laing (ed.), *Clerics and connoisseurs: the Rev. Matthew Pilkington, the Cobbe family and the fortunes of an Irish art collection through three centuries* (London, 2001), p. 61.

72 Berwick, *Rawdon papers*, p. 280.

73 Copy of will of Sir George Rawdon, 19 Oct. 1683, with codicil 30 July 1684 (HA 15697).

who make a trade of begging'; these he saw as 'the plague and pest of the nation'.[74] It was a commonly held view,[75] and perhaps one should be careful not to make too much of the resemblance to Sir George's opinions, except for the fact that it is of a piece with a general similarity of outlook between grandfather and grandson.

The point is accentuated if we look at a particular instance of what might be described as constructive charity: the provision of education for the children of the poor, in which Sir John Rawdon again rehearsed a theme of his grandfather's contribution to public life. Sir George Rawdon had been largely responsible for putting into effect the Conways' scheme for a school at Lisburn: this had been established under the Protectorate, and rebuilt after the Restoration. It became 'the foremost centre for education east of the Bann and rivalled the Royal Schools at Armagh and Enniskillen for quality of education'. Shortly before his death Sir George was working towards further expansion.[76] Of course, philanthropy was only one aspect of the endowment of the Lisburn school, and probably not the most significant: the encouragement of education was an end in itself and part of a broader programme for the social advancement of Ireland. When Sir John Rawdon applied himself to the same ends, the context of educational reform had changed. The two schools that he established on his property, at Moira and Ballynahinch, were part of the movement that developed in the post-Revolution period, combining moral reform, anxiety for the preservation of the reformed religion, and an ambition for local economic regeneration.[77] Charity schools had been founded across the country, at first through a series of independent initiatives, and then brought together by a 'Society for Promoting Christian Knowledge in Ireland by the Method of Charity Schools', imitating, and in communication with, the Society for Promoting Christian Knowledge (S.P.C.K.) in London.[78] Typically, a charity school would take one or two dozen boys and/or girls, mainly but not exclusively Church of Ireland Protestants, teach them the rudiments of literacy and numeracy, catechise them in the doctrines of the established church, and seek to inculcate industriousness, leading to an apprenticeship in a useful trade. As befitted a patron who was active in the 'Society for Promoting Christian Knowledge in Ireland …' and was a corresponding

74 Wilkins, *A sermon preached at Magheralin …*, p. 21.

75 Paul Slack, *Poverty and policy in Tudor and Stuart England* (London, 1988), chs 5, 9; Steve Hindle, 'Dependency, shame and belonging: badging the deserving poor, c. 1550–1750' in *Cultural and Social History*, i (2004), pp 6–35.

76 Gillespie, 'George Rawdon's Lisburn'; Bp Ezekiel Hopkins of Derry to [?Sir George Rawdon], Mar. 1682[/3] (HA 14980).

77 Edward Synge, *An account of the erection … of charity schools in Ireland …* (Dublin, 1717), p. 22; *Methods of erecting, supporting and governing charity schools: with an account of the charity schools in Ireland* (2nd ed., Dublin, 1719), p. 22; Smith, *Ancient and present state of … Down*, pp 77–8. See above, ch. 7.

78 T. C. Barnard, 'Protestants and the Irish language, 1675–1725' in *Journal of Ecclesiastical History*, xliv (1993), pp 243–72. See also, in general, M. G. Jones, *The charity school movement: a study of eighteenth-century puritanism in action* (Cambridge, 1938); C. M. Rose, 'Evangelical philanthropy and Anglican revival: the charity schools of Augustan London, 1698–1740' in *London Journal*, xvi (1991), pp 35–65.

member of the S.P.C.K. in London,[79] Sir John's schools followed this pattern. The school at Moira, for example, accommodated 24 children, half of them 'conformists' and half Catholics or Presbyterians, who were to be taught to read, write and cast accounts, to attend the service of the established church, and to be bound out apprentices to Protestant masters and mistresses.[80]

Clearly one purpose of Sir John's schools was to reinforce the position of the established church, and their proselytising function was directed as much towards local Presbyterians as against Catholics. This seems to be of a piece with what we know of his religious views. Wilkins's funeral sermon gives testimony – if allusive – to its subject's attachment to the Church of Ireland. Sir John 'had a strong aversion to all separations in matters of religion'; he 'contented himself with the known stated forms of worship'; and so on.[81] The correspondence with Prior shows a landlord who not only sought to make provision for his tenants' spiritual needs, through church building, but also took care to nurture those among them who were 'church people' by offering leases on favourable terms.[82] Again, this was in the family tradition. Sir George Rawdon had a history of antagonism towards Presbyterians. In 1639 he had assisted in the enforcement in Ulster of the 'black oath' that obliged Scots to repudiate the national covenant, and after the Restoration he sought to suppress all manifestations of Presbyterianism, refusing in 1681 to allow the Lisburn congregation to build a meeting-house, which he considered would be an 'interruption' to the ongoing peace of the neighbourhood.[83] Indeed, he took pleasure in the notion that 'the Scots presbytery ... esteem me one of the horns against the Kirk'.[84] Sir Arthur, to judge by the letters written to him by his agents, took the same view of the 'rigid Presbyterians' in and about his estates, and continued to refuse requests for a meeting house. 'You may expect little friendship from the Presbyterians and other fanatics', he was told, for they 'are all against your interest.'[85] Nor does it seem as if Sir John was any more accommodating. The rentals of his estate show that the 'meeting house' at Moira was still occupied by the same tenant in 1724 as in 1685,[86] while his letters suggest that one imperative of his estate management was the protection of Anglican tenants from oppression by Presbyterian landlords.[87]

By the time Sir John Rawdon attained his majority, vigorous support for the established church implied a party-political stance. In Queen Anne's reign the main-

79 Prior to Sir John Rawdon, 20 Jan. 1718[/19], 27 June 1719 (HA 15566, 15581); S.P.C.K. minute book, 3 Nov. 1720 (S.P.C.K. archives, now in Cambridge University Library, minute book 9, p. 121).

80 Synge, *Account* ..., p. 22; *Methods of erecting ... charity schools in Ireland*, p. 20.

81 Wilkins, *A sermon preached at Magheralin* ..., pp 15–17.

82 Prior to Sir John Rawdon, 26 Aug. 1718, 20, 22 June 1719 (HA 15564, 15579–80).

83 W. D. Baillie, 'Sir George Rawdon; one of the horns against the kirk in the seventeenth century' in *Bulletin of the Presbyterian Historical Society of Ireland*, xiii (1984), pp 2–9.

84 George Rawdon to [Ld Conway], 13 Feb. 1658 (*C.S.P., Ire.*, 1647–60 and addenda 1625–60, p. 662).

85 Edmond Ellis to [Sir Arthur Rawdon], 27 June 1689 (HA 14660). See also Thomas Stanhope to same, 18 Apr., 3 May 1685 (HA 15869–70)

86 Rentals of Sir John Rawdon's estate, 1717–23 (P.R.O.N.I., T/3765/L/2/19/1–6).

87 See below, p 195.

tenance of the privileged position of the Church of Ireland, and more especially the exclusion of Protestant Dissenters from political rights and even in some cases freedom of worship, became the touchstone of political allegiance, with the Irish parliament and local communities divided along 'Tory' and 'Whig' lines. In England, of course, such allegiances can be traced back to the period of the so-called Exclusion Crisis of 1679–81, when the terms 'Tory' and 'Whig' first appeared as designations for political groupings. In Ireland the pre-history of party politics is more confused, and the case for continuity between the 1680s and 1700s much weaker.

The most important difference between the two kingdoms was that the cavalier tradition of the English Civil War, on which English Toryism drew heavily, was much less substantial in Ireland. Nevertheless, in the parts of Ulster where Presbyterians were numerous, the effect of the covenanter disturbances in Scotland (rather than the activities of English Exclusionists) was to provoke a loyalist reaction from the Church of Ireland population, and what was in essence an ongoing sectarian antagonism took on a party-political colouring. In the 1680s the words Whig and Tory were part of the vocabulary of the Rawdons' local agents, though the precise value attached to these terms is unclear, and complicated by the simultaneous use of 'tory' in its original meaning to denote exponents of customary forms of rural brigandage.[88] However, in some circumstances, especially in the years 1681–6, 'Tory' was being used to refer to an ultra-monarchist outlook, distinguishing what one Ulsterman called 'the king and loyal party'.[89]

The second complicating factor was the greater vulnerability of Irish Protestants to the consequences of the shift in royal policy that followed the accession of the Catholic King James II, especially the changes that occurred in Ireland following the promotion of Lord Tyrconnel, to the command of the Irish army and then to the chief governorship as lord deputy. The experience of Catholic rule, especially the reversal of the land settlement and the mass attainder of Protestants by the Jacobite parliament in 1689, created among the Irish Protestant gentry a consensus in support of the Glorious Revolution, and a common political outlook that in English terms would have been defined as Whig, since it stood four-square behind the Williamite settlement. To a considerable extent, therefore, Irish Toryism had to be reinvented after 1692. When Tories did reappear they were defined principally by hostility to Protestant Dissent rather than by an historic attachment to monarchy. And in ecclesiastical terms this was a new world, with a Presbyterian kirk re-established in Scotland, the Toleration Act in England, and during the 1690s another wave of Scottish Presbyterian immigration into Ulster. Alarmed by these developments, some families with impeccable Whig credentials, and even firm Parliamentarian loyalties from the 1640s, began to identify themselves with the emerging 'Church party'.

The political trajectory taken by the Rawdon family in the 1680s and 1690s resembled that of other Protestant families from north-east Ulster, in taking them

88 For an example, see Thomas Stanhope to [Sir Arthur Rawdon], 18 Apr. 1685 (HA 15869), which also includes a reference to 'the Whigs' in a party-political sense.
89 Edmond Ellis to [same], 27 June 1685 (HA 14660).

from a position of conservative loyalism through the adoption of 'Revolution principles' in the crisis of 1688–92, on to the 'new Toryism' of c.1695–1714. In c. 1675–85 they had occupied a position close to that of English Tories, but having transferred their allegiance from King James to King William, they moved in the aftermath of the Jacobite war into participation in an ultra-Protestant parliamentary opposition in Ireland that in its principles resembled an old-fashioned 'Country party', and included future Tories as well as Whigs. Sir George, not unexpectedly, turns out to have been a loyal supporter of King Charles II against the 'plague of rebellion' in England and Scotland in the early 1680s.[90] And at first Arthur followed this example.[91] His agents certainly referred to his enemies as 'Whigs' (whatever that meant in a local context).[92] He himself took a commission in an Irish cavalry regiment in 1682, which was renewed by James II;[93] and he seems to have greeted with enthusiasm the accession of the new king, despite James's Catholic faith, offering to raise troops to help suppress the Monmouth rebellion.[94] But with Tyrconnel's assumption of authority over the Irish army he lost his troop,[95] and his growing alienation from the Jacobite regime (worsened by what he saw as unfair treatment from Irish judges over the Conway will) led eventually to his taking up arms in support of the prince of Orange.[96] In consequence he was attainted by James II's Irish parliament, which can only have confirmed his commitment to the Revolution. When elected to King William's first Irish parliament in 1692, he joined critics of the administration, and was replaced as governor of County Down and removed from the privy council,[97] only to be reinstated as a privy councillor shortly before his death in 1695 as part of a reconstruction of the Irish ministry, which advanced a number of other ex-oppositionists.[98] Several of his fellow beneficiaries were future leaders of the Irish Whigs, but the 1692 opposition was by no means exclusively Whiggish in its orientation,

90 Sir George Rawdon to Ld Conway, 2 July 1683 (*C.S.P., dom.*, July–Sept. 1683, p. 77. See also R. L. Greaves, *God's other children: Protestant nonconformists and the emergence of denominational churches in Ireland, 1660–1700* (Stanford, Calif., 1997), p. 114.

91 For Arthur's political career see *Hist. Ir. parl.*, vi, 145–6.

92 For example, Edmond Ellis to Arthur Rawdon, 9 Feb. 1683[/4], 5 May, 19 July 1684, 8 Feb. 1684/5 (HA14653–5, 14657); Thomas Stanhope to [same], 24 Nov. 1684, 16 Nov. 1685 (HA 15849, 15884).

93 *C.S.P., dom.*, 1685, p. 76; 1686, pp 51–2.

94 Thomas Stanhope to Sir Arthur Rawdon, 11, 21 Feb. 1684/5 (HA 15861–2, reported in H.M.C., *Hastings MSS*, ii, 395); Raymond Gillespie, 'The Irish Protestants and James II, 1688–90' in *I.H.S.*, xxviii, no. 110 (Nov. 1992), p. 127.

95 Edmond Ellis to [Sir Arthur Rawdon], 24 Mar. 1685/6 (HA 14664).

96 Thomas Stanhope to same, 19 June 1686 (H.M.C., *Hastings MSS*, ii, 397); *A true account of the siege of London-Derry by the Reverend Mr George Walker* ... (London, 1689), pp 41, 42, 47–8.

97 Francis Annesley to Sir Arthur Rawdon, 24 Feb. 1693 (Berwick, *Rawdon papers*, pp 373–5); petition of Sir Arthur Rawdon et al. [Nov. 1692] (*C.S.P., dom.*, 1695 and addenda, p. 219); *The parliamentary diary of Narcissus Luttrell 1691–1693*, ed. Henry Horwitz (Oxford, 1972), p. 442; notes on House of Commons debate [22 Feb. 1693] (Huntington Library, Ellesmere papers, EL 9930a).

98 John Reading to Sir Arthur Rawdon, 13 Oct. 1694 (Berwick, *Rawdon papers*, p. 380); warrant for Sir Arthur Rawdon to be a privy councillor in Ireland, 10 May 1695 (*C.S.P., dom.*, 1694–5, p. 469); C. I. McGrath, 'English ministers, Irish politicians and the making of a parliamentary settlement in Ireland, 1692–5' in *E.H.R.*, cxix (2004), pp 585–613.

especially in Ulster, and included some friends of Rawdon such as Francis Annesley, whose ultimate destination would be the Tory party.[99]

Immediate family example, therefore, would most probably have predisposed Sir John Rawdon to adopt a Tory political outlook – albeit with a 'Country' flavour – which would have been a natural extension of his steadfast loyalty to the established church. The family's connexions also tended in the same direction. Sir John was related to many leading Tories in England, not just through the Conway connexion, but on his mother's side to the Finches (earls of Winchelsea and Nottingham), and through his paternal grandmother to the political dynasty presided over by Robert Harley, himself a Tory convert (of sorts) from Whiggism.[100] Of course, the bitter struggle over the Conway inheritance complicated matters. Sir Edward Seymour was a leading light in the Tory party – by Queen Anne's reign its elder statesman at Westminster – and his accomplices in the affair included several other prominent English Tories. The former solicitor- general Heneage Finch (subsequently first earl of Aylesford) had drawn up the dubious will; the Tory M.P. Francis Gwyn and Sir Jonathan Trelawny, bishop of Winchester, had been witnesses.[101] Also involved at one remove were the Hyde brothers; Henry, earl of Clarendon, and Laurence, earl of Rochester.[102] Later, in 1706, the private bill introduced on the Seymours' behalf at Westminster was managed in the Lords by Rochester, and in the Commons by Gwyn.[103] In Ireland, on the other hand, support for the Seymour claim – if we are to believe the Rawdons' agents – was confined to local 'Whigs' and those who expected direct pecuniary benefit from a change of landlord.[104] From the first the loyalist – later 'Tory' – element in east Ulster, families like the Brownlows, Skeffingtons and Warings, gave what assistance they could to Sir Arthur and his son,[105] while the first duke of Ormond, who might be said to have embodied Stuart loyalism in Ireland, showed a public, and active, sympathy.[106]

99 Sir Arthur Rawdon to Hans Sloane, 24 June 1691 (B.L., Sloane MS 4036, f. 105); Francis Annesley to Sir Arthur Rawdon, 24 Feb. 1693 (Berwick, *Rawdon papers*, pp 373–5); D. W. Hayton, *Ruling Ireland, 1685–1742: politics, politicians and parties* (Woodbridge, 2004), pp 44–9, 97.

100 Dorothy Rawdon to Brilliana Rawdon, 29 Sept. 1705 (HA 15632). Sir John tried to activate this connexion in 1711 when a private bill drawn up on his behalf was sent from Ireland to the privy council in Whitehall (Rawdon to earl of Oxford, 20 Aug. 1711 (B.L., Portland papers, Add. MS 70205)).

101 John Coghill to Sir George Rawdon, 29 Sept., 16 Oct. 1683 (HA14285, 14289); Thomas Stanhope to Sir Arthur Rawdon, 27 Jan. 1684[/5] (HA 15858); Edmond Ellis to same, 8 Feb. 1684/5 (HA 14657).

102 Edmond Ellis to Sir Arthur Rawdon, 8 Feb. 1684/5 (HA 14657); Rochester to Catherine O'Brien, 29 Nov. 1705 (N.L.I., Inchiquin papers, MS 45,295/2).

103 *L.J.*, xviii, 82, 130–1; *C.J.*, xv, 139–40, 180–1; Dorothy Rawdon to Brilliana Rawdon, 9 Jan. [1706] (HA 15636).

104 By the 1700s even Irish Whigs seem to have turned against them: see Dorothy Rawdon to Brilliana Rawdon, 7, 9 Jan. [1706], 2 Mar. 1705/6 (HA 15635–6, 15633).

105 Arthur Brownlow to Thomas Stanhope, 2 Oct. 1685 (HA 14906); Clotworthy Skeffington to [?Sir George Rawdon], 6 Feb. 1683/4 (HA 15783); Edmond Ellis to Arthur Rawdon, 9 Feb. 1683[/4] (HA14653).

106 Arthur Rawdon to Sir George Rawdon, 5 Feb. 1683/4 (HA 15607).

Given his background and connexions, therefore, it might seem odd that when Sir John Rawdon was first thought of as a parliamentary candidate, in the general election of 1713, a source connected with the Tory administration in Ireland seems to have considered that his return would be 'bad' for the Court party.[107] But in the political crisis of 1713–14, when Irish Protestants were gripped by anxiety over the royal succession, a significant number of Tories in Ireland were sceptical of the intentions of ministers, and deserted to opposition when the parliament assembled.[108] These 'moderate', or pro-Hanoverian, Tories were also the first to abandon their party after the accession of George I. Some went so far as to take office under the new Whig administration, as party loyalties seemed less relevant to parliamentary politics. The importance of this group as far as Rawdon is concerned is that it included two individuals who were particularly close to him, and some others with whom he was more distantly connected. The key figures were his father-in-law, Sir Richard Levinge,[109] and his distant kinsman and closest legal adviser, Marmaduke Coghill.[110]

Levinge was a lukewarm Tory who had been nominated for the Speakership of the Irish Commons in November 1713 by the viceroy, Shrewsbury, as a compromise candidate, in the vain hope that he might secure support from both parties. He subsequently accepted a judicial appointment under George I.[111] The link between the Rawdon and Levinge families was very close: Sir Richard and his wife lived with their daughter and son-in-law for a time,[112] and after Sir John's marriage to Dorothy Levinge his sister Isabella also became the wife of Sir Richard's son Charles. Apart from a disagreement over the terms of Isabella's settlement (which was resolved amicably), Rawdon and his father-in-law were on good terms and Levinge's advice was sought on family matters.[113]

Coghill is the more interesting. A civil lawyer, he was a judge of the primate's prerogative court, and a resolute defender of the privileges of the established church. But he was also a pragmatist, a 'man of business' with friends on both sides of the party-political divide.[114] Before 1714 he was a Tory, but described by one contem-

107 'Parliament list, r[eceive]d. 14 June 1713' (B.L., Southwell papers, Add. MS 34777, ff 42–4). The entry in *Hist. Ir. parl.*, vi, 149, assumes that this value judgment refers to Rawdon, although the inference is not entirely certain (cf. 'Parliament recom[mendation]s' [1713] (B.L., Add. MS 34777, ff 28–9)).

108 Hayton, *Ruling Ireland*, pp 172–4.

109 The date of Rawdon's marriage is unknown, but it must have taken place before January 1714 (George Berkeley to Prior, 6 Jan. 1714 N.S. (*The works of George Berkeley, bishop of Cloyne*, ed. A. A. Luce and T. E. Jessop (9 vols, London, 1948–1957), viii, 75–6.)).

110 They were eventually to be joint executors of his will. See above, n. 70.

111 For Levinge see *H.C. 1690–1715*, iv, 623–7; *Hist. Ir. parl.*, v, 89–91. See also Sir John Perceval's 'Character of Sr Richd Levinge', 18 Mar. 1711–12 (B.L., Egmont papers, Add. MS 47087, ff 17–18); Levinge to Edward Southwell, 7 Oct. 1721 (Sir Richard G. A. Levinge, *Jottings of the Levinge family* (Dublin, 1877), p. 68).

112 Prior to Sir John Rawdon, 26 Aug., 16 Dec. 1718 (HA 15564–5).

113 Levinge to Marmaduke Coghill, 16 Dec. 1718, 9 Feb. 1718/19 (HA 15191–2); Prior to Sir John Rawdon, 3 May 1718, 20 Jan., 7 Feb. 1718[/19] (HA 15561, 15566, 15568).

114 For Coghill see *Hist. Ir. parl.*, iii, 442–5; *Coghill letters*, pp xi–xxii.

porary as 'a Tory more by dependence than principle'.[115] Under the Hanoverians he moved smoothly across from opposition to government, and became a close ally of the new Speaker, the arch-Whig William Conolly, with whom, in fact, he had always maintained a close friendship.[116] A wealthy man, he spent lavishly in developing his private estate, but also took a strong interest in charitable enterprises – schools, hospitals and workhouses – and in government promoted a constructive 'patriotism' which did not challenge the constitutional superiority of the English council and parliament but sought to work within the existing system of governance for the betterment of Ireland.[117] Like the Rawdons, the Coghill family had originated in Yorkshire and still maintained a small estate there.[118] Marmaduke's father, Sir John Coghill, had acted as a legal adviser to his 'cousin' Sir George Rawdon, and had been named as an 'overseer' of Sir George's will.[119] After Sir George's death he took prime responsibility for sorting out the family's affairs, and Marmaduke inherited his mantle.[120] He it was who petitioned the Irish House of Commons on Sir John Rawdon's behalf in 1710 for a bill to explain Dorothy Rawdon's Act, and a year later, when Sir John had reached his majority and could petition for himself, Coghill piloted his bill through the Commons and organised the necessary lobbying at Whitehall.[121]

Sir John Rawdon's political opinions – in so far as these can be determined – and his behaviour as a member of the Irish House of Commons, show strong similarities to those of Coghill and other 'moderate' Tories.[122] The description of his churchmanship in Wilkins's funeral sermon seems deliberately to imply 'moderation' in party terms: 'He had … love for the Church without a fiery, consuming zeal, and he was devout without becoming a bigot'.[123] In secular matters he appears as almost the archetype of the 'independent country gentleman', staying aloof from parties and 'the cabals of faction': 'in him we might see revived the true Roman spirit; he would not betray his country for private gain, or go into any measures but such as he was convinced, had a real tendency to the good of the community'.[124] The simple facts of his parliamentary career seem to bear out the essential thrust (if not the moral elaboration) of this judgment. Rawdon did not achieve distinction as a member, and we know relatively little about his conduct in the Commons, except that he voted in 1721 against the scheme for a national bank, which would imply a 'Country' cast

115 Bp Godwin to [Abp Wake], 27 Feb. 1715/16 (Christ Church, Oxford, Wake papers, Arch. W. Epist. xii). See also Arthur Hill to Boyle, 15 Apr. 1729 (P.R.O.N.I., Shannon papers, D/2707/A/1/2/39), where he was referred to expressly as a 'moderate'.

116 See above, pp 128–30.

117 *Coghill letters*, p. xix; above, pp 138–42.

118 J. H. Coghill, *The family of Coghill* … (Cambridge, Mass., 1879), pp 13–28.

119 Copy of will of Sir George Rawdon, 19 Oct. 1683, with codicil, 30 July 1684 (HA 15697).

120 See, for example, Jonathan Ball to Sir John Rawdon, 23 May 1710 (HA 13922); Edmond Ellis to same, 6 May 1712 (HA 14666); Sir Richard Levinge to Coghill, 16 Dec. 1718, 9 Feb. 1718/19 (HA 15191–2).

121 *C.J.Ire.* (2nd ed.), iii, 740, 835, 837, 842, 845, 871; Thomas Trotter to Coghill, [1711] (HA 15937).

122 For Sir John Rawdon, see *Hist. Ir. parl.*, vi, 149.

123 Wilkins, *A sermon preached at Magheralin* …, p. 24.

124 Ibid., pp 18–19.

of mind (although this was a complex issue with factional cross-currents).[125] The few references to him in the Commons *Journals* suggest interest in matters involving moral, social or economic improvement. Returned for County Down in a by-election in 1717, he was named to his first committee the day after he had taken the oaths, and served in three other committees in his first session, all of which were of some importance: to compare engrossed bills with transmisses from Great Britain (a particularly high-powered committee consisting almost entirely of politicians of the first rank), to consider methods for stating the public accounts, and to investigate a publication reflecting on the honour of the House.[126] But his later parliamentary career failed to live up to this promising beginning: three committee nominations in 1719, and only two in 1721/2. Clearly he had been expected to make an impact, but failed to do so. However, the three committees to which he was named in the 1719 session give clues to his interests: one was to consider the petition of the Dun Professor of Physic at Trinity, which reflected Rawdon's own scientific bent; the second to inspect the management of the Dublin workhouse, implying support for initiatives for poor relief; and the third to consider the petition of a papermaker seeking monetary 'encouragement' for a new manufacturing venture.

Sir John's brief history, especially if we view it in the perspective of the two preceding generations, would thus provide a context for the 'patriotic' and 'improving' cast of mind exhibited in due course by his son, Lord Moira. A commitment to learning and to the established religion may also have been carried on by his widow, whose piety has already been noted and who seems to have maintained an interest in scholarship.[127] And of course Thomas Prior's involvement in the education of the future Lord Moira provides a third strand of continuity. But it is the argument of this essay that his contribution was a reinforcement of family tradition rather than a decisive intervention. Prior's own intellectual formation may well have owed as much to the Rawdons – and to the milieu in which they lived – as the next generation of the family owed to him.

Prior's own family background was relatively modest: he was the younger son of an army colonel whose father had come to Ireland in the 1630s and had acquired land in Queen's County in the Cromwellian settlement. But his education had been extensive.[128] From Kilkenny school he went to Trinity College Dublin, taking his BA in 1703, and retained a connexion with the college for some time since he gave his address as Trinity as late as 1716. He also travelled in England, where his uncle Richard resided, and received an MA by incorporation at Oxford in 1712.[129] It seems that by this time he had entered into the employ of the Rawdons, for in 1712 he

125 Michael Ryder, 'The Bank of Ireland, 1721: land, credit and dependency' in *Hist. Jn.*, xxv (1982), pp 557–82.

126 *C.J.Ire.* (2nd ed.), iv, 391, 393, 431, 440, 471.

127 Her name was included in the list of subscribers to Richard Cumberland, *A treatise of the laws of nature* (Dublin, 1727).

128 For a general discussion of the social background of agents in this period, see T. C. Barnard, *A new anatomy of Ireland: the Irish Protestants, 1649–1770* (New Haven, Conn., & London, 2003), ch. 8.

129 Clarke, *Prior*, pp 6–11.

witnessed the will of Sir John's maiden aunt, Brilliana.[130] He may well have been brought into the family's orbit by Marmaduke Coghill.[131] By the winter of 1713–14 Prior was a close companion of Sir John and Lady Rawdon in London, introducing them to a circle of friends that included several of his contemporaries at Trinity: the astronomer and Fellow of the Royal Society, Samuel Molyneux, the clergyman and poet Thomas Parnell, and George Berkeley.[132] His education had produced a cultivated intellect, as his book-buying recommendations to Sir John make clear. He wrote in January 1719:[133]

> I would recommend you to buy in sheets Dean Prideaux's history of the Old and New Testament connected with profane history in two volumes;[134] I reckon these are the most valuable books that have come out this age. Nothing can be more entertaining than the memoirs of the Academy of Sciences at Paris; they are printed cheap in Holland, and I believe you may get them second-hand in London.[135] I don't think they are translated into English ...

Nevertheless, he was still a dependant, a position reinforced rather than relieved by the generosity shown him by the family in 1717 in making him a tenant to properties in Counties Dublin and Wicklow on advantageous terms.[136]

In his outlook, Prior closely resembled his employer, and the other members of Sir John's circle, especially Coghill. The commitment to economic 'improvement' through the expansion of trade, and the promotion of new manufactures, is the most obvious similarity; but he also showed an interest in scientific discovery that recalled the Rawdons' correspondence with Sloane and Maple (who in due course was to join Prior as a founder-member of the Dublin Society). 'Nothing enlarges our knowledge so much', he wrote, 'or makes us so useful to the world as accurate experiment and observation.'[137] In relation to religion or party-politics his letters contain little that is explicit, but we may infer from the nature of the references to

130 Will of Brilliana Rawdon, 21 Aug. 1712 (Huntington library, Hastings papers, box 27, folder 50). See also Edmond Ellis to Sir John Rawdon, 6 May 1712 (HA 14660).

131 For Prior's subsequent connexion with Coghill see James Smyth to William Smyth, 23 Dec. 1729 (N.L.I., Smythe of Barbavilla papers, MS 41,582/7); Coghill to Ld Perceval, 12 Mar. 1730/1 (*Coghill letters*, p. 108).

132 Clarke, *Prior*, pp 10–11; Berkeley to Samuel Molyneux, 26 Nov. 1709, same to Prior, 25 Nov. 1713, 6 Jan., 26 Feb. 1714 N.S. (*Works of Berkeley*, ed. Luce & Jessop, viii, 25, 75–6, 78, 81–2).

133 Prior to Sir John Rawdon, 17 Jan. 1718[/19] (HA 15567). See also same to same, 14 Jan. 1723 (HA 15584).

134 Humphrey Prideaux, *The Old and New Testament connected in the history of the Jews and neighbouring nations* (2 vols, London, 1716–18).

135 In fact already in print in English as *The lives of the French, Italian and German philosophers, late members of the Royal Academy of Sciences in Paris ... to which is added, The preface of the ingenious Monsieur Fontenelle, secretary and author of the history of the said academy* (London, 1717), republished as *Memoirs of the Royal Academy of Sciences in Paris epitomized. With the lives of the late members of that society. And a preface by Monsieur Fontenelle ...* (London, 1721).

136 Lease, 2 Mar. 1716/17 (Cheshire and Chester Archives, Denton papers, CR 132/12). In this context it is worth noting Toby Barnard's observation that the profession of estate agent was 'on the margins of respectability' (Barnard, *New anatomy*, p. 212).

137 Prior, *Absentees*, pp 93–4.

Churchmen and Dissenters that he shared the principles espoused by generations of Rawdons. His comments on proposed relief for the statutory disabilities suffered by Presbyterians (including the sacramental test) certainly imply concern lest the process go too far, while his suggestion that speculation by Jewish and foreign financiers had been largely responsible for the miserable state of the Irish coinage is a fine example of gratuitous High Church bigotry.[138] On behalf of his employer he paid social visits to clergy, arranged for the building and endowment of churches, and encouraged Anglican tenants;[139] and like Sir John, he was an enthusiastic supporter of Church of Ireland charity schools and a corresponding member of the S.P.C.K.[140] In political terms he was clearly anti-Jacobite, and was occasionally amused by the visceral prejudices of Tories who could be manipulated through simple invocations of party loyalty, but at the same time he was no Whig: he seems to have regarded the Tory primate, Thomas Lindsay, with sympathy and approval, and to have been on friendly terms with another leading figure in the party, Lord Anglesey.[141] Like his master, he may be most satisfactorily described as a moderate Tory. Certainly before he came into Rawdon's service his closest personal friendships had been with men of this type: Molyneux was a Whig, but a mild one, while Parnell belonged to the Scriblerus Club, whose members put their literary talents at the disposal of Robert Harley's Tory administration, and the young Berkeley (for all the attempts of some historians to impute to him high-flying notions) seems at this time to have shared the 'Hanoverian' Toryism of his friend Sir John Perceval, the future earl of Egmont.[142]

Besides imbibing from the Rawdons the family ethos of intellectual enterprise, orthodox piety and social conscience, Prior's character and ideas, at this formative period of his development, may also have been influenced by practical considerations. It is easy to see how the hands-on experience of a land agent would have brought him into direct contact with the economic problems that his later writings sought to address: the poverty of the countryside and the beneficial effects of introducing new manufactures.[143] We know, for example, that he was preoccupied in the late 1710s by the chaotic state of the Irish coinage, about which he inveighed in a private letter to Rawdon,[144] and he began his most important pamphlet, the *List of*

138 Prior to Sir John Rawdon, 6 July 1719 (HA 15582); same to same, 19 Nov. 1723 (P.R.O.N.I., T/3765/M/2/4/1); same to same, 6 Apr. 1718 (HA 15558).

139 Same to same, 20, 22, 27 June 1719 (HA 15579–81).

140 Same to same, 20 Jan. 1718[/19], 27 June 1719 (HA 15566, 15581); S.P.C.K. min. bk, 3 Nov. 1720 (S.P.C.K. archives, min. bk 9, p. 121).

141 Prior to Sir John Rawdon, 1 May, 26 Aug. 1718, 19 Mar. 1718[/19], 11, 28 Apr., 8 May 1719 (HA 15560, 15564, 15574, 15576–8); extract from same to same, 29 June 1723 (P.R.O.N.I., Johnston papers, D/2924/1, p. 35).

142 See Ian Campbell Ross, 'Was Berkeley a Jacobite? *Passive obedience* revisited' in *Eighteenth-Century Ireland*, xx (2005), pp 17–30.

143 He also had first-hand experience of the clandestine importation of luxury goods, having been an accessory to Sir John Rawdon's smuggling of silks into Ireland in 1719, hidden under other items in a trunk that passed through customs under Prior's care (Prior to Sir John Rawdon, 4 Apr. 1719 (HA 15574)).

144 Same to same, 6 Apr. 1718 (HA 15558). See also same to same, 8 May 1718, 22 June 1719 (HA 15562, 15580).

the absentees of Ireland ... by stating that he had been 'inspired' to meditate upon the subject by observing 'the great scarcity of coin, which of late we have been very sensible of'.[145] It is also tempting to see in his classic denunciation of the deleterious effects of absenteeism some trace of the unhappy experiences of the Rawdons at the hands of powerful absentee English families. Not only were Sir John and his immediate relations resentful of their treatment by Seymour and his sons, they had also been at odds with Lord Shelburne, whose aggressive demands for repayment of debts had harassed Sir Arthur, and continued to make difficulties for Sir John.[146] Certainly Prior shared the Rawdons' bitter hatred of the Seymour family, writing maliciously in 1718, after the death of one of the heirs, 'I am very glad to find more instances of the fatality that attends the males of the Seymours, there are but two strokes more wanting to finish that affair'.[147] However, while the name of Shelburne was among those cited in the *List of absentees* ..., Prior resisted the opportunity to include the new Lord Conway, and indeed somewhat ostentatiously named several of his own friends and connexions, including Berkeley, Perceval, and the secretary of state for Ireland Edward Southwell, as well as Sir Standish Hartstonge and Alderman William Graham of Drogheda, who were both distantly related to the Rawdons.

After Sir John Rawdon's death in 1723 Prior remained closely involved in the family's affairs, but Lady Rawdon's remarriage to Bishop Cobbe intruded another powerful figure, and thereafter he may not have had quite so important a role to play in family business. It seems indicative of a shift in his commitments that he became more heavily involved with the agency for Berkeley's property in the years following Sir John Rawdon's death. However, in a quasi-tutorial capacity he was still able to influence the development of the Rawdon children, especially the future earl of Moira, whose marriage in 1741 to Lord Egmont's daughter may have been facilitated by Prior's connexion (through Berkeley and Coghill) with the Percevals.[148] Egmont was delighted by the personality as well as the property of his prospective son-in-law, whose 'sober and prudent' temperament accorded with his own.[149] The young Rawdon's interest in literature and music, his piety and active churchmanship (exemplified in strong support for the charter school movement), and his commitment to the economic advancement of his country through the practical encourage-

145 Prior, *Absentees*, preface. See also idem, *Observations on coin in general, with some proposals for regulating the value of coin in Ireland* (Dublin, 1729).

146 Thomas Dance to Sir Arthur Rawdon, 24 Nov. 1693, 25 Dec. 1694 (HA 14620–1); Charles Campbell to same, 19 Sept. 1694 (HA 14144); Roth Jones to same, 6 Nov. 1694 (HA 15104); Prior to Sir John Rawdon, 27 June, 11 July 1719 (HA 15581, 15583). Evidently Sir John's mother had also been involved in a lawsuit with the English peer John Sheffield, duke of Buckingham, the absentee landlord of estates in Co. Wexford (Paul Jodrell to Buckingham, 2 June 1708 (Mulgrave Castle archives, Mulgrave Castle, Lythe, North Yorkshire, I 3/266)).

147 Prior to Sir John Rawdon, 6 Apr. 1718 (HA 15558). Two years earlier, a friend had written to Rawdon, 'I forgot to tell you the agreeable news of the death of Lord Conway's son' ([Capel?] Moore to Sir John Rawdon, 17 Apr. 1716 (Berwick, *Rawdon papers*, pp 399–400)).

148 Prior to Sir John Rawdon, 4th Bt, 19 Nov. 1741 (HA 15585).

149 Egmont's diary, 12, 22 Oct. 1741 (H.M.C., *Egmont diary*, iii, 227–8, 229). For Egmont, see *H.C. 1715–54*, ii, 338; *Oxf. D.N.B.*, xliii, 657–8; T. C. Barnard, 'Improvement, imagination and antiquarianism in mid-eighteenth-century Ireland: the earls of Egmont and Lohort Castle, County Cork' in idem, *Improving Ireland?*, pp 120–42.

ment of industry and agriculture, were all reminiscent of his father, and testimony to the power of family tradition, reinforced by Prior's enduring influence.[150]

Occasionally, Prior lapsed from the polite and moderate tone Egmont and his friends customarily adopted in their own presentation of Irish grievances. The *List of absentees* embodied in its text many unexceptionable nostrums, such as the reduction of imported luxuries,[151] and the promotion of native manufacture, emphasising the contribution of the Linen Board as a pattern to follow. It also singled out for praise the Speaker of the House of Commons, William Conolly (who was Marmaduke Coghill's political patron) and exempted from blame resident English office-holders, who, it was acknowledged, were working hard for the country. However, the denunciation of absentees in general provoked anger in ministerial circles, as did the extremism of some of the solutions proposed (a tax on absentees' property, and even the application of the system of gavelkind to the testamentary disposition of larger estates, as had been applied to Catholic property by the Irish Popery Act of 1704). Two years later, a contribution drafted by Prior to the public debate about British restrictions on the Irish woollen trade was considered by Egmont and other Irish lobbyists in London to be insufficiently tactful and more likely to 'disserve than help Ireland', with the result that it remained unpublished.[152]

Thus Prior was not simply a creature of the Rawdons. Indeed it is impossible to say how much he learned from the family, and how much he himself brought to the relationship. Upbringing had weighed heavily on Sir John Rawdon, and presumably in turn influenced Prior. Other important influences must also have played a part in forming the outlook of both landlord and agent, not least the pragmatic ex-Tories Coghill and Levinge, who were a constant presence at Sir John's side.[153] Indeed, one of the most interesting aspects of this story is the involvement of Coghill, who linked the Rawdons with landlords of similar background and outlook, like Sir John Perceval and Edward Southwell. For this particular knot of enthusiastic 'improvers' the promotion of the interests of the established church was an essential concomitant of economic progress. The same applied to others who played a leading role in the movement to 'improve' the Irish economy, whether clergymen like Berkeley and Samuel Molyneux's nephew Samuel Madden, or laymen like the County Down landowner and judge Michael Ward.[154] The Dublin Society, whose founder-members

150 *D.I.B.*, viii, 395–6; Berwick, *Rawdon papers*, p. 4; *An abstract of the proceedings of the Incorporated Society of Dublin, for Promoting English Protestant Schools in Ireland* (Dublin, 1737), p. 9; Rosemary Richey, 'Landed society in mid-eighteenth-century County Down' (PhD thesis, Queen's University Belfast, 2000), pp 209–13; Barnard, *Making the grand figure*, p. 173.

151 See above, n. 143, and cf. Prior, *Absentees*, p. 55, which discusses the smuggling of luxury goods into Ireland.

152 Egmont's diary, 24 Feb. 1731 (H.M.C., *Egmont diary*, i, 148).

153 Prior nominated the late Sir John Rawdon's brother-in-law Sir Richard Levinge for membership of the Dublin Society in 1732 (Dublin Society register, 11 May 1732 (R.D.S., minute book 1, f. 56)).

154 De Vere White, *Royal Dublin Society*, chs 1–2. For another example, see T. C. Barnard, 'The worlds of an improving Galway squire: Robert French of Monivea, 1716–79' in idem, *Improving Ireland?*, pp 143–66.

consisted in the main of this type, may be said to have embodied the earnest evangelicalism of the Rawdons.[155]

In this way the Irish Tory party, which collapsed as a parliamentary force after the general election of 1715, was able to enjoy a continuing influence, in contributing to the discourse and practice of economic 'patriotism'. The association between the Toryism of Queen Anne's reign in Ireland and the 'patriot' oppositions of the 1720s and 1730s is complex. Some unreconstructed Tories, stranded in perpetuity on the opposition benches – or so it must have appeared to them – became active 'patriots' of a narrowly political kind, brandishing constitutional rights and liberties in habitual attacks on government, which were essentially reactive in nature. Those like the Rawdons and Percevals, moderate in their views, and even ministerialist in their disposition and attachments, advanced a different form of patriotism, less strident and more practical, which worked to transform society rather than governance.

By the time the next generation of the Rawdon family came to maturity, the party-political heritage of the late seventeenth and early eighteenth centuries would be forgotten and the disposition of the first earl of Moira towards philanthropy, evangelicalism, and 'improvement' would be attributed less to political ideology than to character and religious conviction, and of course to the personal influence of men like his mentor Prior and his father-in-law Egmont. What the family's history shows is that this commitment to the cause of moral, social, and economic 'improvement' was the product of a long tradition in which both political allegiance and personal circumstances were important.

What it tells us about the idea of 'improvement' is more doubtful. Certainly the ideas that we associate with Prior and his colleagues in the Dublin Society had a long pedigree. It is also true that the various elements conflated by historians under the general notion of 'improvement' – intellectual curiosity, evangelical Protestantism, economic enterprise and conspicuous consumption – can all be traced in the interests and activities of successive generations of Rawdons.[156] Whether the presence of each was necessary to support the others is an open question; nor is it clear whether a hierarchy of importance can be established. What is undeniable in the case of Sir John Rawdon is that upbringing, connexions and financial circumstances were central to the formation of his attitude to estate management, and that the same domestic context also helped to condition the mindset of his agent.

155 The founder-members in June 1731 included four clergymen, and the society had attracted nineteen others by the end of its first year (Dublin Society register, 1731–2 (R.D.S., min. bk 1, ff 1–56)). See also T. C. Barnard, 'Improving clergymen, 1660–1760' in Ford et al. (eds), *As by law established*, pp 136–51; D. W. Hayton, 'The development and limitations of Protestant ascendancy: the Church of Ireland laity in public life, c. 1660–1740' in W. G. Neely and Raymond Gillespie (eds), *The laity and the Church of Ireland, 1000–2000: all sorts and conditions* (Dublin, 2002), p. 130.

156 And in other noted 'improvers' such as Arthur Dobbs: see Clarke, *Arthur Dobbs*, ch. 2; Dobbs to Michael Ward, [1746] (P.R.O.N.I., Castle Ward papers, D/2092/1/3/1, f. 10).

Bibliography of secondary works

Agnew, Jean, *Belfast merchant families in the seventeenth century* (Dublin, 1996)

Allen, W. O. B. and Edmund McClure, *Two hundred years: a history of the S.P.C.K.* (London, 1888)

Armitage, David, *The ideological origins of the British empire* (Cambridge, 2000)

——, *Greater Britain, 1516–1776: essays in Atlantic history* (Aldershot, 2004)

Ashton, John, *Humour, wit, and satire of the seventeenth century* (London, 1883)

Atherton, H. M., *Political prints in the age of Hogarth* (Oxford, 1974)

Auchmuty, J. J., *Irish education: a historical survey* (Dublin, 1937)

Bahlman, D. W. R., *The moral revolution of 1688* (New Haven, Conn., 1957)

Baillie, W. D., 'Sir George Rawdon; one of the horns against the kirk in the seventeenth century' in *Bulletin of the Presbyterian Historical Society of Ireland*, xiii (1984), pp 2–9

Ball, F. E., *A history of the County Dublin* (6 parts, Dublin, 1902–20)

——, *The judges in Ireland 1221–1921* (2 vols, New York, 1927)

Baltes, Sabine, *The pamphlet controversy about Wood's Halfpence (1722–25) and the tradition of Irish constitutional nationalism* (Frankfurt am Main, 2002)

Barnard, T. C., *Cromwellian Ireland: English government and reform in Ireland 1649–1660* (Oxford, 1975)

——, 'Crises of identity among Irish Protestants, 1641–1685' in *Past and Present*, no. 127 (May 1990), pp 39–83

——, 'Gardening, diet and "improvement" in later seventeenth-century Ireland' in *Journal of Garden History*, x (1990), pp 71–85

——, 'Reforming Irish manners: the religious societies in Dublin during the 1690s' in *Hist. Jn.*, xxxv (1992), pp 805–38

——, 'Lawyers and the law in later seventeenth-century Ireland' in *I.H.S.*, xxviii, no. 111 (May 1993), pp 256–82

——, 'Protestants and the Irish language, c. 1675–1725' in *Journal of Ecclesiastical History*, xliv (1993), pp 243–72

——, 'Improving clergymen, 1660–1760' in Alan Ford, J. I. McGuire and Kenneth Milne (eds), *As by law established: the Church of Ireland since the Reformation* (Dublin, 1995), pp 136–51

——, 'Land and the limits of loyalty: the second earl of Cork and first earl of Burlington (1612–98)' in T. C. Barnard and Jane Clark (eds), *Lord Burlington: architecture, art and life* (London, 1996), pp 167–99

——, *The abduction of a Limerick heiress: social and political relations in mid-eighteenth-century Ireland* (Maynooth Studies in Local History, no. 20, Dublin, 1998)

——, 'New opportunities for British settlement: Ireland, 1650–1700' in *The Oxford history of the British Empire*, i: Nicholas Canny (ed.), *The origins of empire: British overseas enterprise to the close of the seventeenth century* (Oxford, 1998), pp 309–27

——, 'The world of goods and county Offaly in the eighteenth century' in William Nolan and T. P. O'Neill (eds), *Offaly: history and society. Interdisciplinary essays on the history of an Irish county* (Dublin, 1998), pp 371–92

——,'Public and private uses of wealth in Ireland, c.1660–1760' in Jacqueline Hill and Colm Lennon (eds), *Luxury and austerity: Historical Studies xxi* (Dublin, 1999), pp 66–83

——, 'The viceregal court in later seventeenth-century Ireland' in Eveline Cruickshanks (ed.), *The Stuart courts* (Stroud, 2000), pp 256–65
——, *A new anatomy of Ireland: the Irish Protestants, 1649–1770* (New Haven, Conn., & London, 2003)
——, *Irish Protestant ascents and descents, 1641–1770* (Dublin, 2004)
——, *The kingdom of Ireland, 1641–1760* (Basingstoke, 2004)
——, *Making the grand figure: lives and possessions in Ireland, 1641–1770* (New Haven, Conn., & London, 2004)
——, 'Mrs Conolly and Castletown 1720–1752' in William Nolan and Thomas McGrath (eds), *Kildare: history and society* (Dublin, 2006), pp 327–48
——, '"Almoners of Providence": the clergy, 1647 to c. 1780' in idem and W. G. Neely (eds), *The clergy of the Church of Ireland 1000–2000: messengers, watchmen and stewards* (Dublin, 2006), pp 78–105
——, 'The artistic and cultural activities of the Caldwells of Castle Caldwell, 1750–1783' in *Irish Architectural and Decorative Studies*, x (2007), pp 96–8
——, *Improving Ireland? Projectors, prophets and profiteers, 1641–1786* (Dublin, 2008)
——, 'Last stages of plantation' in James Lyttleton and Colin Rynne (eds), *Plantation Ireland: settlement and material culture, c.1550–c.1700* (Dublin, 2009), pp 265–85
——, 'The Dublin Society and other improving societies, 1731–5' in James Kelly and M. J. Powell (eds), *Clubs and societies in eighteenth-century Ireland* (Dublin, 2010), pp 53–88
Barnard, T. C., and Jane Clark (eds), *Lord Burlington: architecture, art and life* (London, 1995)
Barnard, T.C., and Jane Fenlon (eds), *The dukes of Ormonde, 1610–1745* (Woodbridge, 2000)
Barnard, T. C., and W. G. Neely (eds), *The clergy of the Church of Ireland 1000–2000: messengers, watchmen and stewards* (Dublin, 2006), pp 78–105
Bartlett, Thomas, '"A people made rather for copies than originals": the Anglo-Irish, 1760–1800' in *International History Review*, xii (1990), pp 11–25
——, 'The rise and fall of the Protestant nation, 1690–1800' in *Éire–Ireland*, xxvi, no. 2 (1991), pp 7–18
——, 'Protestant nationalism in eighteenth-century Ireland' in Michael O'Dea and Kevin Whelan (eds), *Nations and nationalisms: France, Britain, Ireland and the eighteenth-century context* (Oxford, 1995), pp 79–88
——, '"This famous island set in a Virginian sea": Ireland in the British Empire, 1690–1801' in *The Oxford history of the British Empire*, ii: P. J. Marshall (ed.), *The eighteenth century* (Oxford, 1998), pp 253–75
——, 'Ireland, empire, and union, 1690–1801' in Kevin Kenny (ed.), *Ireland and the British empire* (Oxford, 2004), pp 61–89
Bartlett, Thomas, and Keith Jeffery (eds), *A military history of Ireland* (Cambridge, 1996)
Bartley, J. O., 'The development of a stock character, i: the stage Irishman to 1800' in *Modern Language Review*, xxxviii (1942), pp 438–47
——, 'Bulls and bogg witticisms' in *Irish Book Lover*, xxx (1946–8), pp 59–62
——, *Teague, Shenkin and Sawney* (Cork, 1954)
Beckett, J. C., 'The government and the Church of Ireland under William III and Anne' in *I.H.S.*, ii, no. 7 (Mar. 1941), pp 280–302
——, 'William King's administration of the diocese of Derry, 1691–1703' in *I.H.S.*, iv, no. 14 (Sept. 1944), pp 164–80
——, *Protestant Dissent in Ireland 1687–1780* (London, 1948)
——, *Confrontations: studies in Irish history* (London, 1972)

——, *The Anglo-Irish tradition* (London, 1976)
Bence-Jones, Mark, *Burke's guide to country houses*, i: *Ireland* (London, 1978)
Benn, George, *A history of the town of Belfast from the earliest times to the close of the eighteenth century* (2 vols, London, 1877)
Bennett, George, *The history of Bandon, and the principal towns in the West Riding of County Cork* (enlarged ed., Cork, 1869)
Berry, H. F., 'Justices of the peace for County Cork, 1661–1800' in *Journal of the Cork Historical and Archaeological Society*, ser. 2, iii (1897), pp 58–65, 106–12
Black, J. M., 'The Catholic threat in the British press in the 1720s and 1730s' in *Journal of Religious History*, xii (1983), pp 364–81
Blanning, T. C. W., *The culture of power and the power of culture: old regime Europe 1660–1789* (Oxford, 2002)
Bliss, Alan, *Spoken English in Ireland 1600–1700* (Monkstown, Co. Dublin, 1979)
Borsay, Peter, and L. J. Proudfoot (eds), *Provincial towns in early modern England and Ireland: change, convergence and divergence* (Oxford, 2002)
Bottigheimer, Karl, 'The failure of the Reformation in Ireland: *une question bien posée*' in *Journal of Ecclesiastical History*, xxxvi (1985), pp 196–207
Bowe, Patrick, and Keith Lamb, *A history of gardening in Ireland* (Dublin, 1995)
Boyce, D. G., *Nationalism in Ireland* (London, 1982)
Boyce, D. G., Robert Eccleshall and Vincent Geoghegan (eds), *Political thought in Ireland since the seventeenth century* (London, 1993)
——, (eds), *Political discourse in seventeenth- and eighteenth-century Ireland* (Basingstoke, 2001)
Bradshaw, Brendan, and Peter Roberts (eds), *British consciousness and identity: the making of Britain, 1533–1707* (Cambridge, 1998)
Brooks, E. St J., *Sir Hans Sloane: the great collector and his circle* (London, 1954)
Brown, Michael, 'Francis Hutcheson and the Molesworth connection' in *Eighteenth-Century Ireland*, xiv (1999), pp 62–76
——, *Francis Hutcheson in Dublin, 1719–1730: the crucible of his thought* (Dublin, 2002)
Brown, Michael, C. I. McGrath and Thomas Power (eds), *Converts and conversion in Ireland, 1650–1850* (Dublin, 2005)
Browning, Reed, *Political and constitutional ideas of the Court Whigs* (Baton Rouge, La., & London, 1982)
Bultmann, W. A. and P. A. Bultmann, 'The roots of Anglican humanitarianism: a study of the membership of the S.P.C.K. and S.P.G., 1699–1720' in *Historical Magazine of the Protestant Episcopal Church*, xxiii (1964), pp 3–48
Burke, W. P., *History of Clonmel* (Waterford, 1907)
Burns, R. E., *Irish parliamentary politics in the eighteenth century* (2 vols, Washington, D.C., 1989–90)
Burtchaell, G. D., *Genealogical memoirs of the Members of Parliament for the county and city of Kilkenny* ... (Dublin, 1888)
Butler, D. J., *South Tipperary 1570–1841: religion, land and rivalry* (Dublin, 2006)
Butler, Hubert, *In the land of Nod* (Dublin, 1966)
Caldicott, C. E. J., et al.(eds), *The Huguenots and Ireland: anatomy of an emigration* (Dun Laoghaire, 1987)
Canny, Nicholas, 'Why the Reformation failed in Ireland: *une question mal posée*' in *Journal of Ecclesiastical History*, xxx (1979), pp 423–50
——, 'The formation of the Irish mind: religion, politics and Gaelic Irish literature' in *Past and Present*, no. 95 (May 1982), pp 91–116
——, 'Identity formation in Ireland: the emergence of the Anglo-Irish' in Nicholas

Canny and Anthony Pagden (eds), *Colonial identity in the Atlantic world, 1500–1800* (Princeton, N.J., 1987), pp 159–212
——, *Making Ireland British, 1580–1650* (Oxford, 2001)
Canny, N. P., *The Elizabethan conquest of Ireland: a pattern established, 1565–1576* (Hassocks, Sussex, 1976)
Capp, Bernard, *Astrology and the popular press: English almanacs 1500–1800* (London, 1979)
Carswell, John, *The old cause* (London, 1954)
Casey, Christine, *The eighteenth-century Dublin townhouse* (Dublin, 2010)
Champion, J. A. I., 'John Toland, the druids, and the politics of Celtic scholarship' in *I.H.S.*, xxxii, no. 127 (May 2001), pp 321–42
——, *Republican learning: John Toland and the crisis of Christian culture, 1696–1722* (Manchester, 2003)
Chappell, William, *Popular music of the olden time: a collection of ancient songs, ballads, and dance tunes, illustrative of the national music of England ...* (2 vols, London, 1855–9)
Clark, Peter, *British clubs and societies 1580–1800: the origins of an associational world* (Oxford, 2000)
Clark, Peter, and Raymond Gillespie (eds), *Two capitals: London and Dublin 1500–1840* (Oxford, 2001)
Clarke, Aidan, *Prelude to restoration in Ireland: the end of the Commonwealth, 1659–60* (Cambridge, 1999)
Clarke, Desmond, *Thomas Prior, 1681–1751, founder of the Royal Dublin Society* (Dublin, 1951)
——, *Arthur Dobbs esquire 1689–1765 ...* (Chapel Hill, N.C., 1957)
Clay, Christopher, *Public finance and private wealth: the career of Sir Stephen Fox, 1627–1716* (Oxford, 1978)
Claydon, Tony, *William III and the godly revolution* (Cambridge, 1996)
Claydon, Tony, and Ian McBride (eds), *Protestantism and national identity: Britain and Ireland c. 1650–c. 1850* (Cambridge, 1998)
Coghill, J. H., *The family of Coghill ...* (Cambridge, Mass., 1879)
Colley, Linda, *Britons: forging the nation 1707–1837* (New Haven, Conn., & London, 1992)
Connolly, S. J., 'Law, order and popular protest in early eighteenth-century Ireland: the case of the houghers' in P. J. Corish (ed.), *Radicals, rebels and establishments: Historical Studies xv* (Belfast, 1985), pp 51–68
——, 'The houghers: agrarian protest in early eighteenth-century Connacht' in C. H. E. Philpin (ed.), *Nationalism and popular protest in Ireland* (Cambridge, 1987), pp 139–62
——, *Religion, law and power: the making of Protestant Ireland, 1660–1760* (Oxford, 1992)
——, 'Eighteenth-century Ireland: colony or *ancien régime*' in D. G. Boyce and Alan O'Day (eds), *The making of modern Irish history: revisionism and the revisionist controversy* (London, 1996), pp 15–33
—— (ed.), *Political ideas in eighteenth-century Ireland* (Dublin, 2000)
——, *Divided kingdom: Ireland 1630–1800* (Oxford, 2008)
Corcoran, Timothy, *State policy in Irish education* (Dublin, 1916)
Craig, Maurice, *Dublin 1660–1800* (Dublin, 1952)
Crawford, John, and Raymond Gillespie (eds), *St Patrick's cathedral, Dublin: a history* (Dublin, 2009)
Cronin, D. A., *A Galway gentleman in the age of improvement: Robert French of Monivea, 1716–79* (Dublin, 1995)

Cruickshanks, Eveline, et al. (eds), *The House of Commons 1690–1715* (5 vols, Cambridge, 2002)
Dabhoiwala, Faramerz, 'Sex and societies for moral reform, 1688–1800' in *Journal of British Studies*, xlvi (2007), pp 290–319
Daniel, S. H., *John Toland: his methods, manners and mind* (London, 1984)
Davies, Christie, 'The Irish joke as a social phenomenon' in John Durant and Jonathan Miller (eds), *Laughing matters: a serious look at humour* (Harlow, 1988), pp 44–65
de Vere White, Terence, *The story of the Royal Dublin Society* (Tralee, [1955])
Dickson, David, 'The place of Dublin in the eighteenth-century Irish economy' in T. M. Devine and David Dickson (eds), *Ireland and Scotland 1600–1850: parallels and contrasts in economic and social development* (Edinburgh, 1983), pp 177–92
—— (ed.), *Dublin: the gorgeous mask 1700–1850* (Dublin, 1987)
——, 'In search of the old Irish poor law' in Rosalind Mitchison and Peter Roebuck (eds), *Economy and society in Scotland and Ireland, 1500–1939* (Edinburgh, 1988), pp 149–59
——, *New foundations: Ireland 1660–1800* (2nd ed., Dublin, 2000)
——, 'Jacobitism in eighteenth-century Ireland: a Munster perspective' in *Éire–Ireland*, xxxiv (2004), pp 38–99
——, *Old world colony: Cork and South Munster 1630–1830* (Cork, 2005)
Douglas, Aileen, et al. (eds), *Locating Swift: essays from Dublin on the 250th anniversary of the death of Jonathan Swift, 1667–1745* (Dublin, 1998)
Doyle, Thomas, 'Jacobitism, Catholicism and the Irish Protestant elite, 1700–1710' in *Eighteenth-Century Ireland*, xii (1997), pp 28–59
Dudley, Rowena, 'The Dublin parishes and the poor, 1660–1740' in *Archivium Hibernicum*, liii (1999), pp 80–94
Duffy, Michael, *The Englishman and the foreigner* (Cambridge, 1986)
Duggan, G. C., *The stage Irishman: a history of the Irish play and stage characters* (Dublin, 1937)
Ehrenpreis, Irvin, *Swift: the man, his works, and the age* (3 vols, London, 1962–83)
Fagan, Patrick, *The second city: portrait of Dublin 1700–1760* (Dublin, 1986)
Falkiner, Sir Frederick R., *The foundation of the hospital and free-school of King Charles II, Oxmantown, Dublin* (Dublin, 1906)
Fauske, C. J., *Jonathan Swift and the Church of Ireland 1710–1724* (Dublin, 2002)
——, (ed.), *Archbishop William King and the Anglican Irish context, 1688–1729* (Dublin, 2004)
——, *A political biography of William King* (London, 2011)
Fennelly, Teddy, *Thomas Prior: his life, times, and legacy* (Port Laoise, 2001)
Ferguson, O. W., *Jonathan Swift and Ireland* (Urbana, Ill., 1962)
Fleming, D. A., 'Diversions of the people: sociability among the orders of early eighteenth-century Ireland' in *Eighteenth-Century Ireland*, xvii (2002), pp 99–111
——, *Politics and provincial people: Sligo and Limerick, 1691–1761* (Manchester, 2010)
Ford, Alan, J. I. McGuire and Kenneth Milne (eds), *As by law established: the Church of Ireland since the Reformation* (Dublin, 1995)
Foster, R. F., *Modern Ireland, 1600–1972* (London, 1988)
Froude, J. A., *The English in Ireland in the eighteenth century* (3 vols, London, 1881–6)
Garnham, Neal, *The courts, crime and the criminal law in Ireland 1692–1760* (Blackrock, Co. Dublin, 1996)
——, 'How violent was eighteenth-century Ireland?' in *I.H.S.*, xxx, no. 119 (May 1997), pp 377–92
——, 'The trials of James Cotter and Henry, Baron Barry of Santry: two case studies in

the administration of criminal justice in early eighteenth-century Ireland' in *I.H.S.*, xxxi, no. 123 (May 1999), pp 328–42

Gilbert, J. T., *A history of the city of Dublin* (3 vols, Dublin, 1854–9)

Gillespie, Raymond, 'George Rawdon's Lisburn' in *Lisburn Historical Society Journal*, viii (1991), pp 32–6

——, 'The Irish Protestants and James II, 1688–90' in *I.H.S.*, xxviii, no. 110 (Nov. 1992), pp 124–33

——, *Reading Ireland: print, reading and social change in early modern Ireland* (Manchester, 2005)

Gillespie, Raymond, and Andrew Hadfield (eds), *The Oxford history of the Irish book*, iii: *The Irish book in English 1550–1800* (Oxford, 2006)

Goodwin, Albert, 'Wood's halfpence', in *E.H.R.*, li (1936), pp. 647–74, repr. in Rosalind Mitchison (arr.), *Essays in eighteenth-century history* (London, 1966), pp 117–44

Graham, C. I., 'The right honourable William Conolly, Speaker of the Irish House of Commons' in *Journal of the County Kildare Archaeological Society*, iii (1899–1902), pp 112–17

Greaves, R. L., *God's other children: Protestant nonconformists and the emergence of denominational churches in Ireland, 1660–1700* (Stanford, Calif., 1997)

Gribbon, H. D., 'The Irish Linen Board, 1711–1828' in L. M. Cullen and T. C. Smout (eds), *Comparative aspects of Scottish and Irish economic and social history 1600–1900* (Edinburgh, [1977]), pp 77–87

Hardiman, James, *The history of the town and country of the town of Galway : from the earliest period to the present time* (Dublin, 1820)

Haydon, Colin, 'The anti-Catholic activity of the S.P.C.K., c.1698–1740' in *Recusant History*, xviii (1987), pp 418–21

——, *Anti-Catholicism in eighteenth-century England, c.1714–80: a political and social study* (Manchester, 1993)

——, 'Parliament and popery in England, 1700–1780' in J. P. Parry and Stephen Taylor (eds), *Parliament and the church 1529–1960* (Edinburgh, 2000), pp 48–63

Hayton, D. W., 'Tories and Whigs in County Cork, 1714' in *Journal of the Cork Historical and Archaeological Society*, lxxx (1975), pp 84–8

——, 'Two ballads on the County Westmeath by-election of 1723' in *Eighteenth-Century Ireland*, iv (1989), pp 7–30.

——,'The Stanhope/Sunderland ministry and the repudiation of Irish parliamentary independence', in *E.H.R.*, cxiii (1998), pp 610–36

—— (ed.), *The Irish parliament in the eighteenth century: the long apprenticeship* (Edinburgh, 2001)

——, 'Patriots and legislators: Irishmen and their parliaments, c. 1689–c.1740' in Julian Hoppit (ed.), *Parliaments, nations and identities in Britain and Ireland, 1660–1860* (Manchester, 2003), pp 103–23

——, *Ruling Ireland, 1685–1742: politics, politicians and parties* (Woodbridge, 2004)

——, 'Voters, patrons and parties: parliamentary elections in Ireland, c. 1692–1727' in Clyve Jones, et al. (eds), *Partisan politics, principle and reform in parliament and the constituencies, 1689–1880: essays in memory of John A. Phillips* (Edinburgh, 2005), pp 44–70

——, 'The personal and political contexts of Robert Molesworth's *Account of Denmark*' in Knud Haakonssen and Henrik Horstbøll (eds), *Northern antiquities and national identities: perceptions of Denmark and the north in the eighteenth century* (Copenhagen, 2007), pp 41–67

Hayton, D. W., and Thomas Bartlett (eds), *Penal era and golden age: essays in Irish history 1690–1800* (Belfast, 1979)
Hayton, D. W, James Kelly and John Bergin (eds), *The eighteenth-century composite state: representative institutions in Ireland and Europe, 1689–1800* (Basingstoke, 2010)
Hechter, Michael, *Internal colonialism: the Celtic fringe in British national development 1536–1966* (London, 1975)
Henning, B. D. (ed.), *The House of Commons 1660–90* (3 vols, London, 1983)
Herlihy, Kevin (ed.), *The Irish dissenting tradition, 1650–1750* (Dublin, 1995)
——, *The politics of Irish dissent 1650–1800* (Dublin, 1997)
Hill, J. R., 'Popery and Protestantism, civil and religious liberty: the disputed lessons of Irish history, 1690–1812' in *Past and Present*, no. 118 (1988), pp 96–129
——, 'Corporate values in Hanoverian Edinburgh and Dublin' in S. J. Connolly et al. (eds), *Conflict, identity and economic development: Ireland and Scotland, 1600–1939* (Preston, 1995), pp 114–24
——, 'Ireland without union: Molyneux and his legacy' in John Robertson (ed.), *A union for empire : political thought and the British union of 1707* (Cambridge, 1995), pp 271–96
——, *From patriots to unionists: Dublin civic politics and Irish Protestant patriotism, 1660–1840* (Oxford, 1997)
——, 'Loyal societies in Ireland, 1690–1790' in James Kelly and M. J. Powell (eds), *Clubs and societies in eighteenth-century Ireland* (Dublin, 2010), pp 181–202
Hindle, Steve, 'Dependency, shame and belonging: badging the deserving poor, c. 1550–1750' in *Cultural and Social History*, i (2004), pp 6–35
Holmes, Geoffrey, *Augustan England: professions, state and society 1680–1730* (London, 1982)
Hoppen, K. T., *The common scientist in the seventeenth century: a study of the Dublin Philosophical Society 1683–1708* (London, 1970)
Isaacs, Tina, 'The Anglican hierarchy and the reformation of manners, 1688–1738', in *Journal of Ecclesiastical History*, xxxiii (1982), pp 391–411
Jackson, R. W., *Peter Browne, devotional writer of the eighteenth century* (Dublin, 1963)
James, F. G., *Ireland in the empire, 1688–1770: a history of Ireland from the Williamite wars to the eve of the American Revolution* (Cambridge, Mass., 1973)
——, *Lords of the ascendancy: the Irish House of Lords and its members, 1600–1800* (Blackrock, Co. Dublin, 1995)
Johnston-Liik, Edith Mary, *History of the Irish parliament 1692–1800* (6 vols, Belfast, 2002)
Jones, G. H., 'The Irish fright of 1688: real violence and imagined massacre' in *Bulletin of the Institute of Historical Research*, lv (1982), pp 149–53
Jones, M. G., *The charity school movement: a study of eighteenth-century Puritanism in action* (Cambridge, 1938)
Kelly, James, 'Jonathan Swift and the Irish economy in the 1720s' in *Eighteenth-Century Ireland*, vi (1991), pp 7–31
——, '"The glorious and immortal memory": commemoration and Protestant identity in Ireland 1660–1800' in *Proceedings of the Royal Irish Academy*, xciv (1994), sect. C, pp 25–52
——, *'That damn'd thing called honour': duelling in Ireland, 1570–1860* (Cork, 1995)
——, 'The politics of the "Protestant Ascendancy": County Galway 1650–1832' in Gerard Moran (ed)., *Galway: history and society ...*(Dublin, 1996), pp 229–70
——, *Poynings' Law and the making of law in Ireland 1660–1800* (Dublin, 2007)
Kelly, James, John McCafferty and C. I. McGrath (eds), *People, politics and power: essays on Irish history 1660–1850 in honour of James I. McGuire* (Dublin, 2009)

Kelly, James, and M. J. Powell (eds), *Clubs and societies in eighteenth-century Ireland* (Dublin, 2010)

Kelly, Patrick, 'A pamphlet attributed to John Toland and an unpublished reply by Archbishop William King' in *Topoi*, v (1985), pp 81–90

——, 'Archbishop William King (1650–1729) and colonial nationalism' in Ciarán Brady (ed.), *Worsted in the game: losers in Irish history* (Dublin, 1989), pp 85–94

——, 'Industry and virtue versus luxury and corruption': Berkeley, Walpole, and the South Sea Bubble crisis' in *Eighteenth-Century Ireland*, vii (1992), pp 57–74

——, 'The politics of political economy in mid-eighteenth-century Ireland' in S. J. Connolly (ed.), *Political ideas in eighteenth-century Ireland* (Dublin, 2000), pp 105–29

Kerrigan, John, *Archipelagic English: literature, history and politics 1603–1707* (Oxford, 2008)

Kidd, Colin, 'North Britishness and the nature of eighteenth-century British patriotisms' in *Hist. Jnl*, xxix (1996), pp 361–82

——, *British identities before nationalism: ethnicity and nationhood in the Atlantic world 1600–1800* (Cambridge, 1999)

King, Sir Charles S. (ed.), *A great archbishop of Dublin: William King D.D. ...* (London, 1906)

Laing, Alastair (ed.), *Clerics and connoisseurs: the Rev. Matthew Pilkington, the Cobbe family and the fortunes of an Irish art collection through three centuries* (London, 2001)

Landa, L. A., *Swift and the Church of Ireland* (Oxford, 1954)

Lecky, W. E. H., *A history of Ireland in the eighteenth century* (new ed., 5 vols, London, 1892)

Leerssen, Joep, *Mere Irish and Fíor-Ghael: studies in the idea of Irish nationality, its development and literary expression prior to the nineteenth century* (2nd ed., Cork, 1996)

Leerssen, J. T., 'Anglo-Irish patriotism and its European context: notes towards a reassessment' in *Eighteenth-Century Ireland*, iii (1988), pp 7–24

Leighton, C. D. A., *Catholicism in a Protestant kingdom: a study of the Irish ancien régime* (Basingstoke, 1994)

Lemmings, David, *Gentlemen and barristers: the inns of court and the English bar 1680–1730* (Oxford, 1990)

——, *Professors of the law: barristers and English legal culture in the eighteenth century* (Oxford, 2000)

Lenihan, Maurice, *Limerick; its history and antiquities, ecclesiastical, civil, and military ...* (Dublin, 1866)

Lett, C. H,. 'Botanists of the north of Ireland' in *The Irish Naturalist*, xxii, no. 2 (Feb. 1913), pp 21–33

Livesey, James, 'The Dublin Society in eighteenth-century Irish political thought' in *Hist. Jn.*, xlvii (2004), pp 615–40

——, *Civil society and empire: Ireland and Scotland in the eighteenth-century Atlantic world* (New Haven, Conn., & London, 2009)

Loeber, Rolf, *A biographical dictionary of architects in Ireland 1600–1720* (London, 1981)

Loupès, Philip, 'Bishop Dopping's visitation of the diocese of Meath, 1693' in *Studia Hibernica*, xxiv (1988), pp 127–51

Lowther Clarke, W. K., *A history of the S.P.C.K.* (London, 1959)

Magennis, Eoin, *The Irish political system 1740–1765: the golden age of the undertakers* (Dublin, 2000)

——, 'A "beleaguered Protestant"? Walter Harris and the writing of *Fiction unmasked*' in *Eighteenth-Century Ireland*, xiii (1998), pp 86–111

Malcomson, A. P. W., 'The Foster family and the parliamentary borough of Dunleer,

1683–1800' in *Journal of the County Louth Archaeological Society*, xvii (1969–72), pp 156–63
——, 'The politics of "natural right": the Abercorn family and Strabane borough, 1692–1800' in G. A. Hayes-McCoy (ed.), *Historical Studies* x (Dublin, 1976), pp 43–90
——, *Archbishop Charles Agar: churchmanship and politics in Ireland, 1760–1810* (Dublin, 2002)
——, *Nathaniel Clements: government and the governing elite in Ireland, 1725–75* (Dublin, 2005)
——, *The pursuit of the heiress: aristocratic marriage in Ireland 1740–1840* (2nd ed., Belfast 2006)
Mant, Richard, *History of the Church of Ireland from the revolution to the union of the churches of England and Ireland* (London, 1840)
Matthew, H. C. G., et al. (eds), *Oxford dictionary of national biography* (60 vols, Oxford, 2004)
Maxwell, Constantia, *Country and town in Ireland under the Georges* (rev. ed., Dundalk, 1949)
——, *The stranger in Ireland* (London, 1954)
——, *Dublin under the Georges: 1714–1830* (rev. ed., London, 1956)
McBride, Ian, *Eighteenth-century Ireland: the isle of slaves* (Dublin, 2009)
McCann, Peadar, 'Cork city's eighteenth-century charity schools: origins and early history' in *Journal of the Cork Historical and Archaeological Society*, lxxxiv (1979), pp 102–11
McCarthy, Muriel, and Ann Simmons (eds), *The making of Marsh's Library: learning, politics and religion in Ireland, 1650–1750* (Dublin, 2004)
McCarthy, Muriel, and Ann Simmons (eds), *Marsh's Library: a mirror on the world* (Dublin, 2009)
McClure, Edmund (ed.), *A chapter in English church history: being the minutes of the Society for Promoting Christian Knowledge …1698–1704* (London, 1888),
McCormack, Bridget, *Perceptions of St Patrick in eighteenth-century Ireland* (Dublin, 2000)
McCoy, Gerard, '"Patriots, Protestants and papists": religion and the ascendancy 1714–1760' in *Bullán*, i (1994), pp 105–18
McCracken, J. L., 'Irish parliamentary elections, 1727–68' in *I.H.S.*, v, no. 19 (Mar. 1947), pp 209–30
McGrath, C. I., *The making of the eighteenth-century Irish constitution: government, parliament and the revenue, 1692–1714* (Dublin, 2000)
——, 'English ministers, Irish politicians and the making of a parliamentary settlement in Ireland, 1692–5' in *E.H.R.*, cxix (2004), pp 585–613
——, 'Government, parliament and the constitution: the reinterpretation of Poynings' Law, 1692–1714' in *I.H.S.*, xxxv, no. 138 (Nov. 2006), pp 160–72
——, 'The union representation of 1703 in the Irish House of Commons: a case of mistaken identity' in *Eighteenth-Century Ireland*, xxiii (2008), pp 11–35
McGrath, C. I., and C. J. Fauske (eds), *Money, power, and print: interdisciplinary studies on the financial revolution in the British Isles* (Newark, Del., 2008)
McGuire, James, 'The Church of Ireland and the "Glorious Revolution" of 1688' in Art Cosgrove and Donal McCartney (eds), *Studies in Irish history presented to R. Dudley Edwards* (Dublin, 1979), pp 137–49
McGuire, James, and James Quinn (eds), *The dictionary of Irish biography* (9 vols, Cambridge, 2009)
McLoughlin, Thomas, *Contesting Ireland: Irish voices against England in the eighteenth century* (Dublin, 1999)

McNally, Patrick, '"Irish and English interests": national conflict within the Church of Ireland episcopate in the reign of George I' in *I.H.S.*, xxix, no. 115 (May 1995), pp 295–314

——, 'Wood's Halfpence, Carteret, and the government of Ireland, 1723–6' in *I.H.S.*, xxx, no. 119 (May 1997), pp 354–76

——, *Parties, patriots and undertakers: parliamentary politics in early Hanoverian Ireland* (Dublin, 1997)

McParland, Edward, 'Building the Parliament House in Dublin' in *Parliamentary History*, xxi (2002), pp 131–40

——, *Public architecture in Ireland, 1680–1760* (New Haven, Conn., & London, 2002)

Milne, Kenneth, 'The corporation of Waterford in the eighteenth century' in William Nolan and T. P. Power (eds), *Waterford: history and society* ... (Dublin, 1996), pp 331–50

——, *The Irish charter schools 1730–1830* (Dublin, 1997)

—— (ed.), *Christ Church cathedral, Dublin: a history* (Dublin, 2000)

Moody, T. W., and W. E. Vaughan (eds), *A new history of Ireland*, iv: *Eighteenth-century Ireland 1691–1800* (Oxford, 1986)

Moore, S. D., *Swift, the book and the Irish financial revolution: satire and sovereignty in colonial Ireland* (Baltimore, Md., 2010)

Munter, Robert, *The history of the Irish newspaper, 1685–1760* (Cambridge, 1967)

Murphy, Seán, 'Charles Lucas and the Dublin election of 1748–1749' in *Parliamentary History*, ii (1983), pp 93–111

——, 'Charles Lucas, Catholicism and nationalism' in *Eighteenth-Century Ireland*, viii (1993), pp 83–102

Neely, W. G., *Kilkenny: an urban history, 1391–1843* (Belfast, [1989])

Neely, W. G., and Raymond Gillespie (eds.), *The laity and the Church of Ireland, 1000–2000: all sorts and conditions* (Dublin, 2002)

Nelson, E. C., 'Sir Arthur Rawdon (1662–1695) of Moira: his life and letters, family and friends, and his Jamaican plants' in *Proceedings and Reports of the Belfast Natural History and Philosophical Society*, ser. 2, x (1977–82), pp 30–52

Nokes, David, *Jonathan Swift, a hypocrite reversed: a critical biography* (Oxford, 1985)

Nolan, William, and Kevin Whelan (eds), *Kilkenny: history and society* ... (Dublin, 1990)

Ó Ciardha, Éamon, *Ireland and the Jacobite cause, 1685–1766: a fatal attachment* (Dublin, 2002)

Ó Coindealbháin, Seán, 'Schools and schooling in Cork city 1700–1831' in *Journal of the Cork Historical and Archaeological Society*, ser. 2, xlviii (1943), pp 44–8

O'Flanagan, Patrick, and C. G. Buttimer (eds), *Cork: history and society* ... (Dublin, 1993)

O'Kane, Finola, *Landscape design in eighteenth-century Ireland: mixing foreign trees with the natives* (Cork, 2004)

O'Regan, Philip, *Archbishop William King of Dublin (1750–1729) and the constitution in church and state* (Dublin, 2000)

Phillips, W. A. (ed.), *History of the Church of Ireland* (3 vols, Oxford, 1933–4)

Pilsworth, W. J., *History of Thomastown and district* ([Kilkenny,] 1953)

Pollard, Mary, *Dublin's trade in books 1550–1800* (Oxford, 1989)

Portus, G. V., '*Caritas Anglicana*' (London, 1912)

Potterton, Homan, *Irish church monuments 1570–1880* (Belfast, 1975)

Power, Denis, et al., *Archaeological Inventory of County Cork*, ii: *East and south Cork* (Dublin, 1994)

Power, T. P., *Land, politics and society in eighteenth-century Tipperary* (Oxford, 1993)

Power, T. P., and Kevin Whelan (eds), *Endurance and emergence: Catholics in Ireland in the eighteenth century* (Blackrock, Co. Dublin, 1990)

Proudfoot, Lindsay and William Nolan (eds), *Down: history and society* ... (Dublin, 1997)

Quane, Michael, 'Midleton school, County Cork' in *Journal of the Royal Society of Antiquaries of Ireland*, lxxxii (1952), pp 1–27

——, 'Viscount Weymouth's grammar school, Carrickmacross' in *Journal of the Royal Society of Antiquaries of Ireland*, lxxxvi (1956), pp 26–51

——, 'The diocesan schools 1570–1870' in *Journal of the Cork Historical and Archaeological Society*, ser. 2, lxvi (1961), pp 26–49

——, 'Aspects of education in Ireland 1695–1795' in *Journal of the Cork Historical and Archaeological Society*., lxxiii (1968), pp 120–28

Quinn, D. B., *The Elizabethans and the Irish* (Ithaca, N.Y., 1966)

Rankin, Deana, '"Shet fourd vor general nouddificaushion": relocating the Irish joke, 1678–1690' in *Eighteenth-Century Ireland*, xvi (2001), pp 47–72

Reid, J. S., *History of the Presbyterian church in Ireland*, ed. W. D. Killen (3 vols, Belfast, 1867)

Richardson, Joseph, 'Archbishop William King (1650–1729): "Church Tory and state Whig"?' in *Eighteenth-Century Ireland*, xv (2000), pp 54–76

Robbins, Caroline, *The eighteenth-century commonwealthman* (Cambridge, Mass., 1959)

Rose, Craig, 'Evangelical philanthropy and Anglican revival: the charity schools of Augustan London, 1698–1740' in *London Journal*, xvi (1991), pp 35–65

——, '"Seminarys of faction and rebellion": Jacobites, Whigs and the London charity schools, 1716–1725' in *Hist. Jn.*, xxxiv (1991), pp 831–55

——, 'The origin and ideals of the SPCK 1695–1716' in John Walsh, Colin Haydon and Stephen Taylor (eds), *The Church of England, c. 1689–c. 1873: from toleration to tractarianism* (Cambridge, 1993) pp 172–90

——, 'Providence, Protestant union and godly reformation in the 1690s' in *Transactions of the Royal Historical Society*, ser. 6, iii (1993), pp 151–69

Ross, Ian Campbell, 'Was Berkeley a Jacobite? *Passive obedience* revisited' in *Eighteenth-Century Ireland*, xx (2005), pp 17–30

Ryder, Michael, 'The Bank of Ireland, 1721: land, credit and dependency' in *Hist. Jn.*, xxv (1982), pp 557–82

Sadlier, T. U., and P. L. Dickinson, *Georgian mansions in Ireland* ... (Dublin 1915)

Sedgwick, Romney, *The House of Commons 1715–1754* (2 vols, London, 1970)

Sheldon, E. K., *Thomas Sheridan of Smock Alley* (Princeton, N.J., 1967)

Simms, J. G., *The Williamite confiscation in Ireland 1690–1703* (London, 1956)

——, 'John Toland (1670–1722): a Donegal heretic' in *I.H.S.*, no. 63 (March 1969), pp 304–20

——, *Colonial nationalism 1698–1776: Molyneux's 'The case of Ireland ... stated'* (Cork, 1976)

Simon, Joan, 'From charity school to workhouse in the 1720s: the SPCK and Mr Marriott's solution' in *History of Education*, xvii (1988), pp 113–29

Smyth, Jim, '"Like amphibious animals": Irish Protestants, ancient Britons, 1691–1707' in *Hist. Jn.*, xxxvi (1993), pp 785–97

——, 'Anglo-Irish unionist discourse, c. 1656–1797: from Harrington to Fletcher', in *Bullán*, ii (1995), 17–34

——, *The making of the United Kingdom, 1660–1800* (Harlow, 2001)

Sneddon, Andrew, '"Darkness must be expell'd by letting in the light": Bishop Francis Hutchinson and the conversion of Irish Catholics by means of the Irish language, c. 1720–4' in *Eighteenth-Century Ireland*, xix (2004), pp 37–55

——, 'Bishop Francis Hutchinson (1660–1739): a case study in the eighteenth-century culture of improvement' in *I.H.S.*, xxxv, no. 139 (May 2007), pp 289–310

——, *Witchcraft and Whigs: the life of Bishop Francis Hutchinson, 1660–1739* (Manchester, 2008)

Snyder, E. D., 'The wild Irish: a study of some English satires of the Irish, Scots and Welsh' in *Modern Philology*, xvii (1919–20), pp 687–725

Spufford, Margaret, *Small books and pleasant histories: popular fiction and its readership in seventeenth-century England* (Cambridge, 1981)

Stevenson, John, *Two centuries of life in Down* (Belfast, 1920)

Victory, Isolde, 'The making of the 1720 Declaratory Act' in Gerard O'Brien (ed.), *Parliament, politics and people: essays in eighteenth-century Irish history* (Blackrock, Co. Dublin, 1989), pp 9–29

Walsh, Patrick, *The making of the Irish protestant ascendancy: the life of William Conolly, 1662–1729* (Woodbridge, 2010)

Walsh, T. J., *Opera in Dublin 1705–1797: the social scene* (Dublin, 1973)

Wheatley, C. J., *'Beneath Iërne's banners': Irish Protestant drama of the Restoration and eighteenth century* (Notre Dame, Ind., 1999)

York, N. L., *Neither kingdom nor nation: the Irish quest for constitutional rights, 1698–1800* (Washington, D.C., 1994)

Unpublished theses

Beaumont, D. M., 'The gentry of the King's and Queen's Counties: Protestant landed society, 1690–1760', 2 vols (PhD thesis, T.C.D., 1999)

Bergin, John, 'Irish legislative procedure after the Williamite revolution: the operation of Poynings ' Law, 1692–1705', 2 vols (PhD thesis, University College Dublin, 2005)

Craig, A. G., 'The movement for the reformation of manners, 1688–1715' (PhD thesis, University of Edinburgh, 1980)

de Valera, Ann, 'Antiquarian and historical investigations in Ireland in the eighteenth century' (MA thesis, University College Dublin 1978)

Doyle, Thomas, 'The politics of Protestant ascendancy: politics, religion and society in Protestant Ireland, 1700–1710' (PhD thesis, University College Dublin, 1996)

Duke-Evans, J. B., 'The political theory and practice of the English commonwealthsmen, 1695–1725' (DPhil thesis, University of Oxford, 1980)

Fleming, D. A., 'The government and politics of provincial Ireland, 1691–1761' (DPhil thesis, University of Oxford, 2006)

Gilmore, M. E., 'Anthony Dopping and the Church of Ireland, 1685–1695' (MA thesis, Queen's University Belfast, 1988)

Griffin, Joseph, 'Parliamentary politics in Ireland during the reign of George I' (MA thesis, National University of Ireland (University College, Dublin), 1977)

Lyons, Emma H., 'Morristown Lattin: a case study of the Lattin and Mansfield families in County Kildare, c. 1600–1860' (PhD thesis, University College Dublin, 2011)

Mayo, Hugh, 'Robert Molesworth's *Account of Denmark*: its roots and its impact' (PhD thesis, University of South Denmark, 2000)

McCoy, J. G., 'Court identity in mid-eighteenth-century Ireland: an examination of political culture' (MA thesis, National University of Ireland, Maynooth, 1990)

——, 'Local political culture in the Hanoverian empire: the case of Ireland 1714–60' (DPhil thesis, Oxford University, 1994).

McNally, Patrick, 'Patronage and politics in Ireland 1714–1727' (PhD thesis, Queen's University Belfast, 1993)
Meaney, Lisa, 'Civic society in eighteenth-century Ulster c. 1740–1780' (PhD thesis, Queen's University Belfast, 2011)
Murray, Catherine, 'English schools in Ireland in the seventeenth and eighteenth centuries' (MA thesis, Queen's University Belfast, 1954)
Richey, Rosemary A, 'Landed society in mid-eighteenth century County Down' (PhD thesis, Queen's University Belfast, 2000)
Walsh, Patrick, 'The career of William Conolly, 1689–1729' (PhD thesis, T.C.D., 2007)
Whan, Robert, 'Presbyterians in Ulster, c. 1680–1730: a social and political study' (PhD thesis, Queen's University Belfast, 2009)

Index

Grafton, 2nd duke of, *see* Fitzroy, Charles